Slackware® Li... For Dummie...

Country Code Listing

The following table lists the common codes used on the Internet according to the International Organization for Standardization (ISO) document 3166-1, the International Country Code Standard. This list is accurate as of the printing of this book.

Programs and utilities within Slackware may make reference to the ISO document. One such program is the Slackware `setup` program, which enables you to change the way keys are arranged on your keyboard to suit the country and language of your choice.

The actual list includes 239 countries, but only the ones that affect Slackware software are listed.

ISO 3166-1 Specification Country Codes

Code	Country	Code	Country
be	Belgium	it	Italian
cf	Central African Republic	jp	Japan
ch	Switzerland	no	Norway
de	Germany	pl	Poland
dk	Denmark	ru	Russian Federation
es	Spain	sg	Singapore
fi	Finland	si	Slovenia
fr	France	uk	United Kingdom
gr	Greece	us	United States of America

Slackware Directories

Directory	What it contains	Directory	What it contains
`/bin`	System binaries	`/root`	Super user's home directory
`/boot`	Boot information	`/sbin`	System administration binaries
`/dev`	System device files	`/tmp`	Temporary storage
`/etc`	Configuration files	`/usr/doc`	Documentation
`/home`	User directories	`/usr/local`	Information specific to the local machine
`/lib`	System and program libraries	`/usr/man`	Manual pages
`/mnt`	Optional directory	`/usr/X11R6`	X Windows
`/opt`	Optional directory — also where KDE is installed	`/usr/bin`	Binaries that don't fit into `/bin` or `/sbin`
`/proc`	Current system process information files	`/var`	Variable or changing information, not static

For Dummies®: Bestselling Book Series for Beginners

Slackware® Linux® For Dummies®

File and Directory Commands

Command	What it does
`touch`	Creates a new (empty) file
`rm`	Removes a file or an empty directory
`mkdir`	Creates a directory
`rmdir`	Removes a directory
`ls`	Lists files
`cd`	Changes directories
`pwd`	Prints a working (current) directory (to the screen)
`cp`	Copies files
`mv`	Moves or renames files or directories
`ln`	Creates a symbolic link
`cat`	Shows (concatenates) the contents of a file
`more`	Shows the contents of a file, one screen at a time

Redirection

Director	What it does
`command1 | command2`	Executes command1 and then command2 using the output from command1
`command > file`	Sends output of command to file
`command < file`	Runs command and use the contents of file as input
`command >> file`	Appends the output of command to file

Administrative Commands

Command	What it does
`fsck`	Performs a file system check
`w`	Checks who's doing what on the system
`date`	Shows current date and time
`mount`	Adds a file system to the current system
`umount`	Removes a file system from the current system
`shutdown`	Shuts down the computer
`finger`	Presents information about a user
`adduser`	Adds a user account to the system
`passwd`	Changes the password for the current account

Package Commands

Commands	What it does
`pkgtool`	Acts as all-purpose package manager
`intallpkg`	Installs a package
`removepkg`	Removes a package
`upgradepkg`	Upgrades a package to a newer version
`makepkg`	Creates a package
`explodepkg`	Dumps the contents of a package into your current directory
`rpm2targz`	Converts .rpm packages to .tar.gz format
`rpm2tgz`	Converts .rpm packages to .tgz format

Cheat Sheet $2.95 value. Item 0689-7.
For more information about IDG Books, call 1-800-762-2974.

For Dummies®: Bestselling Book Series for Beginners

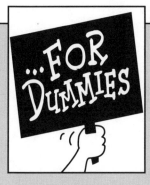

by Paul Gallegos

IDG Books Worldwide, Inc.
An International Data Group Company

Foster City, CA ◆ Chicago, IL ◆ Indianapolis, IN ◆ New York, NY

Slackware® Linux® For Dummies®

Published by
IDG Books Worldwide, Inc.
An International Data Group Company
919 E. Hillsdale Blvd.
Suite 400
Foster City, CA 94404
www.idgbooks.com (IDG Books Worldwide Web site)
www.dummies.com (Dummies Press Web site)

Library of Congress Catalog Card No.: 99-69385

ISBN: 0-7645-0689-7

Printed in the United States of America

10 9 8 7 6 5 4 3 2 1

1O/QU/QV/QQ/IN

Distributed in the United States by IDG Books Worldwide, Inc.

Distributed by CDG Books Canada Inc. for Canada; by Transworld Publishers Limited in the United Kingdom; by IDG Norge Books for Norway; by IDG Sweden Books for Sweden; by IDG Books Australia Publishing Corporation Pty. Ltd. for Australia and New Zealand; by TransQuest Publishers Pte Ltd. for Singapore, Malaysia, Thailand, Indonesia, and Hong Kong; by Gotop Information Inc. for Taiwan; by ICG Muse, Inc. for Japan; by Intersoft for South Africa; by Eyrolles for France; by International Thomson Publishing for Germany, Austria and Switzerland; by Distribuidora Cuspide for Argentina; by LR International for Brazil; by Galileo Libros for Chile; by Ediciones ZETA S.C.R. Ltda. for Peru; by WS Computer Publishing Corporation, Inc., for the Philippines; by Contemporanea de Ediciones for Venezuela; by Express Computer Distributors for the Caribbean and West Indies; by Micronesia Media Distributor, Inc. for Micronesia; by Chips Computadoras S.A. de C.V. for Mexico; by Editorial Norma de Panama S.A. for Panama; by American Bookshops for Finland.

For general information on IDG Books Worldwide's books in the U.S., please call our Consumer Customer Service department at 800-762-2974. For reseller information, including discounts and premium sales, please call our Reseller Customer Service department at 800-434-3422.

For information on where to purchase IDG Books Worldwide's books outside the U.S., please contact our International Sales department at 317-596-5530 or fax 317-572-4002.

For consumer information on foreign language translations, please contact our Customer Service department at 1-800-434-3422, fax 317-572-4002, or e-mail rights@idgbooks.com.

For information on licensing foreign or domestic rights, please phone +1-650-653-7098.

For sales inquiries and special prices for bulk quantities, please contact our Order Services department at 800-434-3422 or write to the address above.

For information on using IDG Books Worldwide's books in the classroom or for ordering examination copies, please contact our Educational Sales department at 800-434-2086 or fax 317-572-4005.

For press review copies, author interviews, or other publicity information, please contact our Public Relations department at 650-653-7000 or fax 650-653-7500.

For authorization to photocopy items for corporate, personal, or educational use, please contact Copyright Clearance Center, 222 Rosewood Drive, Danvers, MA 01923, or fax 978-750-4470.

About the Author

Paul Gallegos is a Digital Metrics Certified Linux Administrator (dmCLA) and freelance Linux consultant who has worked in the system administration, telecommunications, and networking fields since 1989. Along the way he has used and administered systems and networks with various operating systems, but he finally settled on Linux as his OS of choice around 1994. He has used Slackware Linux exclusively since 1995, though he admits to having dabbled with other flavors. Currently, Paul is the Director of Information Systems for Marketplayer.com, a leading provider of global Internet stock competition software and products.

When not working on Linux solutions, Paul can be found spending time with his family in their home in Mesa, AZ, playing fetch with his Shih-tzu dog, Taz, pursuing the latest and greatest Japanese anime series available, playing competitive indoor and sand volleyball, or writing things not Linux-related (it actually does happen).

ABOUT IDG BOOKS WORLDWIDE

Welcome to the world of IDG Books Worldwide.

IDG Books Worldwide, Inc., is a subsidiary of International Data Group, the world's largest publisher of computer-related information and the leading global provider of information services on information technology. IDG was founded more than 30 years ago by Patrick J. McGovern and now employs more than 9,000 people worldwide. IDG publishes more than 290 computer publications in over 75 countries. More than 90 million people read one or more IDG publications each month.

Launched in 1990, IDG Books Worldwide is today the #1 publisher of best-selling computer books in the United States. We are proud to have received eight awards from the Computer Press Association in recognition of editorial excellence and three from Computer Currents' First Annual Readers' Choice Awards. Our best-selling *...For Dummies®* series has more than 50 million copies in print with translations in 31 languages. IDG Books Worldwide, through a joint venture with IDG's Hi-Tech Beijing, became the first U.S. publisher to publish a computer book in the People's Republic of China. In record time, IDG Books Worldwide has become the first choice for millions of readers around the world who want to learn how to better manage their businesses.

Our mission is simple: Every one of our books is designed to bring extra value and skill-building instructions to the reader. Our books are written by experts who understand and care about our readers. The knowledge base of our editorial staff comes from years of experience in publishing, education, and journalism — experience we use to produce books to carry us into the new millennium. In short, we care about books, so we attract the best people. We devote special attention to details such as audience, interior design, use of icons, and illustrations. And because we use an efficient process of authoring, editing, and desktop publishing our books electronically, we can spend more time ensuring superior content and less time on the technicalities of making books.

You can count on our commitment to deliver high-quality books at competitive prices on topics you want to read about. At IDG Books Worldwide, we continue in the IDG tradition of delivering quality for more than 30 years. You'll find no better book on a subject than one from IDG Books Worldwide.

John Kilcullen
Chairman and CEO
IDG Books Worldwide, Inc.

Eighth Annual Computer Press Awards 1992

Ninth Annual Computer Press Awards 1993

Tenth Annual Computer Press Awards 1994

Eleventh Annual Computer Press Awards 1995

IDG is the world's leading IT media, research and exposition company. Founded in 1964, IDG had 1997 revenues of $2.05 billion and has more than 9,000 employees worldwide. IDG offers the widest range of media options that reach IT buyers in 75 countries representing 95% of worldwide IT spending. IDG's diverse product and services portfolio spans six key areas including print publishing, online publishing, expositions and conferences, market research, education and training, and global marketing services. More than 90 million people read one or more of IDG's 290 magazines and newspapers, including IDG's leading global brands — Computerworld, PC World, Network World, Macworld and the Channel World family of publications. IDG Books Worldwide is one of the fastest-growing computer book publishers in the world, with more than 700 titles in 36 languages. The "...For Dummies®" series alone has more than 50 million copies in print. IDG offers online users the largest network of technology-specific Web sites around the world through IDG.net (http://www.idg.net), which comprises more than 225 targeted Web sites in 55 countries worldwide. International Data Corporation (IDC) is the world's largest provider of information technology data, analysis and consulting, with research centers in over 41 countries and more than 400 research analysts worldwide. IDG World Expo is a leading producer of more than 168 globally branded conferences and expositions in 35 countries including E3 (Electronic Entertainment Expo), Macworld Expo, ComNet, Windows World Expo, ICE (Internet Commerce Expo), Agenda, DEMO, and Spotlight. IDG's training subsidiary, ExecuTrain, is the world's largest computer training company, with more than 230 locations worldwide and 785 training courses. IDG Marketing Services helps industry-leading IT companies build international brand recognition by developing global integrated marketing programs via IDG's print, online and exposition products worldwide. Further information about the company can be found at www.idg.com.

1/26/00

Dedication

This book is dedicated to my son Dominic, who arrived in this world just prior to the publishing of this book, and my wife Theresa. Home is where your family is, after all.

Author's Acknowledgments

Many thanks go out to Jennifer Rowe and Laura Lewin (both at IDG Books Worldwide), who encouraged me to write this book. Also, thanks to Jade Williams for being such an understanding editor through all the trials and tribulations (wherever would this book be without you?); Jeremy Zucker for esteemed work in making me rethink my words; James Russell for his thorough inspection of the installation chapters; Mohammed Kabir for his technical editing; and the rest of the nameless crew at IDG Books whose tireless work in publishing rarely get noticed, much less receive acknowledgment.

More thanks go to Keith Holguin for his early suggestions and helpful ideas in getting started; John Joganic for technical help with GNOME and The GIMP and for making sure I have my head above water at all times; Dr. Eric B. Schorvitz for providing motivation exactly when I needed it; and the Tucson Animation Screening Society for graciously lending me the use of their systems these last three years in order to further my Slackware and Linux knowledge base.

Belated thanks go out to Linus Torvalds and Patrick Volkerding for creating Linux and Slackware, respectively. I may never meet you guys, but you both have created something completely unparalleled, and for that you have my utmost respect.

Special thanks go out to David Tai, John Biles, and Jeff Hosmer for upping the standard of writing so far that I get nosebleeds. Thanks, guys.

Last but not least, my deepest thanks go to my wife Theresa for understanding and encouraging this project despite all the setbacks, and for giving me a son, for which I'll be forever grateful. Love you both!

This book was written while listening to the *Video Girl Ai* soundtrack, Foreigner's *Mr. Moonlight*, Def Leppard's *Euphoria*, Enrique Iglesias' *Enrique*, Savage Garden's *Affirmation*, and Michael W. Smith's *Live the Life* and *This Is Your Time*. (I have a wide range of musical tastes . . . ;-)

Publisher's Acknowledgments

We're proud of this book; please register your comments through our IDG Books Worldwide Online Registration Form located at http://my2cents.dummies.com.

Some of the people who helped bring this book to market include the following:

Acquisitions, Editorial, and Media Development

Project Editor: Jade L. Williams

Acquisitions Editor: Laura Lewin

Copy Editors: Jeremy Zucker, James H. Russell

Technical Editor: Mohammed Kabir

Permissions Editor: Carmen Krikorian

Associate Media Development Specialist: Megan Decraene

Media Development Coordinator: Marisa Pearman

Editorial Manager: Leah P. Cameron, Kyle Looper

Media Development Manager: Heather Heath Dismore

Editorial Assistant: Beth Parlon

Production

Project Coordinator: Emily Perkins

Layout and Graphics: Amy Adrian, Joe Bucki, Barry Offringa, Tracy K. Oliver, Jacque Schneider, Brian Torwelle, Erin Zeltner

Proofreaders: Laura Albert, Corey Bowen, Sally Burton, John Greenough, Joanne Keaton, Marianne Santy

Indexer: Sharon Hilgenberg

Special Help

Patrick Volkerding, Slackware Creator

General and Administrative

IDG Books Worldwide, Inc.: John Kilcullen, CEO

IDG Books Technology Publishing Group: Richard Swadley, Senior Vice President and Publisher; Walter R. Bruce III, Vice President and Publisher; Joseph Wikert, Vice President and Publisher; Mary Bednarek, Vice President and Director, Product Development; Andy Cummings, Publishing Director, General User Group; Mary C. Corder, Editorial Director; Barry Pruett, Publishing Director

IDG Books Consumer Publishing Group: Roland Elgey, Senior Vice President and Publisher; Kathleen A. Welton, Vice President and Publisher; Kevin Thornton, Acquisitions Manager; Kristin A. Cocks, Editorial Director

IDG Books Internet Publishing Group: Brenda McLaughlin, Senior Vice President and Publisher; Sofia Marchant, Online Marketing Manager

IDG Books Production for Branded Press: Debbie Stailey, Director of Production; Cindy L. Phipps, Manager of Project Coordination, Production Proofreading, and Indexing; Tony Augsburger, Manager of Prepress, Reprints, and Systems; Laura Carpenter, Production Control Manager; Shelley Lea, Supervisor of Graphics and Design; Debbie J. Gates, Production Systems Specialist; Robert Springer, Supervisor of Proofreading; Kathie Schutte, Production Supervisor

Packaging and Book Design: Patty Page, Manager, Promotions Marketing

◆

The publisher would like to give special thanks to Patrick J. McGovern, without whom this book would not have been possible.

◆

Contents at a Glance

Cartoons at a Glance

By Rich Tennant

The 5th Wave
By Rich Tennant
©RICHTENNANT

"Philip– come quick! David just used Slackware to connect the amp and speakers to his air-guitar!"

page 333

The 5th Wave
By Rich Tennant
©RICHTENNANT

"I don't mind dealing with Slackware's little quirks, Martin, but I'd appreciate it if you kept yours to yourself."

page 247

The 5th Wave
By Rich Tennant
IT WAS KEVIN'S FIRST ATTEMPT AT INSTALLING GHOSTSCRIPT. AN ICY CHILL WENT DOWN HIS SPINE AS HIS OUIJA BOARD SUDDENLY FELL FROM THE SHELF CAUSING HIS CANDLE TO FLICKER WILDLY.
©RICHTENNANT

page 75

The 5th Wave
By Rich Tennant
©RICHTENNANT

"Before installing Slackware, partition your hard drive, make boot and root disks, and select an appropriate morphine drip."

page 7

The 5th Wave
By Rich Tennant
©RICHTENNANT

"Drive carefully, remember your lunch, and always make a backup of your directory tree before modifying your hard disk partition file."

page 149

The 5th Wave
By Rich Tennant
©RICHTENNANT

My job consists of working with the kernel all day.

page 275

The 5th Wave
By Rich Tennant
©RICHTENNANT

"Slackware does a lot of great things, I'm just not sure running a word processing program sideways without line breaks on butcher's paper is one of them."

page 313

Fax: 978-546-7747

E-mail: richtennant@the5thwave.com

World Wide Web: www.the5thwave.com

Table of Contents

Introduction

In 1991, University of Helsinki student Linus Torvalds created the Linux operating system. Since then, a number of software packages based on the Linux system have been designed. One such package is Slackware.

Slackware is one of the most widely used Linux distributions in the world — and now it's in your hands. This book is your friendly guide to Slackware and its installation. You don't need a rocket science degree to understand Slackware — I've boiled it down to the basics. My aim is to bring the concepts of Slackware down to earth. You have no reason to fear what some believe is at the forefront of the next generation of computing. You may even like it.

About This Book

This book is meant to be a reference manual — you should feel comfortable turning to any page and reading what you find. You can read the book from cover to cover, but it isn't necessary. (For those new to Slackware, however, I do recommend reading the early installation chapters in sequence.)

In this book, you find information on the following:

- Installing Slackware
- Getting hooked up to the Internet with Slackware
- Manipulating X Windows setting
- Optimizing the performance of Slackware

How to Use This Book

Start with the topic that you want to know more about and look for it in the table of contents or index. After you find your topic in the table of contents or index, turn to the area of interest, read as much or as little as you need, and then get started.

Conventions used in this book

When I describe a message or information that you see on screen, it appears like this:

```
Hi mom!
```

Anything that I instruct you to type appears in **bold font**.

When you see a menu command, like Start⇨Programs, this means to use the mouse to click the Start button and then choose the Programs option.

Sometimes the book directs you to use specific keyboard commands to get things done. For example, when the text instructs you to press Ctrl+C, it means that you should hold down the Ctrl key while pressing the C key, and then release both together. Don't type the plus sign.

Some other conventions to beware of are

- Text not in [ ] or { } must be typed exactly as stated.
- Anything inside { } is mandatory, meaning that you must substitute the appropriate value there. I try to use generic words whenever possible to state what kinds of values are being looked for.
- Anything inside [ ] is optional, meaning that you can omit values here if you want.

Gotchas

What are gotchas? *Gotchas* are those little subtle differences that can make all the difference in the world if you are not careful.

- Slackware is case-sensitive — there is a difference between *file* and *FILE*.
- An asterisk (*) matches anything from that point on to the *right*. A question mark (?) matches any *one* character.
- Variables are preceded by a dollar sign ($).
- Ctrl+C interrupts almost any command. Ctrl+Z only *suspends* a command.
- Netscape doesn't work without X Windows. Lynx works both in text-only mode and X Windows.
- `!!` repeats the last command you just ran. `!comm` repeats the last command that begins with `comm`.

- A regular user and a super user are different. Most system administration tools are unavailable to a regular user.
- Removing a link doesn't remove the file on the other end and vice versa.
- The Perl programming language is one of the best inventions of the late 20th century. Learn Perl or be prepared to do lots of tasks the long way.
- Doing a `kill -9 1` is a *very* bad idea.

What You Don't Need to Read

You can safely skip over anything marked with the Technical Stuff icon and any sidebars that you find. Most of the information that you find within those two items is for the techie who wants more data. You can also skip Chapter 1 if you're not interested in the history of Slackware (but you may find it enlightening). What you do with the book is your business — including if you decide to use it to prop your monitor up to a viewable height.

Foolish Assumptions

Because of the nature of Slackware, I'm forced to make some assumptions about you such as:

- You have a computer.
- You have a copy of Slackware — conveniently, a copy is enclosed with this book.
- You have never used Slackware or Linux before or are trying to find out more information about it.
- You are an intelligent human being — Slackware assumes that you know exactly what you're doing with each command you enter.

How This Book Is Organized

This book is arranged into seven parts, and each part is broken down into chapters that cover various topics of Slackware Linux. The chapters have a logical sequence, so it makes sense to read them in order. But you can open the book to any page and start reading if you wish.

This section contains a breakdown of what's in each of the seven parts.

Part I: Presenting Slackware Linux

This part gives you the basics of Slackware — the history behind Linux, the things Slackware is capable of doing, and the advantages of using Slackware. Then you're shown how to find out the exact type of hardware you have, how to make the boot and root disks necessary for installing Slackware, and how to prepare the hard drive space you have for the install.

Part II: Installing and Configuring Your System

In this part, you find out how to run the Slackware setup program to install software on your computer, perform the initial configuration of your computer (which you can change at a later time), reboot, and run Slackware for the first time. You also figure out how to create your own account, install new software packages, and set up a printer. Part II really gives you a sense of what system administrators do.

Part III: Utilizing Slackware Basics

Part III breaks down what Slackware users do with their shells, how Slackware organizes its files and directories (called folders in Windows), how to use an editor, how to set up the X Windows system, and what KDE and GNOME are (no, they're not the lost dwarfs from *Snow White* either).

Part IV: Networking and the Web

The chapters in Part IV show you how to connect to the Internet by giving you a heads up on Internet Service Providers, setting up your modem, and making that first connection. You also see how to use Netscape within Slackware to surf the Web and read e-mail.

Part V: Managing Your System

This part contains tips for the advanced user, such as optimizing your system, working with the hard drive and other special drives, finding out more about file and directory permissions, controlling jobs, and what to do in case of an emergency.

Part VI: The Part of Tens

Every *For Dummies* book includes a collection of chapters with lists of interesting tidbits, and this book is no different. Part VI contains chapters on installation problems, questions about X Windows, tips for working with packages, and places to go for help.

Part VII: Appendixes

Part VII features three appendixes, including an abridged hardware compatibility guide, a listing of common country codes (because Slackware software is worldwide, some programs may refer to codes found here), and a little blurb about the enclosed CDs.

Icons Used in This Book

For the technically curious, this information is just for you. You can safely skip this information if you find yourself confused early in the procedures.

By ignoring this icon, you can cause your computer to crash, lose data, or both. For safety reasons, read the information next to this icon carefully.

You find some particularly useful info here, such as a shortcut for repetitive commands or a helpful procedure.

Information you should commit to memory, or at least paper.

Information, programs, or tools found on the enclosed CDs.

Where to Go From Here

Armed with this book, you're ready to take on the new domain of Slackware. Start with the table of contents and go from there. Understanding Slackware Linux places you on the cutting edge of computing. Good luck!

Part I

Presenting Slackware Linux

"Before installing Slackware, partition your hard drive, make boot and root disks, and select an appropriate morphine drip."

In this part . . .

Chapter 1 introduces you to Linux and the Slackware distribution, featuring a brief history, a short tour of what's inside, and what Slackware can do for you. Chapters 2 through 4 prepare you to perform the actual installation of Slackware. This includes finding out what specific hardware you have in your computer, consolidating space on your hard drive, rebooting, and divvying up your hard drive to make room for the Slackware installation.

Chapter 1

Introducing Slackware Linux

In This Chapter

- Getting familiar with Linux and the Slackware distribution
- Understanding Open Source and Free Software
- Discovering who's using Slackware and why
- Previewing the Slackware distribution
- Examining the advantages of Slackware Linux

That old computer that you bought back in 1991 is stacked in the corner and starting to collect dust. You're debating what to do with it. Your friends mentioned that they need a new boat anchor. At one time, you considered giving it away to charity but thought the donation might be rejected.

Then you heard about this thing called Linux that's making headlines all over the country. Rumor has it that this Linux thing can run on your old computer better than DOS or Windows ever did! Ah, but it's just a rumor, right? Wrong!

Discovering Linux Basics

Linux isn't just the latest anti-big-company-in-Redmond fad — Linux has been around for a long time. Of course, being around for a long time also means that history has a tendency to embellish certain facts. But here's one fact that's remained the same: "Linux" is pronounced LIH-nucks, not LIE-nucks.

Just because you can pronounce the name, however, doesn't mean that you automatically know what Linux can do for you. Linux is an *operating system* that manages all aspects of a computer, making your computer more powerful, faster, and cost efficient, no matter what you are doing with your computer. Here's the difference between Linux and other operating systems, like DOS or Windows.

- Linux is a multiple-user (multiuser), multiple-function (multitasking) operating system that runs on a wider range of computer equipment than any other operating system in existence.
- Linux enables you to fine-tune your computer down to the smallest part without all the unnecessary parts that come with other operating systems, like program libraries that duplicate each other's duties or Web browsers integrated into the operating system.
- Linux is also stable, secure, and cheap — and that's just the tip of the iceberg! The Linux *source code* (the version of a program before it's *compiled,* or turned into a language that the computer recognizes) is freely distributable to everyone. This means that anyone can get a copy to install and/or run their own version of Linux by compiling the source code. Notably, the Linux kernel doesn't use code from any proprietary or copyrighted source, which means that no company can charge you for using the software because the software doesn't contain any code owned by that company. Much of the software available is developed by the GNU project at the Free Software Foundation in Cambridge, Massachusetts. GNU stands for GNU's Not UNIX — this group is notorious for creating recursive acronyms.
- Currently, there are dozens of ongoing projects for *porting* Linux into various hardware configurations. Porting is the writing of Linux code for a specific hardware like the Apple PowerMac. A team of programmers usually does this, although single programmers are known to undertake porting projects as a form of self-torture. Examples include the LinuxPPC project, which ports Linux to the Apple PowerMac computer, and UltraPenguin, which ports Linux to the Sun UltraSPARC machines. You can get a list of these and other versions of Linux from the Web at `http://kernelnotes.org/dist-index.html`.

Presenting . . . Linux!

Linux was initially created as a hobby by Linus Torvalds (pronounced LEE-nus, not LIE-nus — he isn't a Peanuts character!) in 1991 when he was a student at the University of Helsinki in Finland. Torvalds wanted to run *UNIX*, an operating system for multiprocessing computers, on his AT-386 computer. He needed to do some intense programming — something not possible in DOS. After trying out a version of UNIX called Minix, he decided to develop his own operating system, which he felt would be better. The first version of the Linux *kernel* — the center of the computer's operating system — was released in October of 1991. The *stable* — (mostly) error-free version — wasn't released until mid-1994.

Linux has become popular worldwide because of its availability and capability to perform multiple functions effortlessly. Many software programmers have adapted the Linux source code to meet their individual needs, such as for networking, software development, and as an end-user platform. Linux is considered an excellent, low-cost alternative to other more expensive operating systems or platforms.

Presenting . . . Slackware!

Patrick Volkerding discovered the Softlanding Linux System (SLS Linux) distribution in 1994 but found it had way too many shortcomings — it didn't always work, for example. So, Volkerding decided to fix the distribution while adding some new features that he thought may be handy. His distribution, a mostly repaired version of SLS, was the first known distribution of Slackware.

Slackware 7.0 is based on the 2.2 Linux kernel series and the GNU C Library version 2.1.x (glibc2). The Linux kernel v2.2 is the latest, most stable version of the Linux kernel, and glibc2 is the latest version of the GNU C Library. Slackware 7.0 contains an easy to use installation program, extensive online documentation, and a menu-driven package system. A *full* Slackware Linux 7.0 installation (see the accompanying CD) provides you with the X Window System, your choice of the KDE or GNOME desktops, C/C++ development environments, Perl, networking utilities, a mail server, a news server, a Web server, an FTP server, the GNU Image Manipulation Program (GIMP), Netscape Communicator, and many other programs. Slackware Linux can run on anything from a slow 386 system to the fast Compaq (formerly Digital Equipment Corporation) Alpha processor to the latest Intel Pentium III and AMD Athlon system.

Slacking with Slackware

Slackware. The name itself has certain connotations, like "no support" and "for slackers only." The name actually originates from an Internet group called the Church of the SubGenius, whose goal is to acquire more "slack" by doing less work — hence *slackware*, meaning doing more with less. Then again, maybe the name just sounded cool.

Slackware is a Linux distribution. A *Linux distribution* is created by taking the Linux kernel, which is the center of the computer's operating system, bundling it together with a collection of software, and adding an installation program. Slackware is not only one of the oldest Linux distributions, but the first Linux distribution to achieve mass distribution. (As mentioned earlier in this chapter, Linux is a distributable operating system that anyone can download and use.)

Understanding Open Source

Most, but not all, Linux programs are open source software programs, including Linux distributions like Slackware. An open source program is freely distributable (anyone can get a free copy) and must contain the source code. This doesn't mean that the program is free, as in "free food;" companies and developers may charge money for the program as long as the source code is *freely available* (you don't have to pay to see it) via the Internet. So, when companies and developers charge for a program or distribution that is open source, you are really paying for the leg work and time that it took to bundle the various software programs and source code into one package. These packages are offered at a very low price and are considered a timesaver for those who are very busy.

Open source enables users to modify or change the program, as long as the modifications are also freely distributable. In other words, if you change something in the program, you must allow other people to make changes to your changes. This doesn't apply if you're changing the program for your own personal use, though. The open source *license for use*, or permission to use the program, must be nondiscriminatory toward any person, group, or field of endeavor, and not specific to any one product. For example, this means that you can not create a program for university professors only or stipulate that a program can not be used with the compatible Generic Product B.

Slackware Linux is developed under the *GNU General Public License (GPL)*, which is one of the main licenses for open source programs. The GPL is commonly called "copyleft" as a jeer towards general copyright restrictions.

Getting support for free software

Free software usually doesn't offer the luxury of a toll-free number or dedicated customer support; if the author decides to help you out with a problem you're having, it's a cause for celebration. Linux, however, is a special case. For example, when you purchase a Slackware CD-ROM from a company like Walnut Creek, you get the same kind of 24-hour customer support for 30 days enjoyed by commercial software customers.

Examining shareware and commercial software

Make no mistake, Slackware is not shareware or commercial software. *Shareware* is like a demo version of software — after a specific time period or number of uses, you're expected to pay the developer or owner a small fee in return for continued usage (Scout's honor). *Commercial software* is a pay-as-you-go program. You pay a *licensing fee* (a dollar amount that gives you the right to use the program) up front, usually as part of the software's purchase price, before you can even use the program.

Commercial software has some good attributes, too — you normally get 24-hour support via a toll-free phone number for up to 30 days after purchase. Shareware sometimes offers this feature as well, assuming you pay the fee.

Wondering about the penguin logo?

The official Linux mascot, Tux the Penguin, was selected by Linus Torvalds to represent the image that he associates with the operating system he created. When Torvalds was asked how a penguin became the Linux mascot, he answered that it was due in part to having once been bitten by a "fairy penguin" at a zoo, and the image stayed with him. Torvalds is happy to be associated with an irreverent logo, rather than a boring commercial logo. (As for what a "fairy penguin" is, I think it has to do with just how unferocious penguins actually are.)

Larry Ewing drew the now-famous image of Tux the Penguin by using the GNU Image Manipulation Program (GIMP), a program included in most Linux distributions (including Slackware).

When Linux kernel v2.0 was released, Torvalds was quoted on the Usenet newsgroup `comp.os.linux` as saying, "Some people have told me that they don't think a fat penguin really embodies the grace of Linux, which just tells me that they have never seen an angry penguin charging at them in excess of 100 mph. They'd be a lot more careful about what they say if they had."

What happens after that 30-day customer support runs out? Commercial software customers are usually up the creek without a paddle, but Slackware Linux users . . . well, they tend to take care of their own. As a Linux user, you can ask other Linux users for help by posting to newsgroups or mailing lists, asking questions of your local Linux Users Group (LUG), or even just searching the World Wide Web. Major developers or development groups of every Linux program read these forums and respond to all questions out of a genuine interest in your concerns or problems with their programs. Some of the major newsgroups are listed in Chapter 23.

Discovering Who's Using Slackware

Slackware is so flexible that it's no longer just the domain of computer geeks who sit for hours in front of monochrome monitors. Slackware is used for a number of specific purposes, such as Web servers, news servers, computing labs, and software development. Some people use Slackware to create Web pages, write stories, or just surf the Internet. For example, I use Slackware at home on my old Pentium 120. It runs a myriad of programs (some of which are listed later in this chapter) and allows me to work from home in a capacity that I can't do with DOS or Windows. (Ironically, I have to run Windows to write this book, because the good people at IDG Books Worldwide, Inc. aren't running Linux quite yet.)

Here's a list of how professionals are using Slackware:

- Large corporations, like Allot Communications, Ltd., are using Slackware for almost every aspect of their internal communications, from e-mail to Web servers, and for client workstations and customer file storage areas.
- Small businesses are using Slackware as a low-cost alternative to traditional operating systems, like Windows and Sun Microsystems Solaris, with high-end performance gains. This enables small businesses to compete in areas dominated by businesses with more expensive workstations and databases.
- Universities are using Slackware to teach courses in operating systems and systems design and as a research tool.
- Business schools are using Slackware to teach their students the latest practices, techniques, and standards for e-mail, Web, and Usenet news.
- Teachers are using Slackware as a teaching tool for programming classes and computer science logic in high schools and middle schools.

Software companies and various organizations are finding that with Slackware, you can go home for the weekend and know that your servers aren't going to crash or get broken into through an undiscovered back door.

Breaking the Seal on Slackware

One of the big questions asked about Slackware is "What do I get with this thing?" A complete list of what's included would take up its own book, but you can break down the list into four distinct categories: office utilities, multimedia programs, Internet and Web applications, and games.

Building an office with utilities

Whether you're writing a novel, crunching numbers in a spreadsheet, or calculating next year's taxes, Slackware has the utilities you need. Office utilities such as spreadsheets, word processors, and presentation applications are essential tools that many people rely on. The Slackware distribution includes two spreadsheet programs, a spell checker, a calendar and scheduling program, a paint program, a jot-pad program, a scientific calculator, and several file managers. Most of these programs are a standard part of Slackware's desktop managers (you have a choice between the KDE or GNOME desktop package), though some are simple command-line programs that are not run within X Window. See Chapter 12 for more information on the KDE and GNOME desktop packages.

Sun Microsystems offers the StarOffice office suite, which is similar to Microsoft Office, for free via the Internet or for a small fee via mail order. This office suite runs on Slackware and contains a word processor, a spreadsheet, a presentation maker, a scheduler, a database program, and graphics utilities. In addition, StarOffice can share files with Microsoft Office!

Yet there are other office utilities that are taken for granted. What about Postscript and Postscript Document Format (PDF) viewing utilities? Ghostscript, a useful utility for reading such PDF documents, is ready for your command. Plotting utilities? Gnuplot is available for you to plot away. Image manipulation utilities? The GIMP and Kpaint are two paint and imaging programs that come with Slackware. Fractal drawers? Kfract will draw your every pixel. For more information on these applications, check out the `PACKAGES.TXT` file on the Slackware CD-ROMs included with this book.

Playing with multimedia

For whistling while you work, Slackware includes a variety of multimedia programs to help time pass faster or just to enlighten your day. For example, if you have a favorite CD (I'm listening to mine as I write), you can play it in the background by using Workbone (a text-based audio CD player) or KSCD (a CD player included with the KDE desktop). If you like digitally synthesized music in the form of MIDI files or audio sound in the form of WAV sound files, the Kmidi program is available. And if you want to create your own audio or data CDs, Slackware's gotcha covered with the cdwrite or cdrecord programs, both of which will write information to recordable CD-ROMS. For more information on these applications, check out the `PACKAGES.TXT` file on the Slackware CD-ROMs included with this book.

Surfing the Internet and Web

The Slackware distribution features two popular Web browsers — Netscape Communicator (graphical) and Lynx (text-based) — and utilities to set up an in-home network, just in case you have more than one computer. Slackware also offers you a choice of more than six different e-mail programs — some graphical and some text-based. See Chapters 13 and 14 for more information on setting up your Internet connection and browsing the Web.

As an added bonus, Slackware includes Seyon, a full-featured telecommunications package that does everything from maintaining a dialing directory of frequently called numbers, supporting various terminal emulations, and automating tasks (such as logging in to remote computers) to supporting automatic file transfers. What else could you ask for in a telecommunications package?

Relaxing with games

Slackware lets the games begin with an installation including chess, poker, Hangman, Asteroids, and xbill (which you have to play to appreciate). Slackware Linux also has many commercial games that are available in stores now, such as Quake III Arena, Unreal, and Civilization: Call to Power.

Working with Slackware

Slackware enables you to determine what your computer can do instead of letting the computer dictate what you can do. For example, Windows installs many different kinds of program libraries to support a multitude of hardware pieces. With Slackware, you can remove programs and hardware that you don't need, and the computer won't complain one bit. If you have Sound Card A, Windows forces you to maintain support for Sound Cards B through Z as well. Slackware only requires Sound Card A support and nothing more. This applies to Web browsers as well. Windows forces you to use Internet Explorer, but with Slackware, you may choose from several Web browers, such as Lynx, Netscape, and KDE. It's kind of nice to have such power in one little package.

You can set up your computer as a workstation, as a file or print server, or as a database engine for starters, but that's not to say that's all you can do with Slackware.

Running as a workstation

A workstation is the place where you expect to sit down and, well, work. Slackware understands the need for working well, but it also understands that not everyone works the same. With a Slackware workstation, you can run multiple programs at the same time without worrying about having one program crash and taking down the entire system with it. (Fact is, most of the Slackware programs don't crash!) On my personal workstation, I'm using a word processor, a spreadsheet, the KDE world-time watch, Communicator, the KDE process monitor (which monitors all currently running Slackware processes on my computer), and elm (a text-based e-mail program) all at the same time. My workstation is as happy as a clam.

Slackware Linux can handle large files and large programs. If you got data from work on two CD-ROMs and you need to analyze it by Thursday while at home, Slackware allows you to copy all of the data to the computer (that's more than 1.2GB of data in one file) and work at your leisure. In comparison, other operating systems may complain that the file size is too large for the program in question to handle. Although Slackware supports most files created on systems like Microsoft Windows, IBM's OS/2, and most UNIX variants, you can not run executable programs that are specific to other operating systems on Slackware.

Slackware also includes a highly sophisticated windowing system called X Window, which is the graphical display for Slackware. X Window is so powerful that if you turn its settings too high, you can burn out your monitor by causing it to try and display images outside its normal operating range! X Window is covered in more detail in Chapter 11.

Slackware comes with program compilers, networking programs, e-mail readers, and even Web browsers. In addition, many companies have created or *ported* (translated) commercial applications, such as databases, office suites, data management, and even graphic design programs to run on the Linux operating system. Whatever you may need, chances are good that it's included in your version of Slackware, or you can download it for free from the Web.

Serving files or printouts

You have two PCs and you're content running DOS or Windows on one computer, but you're running out of space! Slackware can help. Slackware works extremely well as a file server. By using *SAMBA,* you can share directories with other Linux or UNIX Windows machines. SAMBA is a software suite that provides seamless file and print services to clients. Like Slackware, SAMBA is available as an open source program under the GNU General Public License at `http://www.samba.org/`.

SAMBA enables you to share files or directories on your Slackware system's hard drives. You don't have to worry about running out of space on your DOS or Windows PC because you can use the hard drive from your Slackware machine!

If you have two computers at home (yours and the kids') that need connecting to one printer, just hook the printer up to your Slackware machine, turn on SAMBA, and you can change that old 486 computer/doorstop into an inexpensive printer station.

Organizing your data as a database

Number crunching is the bane of many businesses. But Slackware can alleviate the headache of converting from your database engine of choice to a format usable by your PC.

Oracle, MySQL, and Postgres are just three of the more common database engines that businesses and corporations are using for their critical data and are available for Slackware Linux. Any one of these may cost hundreds or even thousands of dollars for a company or business, but for a single user like you, there's no charge. This is because software companies believe that corporations should pay for resources that enable them to make money. On the other hand, individuals who are using the programs, perhaps to teach themselves database applications or maybe to organize household tasks, may do so for free.

The following is a list of URLs from which you can download your free personal copy of a database engine:

- **Oracle:** Go to `www.oracle.com/database/prodfam/personal.html` for your personal copy of Oracle.
- **MySQL:** Go to `www.mysql.com/download.html` for your personal copy of MySQL for Linux.
- **Postgres:** Go to `www.postgresql.org/` for your personal copy of Postgres.

Increasing your Internet security

The Internet is probably the biggest moneymaker in the history of the world next to the lottery. In fact, several countries don't have lotteries, but they have Internet access! The success stems from connecting people and businesses all over the world together through a portal to transact business. For example, my cousin wanted a backpack with a specific Japanese animation character on it. This backpack was not available anywhere in the Phoenix area. Following a quick Web search, I found one in New York, ordered it by using my credit card, and had it delivered to my cousin's doorstep in three days.

Although e-commerce generates a lot of revenue, the *real* moneymakers are the Internet service providers (ISPs). Slackware helps decrease the overhead costs of ISPs — that's more money for the shareholders or company executives — by worrying less about budgeting money for licenses and concentrating on keeping their clientele happy.

Slackware increases the stability, or consistency, of the ISP with its ability to stay up and running even under the most trying of conditions, which is good in an industry where server *downtime* — when the server is not running or has crashed unexpectedly — can mean hundreds of thousands of dollars in lost business. Slackware's built-in security features increase the security of the ISP by ensuring that e-mail is private and that files are stored safely. For example, bugs, errors, or security holes found in the open source software

are usually patched within hours, not days or weeks like other operating systems. Slackware is also immune to all virus attacks. This is because viruses attack the connections between applications and the operating system, just like real human viruses attack the connections between cells. Because applications like a Web server are not tied directly to the operating system itself, viruses are powerless. Finally, Slackware can be configured to be a *firewall,* which limits access to the systems or networks to only certain users.

Finding other uses

You can find your own use for Slackware, like serving Web pages (being a machine that other people visit to see Web content), playing games, running a voice-mail for your phone, or setting the air conditioning automatically in your house! There's no limit to what you can do with Slackware — people are finding more uses for it everyday. For examples of other Slackware usages, go to `http://linuxtoday.com` and read the latest news on Slackware and Linux or go to `http://freshmeat.net` for the latest Linux programs and uses.

Benefiting from Slackware

Slackware users are finding that the advantages of Slackware over other operating systems are cost-efficient on a short-term and long-term basis. This is because Slackware promotes learning by steps instead of learning by the shotgun method.

Zipslack and Bigslack

Slackware has two other official distributions, *zipslack* and *bigslack.*

Zipslack is an easy-to-install version for use on a very small partition or 100MB zip drive. Zipslack is included on the accompanying CD-ROMs at the back of book. Its advantage is you get the functionality of Slackware crammed into a very small (100MB) space.

Bigslack, on the other hand, is an almost full version of Slackware packaged as zip files for an existing DOS or Windows partition. You need nearly 800MB of free space to install. (Because a CD-ROM only holds 650MB of data, Bigslack is not included on the accompanying CD-ROMs.) Its main advantage is that you get to use Slackware within another operating system, like DOS or Windows. Bigslack is available from the main Slackware FTP site at `ftp://ftp.cdrom.com/pub/linux/slackware-7.0/bigslack/`.

In either case, you need a compression utility like PKZIP to unzip the files. You can get a nice compression utility from `http://www.pkware.com`.

Slackware also adheres to most of the Linux standards, thus saving you time and effort in administration tasks. And that's just the beginning of the benefits enjoyed by Slackware users.

Considering the cost

When you purchase a new computer with an operating system other than Linux, a hidden software cost is included. The office products that come with your computer are also not free, even if you never use them. You end up paying for more than you bargained for, and most places don't give refunds, either.

Well, you won't have that problem with Slackware. Slackware is so cheap that it's scary. In fact, Slackware won't cost you a penny more than the amount you purchase it for — and in some cases, that amount is literally nothing. Some Linux User Groups (LUGs) gladly make copies of Slackware or other Linux distributions on CD-ROMs and give them away for free.

Perhaps you've got a couple of outdated computers lying around the house and want to put them to good use. Certain other operating systems may not run on your system, but Slackware can! You can still use your old computer, and save money.

Maybe you want to teach yourself UNIX but can't afford to buy a high-end workstation. Using Slackware enables you to get that training without costing an arm and a leg because Slackware has all the functionality of UNIX without the high-end hardware cost.

What if you're a video game player and want to set up a network at home to try the latest first-person shoot-'em-up game against your friends? Slackware lets you set up multiple computers in an in-home network just so you can see your favorite character get blasted to tiny pieces. Some of the most popular games available can be played on Linux!

Evaluating compatibility

Compatibility is key for Slackware Linux. Programs need to run on every distribution of Linux, just as programs for Windows 95 are supposed to run on Windows 98. Given the source code, any Linux program can run on Slackware Linux. It's as simple as recompiling the program and turning it into a form that the operating system can understand. Likewise, any program developed on Slackware can run easily on other Linux distributions. The source code is available from wherever you copied the program (a CD or from the Internet).

Slackware includes the rpm2targz (.tar.gz or .tgz being the format for Slackware packages) program to convert RPM packages — packages with the

.rpm extension that are intended for use on the Red Hat Linux distribution — to Slackware-compatible versions. See Chapter 7 for more information on installing and upgrading packages.

Analyzing security

Security is necessary for keeping your information private and safe. Viruses and Web browser security holes are, unfortunately, a common obstacle.

When a bug or security hole is found in Slackware, a patch or fix for that bug or security hole is available online within hours, as compared with operating systems like Windows or OS/2 (another PC operating system) that may take weeks to have a repair released.

Slackware is immune to viruses that would otherwise plague Windows users. Viruses rely on exploiting back doors in the way that Windows applications talk to the Windows operating system. Because Slackware isolates applications from the kernel, there's no way for a virus to work its way through from the application to the operating system. The Melissa virus? Not a problem. The Bubble Boy virus? Hah! The Back Orifice Windows cracking program? Denied! Oh, and macro attacks don't work either because Slackware doesn't use Windows macros.

Finding stability

Compared with other Linux distributions that are backed by entire companies dedicated to their development, Patrick Volkerding single-handedly maintains the Slackware distribution. Volkerding personally selects each and every package that is included as part of Slackware Linux. Stability is the primary goal of the Slackware distribution.

An unstable system is unreliable, so every version of Slackware includes only the most stable packages available, not necessarily the most recent packages. (You can see for yourself what packages are included with Slackware Linux in Appendix B of this book.) A good example of this is the libc programming libraries — Slackware didn't use the glibc or libc6 libraries as part of the operating system until version 7.0 because those libraries were still considered experimental and unstable . . . until now.

As a result of Volkerding's work, Slackware has far fewer bug reports or incompatible programs than any other distribution. I'm a subscriber to the Slackware security mailing list and have seen only one item come across in the last half of 1999. That's an indication of how good his package selections are. See Chapters 8 and 17 for more information about Slackware's stability.

Crushing libc5 and glibc rumors

In the past, one of the biggest myths about Slackware was that you couldn't run certain programs due to the program libraries (library of routines used by programs to execute quickly) being used. Slackware originally used the GNU libc5 libraries because they were the most stable at the time. However, the libc5 libraries didn't contain the support necessary for usage by the newer programs created after 1997.

Although the old libc5 libraries are smaller and faster then the newer glibc (or libc6) libraries, the glibc library includes features that did not exist in libc5, such as support for more hardware architectures and operating systems than libc5 ever could support and stronger encryption methods. Another difference is that glibc is actively being developed — thus there's more support for it. The intent for glibc5 has always been to replace libc5, and it has succeeded. The glibc runtime library enables you to compile and link programs that use the glibc libraries, even though the Linux kernel may be running libc5.

As of Slackware 7.0, glibc is the library of choice for both programming and the Linux kernel, effectively rendering this point moot.

Making systems easy to use

Ease of use is a major reason for Slackware Linux's success. After all, if it's not easy to use, then why use it? For example, the Slackware setup program, which I cover in Chapter 5, is still one of the simplest installation programs today. The entire install process takes less than 30 minutes and is completely flawless, something the previous Win98 installation on the same machine was lacking. The Slackware programs for installing and removing new packages are as easy to use as typing **installpkg** to install and **removepkg** to remove. Pretty simple, eh?

Because Slackware is one of the oldest distributions available, it is one of the most documented distributions with help files, tips and tricks, manual pages, archives, and HOWTO documents. See the accompanying CD-ROM in the back of the book or go to the Linux Documentation Project at `http://www.linuxdoc.org/`.

You can find more help on the Web for Slackware dating back to 1995! In fact, some of the Linux how-to documentation still in use today was written for and on Slackware systems. Almost any sort of help that you may need is available via the Slackware Forum at `http://www.slackware.com/forum`, the Usenet newsgroups at `alt.os.linux.slackware` and `comp.os.linux`, or other people's personal pages on the Web (use a search engine like AltaVista, `http://www.altavista.com`, and look for the word "Linux"), just to name a few. See Chapter 23 for additional places to get help with Slackware.

Getting Slackware

A full distribution of Slackware 7.0 is on the accompanying CD-ROMs in the back of this book. However, if you misplace your CDs, you can download the Slackware Linux distribution for free from a variety of FTP, Web, or *mirror sites* (a mirror site is a Web site that *mirrors*, or creates a duplicate of, the contents of another Web site) off the Internet. You can also purchase Slackware for a nominal cost from a myriad of Web sites (usually around $1.99 plus shipping) or from your local electronics store (which will definitely cost more). This purchasing fee covers the cost of a middle person bundling the various software and source codes into one package. These packages are a timesaver for individuals who are too busy to download from the Internet. And, if you're too busy to install Slackware yourself, you can purchase a computer with Slackware preinstalled.

The following is a list of Web sites where you can download Slackware Linux for free:

- **Walnut Creek CD-ROM.** This is the main Slackware archive home. All updates go here first and then are propagated to other sites. `ftp://ftp.cdrom.com/pub/linux/slackware`
- **Metalab at UNC.** As a major Linux mirror (carbon copy of the main Slackware archive at Walnut Creek), Metalab also houses copies of the Linux Documentation Project, where you can find almost every handbook or guide on any Linux-related topic or software program. `ftp://metalab.unc.edu/pub/Linux/distributions/slackware`
- **Higher Education National Software Archive.** HENSA is a major Slackware mirror outside the U.S. `ftp://Unix.hensa.ac.uk/mirrors/ftp.cdrom.com/pub/linux/slackware`

Following is a list of Web sites where you can purchase Slackware for a nominal fee:

- **Walnut Creek CD-ROM.** By ordering directly from the creator Walnut Creek, you will get commercial telephone support not offered by other vendors. `http://www.cdrom.com`
- **CheapBytes.** You can get almost any distribution of Linux from CheapBytes much cheaper than most places, but the drawback is there's no telephone support. `www.cheapbytes.com`
- **InfoMagic.** As an alternative to Walnut Creek, InfoMagic offers a CD set containing several distributions of Linux bundled together (not just Slackware) and an additional CD set containing the complete archives of several FTP sites. `www.infomagic.com`
- **Linux Mall.** Allegedly, the largest online shopping center for Linux products, which means it's a distribution center, not a support center. `http://www.linuxmall.com`

The following is a list of businesses that preinstall Slackware Linux on computers:

- **Sunset Systems.** Provides preconfigured ready to run Slackware systems on high quality hardware at affordable prices. www.sunsetsystems.com
- **Net Express.** As the first vendor to sell exclusively on the Internet and to offer Linux computers, Net Express provides competitive prices on their equipment. www.tdl.com/~netex
- **ASA Computers.** ASA Computers, located in the middle of Silicon Valley, CA, has clientele that range from home users to corporations. www.asacomputers.com

Chapter 2

Identifying Your Hardware

In This Chapter

- Sorting through Slackware's requirements
- Identifying commonly supported hardware
- Itemizing your hardware
- Creating backup disks

Slackware enables you to get the maximum performance out of your computer by talking to each individual piece of hardware. Slackware figures out the strengths and limitations of each piece of hardware, and sets itself to work in those parameters. You then benefit from a faster machine, which can handle more simultaneous processes than any Windows 9x machine. But Slackware needs a little help from you to know exactly what it has to work with.

Every good piece of software lists the minimum hardware requirements that it needs to run properly; Slackware is no exception. Many times, however, the minimum requirements work only if you plan on not doing anything useful for the next couple of hours.

Never fear! Because Slackware doesn't need the latest and greatest hardware, it can run on just about any old PC. In this chapter, I show you how to determine what kind of hardware you have. Establishing the limitations of your hardware is crucial for when you later set up Slackware. (See Appendix A for an abridged list of Slackware's minimum requirements.)

Acquiring the Bare Minimum Hardware Standard

Technology is constantly advancing on the previous day's breakthroughs. What's cutting-edge today is likely to be out-of-date within a month. But with Slackware, it doesn't matter whether you're using today's hottest toy or yesterday's news. Slackware can run on some of the most basic hardware.

Although I recommend using the best system available, the following is a list of the minimum requirements necessary to run Slackware:

- **486 computer system.** The number 486 denotes the type of central processing unit (CPU) in the computer; the 486 is common in computers built between 1994 and 1997.

  (The IBM PS/2 is *not* supported under Slackware — it has some really weird stuff inside that IBM doesn't want us to know about.)

  Some computers may tell you that you have a math coprocessor inside to calculate mathematical functions. You don't need a math coprocessor — Slackware can fake having one.

- **16MB of RAM.** This is the minimum requirement of RAM you need if you want to install X Windows (X). X is the graphical display for Slackware, as opposed to character display or text-only mode (just straight text, no graphics). If you don't want to install X Windows, and some people don't, then you only need 8MB of RAM.

  The more memory you have in your system, the more applications you can run!

  Although most hard drives work with Slackware, check to see what type of *drive controller* you have. A drive controller is a piece of hardware that controls how the computer interacts with the hard drives and floppy drives. (See Chapter 4 for more information on determining your hard drive type.)

- **Floppy disk drive.** You need a floppy disk drive on your computer — either a 5¼-inch drive or a 3½-inch drive — to create boot and root disks, and possibly to run the emergency disks. (See Chapter 3 for information on building boot and root disks.)

  A CD-ROM drive isn't needed but highly recommended, unless you're willing to sit in front of a computer flipping disks back and forth for a couple of hours. Slackware's A and N software-application series fit nicely onto about 25 floppy disks. If you decide to get a CD-ROM, the speed doesn't matter; just having a CD-ROM on your computer can quicken the installation process and enable you to install Slackware Linux from the free CD in the back of this book.

- **Disk space.** You need at least 40 to 80MB of disk space on your hard drive for a minimal Slackware installation. A minimal installation is just the necessities to get Slackware up and running, nothing more.

  To check how much disk space you have available on your computer, follow these steps if you're using DOS:

  1. **Turn on your computer and monitor. (Windows 3.x users must exit Windows.)**

2. **At the prompt that appears, type** dir **and press Enter.**

   A directory and file listing appears, displaying something like 971MB free. Write that bit of information down for later use.

To check how much disk space you have available on your computer, follow these steps if you're using Windows 9x:

1. **Turn on your computer and monitor.**
2. **Double-click the My Computer icon.**

   The My Computer window appears with your hard drive(s) and floppy drive(s) listed.

3. **Click the C: drive to select.**
4. **Choose File⇨Properties.**

The C: Properties dialog box appears with a graphical pie chart, showing the amount of free and used disk space. Write down the amount of available space.

Disk space isn't the same as *RAM.* RAM is the computer's primary working memory where program instructions and data are stored. Disk space is the place where all the applications and programs reside.

Slackware can coexist on a hard drive with other operating systems, like DOS, OS/2, and even Windows. See Chapter 3 for information on how to *partition* your disk, or set up your disk to enable Slackware to live peacefully with other operating systems that you may have.

A full Slackware installation, as found on the accompanying CD-ROM, can require as much as 900MB. This means that you have installed every single program on the two CD-ROMs, including some of the unnecessary X software and Slackware development programs. I personally recommend a minimum of 400MB of disk space; that way you can install Slackware and some other programs. If you have a 486 or a computer built after 1994, chances are you have at least a 540MB hard drive or bigger, which is more than you need. Note that if you want more disk space, you will have to purchase a new hard drive. Slackware can do many things, but creating more space on your hard drive is not one of them.

- **Compatible video card and monitor.** I know this sounds weird, but there are people out there with very old computers that go out and buy brand new monitors and then wonder why the two don't work together. The reality is that any *supported* video card, or a video card that Slackware has built-in components for (and there are quite a few), enables you to run Slackware in text mode (no graphics). X (Slackware's graphical display), however, may require a different video card that can handle lots of different colors and screen sizes. See Chapter 11 for more information on X.

You can run Slackware without a modem, but if you want to connect to the Internet, you need at least a 14,400 bits per second (bps) modem (abbreviated as 14.4K). The current standard for modems is 56,000 bps (abbreviated as 56K); therefore, a 14.4 modem runs a bit slow. Keep in mind that some people using 56K modems only connect at a speed of 28,800 bps, so a 14.4K modem isn't that bad.

Soon, you'll discover that the more programs you want to run at a faster speed — like games, business applications, and graphic programs — requires more memory and a faster processor. For example, a 486 DX2/66 with 32MB RAM outperforms several cheap workstations in many areas, and that's without X running. However, a Pentium II-class machine with 96MB of RAM running X will outperform many business-class file and Web servers.

Collecting Hardware Information

You're pretty sure that you have most of what you need to run Slackware, but you're not certain about the *video card* — the adapter that creates the output required to display text and graphics on a monitor or hard drive. Knowing the details of your hardware is useful to both you and Slackware — Slackware needs this information to determine how it is to run, and you need this information to better troubleshoot problems and to eventually upgrade your hardware.

If gathering this information about your computer seems overwhelming, don't worry. Several tools exist to help you if you get stuck. I recommend opening your computer case and looking inside at least once just to get a feel for what's inside. You'll discover that there's no gerbil turning a wheel in there, or is there?

If you already have an operating system on your computer like DOS or Windows 3.1, you can use the built-in program called MSD (Microsoft Diagnostic Utility) to determine what exactly is inside your computer. I've used it many times in troubleshooting problems and found it invaluable. Turn to the section entitled "Accessing your hardware details in DOS or Windows 3.1" further in this chapter.

For those using Windows 95 or 98 (usually denoted as Win9x), you can use your system's Control Panel to get a list of all the hardware in your computer. See the "Accessing your hardware details in Win9x" section later in this chapter.

Accessing your hardware details in DOS or Windows 3.1

The first order of business is determining exactly what programs and configurations you have in your computer. You must be prepared for any questions that Slackware may pose during the installation process. In the past, this may have included taking off your computer's outer case and looking at each individual part, trying to decide if that little chip was part of the video card, or if it controlled the disk drives.

Fortunately, Microsoft provides MSD with the operating systems DOS 6.0, Windows 3.1, and Windows for Workgroups 3.11. MSD finds out what hardware you have without you resorting to the old take-off-the-case method. The MSD program is usually in your DOS or Windows directory. If you don't have this program, or can't seem to find it, you can download it from the Internet at `ftp://ftp.microsoft.com/Softlib/MSLFILES/MSDZIP.EXE`. MSD is useful for getting a list of what's in your system and for troubleshooting.

You need to know six things about your computer. Get a pen and piece of paper to write down the information, unless you have a photographic memory.

- Video settings
- Type of disk drive
- Available free space on the drive
- LPT (line print terminal) port settings
- COM (communication) port settings
- IRQ (interrupt request) status

To use MSD, you need to have a DOS prompt ready, which is usually seen as the `C:\>` prompt. If you're using DOS to begin with, you're ready to go. If you're using Windows 3.x, you need to exit Windows first and follow these steps:

1. **Type** msd **and press Enter.**

   The MSD menu appears, as shown in Figure 2-1.

   Note that a highlighted letter appears in each menu listing. You can select any of the menu listings by simply typing the appropriate key that corresponds to the highlighted letter.

   You can use the mouse to navigate the MSD menu instead of the keyboard by pointing and clicking on the appropriate menu item.

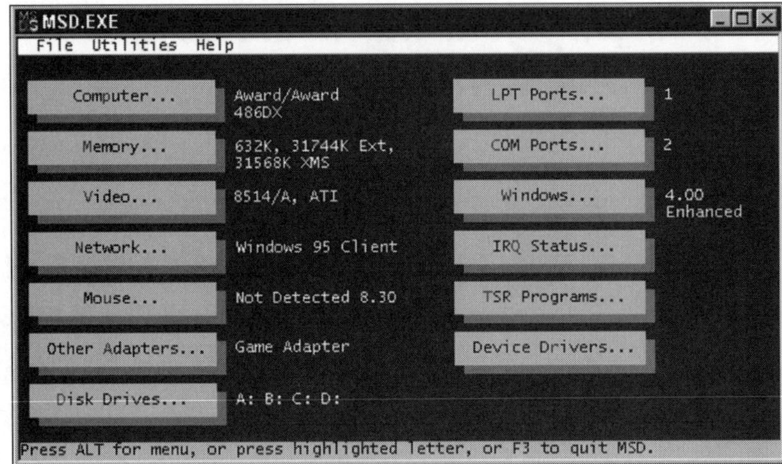

Figure 2-1: The MSD main menu.

2. **Type** V **to open the Video dialog box.**

   The Video dialog box appears, as shown in Figure 2-2.

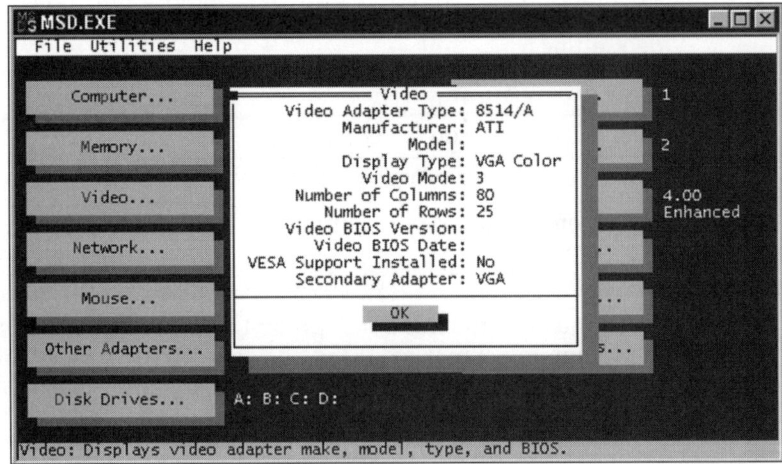

Figure 2-2: The MSD Video dialog box.

   Write down the information on this screen, including the video adapter type (which is just the video card) and model number. You need this information to set up X Windows (see Chapter 11).

3. **Press Enter to return to the MSD main menu.**
4. **Type** D **to open the Disk Drives dialog box.**

   The Disk Drives dialog box appears, as shown in Figure 2-3.

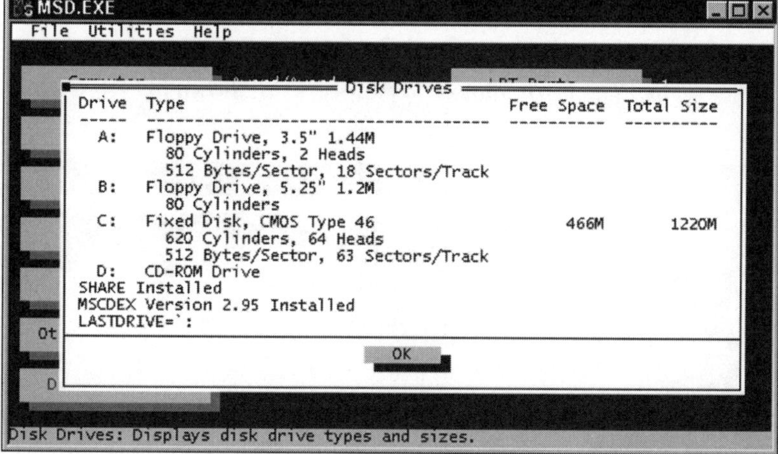

Figure 2-3: The MSD Disk Drives dialog box.

From the Disk Drives dialog box, write down the name and size of each hard, floppy, and CD-ROM drive. Then write down the number of cylinders, heads, and the total size of the hard drive(s).

5. **Press Enter to return to the MSD main menu.**
6. **Type** L **to open the LPT Ports dialog box.**

   The LPT Ports dialog box appears, as shown in Figure 2-4.

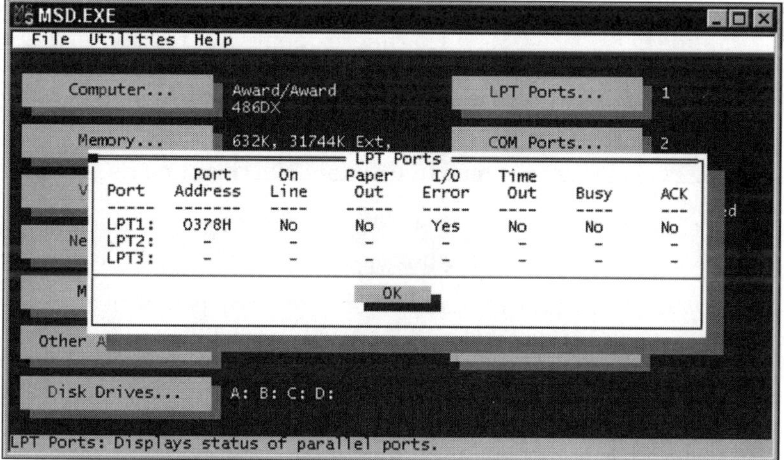

Figure 2-4: The MSD LPT Ports dialog box.

Write down the information on screen, including the corresponding port address noted for each LPT port listed.

7. **Press Enter to return to the MSD main menu.**

8. **Type** C **to open the COM Ports dialog box.**

   The COM Ports dialog box appears, as shown in Figure 2-5.

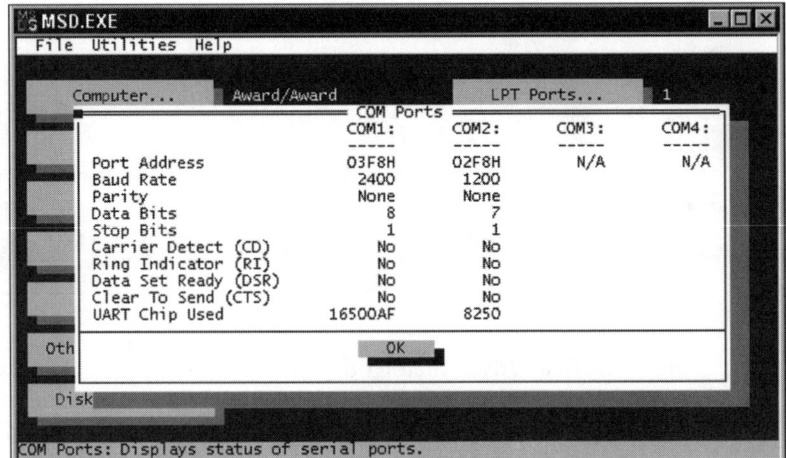

Figure 2-5: The MSD COM Ports dialog box.

   Write down the information on screen, including the port addresses and baud rates. Again, make sure that you have the corresponding port address noted for each COM port listed.

   The mouse is usually connected to COM1 or COM3, while the modem is on COM2 or COM4. (This information is not readily apparent, which is why I'm telling you this now.) Later in the setup process for Slackware, you will be asked what COM port your mouse uses and what COM port your modem uses.

9. **Press Enter to return to the main MSD main menu.**

10. **Type** Q **to open the IRQ Status dialog box.**

    The IRQ Status dialog box appears, as shown in Figure 2-6.

    Write down the information on screen. No two devices can have the same *interrupt* (IRQ). An interrupt is a signal from a device attached to a computer that causes the operating system to stop and figure out what to do next. Without this information, IRQs are headaches if not configured properly.

11. **Press Enter to return to the MSD main menu.**

12. **Press the F3 key to exit MSD.**

Now that you have the information on your computer handy, you can skip ahead to the "Backing Out" section at the end of this chapter.

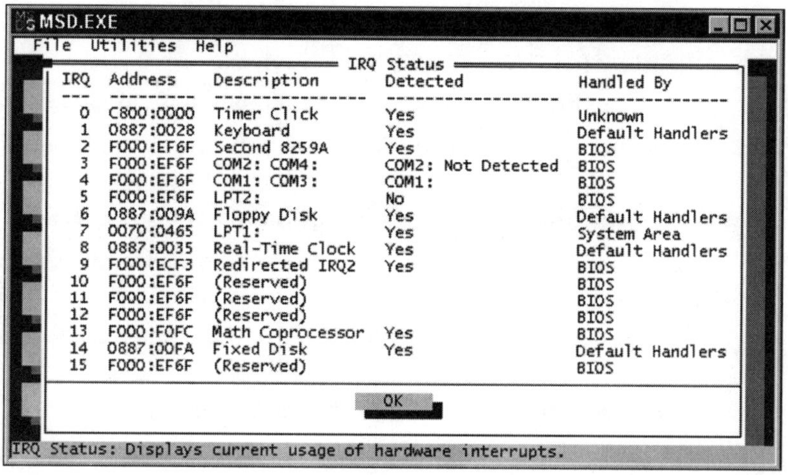

MSD.EXE

File Utilities Help

IRQ Status

IRQ	Address	Description	Detected	Handled By
0	C800:0000	Timer Click	Yes	Unknown
1	0887:0028	Keyboard	Yes	Default Handlers
2	F000:EF6F	Second 8259A	Yes	BIOS
3	F000:EF6F	COM2: COM4:	COM2: Not Detected	BIOS
4	F000:EF6F	COM1: COM3:	COM1:	BIOS
5	F000:EF6F	LPT2:	No	BIOS
6	0887:009A	Floppy Disk	Yes	Default Handlers
7	0070:0465	LPT1:	Yes	System Area
8	0887:0035	Real-Time Clock	Yes	Default Handlers
9	F000:ECF3	Redirected IRQ2	Yes	BIOS
10	F000:EF6F	(Reserved)		BIOS
11	F000:EF6F	(Reserved)		BIOS
12	F000:EF6F	(Reserved)		BIOS
13	F000:F0FC	Math Coprocessor	Yes	BIOS
14	0887:00FA	Fixed Disk	Yes	Default Handlers
15	F000:EF6F	(Reserved)		BIOS

OK

IRQ Status: Displays current usage of hardware interrupts.

Figure 2-6: The MSD IRQ Status dialog box.

Accessing your hardware details in Win9x

Win9x makes finding your hardware much easier when compared with older versions of Windows and DOS. MSD is included on the retail version of the Windows 95 CD (that's the version you buy at the store, not the version that comes with your computer). MSD does not come on the Windows 98 CD. You can download a copy from the Microsoft Web site at `ftp.microsoft.com/Softlib/MSLFILES/MSDZIP.EXE`.

Win9x's Control Panel makes finding hardware simpler than MSD because it's better organized and easier to read. To find your hardware in Win9x, follow these steps:

1. **From the Start menu, choose Settings⇨Control Panel.**

   The Control Panel window appears.

2. **Double-click the System icon.**

   The System Properties dialog box appears with a selection of tabs across the top. The type of CPU and the amount of RAM appears in the lower-right corner.

3. **Click the Device Manager tab.**

   The Device Manager page shows a variety of information. Several small circular buttons are at the top of the window.

4. **Click the View Devices By Type options button, if it's not already selected.**

   The Device Manager Page shows its information in a different format. A Computer icon appears near the top of this page.

5. **Click the Computer icon to highlight.**

   The Computer icon highlights.

6. **Click the Properties button at the bottom of the dialog box.**

   The Computer Properties dialog box appears with four button selections at the top.

7. **Click the Interrupt Request (IRQ) button, if it's not already selected.**

   The Computer Properties dialog box changes how it lists its information, as shown in Figure 2-7.

   Write down all the information listed in the Computer Properties dialog box.

8. **Click the Input/Output (I/O) options button.**

   The Computer Properties dialog box changes how it lists its information. Use the scroll bar on the right of the window and look for the following entries:

   - COM and LPT
   - Video card
   - Sound card (if you have one)

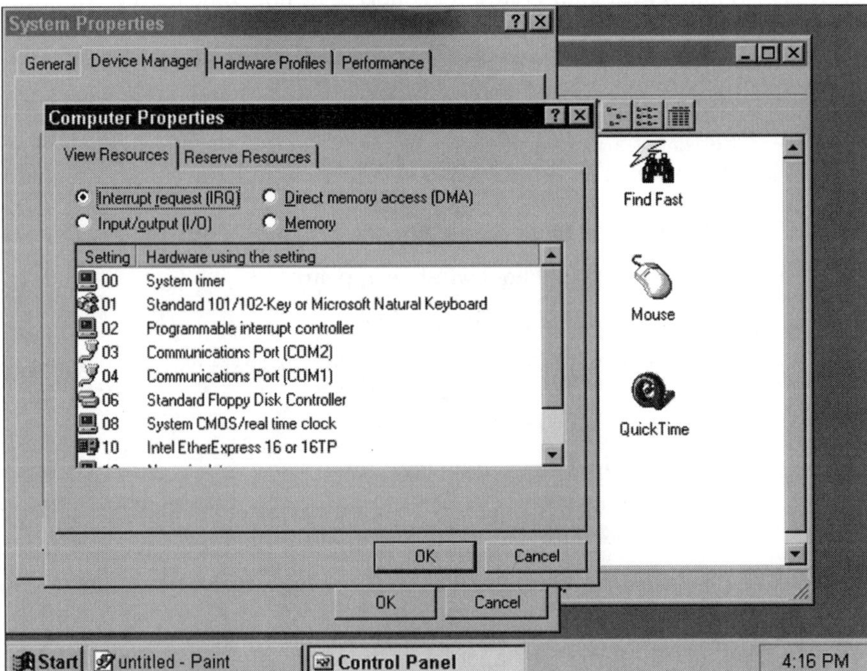

Figure 2-7: The Computer Properties IRQ window.

9. **Click the OK button.**

   The Computer Properties dialog box disappears, and the Device Manager dialog box returns. Again, make sure that the Computer icon is highlighted.

10. **Click the plus (+) sign next to Hard Disk Controllers.**

    The entry expands. Copy down which type of controller you have (IDE or SCSI) and brand name (if any).

11. **Click the plus (+) sign next to Disk Drives.**

    At least one disk appears as a submenu entry, as shown in Figure 2-8.

    Write down all information listed in the Disk drives submenu.

12. **Now repeat Step 11 for the following:**

    - **CDROM (not CD-ROM controllers)**
    - **Display Adapters**
    - **Keyboard**
    - **Modem**
    - **Monitor**
    - **Mouse**
    - **Ports (both COM and LPT)**

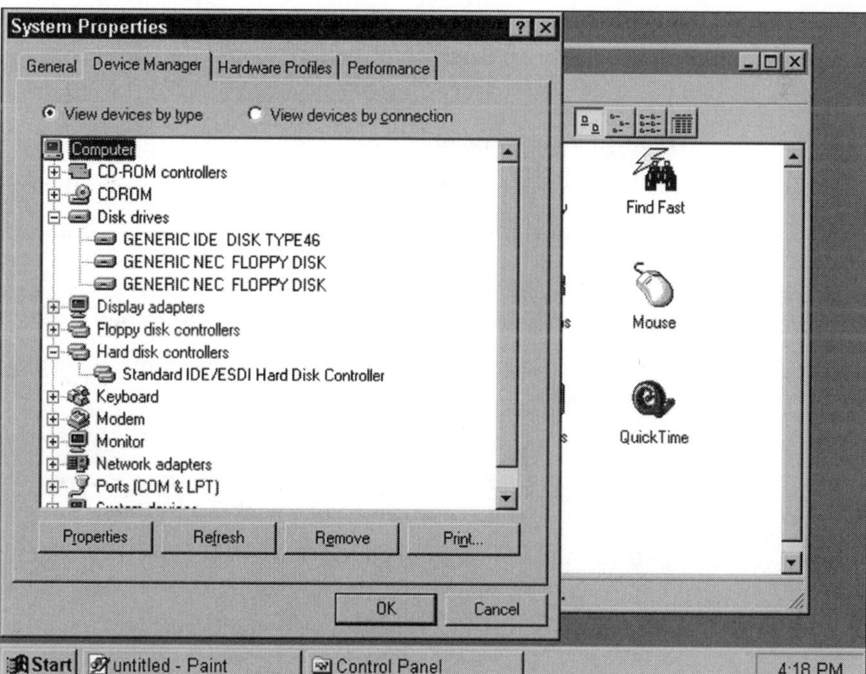

Figure 2-8: The System Properties dialog box.

13. **Click the plus (+) sign next to Sound, Video, and Game Controllers.**

    If you don't have a sound card, you will not have a listing for Sound, Video, and Game Controllers. Therefore, go to Step 19.

    Several entries may appear in a submenu, depending on the number of controllers that you have in your system. If you have a sound card in your computer, you should have at least one entry.

14. **Click the first entry listed in the Sound, Video, and Game Controllers submenu.**

15. **Now click the Properties button.**

    A dialog box for the first entry appears with several tabs across the top.

16. **Click the Resources tab at the top of the dialog box.**

    The entry's Resources page appears. Write down the resource types and corresponding settings.

17. **Click OK.**

    The entry's Resources page disappears.

18. **Repeat Steps 14 through 17 for each entry listed in Sound, Video, and Game Controllers.**

19. **In the Device Manager dialog box, click the OK button.**

    The Control Panel window returns.

You've gotten through most of the nitty-gritty information, but you still need to know a few things. To get information about your monitor, video card, and printers, follow these steps:

1. **Double-click the Display icon.**

   The Display Properties dialog box appears with several tabs at the top.

2. **Click the Settings tab.**

   The Settings dialog box appears.

3. **Click the menu arrow next to the Color Palette box.**

   The Color Palette menu appears, shown in Figure 2-9, displaying your color options.

   Write down all the information from the Color Palette Settings menu.

4. **In the Desktop area, click and hold the horizontal scrolling bar to move back and forth to view your desktop setting.**

   Note that the information changes below the bar as you scroll back and forth.

   Write down all the possible screen resolutions (how many colored dots can display) for your monitor.

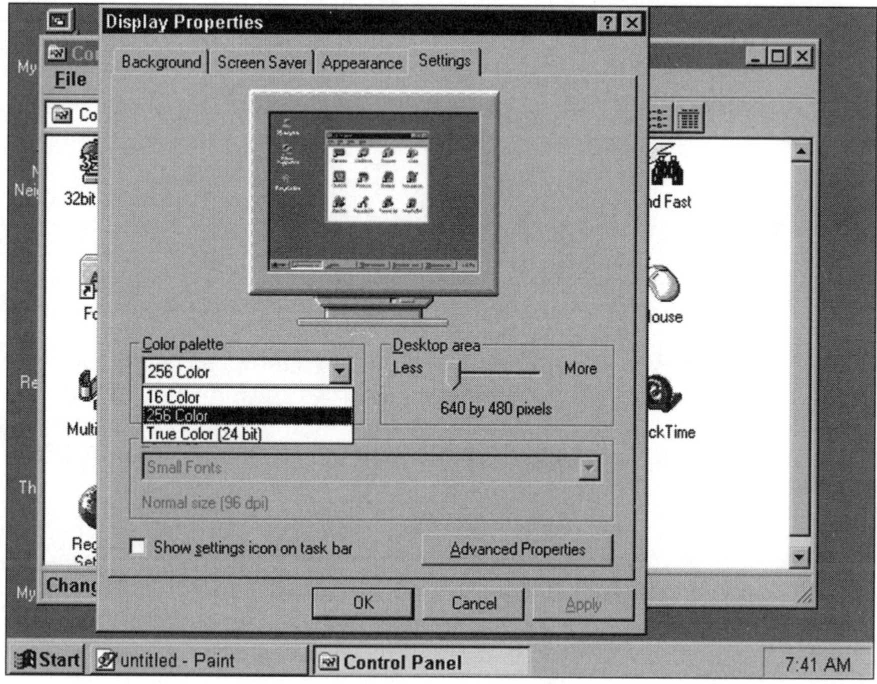

Figure 2-9: The Display Properties dialog box.

5. **Click the Cancel button to close the Display Properties dialog box.**

   The Control Panel window returns.

6. **Double-click the Printers icon.**

   The Printers window appears listing all the printers currently attached to your computer.

7. **Click the first printer entry next to the Add Printer icon.**

   Your printer's window opens with a menu bar across the top. This window lists the files that are currently printing (it's most likely empty).

8. **Choose File⇨Properties.**

   The Properties dialog box appears with several tabs across the top.

9. **Click the Details tab.**

   The dialog box changes how it lists its information. Make a note of the make, model, and COM port that the printer is using.

10. **Click the OK button.**

    The printer Properties dialog box closes.

11. **Close all remaining open windows by clicking the X in the top right corner of each window.**

Whew! That was a bit of work, but it's worth it to have this information if the Slackware setup program needs to know something particular about your printer or display. In any case, you now have almost every bit of information you can possibly get out of your computer!

Backing Out

If you choose to install Slackware Linux, you will make major changes to your computer that can possibly destroy data already on your computer. Therefore, I can't stress enough the need to back up your system right now, just in case something happens later. Windows 95 has its own backup utility, but you can purchase other commercial software as a backup or create your own boot disk. This makes your valuable data, like that research paper you're working on, or the monthly family budget, salvageable from possible destruction and restorable later if necessary.

By creating a *boot disk* of your operating system, you can boot your computer from a floppy disk containing the essential boot files, just in case you need to go back to the way things were.

To create a boot disk from DOS, follow these steps:

1. **Insert your blank floppy disk into the disk drive.**
2. **Type** format a: /s **and press Enter.**

   The disk formats and the operating system copies its essential files to the disk.

To create a boot disk from Win9x, follow these steps:

1. **Insert a blank floppy disk into the disk drive.**
2. **Double-click the My Computer icon on your desktop.**

   The My Computer window opens, listing all the drives currently in your system, plus several folders.
3. **Right-click the A: drive and select Format from the pop-up menu.**

   The Format A: drive dialog box appears.
4. **Click the button marked Copy System Files Only.**

   Several menu items may disappear or become grayed out.
5. **Click the Start button.**

   The disk formats and the operating system copies its essential files onto the disk.
6. **Click the Close button.**

   The Format A: drive dialog box closes. You can now close all other windows.

Keep the boot disk safe — you never know when you may need it.

Chapter 3

Making Boot and Root Disks

In This Chapter

- Creating boot and root disks in Windows and Linux
- Optimizing your free space
- Cleaning up your hard drive
- Making use of FIPS
- Using your boot disk

Your journey with Slackware needs to start somewhere, and that somewhere is with making boot and root disks to start your installation. If you think you can boot from your CD, see the beginning of the next section, in which case you can skip this chapter entirely. In this chapter, I assume that you're using the CD-ROM that came with this book, though these steps work for any version of Slackware after version 3.5.

In this chapter, I assume that the main partition of your hard drive is `C:`. If you've named your main partition something other than C:, substitute that name for C: wherever you see it in this chapter. I also assume that your first floppy drive (or only floppy drive if you only have one) is `A:`.

Getting Ready with Boot and Root Disks

Before you can begin the installing Slackware, if you have a computer built before 1997 you must have an operating system — any operating system, whether it be OS/2, Windows, DOS, or another form of Linux — already on your computer. If you have a computer purchased after 1997, you may be able to boot from the CD-ROM drive by doing the following:

1. **Turn on your computer and monitor.**
2. **Place the Slackware Install CD in the CD-ROM drive and close the drive.**

   If the Linux deities are smiling upon you, Slackware boots from the CD-ROM. If so, jump once for joy and then skip ahead to Chapter 4. The CD-ROM is now both your boot and root disk.

If you can't boot from your CD, you need to have two things before you start installing Slackware. These are:

- **A boot disk:** A floppy disk containing the basic booting process for the computer.
- **A root disk:** A stripped-down (bare essentials only) version of the operating system.

Why do you need these things? Making boot and root disks is essential for installing Slackware because Slackware needs a foundation or platform on which it can work. By using boot and root disks, you start from a blank slate instead of starting from another operating system. You also minimize the chance for errors when using boot and root disks as compared with running the install process under another operating system like DOS or Windows.

Windows actually uses a boot disk, too, but most never see it because the vast percentage of PC-buyers buy a computer with Windows preinstalled, or upgrade their copy of Windows, which usually runs from a CD.

If you're not starting from a clean hard drive — that is, if you have data you'll be keeping (such as a Windows partition, for example) — you also need to shuffle any existing data around so that you can get the most out of the free space available. Slackware can be very compact when it needs to be, but it doesn't hurt to squeeze that last kilobyte of space out of your hard drive.

Don't get me wrong, it's possible to run Slackware from DOS or Windows, but there really isn't any reason to if you can help it! Slackware is its own operating system — it doesn't need help from another one. Slackware is much faster than Windows in general, and doesn't crash as often as Windows, if at all.

Before you start, you need at least three blank, formatted floppy disks. Two are used immediately, while the third is used later for a FIPS disk. (FIPS is explained in greater detail in Chapter 4.) You must also make sure that you back up anything important on your hard drive. That way, if, for some reason you accidentally destroy something valuable you can always restore it later. If you don't have anything on your hard drive you want to save, you can skip using FIPS entirely.

I recommend having a box of ten blank, formatted floppy disks available. (The most common way to buy floppy disks is to purchase a box of ten from your local office-supply store.) Sometimes, you just need to have a floppy disk handy. Loss of information isn't a common problem with Slackware's installation, but it never hurts to plan ahead.

Making startup disks with DOS or Windows

As the previous section makes abundantly clear, you need a boot disk and a root disk to start up the Slackware installation process. DOS and Windows put their equivalent of boot and root disks on your `C:` drive by default. After installation, Slackware does the same thing, overwriting the DOS or Windows equivalent. In the meantime, you need to create these disks.

Getting the boot

On the CD-ROM are two folders that have names starting with `bootdsks`, namely the `bootdsks.144` folder (for those with 3½-inch floppy disk drives) and the `bootdsks.122` folder (for those with 5¼-inch disk drives). In each folder are many files like `net.i`, `bare.i`, and `xt.i`. These files are the boot disk images that you will need to start your Slackware system.

Throughout these instructions, I assume you have a 3½-inch floppy disk drive, but if you have a 5¼-inch floppy disk drive instead, substitute `bootdsks.122` for `bootdsks.144`. I also assume that you have an IDE hard drive, but if you have a SCSI hard drive, substitute `scsi.s` wherever you see `bare.i` in the following instructions.

Before making your disks, take note of the following:

- In the following steps, I assume that your floppy drive is the `A:` drive, and that your CD-ROM drive is the `D:` drive.
- If you're using DOS or Windows, make sure that no other applications are running. Also, if you're running Windows 3.*x*, exit Windows and get back to DOS.

In the `bootdsks.144` directory on the CD-ROM is a program called RAWRITE. To use RAWRITE to transfer the necessary boot images to your boot disk, follow these steps:

1. **If you're using Windows, open a DOS prompt by clicking the Start button and choosing Programs⇨MS-DOS Prompt.**

   In Windows, the MS-DOS Prompt window appears with a `C:\WINDOWS>` prompt. If you're using DOS, any prompt is fine.

2. **Insert a blank floppy disk into the `A:` drive.**
3. **Type one of the following lines at the DOS prompt (depending on your floppy disk drive type) and then press Enter:**

If you have a 3½-inch disk drive, type **d:\bootdsks.144\rawrite.exe d:\bootdsks.144\bare.i a:**

If you have a 5¼-inch disk drive, type **d:\bootdsks.122\rawrite.exe d:\bootdsks.122\bare.i a:**

These commands copy the `bare.i` boot program to your floppy disk; bare.i is the standard boot program.

The following text appears on the screen (though the numbers may differ, as well as the drive letters if yours are not standard):

```
Number of sectors per track for this disk is 18
Writing image to drive A:.  Press ^C to abort.
Track: 44  Head:  0 Sector:  4
Done.
```

RAWRITE writes the `bare.i` image from the CD to your floppy disk. The numbers next to track, head, and sector change as it writes the image. Eject your floppy disk and label it "Slackware boot."

Don't be fooled into thinking that the above process is just a plain file-copy process, and that you can just use the COPY command to do this instead of RAWRITE. RAWRITE writes specific information to the floppy disk that enables the system to boot from that floppy disk. The DOS `copy` command doesn't do this!

Making the root

Now you need to create the root disk. On the CD-ROM is a directory called `rootdsks` that contains many images — or root systems — for your computer, along with another copy of RAWRITE.

To copy the necessary root images to your disk, follow these steps:

1. **If you're using Windows, open a DOS prompt by clicking the Start button and choosing Programs⇨MS-DOS Prompt (any DOS prompt is fine).**

   If you already have the MS-DOS Prompt window open, you can skip this step. You don't have to open a second one.

   If you're using DOS, make sure that no other applications are running.

   Otherwise, the MS-DOS Prompt window appears with a `C:\WINDOWS>` prompt.

2. **Insert a blank floppy disk into the `A:` drive.**

3. **Type** d:\rootdsks\rawrite.exe d:\rootdsks\color.gz a: **and press Enter.**

   I assume that your CD-ROM drive is designated on your computer as `D:`. If this is not the case, substitute the designation of your CD drive accordingly wherever you see `D:`.

The following text appears on the screen (the numbers may differ, as well as the drive letters if yours are not standard):

```
Number of sectors per track for this disk is 18
Writing image to drive A:.  Press ^C to abort.
Track: 67  Head:  0 Sector: 13
Done.
```

RAWRITE writes the `color.gz` image from the CD to your blank disk. The numbers next to track, head, and sector change as it writes the image.

4. **Eject your floppy disk and label it *root*.**

Making disks with Linux

Suppose that you want to make boot and root disks for friends, but you're already running Linux, such as another distribution of Linux or an older version of Slackware, instead of DOS or Windows. No problem! Making boot and root disks in Slackware is even simpler than the RAWRITE program that you use when making the disks in Windows (as the previous section describes).

Under DOS or Windows, your first floppy drive (either a 3½-inch or a 5¼-inch floppy drive) is listed as `A:`. Slackware sees this floppy drive as `/dev/fd0`, which is important to note because using the wrong device in the following instructions can wreak serious havoc on your system.

To create boot and root disks in Linux, you use the same boot and root images that you would use if making the disks in Windows (as mentioned in the previous section). To make boot and root disks within Slackware or another Linux distribution, follow these steps:

1. **Insert the CD from the back of the book into your CD-ROM drive.**
2. **At the `login:` prompt, type** root **and press Enter.**
3. **At the password prompt, enter the root user's password (if one exists).**

   A command prompt ending with # (the pound sign) is displayed on your screen. This prompt is where you type commands.
4. **At the # command prompt, type** `mount /dev/cdrom /cdrom` **and press Enter.**

   Your computer mounts the CD so that Slackware can use it. *Mounting* means that the CD is set up for use by the computer. Slackware then displays the message `Mounting /cdrom read-only` and gives you another command prompt.
5. **Insert a blank floppy disk into the floppy drive.**

6. **At the # command prompt, type** dd if=/cdrom/bootdsks.144/bare.i of=/dev/fd0 **and press Enter.**

   This creates the boot disk. Another command prompt displays.

7. **Eject the disk and label it *boot.***
8. **Insert another blank floppy disk into the floppy drive.**
9. **At the # command prompt, type** dd if=/cdrom/rootdsks/color.gz of=/dev/fd0 **and press Enter.**

   This creates the root disk.

10. **Eject the disk and label it *root.***

Chapter 4

Discovering the Joy of Partitioning

In This Chapter

- Calculating your partition space
- Creating swap space
- Using `fdisk` or `cfdisk` to carve up your disk

Partitions are areas on your hard drive set aside like little virtual hard drives. The most common use for a partition is to install multiple operating systems, such as Slackware and Windows, on the same hard drive (which isn't allowed without partitions). To run Slackware, you need at least one partition on your hard drive, and that's what this chapter is all about.

In this chapter you also get to deal with *swap space* (lucky you!), which is the area on your hard drive reserved for passing information back and forth between the system and the application. Fortunately, I show you how to set up an appropriate swap space for Slackware so that your system can run smoothly.

Finally, after you have a handle on your disk space and swap space, I show you how the `fdisk` and `cfdisk` utilities can help divide both disk space and swap space.

So now it's time to take off the kid gloves and get your hands dirty. You can always wash up after you're done, just don't drip on the keyboard — it really hates that.

Preparing to Partition Your Hard Drive

Before you can install Slackware, you have to make room for it on your hard drive. Usually, the easiest (albeit the most expensive) way to do this is to physically add another hard drive to the computer. A less expensive option is to remove Windows or any other operating system that you may already have, though that's a radical method. If you don't have a big enough hard drive to install Slackware, you will have to exercise one of these options.

After you know that your hard drive is big enough for your needs (which you can determine by visiting the "Making sure your hard drive is worthy" section a little farther into this chapter), you find yourself in one of the following two groups:

- **Your hard drive is big enough to handle Slackware and the software you want to install on it, but you want to keep Windows and/or information on your hard drive.**

  What you should do now: You need to use FIPS. You should continue with this section to defrag your drive and check it for errors to prepare it for FIPS.

- **Your hard drive is big enough to handle Slackware and the software you want to install on it, but is either blank or has information you don't mind erasing.**

  What you should do now: You may skip to the "Rebooting with your Slackware boot disk" section in this chapter now.

Manipulating your free space

Before installing Linux or any program on your system (or before installing any program, for that matter), you need to know how much hard drive space you have available on your computer, as well as how much hard drive space is required to install your programs. Without this information, you may run out of space before you can get started! See the following section to make sure your hard drive is worthy of Slackware.

Making sure your hard drive is worthy

Before you go to all the silliness in the following sections with your hard drive, you should make sure your hard drive is of a size to meet your needs. If you don't know what size your hard drive is, take a gander at Chapter 2 and follow the instructions there to find out.

Unless you have about 1GB of hard drive space available, you won't be able to install all the packages that come with Slackware. Table 4-1 lists the common sizes of some typical installations.

Table 4-1 Typical Installation Sizes

Size (in MB)	*What's Installed*
150	Minimum Slackware installation (no graphics)
250	Minimum Slackware installation plus X Windows

Size (in MB)	What's Installed
325	Average Slackware installation plus X Windows
350	Minimum Slackware installation, X Windows, KDE
400	Average Slackware installation, X Windows, KDE
425	Minimum Slackware installation, X Windows, GNOME
500	Average Slackware installation, X Windows, GNOME
700	Average Slackware installation, X Windows, KDE and GNOME
900	All contents of CD-ROM

X Windows is the graphical display for Slackware. KDE and GNOME are graphical desktops for Slackware (to make your screen look like a hybrid between Windows, Macintosh, and Unix).

All these options are software packages available to install on your computer once Slackware is installed. Note that some of these examples are of *minimum* installations, which means that only the bare essential files are installed and not a byte more. Having a robust system means having more programs and files installed, which in turn means more disk space necessary. An average installation size — including a standard X Windows install, plus the KDE or GNOME desktop, and installation of accessory programs like games, CD-ROM music players, and chat programs — is usually over 700MB.

Add up the amount of space the software packages you want to install take up and make sure that this number is less than the amount of hard drive space you currently have by a good 20MB or more. If it isn't, your hard drive is not big enough to handle what you want to install on it! If this is the case, you either need to rethink how much software you want to install, see if you can free up any more room on your hard drive to accommodate what you want to install on it (by deleting Windows, for example), or get a new hard drive.

Scanning your disk for errors

Before attempting the Slackware installation, you first need to ensure that everything's okay with the hard drive. The fastest way to do this is to run the Scandisk program, which checks the `C:` drive for errors and then fixes the errors or moves the data (if possible) to another part of the disk. Scandisk is included with the MS-DOS, Windows 3.*x*, and Windows 9*x* operating systems.

To start Scandisk in DOS, type **c:\dos\scandisk c:** at the `C:\ >` prompt and then press Enter.

If you're using Windows 9*x*, follow these steps to start Scandisk:

1. **Double-click the My Computer icon on your desktop.**

   The My Computer window appears.

2. **Click your `C:` drive once to select it.**

3. **Choose File⇨Properties.**

   The `C:` Properties dialog box appears with details about your C: drive. Figure 4-1 shows the menu that pops up after right-clicking the `C:` drive icon.

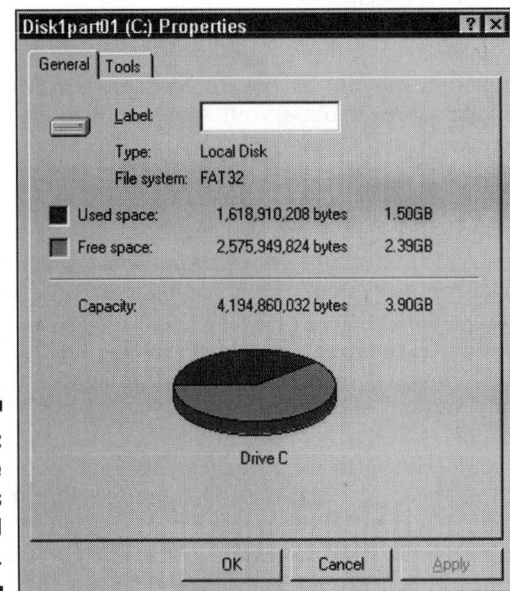

Figure 4-1: The properties of your hard drive.

4. **Select the Tools tab.**

   Figure 4-2 shows the Tools tab.

5. **Click the Check Now . . . button.**

   The Scandisk options dialog box appears.

6. **Select the Thorough option if it's not already selected.**

7. **Select the Automatically Fix Errors option if it's not already selected.**

8. **Click Start.**

   Scandisk runs, and runs, and runs. Depending on the size of your hard drive, this process may take some time.

9. **When Scandisk finishes, click the Close button.**

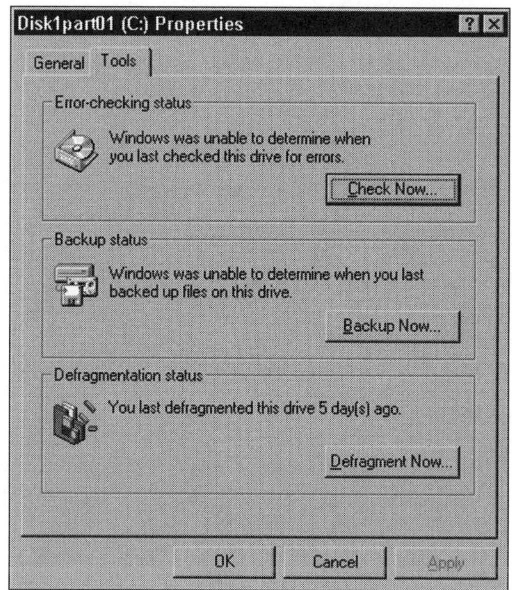

Figure 4-2: The Tools tab of the Properties window.

Defragging your hard drive

The next step in preparing for installation is to consolidate the free space available on your hard drive, or *defragment* the drive. In DOS or Windows, it's important to use the Disk Defragmenter program to defragment your hard drive at least once a month as a precaution. In Slackware defragging is not usually necessary because Slackware checks the disk to see if defragging is needed every time it boots up — if defragging is necessary, Slackware does it for you.

If you're planning to remove your old operating system and use Slackware only, you can skip to the "Rebooting with Your Boot Disk" section later in this chapter. Defragging to get your files in order is hardly necessary when you're going to erase those files, after all.

When it comes to free space, computers store information on a first-come, first-served basis. When you delete a file, you leave a hole in the disk where the file used to be. Defragmenting fills the holes by shuffling everything as close to the beginning of the disk as possible.

Windows' Disk Defragmenter checks the hard drive and tells you whether or not your hard drive needs to be defragged. Defrag the drive whether Disk Defragmenter says you need to do so or not. Disk Defragmenter is programmed to say you don't need to defragment your drive if your drive is less than 9 percent fragmented. However, those data fragments are still lying around the drive, and FIPS will have problems if the disk is not defragged.

In DOS, type the following at the C:\> prompt and then press Enter:

```
c:\dos\defrag c:
```

If you're using Windows 9*x*, follow these steps:

1. **Double-click the My Computer icon on your desktop.**

   The My Computer window appears.

2. **Click the icon for your `C:` drive to select it.**
3. **Choose File⇨Properties.**

   The C: Properties dialog box appears with details about your `C:` drive.

4. **Select the Tools tab.**
5. **Click the Defragment Now . . . button.**

   Disk Defragmenter scans the drive and tells you how fragmented your hard drive is.

6. **Click Start.**

   Disk Defragmenter runs (and runs, and runs). Depending on the size of your hard drive, this process may take some time.

After the defragment procedure is complete, you're ready to move your data around and free up some space for Slackware.

Using FIPS

FIPS (which stands for First nondestructive Interactive Partition Splitting) is a program that enables you to move things around (like your programs, data, files, and folders) on your hard drive, leaving plenty of room for both your old operating system and Slackware. This is called *nondestructive repartitioning*. The "nondestructive" part stems from FIPS's ability to move data around your hard drive without destroying it.

If you have a blank hard drive or one that you don't mind completely erasing, you don't need to use FIPS and can skip to the next section. You need to use FIPS only if you have an existing partition (with Windows or another operating system on it, for example) that you do not want to get rid of.

You should scan your disk for errors and defrag your hard drive before you follow the instructions in this section. See the "Scanning your disk for errors" and "Defragging your hard drive" sections earlier in this chapter to get these chores out of the way.

Before you can run FIPS, you need to boot your computer from a Windows or DOS floppy disk, which means you need to format a blank floppy disk as a Windows or DOS boot disk. Your floppy disks are probably preformatted, but in order for a floppy to become a Windows or DOS boot disk, certain system files need to be copied onto it. To add the system files to your floppy disk, follow these steps:

Make sure for the two numbered lists that follow (you only need follow one or the other) that you use a *new* blank disk, not your boot or root disks!

To create a DOS boot disk:

1. **Insert a blank floppy disk into the disk drive.**
2. **At the** `C:\>` **prompt, type** format a: /s **and press Enter.**

   The disk is formatted and the operating system files are copied to the disk.

To create a Windows 9*x* boot disk:

1. **Insert a blank floppy disk into the disk drive.**
2. **Double-click the My Computer icon on your desktop.**

   The My Computer window appears.
3. **Right-click the** `A:` **drive and select Format from the pop-up menu.**

   The Format A: dialog box appears.
4. **Click the Copy System Files Only button.**

   Several menu items disappear or become grayed out, meaning that these items are not relevant to the current process.
5. **Click Start.**

   The disk is formatted and the operating system files are copied to the disk.
6. **Click Close.**

Now you can copy the FIPS program from the Source CD that comes with this book to the floppy disk. To copy the FIPS program from the Source CD to the floppy disk in DOS, follow these steps:

1. **Make sure that the floppy disk that you just formatted with the system files is in the** `A:` **drive.**
2. **At your** `C:\>` **prompt, type** copy d:\install\fips-20\restorrb.exe a: **and press Enter.**

   The RESTORRB program copies to the disk in the A: drive.
3. **At the** `C:\>` **prompt, type** copy d:\install\fips-20\fips.exe a: **and press Enter.**

   The FIPS program copies to the disk in the A: drive.

4. **At the** `C:\>` **prompt, type** copy d:\install\fips-20\errors.txt a: **and press Enter.**

   The FIPS errors file copies to the disk in the `A:` drive.

5. **Leave the disk in the** `A:` **drive and reboot your computer.**

   When the computer reboots, it boots from the floppy disk. If you've finagled your BIOS to not allow booting from a floppy disk (or someone else has) you need to turn this option back on or find someone who can.

To copy the FIPS program from the CD to the floppy drive in Windows 9*x*, follow these steps (make sure that the floppy disk that you just formatted with the system files is in the `A:` drive):

1. **Open Windows Explorer by clicking the Start button and choosing Programs⇨Windows Explorer from the Start menu.**

   Windows Explorer appears.

2. **Double-click the** `D:` **drive listing.**

   The `D:` drive expands to list all the folders in the drive.

3. **Double-click the** `Install` **folder.**

   The `Install` folder expands to list all the folders inside.

4. **Double-click the** `fips-20` **folder.**

   The `fips-20` folder expands to list all the files inside.

5. **Click and drag the** `restorrb.exe` **file to your** `A:` **drive.**

   The RESTORRB program copies to the `A:` drive.

6. **Click and drag the** `fips.exe` **file to your** `A:` **drive.**

   The FIPS program copies to the `A:` drive.

7. **Click and drag the errors.txt file to your** `A:` **drive.**

   The FIPS errors file copies to the `A:` drive.

8. **Leave the disk in the** `A:` **drive and reboot your computer.**

   When the computer reboots, it boots from the floppy disk. If your BIOS does not allow booting from a floppy disk, you'll need to turn this option back on or find someone who can.

By using the copy of the operating system on the floppy disk, FIPS can run without worrying about moving files currently in use by DOS or Windows.

Make sure that you label this disk "FIPS" at a later time! If you want to label it now, just make sure you do so and then put the disk back into the drive before you reboot.

After you reboot, the `A:\>` prompt appears:

If at any time you want to exit FIPS (such as after making a typo, for example), just press Ctrl+C.

To use FIPS, follow these steps:

1. **At the** `A:\>` **prompt, type** fips **and press Enter.**

   A bunch of text appears on your screen, and at the end of the text it says `Press any Key.`

2. **Press the space bar.**

   A small partition table appears, similar to Figure 4-3.

   The only information in this listing that is useful to you is the last column, under MB. The last column lists the total amount of space on your hard drive. You should make a note of the total amount of space you have according to FIPS. If you have multiple partitions, add together all the numbers in the last column to get the total amount of space available.

```
Partition table:

     |        |      Start        |      |       End         | Start  |Number of|
Part.|bootable|Head Cyl. Sector|System|Head Cyl. Sector| Sector |Sectors  |  MB
-----+--------+----------------+------+----------------+--------+---------+----
1    |     yes |   1     0        1|   06h|  63   619        63|       63|  2499777|1220
2    |      no |   0     0        0|   00h|   0     0         0|        0|        0|   0
3    |      no |   0     0        0|   00h|   0     0         0|        0|        0|   0
4    |      no |   0     0        0|   00h|   0     0         0|        0|        0|   0

Checking root sector ... OK

Press any Key
```

Figure 4-3: The FIPS partition table listing.

3. **Press the space bar.**

   FIPS proceeds to check your hard drive to see where to begin the free space partition. Don't worry, this is normal. When it's finished, FIPS asks if you want to make a backup copy of your partition information.

   FIPS is checking your drive to see if any stray fragments are lying around. I tried this once without defragging first, and discovered that wherever the last fragment is on the disk, FIPS uses that point to start calculating your free space area. In my case, I had a fragment on the next-to-last cylinder, so FIPS reported I had 10MB of space free when in fact I had 560MB free. Oops! This is why it's important to defrag your disk!

4. **Press *y* to backup your partition information, or press *n* if you don't want to bother.**

   Backing up your partition information can save you headaches in case you decide not to follow through with the Slackware installation. By backing up your partition information, you can use FIPS if you wish to restore your machine back to the way it originally was.

   FIPS now tries to trick you — it asks if you have a bootable floppy disk in the `A:` drive "as described in the documentation." You can use *any* floppy disk that has about 75KB of free space, including the floppy disk that you just booted your computer with, as there is enough free space on that disk for at least ten backup copies of your partition table.

5. **Press *y*.**

   FIPS writes a backup copy of your partition info to the floppy disk, calling it `rootboot.000`. If you repeat this process, FIPS changes the 000 to 001, 002, 003, and so on.

   Next a table that lists the cylinders of your hard drive appears, similar to Figure 4-4. The format of the table is the same for any hard drive used, but the numbers are different depending on the total space available in the hard drive.

   FIPS automatically assumes that you want to use all available free space so it dedicates all available space to your new partition. You can change this amount or just leave it alone.

6. **Use the left and right arrow keys to choose how much space to give the new partition.**

   Unless you have about 1GB of hard drive space available, you won't be able to install all the packages that come with Slackware. For more information about space requirements for Slackware, see the "Making sure your hard drive is worthy" section earlier in this chapter.

```
Enter start cylinder for new partition (379 - 619):

Use the cursor keys to choose the cylinder, <enter> to continue

Old partition      Cylinder       New Partition
  746.2 MB           379            474.5 MB
```

Figure 4-4: FIPS cylinder information.

The numeric keypad arrow keys don't work in this situation. The third column, New Partition, increases or decreases as you press the left or right arrow keys. Once you are satisfied with the amount of space shown, go on to Step 7.

You need to leave some room for your other operating system if you intend to make any real use of it again. Your other operating system already has the room it needs to run, but if you decide to create or save new files or to install new programs, leave some extra space. If you have an extra 200MB of disk space to spare, consider giving that space to your other operating system.

7. **Press Enter.**

   FIPS tests to see if the space in your new partition is really empty. FIPS does this test because some people don't run Scandisk and Defrag before performing these steps, and the empty space isn't consolidated into one large area. When the test is complete, a new partition table similar to the one shown in Figure 4-5 appears on the screen (the actual information within the table differs depending on the size of your hard drive).

   Notice that at the bottom of the screen, FIPS asks if you want to continue or to reedit the table. If you want to change anything, press *r* to repeat Steps 6 and 7.

```
Enter start cylinder for new partition (379 - 619):

Use the cursor keys to choose the cylinder, <enter> to continue

Old partition      Cylinder       New Partition
  750.1 MB           381             470.5 MB

First Cluster: 23998
Last Cluster: 39054

Testing if empty ... OK

New partition table:

     |        |      Start       |      |       End        | Start   |Number of|
Part.|bootable|Head Cyl. Sector|System|Head Cyl. Sector| Sector  |Sectors  |  MB
-----+--------+----------------+------+----------------+---------+---------+----
1    |    yes |  1    0       1|   06h|  63  380      63|       63|  1536129| 750
2    |     no |  0  381       1|   06h|  63  619      63|  1536192|   963648| 470
3    |     no |  0    0       0|   00h|   0    0       0|        0|        0|   0
4    |     no |  0    0       0|   00h|   0    0       0|        0|        0|   0

Checking root sector ... OK

Do you want to continue or reedit the partition table (c/r)?
```

Figure 4-5: A new FIPS partition table.

8. **Press *c* to continue.**

   FIPS asks whether you're ready to write the new partition information to the hard drive.

9. **Press *y* if you're ready, or press *n* if you're not.**

   FIPS writes the new partition table to the floppy disk.

10. **Eject your floppy disk and label it "FIPS + partition info (bootable)" or something similar.**

11. **Reboot your computer.**

The computer boots up in your old operating system (such as Windows or DOS).

Rebooting with your Slackware boot disk

Booting your computer with your new boot disk is crucial to the installation process. This is because Slackware needs its own platform to work with, instead of using DOS, Windows, an older version of Slackware, or another distribution of Linux.

After you've completed the necessary tasks in the previous sections and you're sure that you have a good boot and root disk, follow these steps:

1. **Put the disk labeled "Slackware boot" (you did label your disks, didn't you?) into your `A:` drive and reboot your computer.**

   Some general information displays on your screen and a `boot:` prompt appears.

2. **Press Enter.**

   The following message appears:

   ```
   Loading ramdisk..................
   Uncompressing Linux...
   ```

   Then your screen starts scrolling with information. Slackware is finding out exactly what kind of hardware you have.

   Don't worry about any warning messages that you may receive; Slackware is actually writing copies of these warnings to its own files for future reference. Most of the warnings are caused by Slackware trying to probe for hardware that isn't there, like a second CD-ROM drive or another video card.

   When the information is done scrolling, you see a message that reads:

   ```
   VFS: Insert root floppy disk to be loaded into RAM disk
            and press ENTER
   ```

3. **Eject your boot disk, insert your root disk, and press Enter.**

   The following message appears:

   ```
   RAMDISK: compressed image found at block 0
   ```

   Now the computer begins loading the Slackware root, or kernel.

   The *kernel* is the essential center of a computer, the core that provides basic services for all other parts of the operating system.

   When the computer is finished loading the kernel, another screen of information appears.

4. **Read the information that appears carefully, as it contains important information about what to do if you have less than 8MB of RAM or if you don't have a color monitor.**

5. **At the `login:` prompt, type** root **and press Enter.**

   You are brought to the command prompt (the # prompt).

Congratulations! You have successfully booted with your Slackware boot and root disks!

Calculating your partition space wisely

You can't run pell-mell into an installation without knowing exactly where you're going to put everything on the drive. You must have enough space for what you want — you wouldn't install a new whiz-bang spreadsheet program that takes up 45MB if you only had 30MB left, would you? Of course not! The same principle applies with Slackware.

First you need to know that, unlike Windows, Slackware places its software in certain directories on the hard drive instead of just tossing everything into one directory. These directories can then be broken up into different areas of the hard drive so that if for some reason the hard drive dies, it's easier to recover information. Breaking up the hard drive into sections is called *partitioning.*

See the `README7.TXT` file on the CD for a list of approximately how much space each Slackware software package uses, or see the "Making sure your hard drive is worthy" section earlier in this chapter to see if your hard drive is up to par with what you want to do with it. Add up the amount of space the software packages you want to install take up. Make sure that this number is less than the amount of hard drive space you currently have by a good 20MB or more. If this is the case, you can safely partition your hard drive.

By this point you should know how large your hard drive is, and how much space is available on it. If you don't, turn to Chapter 2.

If you have a SCSI hard drive, your drives will appears as devices like `/dev/sda1`, `/dev/sda2`, and `/dev/sda3` instead of `/dev/hda1` and so on.

Partitions can appear as two different types — data or swap. *Swap partitions* are used as virtual memory and are not visible to the user, but the system knows the swap partition exists and uses it. *Data partitions* are visible partitions that the user can see — these partitions become directories containing the files on your Slackware system.

What's easy for Slackware may not be easy for you. Slackware can interchange partitions as easily as you can switch the letters in "interchange." If you tell Slackware to use partition A for one purpose and then accidentally tell Slackware to use partition A for another, completely different purpose, Slackware will follow your instructions and probably destroy the data on partition A. In other words, Slackware does exactly what you tell it to do, even if you tell Slackware to do something you later regret.

You may wonder why you need swap space when you have *x* amount of memory or RAM on your computer. Ah, Windows has you fooled. Even though Windows says that it is using RAM to run, it's also using swap space to help handle programs.

Slackware knows how to use partitions to the fullest extent, so it can squeeze the most data into all the available space without fragmenting or leaving holes of free space on the disk.

You may be wondering if your hard drive isn't already partitioned. The answer is a conditional "no." If you have a hard drive that's less than 2GB, you most likely have only one partition. Windows and DOS use the all-in-one method, placing everything on one partition. If you've purchased a computer recently, then you probably have more than one partition because the vendor will have partitioned your hard drive into two drives (`C:` and `D:`). And if you have a brand-new, never used, just-out-of-the-box hard drive (minus the computer), you definitely don't have any partitions.

Creating multiple partitions is a good idea because keeping information stored in multiple partitions is safer than having everything on one partition (or no partition at all). The theory goes that if one partition dies, you're less likely to lose information on the rest of the partitions. The steps you go through further along in this chapter assume that you are partitioning your disk into multiple partitions.

To install Slackware, you need at least three partitions in addition to any partitions you have with other files or operating systems on them. Partitions show up in Windows as new drive letters, such as `D:`, `E:`, `F:`, and so on. But with Slackware, partitions appear as devices like `/dev/hda1`, `/dev/hda2`, and `/dev/hda3` (hda1 meaning hard drive one, hda2 meaning hard drive two, and so on). The `/dev` names may look a little confusing, but trust me, Slackware keeps track of what's what quite well.

The following sections describe how to create these partitions using either `fdisk` or `cfdisk`, but first here's a list of the partitions you need and the purpose each serves:

The following partitioning scheme is probably the most widely used, with three partitions dedicated to the following directories:

- `/` — This partition is the basis for all the directories in the computer. It is literally the main, or root, directory. You need this directory to be on its own partition in order to boot Slackware because Slackware by default places the Linux kernel (core of the operating system) in `/`.
- `/usr` — This partition contains most, but not all, of the system files and applications specific to your computer. This directory should be on its own partition in case of hard drive failure so that files are more easily recovered or replaced.

- swap — This partition is used as virtual memory instead of a directory for storing files and data. A swap partition is necessary when you have a small amount of memory or RAM. But that doesn't mean that robust systems with 128MB of RAM can't benefit from having a swap partition. Even the most mundane of tasks for a Slackware machine can benefit from a little swap space, freeing up conventional (normal) RAM for other, more important tasks. Slackware's setup program requires a swap partition before installation can take place.
- /home — The directory where all personal user documents and files reside. This directory is completely optional; no system files depend on /home.

A good guideline is to use at most three times the amount of physical RAM that you have for a swap partition. For example, if you have 8MB of RAM, the most swap space that you want to have is 24MB. Most systems work well with only double the amount of RAM for swap space, like systems with 64MB of RAM. However, you should not have a swap partition larger than 128MB. If you have the disk space available and want to create a 128MB swap partition, that's fine. Slackware can use a *swap file* (that is, a file on a partition used for virtual memory) if necessary, but Slackware runs much faster using a dedicated partition as a swap partition. Having multiple swap partitions is okay, as is the use of swap files in conjunction with swap partitions (see the "Swap files — going with the alternative" sidebar in this chapter).

You should have at least 150MB of disk space reserved for the root directory, and at least 350MB for the applications on the included CDs to have a minimum Slackware installation. You also should have at least 32MB reserved for swap space.

Partitioning Your Hard Drive for Slackware

Carving up your hard drive into usable Slackware partitions isn't as daunting as you may think. Slackware includes two utilities, fdisk and cfdisk, which are partition manipulator programs that can help you along in your repartitioning scheme. You only have to use one of the two programs to partition your hard drive. These utilities aren't graphical, like Windows' Scandisk and Defrag utilities. Don't look for point-and-click interfaces here. However, cfdisk does take advantage of using highlighted characters and the arrow keys to navigate through the program, so it looks like a graphical program. cfdisk is actually the easier program to use of the two, but either way, both fdisk and cfdisk are powerful enough to get the job done.

Partitioning your hard drive with information on it will very likely damage any existing data on your hard drive unless you used the FIPS utility beforehand (see the "Using FIPS" section earlier in this chapter for instructions on using FIPS).

If you used FIPS earlier in this chapter, you still need to partition your drive with either `cfdisk` or `fdisk`. FIPS is not an alternative to `cfdisk` or `fdisk` because FIPS does not create Linux native or Linux swap partitions. FIPS only reallocates used disk space (indiscriminate of the type of partition) into a giant partition and creates another nondenominational partition out of the unused space.

`fdisk` is an old and text-based (but very reliable) utility for setting up brand-new Slackware-friendly partitions on your hard drive. `fdisk` also enables you to specify which hard drive you want to partition instead of taking the first available hard drive and assuming that's the one you want to partition. This ability is important when you have multiple hard drives and you want to partition the second or third one instead of the first one.

`fdisk` doesn't have a nice graphical interface. Then again, when `fdisk` was developed back around 1994, a graphical interface wasn't necessary. The idea was to have something that was simple, straightforward, and effective, without a ton of bells or whistles weighing it down. `fdisk` was designed to do a job — namely disk partitioning — and do it well.

Other programs have been developed around `fdisk`, like the `cfdisk` package included with Slackware 7.0. `cfdisk` is a little more graphical, but not much. Then again, do you need a talking digitized paper clip just to partition a disk?

`cfdisk` is the easier program to use since it takes advantage of the use of arrow keys to navigate through the program's options and highlights characters to make the information more readable. I highly recommend using `cfdisk` to do your partitioning. Really, I think the only reason `fdisk` is still around is that some people are used to using it and just expect it to be there.

By using `fdisk` or `cfdisk`, you're able to remove other operating systems completely from your hard disk (instructions for doing so are in each of the following two sections for using `fdisk` and `cfdisk`). If it is not your intent to remove an operating system already on your hard drive, then please follow the instructions below extra carefully! Also, make certain you have followed the instructions in the "Using FIPS" section of this chapter on using FIPS. If it *is* your intent to wipe out any existing operating systems and data then you should have no problems.

A good reason for removing any other operating system from your hard drive is to simply give yourself more space to work with. The drawback is that you're unable to access any files that you previously were able to use with that other operating system.

Swap files — going with the alternative

You can use a file for virtual memory (called a *swap file*) in addition to a dedicated partition. This is what Windows 9*x* does. However, to use a swap file in Slackware, Slackware must first be installed.

Swap files are useful if you have a temporary need for more swap space, like if you're compiling the new test version of your favorite game (including the latest in weaponry systems — the railroad spike gun) and you want to speed things up a bit. Swap files can also come in handy if you've noticed that your system is responding a bit slow lately when you're running 20 or so applications simultaneously. If you have a swap partition and a swap file, both are used, but the swap partition is filled first before the swap file is touched.

The drawback to swap files is that because you're using the file system for a swap file, performance may be less than if you use a partition. This is because the blocks (or areas of space) used by a partition are consecutive, while the areas of space used by the swap file may not be adjacent to each other.

You can only create and turn on swap files as the super user! (For more information on using the super user account, see Chapter 6.)

To create a swap file of about 8MB, follow these steps:

1. **Type the following command at your # command prompt:**

   ```
   dd if=/dev/zero of=/swapfile
   bs=1024 count=8208
   ```

   where *swapfile* is the name you choose (swapfile is as good a name as any). Whatever name you choose, subsitute it for "swapfile" throughout the rest of this list.

   The above command creates an empty file called swapfile containing null (meaningless) characters that's exactly 8.4MB in size. The command then places the swap file in the root directory (which is why there's a / in front of the filename).

2. **Type the following command to initialize your new swap file:**

   ```
   mkswap /swapfile 8208
   ```

   The swap file can now be turned on or off at the super user's whim.

3. **Type the following command to turn on the swap file:**

   ```
   sync; swapon /swapfile
   ```

   This command synchronizes all the file systems whether they are Linux file systems, Windows (FAT 16/32), OS/2, or some other file system. This synchronization forces all programs to write cached data (any data sitting in RAM) to the hard drive, and updates the hard drive's data information. This step is a precautionary step before the computer enables the swap file. The entire command ensures that the swap file starts from a definitive point for all of the currently running processes so that the processes may have some point of reference for any data they are or will be calculating, storing, or creating.

To turn off a swap file, type the following command:

```
swapoff /swapfile
```

To remove a swap file from the disk, type the following command:

```
rm /swapfile
```

which will delete the swap file from the disk.

Remember that you can only create and turn on swap files as the super user! (For more information on using the super user account, see Chapter 6.)

Partitioning with cfdisk

`cfdisk` is a partitioning tool to slice and dice your hard drive into more manageable chunks. This repartitioning is necessary for system management, organization, and stability. `cfdisk` creates partitions one at a time and then writes the new partitioning scheme to the hard drive. `cfdisk` also enables you to change the type of partitions from one type to another (such as from Linux to Macintosh, for example).

If you compared `cfdisk` and `fdisk`, you'd find that `cfdisk` is very similar to `fdisk`, except that `cfdisk` uses menus that stay on the screen at all times, thus providing a better point of reference. `cfdisk` also uses the arrow keys to navigate around. Not exactly a killer graphical application, but then again, hard drive space *is* a premium.

Figure 4-6 shows what `cfdisk` looks like while running. Notice the options listed along the bottom of the screen. You can use your left or right arrows to navigate those options, and pressing Enter selects the option that you've highlighted. Using the up and down arrows selects which partition you're working on.

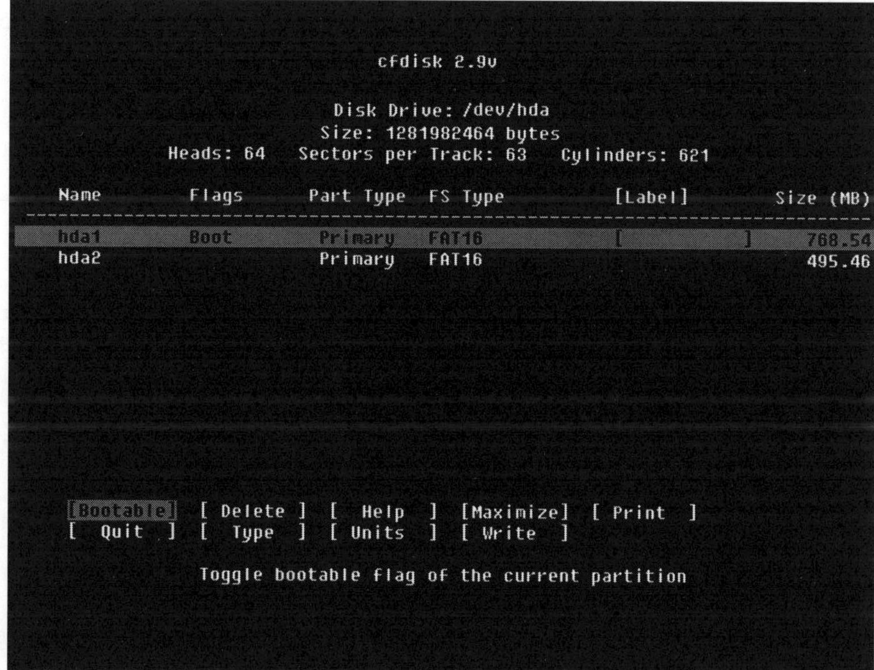

Figure 4-6: The cfdisk graphical disk partitioning utility.

In the following list, I show you how to partition your hard disk into four total partitions, the first one being where your old operating system resides.

If you have IDE hard drives, which are the most common types of drives (see Chapter 2 if you don't know which type you have), you use `/dev/hda` or `/dev/hdb` for your drive names (`hda` is the first drive, `hdb` is the second drive, and so on). SCSI hard drives use `/dev/sda` or `/dev/sdb` for the drive names. Therefore, if you have SCSI drives, substitute `/dev/sda` for `/dev/hda` in the examples below. Partitions are numbered in the order in which they're created. The first partition of the first IDE drive is named `/dev/hda1`; the second partition of the first IDE drive is `/dev/hda2`, and so on.

To use `cfdisk`, make sure that you've rebooted your computer with your boot and root disks. See the "Rebooting with Your Slackware Boot Disk" section in this chapter for more help on rebooting with your boot disks, and see Chapter 3 if you don't know what the heck boot and root disks are. After you reboot, you are presented with a `login:` prompt. Just type **root** and press Enter.

Be careful not to confuse the following: `root` (the super user account), `-` (the root directory), and # (the root account command prompt). It's a very easy mistake to make!

After you log in to your Slackware system as root, about half a screen of information appears along with a # command prompt. The important part is at the bottom of the information:

```
To partition your hard drive(s), use cfdisk or fdisk.
To start the main installation, type 'setup'.
```

You need to partition your hard drive before you can run `setup`. To use `cfdisk` to partition your hard drive for Slackware, follow these steps:

1. **To partition the first hard drive (usually `/dev/hda`), type** cfdisk **at the # prompt and press Enter. If you want to partition a different drive, type** cfdisk /dev/hd*x* **instead, where *x* is the letter in the name of the hard drive you want to partition.**

   If you are partitioning a different hard drive than `/dev/hda`, from now on just substitute the correct name of the hard drive (`hdb` or `sda`) wherever you see `hda` in the following steps.

2. **Use your down arrow key to highlight any partition you want to delete.**

3. **Use your right arrow key to highlight the option marked Delete and press Enter.**

   The hard drive's entry is replaced by the words *Free Space*, as shown in Figure 4-7. Cool, eh?

   Notice also that the options on the bottom have changed — you now have a new option called `New`, while the `Bootable`, `Delete`, `Maximize`, and `Type` options have disappeared.

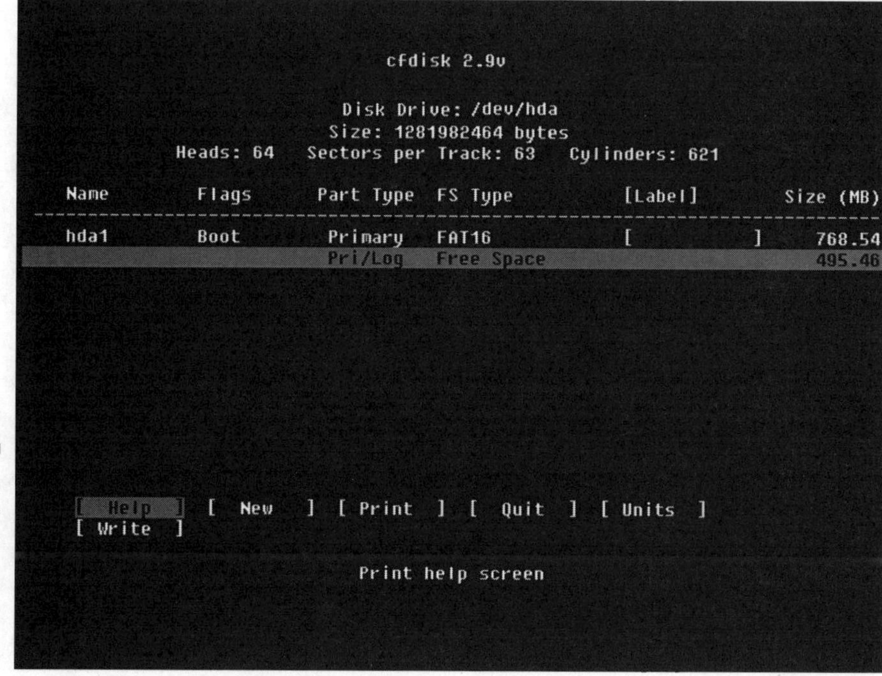

Figure 4-7: cfdisk — after deleting the second partition.

4. **Repeat Steps 2 and 3 to delete as many partitions as you want.**
5. **Highlight the entry marked** `Free Space`.
6. **Use your right arrow key to highlight the New option and press Enter.**

   You are presented with three more options.
7. **Highlight Primary and press Enter.**

   A *primary partition* is a base partition, as opposed to secondary or extended partitions that are built from the primary partition.

   `cfdisk` now asks you what size you want the new partition to be. This first partition will be the / (root) directory.
8. **Type the number of MB you want to devote to this partition and press Enter.**

   A good size for the main partition is anywhere from 150MB to 350MB.

   Three more options are presented, asking you where you want to have this partition created in the free space.
9. **Highlight the Beginning option and press Enter.**

   A new entry appears, as shown with the `hda2` listing in Figure 4-8.

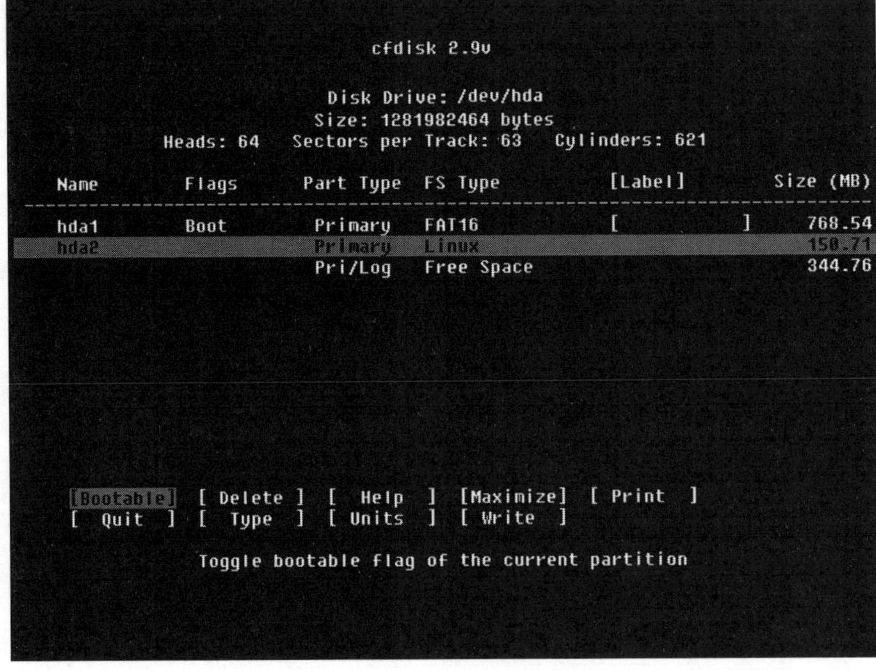

Figure 4-8: cfdisk — after re-creating the second partition as a Linux partition.

10. **Repeat Steps 5 through 10 and create two more partitions, keeping the following two points in mind when performing Step 8 again:**

    The second partition you create is for a swap partition. A good guideline to follow is to allot at most three times the amount of physical RAM that you have for the swap partition. If you have 8MB of RAM, the most swap space you want to have is 24MB. Most systems work well with only double the amount of RAM for swap space, like systems with 64MB of RAM. However, you should not have a swap partition larger than 128MB. Having multiple swap partitions is okay, as is the use of swap files (see sidebar titled "Swap files — going with the alternative").

    The third partition is for the `/usr` partition. If you want to have this partition encompass the rest of your hard drive's free space, just accept the default size that `cfdisk` suggests.

11. **Use your down arrow key to highlight the second partition you created for a swap partition and then use your right arrow key to highlight the Type option.**

    Figure 4-4 shows my swap partition highlighted and ready for me to change its type from Linux to Linux swap. (Changing the type this way lets Slackware know that this partition is not a data partition but one specifically for swapping.)

12. **Press Enter.**

    A list of partition type codes appears — this list may scroll to the next page.

13. **Use your right arrow key to highlight the option marked, as shown in Figure 4-9, and press Enter.**

14. **Press the space bar to move to the next screen of codes.**

    Luckily, 82 is the default selection, and it happens to be the code for Linux swap.

15. **Double check that the 82 option is highlighted and press Enter.**

    The partition type changes to Linux swap. Your table looks similar to Figure 4-10 (remember that the numbers may differ depending on the sizes you used earlier).

    Now you need to make sure your Slackware partition is the bootable partition, or the partition that your hard drive boots from when starting your computer. If the partition you created for your Slackware installation already says Boot under the Flags column on your partition table, skip ahead to Step 20. (But if you followed all instructions in this table verbatim, your Slackware partition should not be bootable yet.)

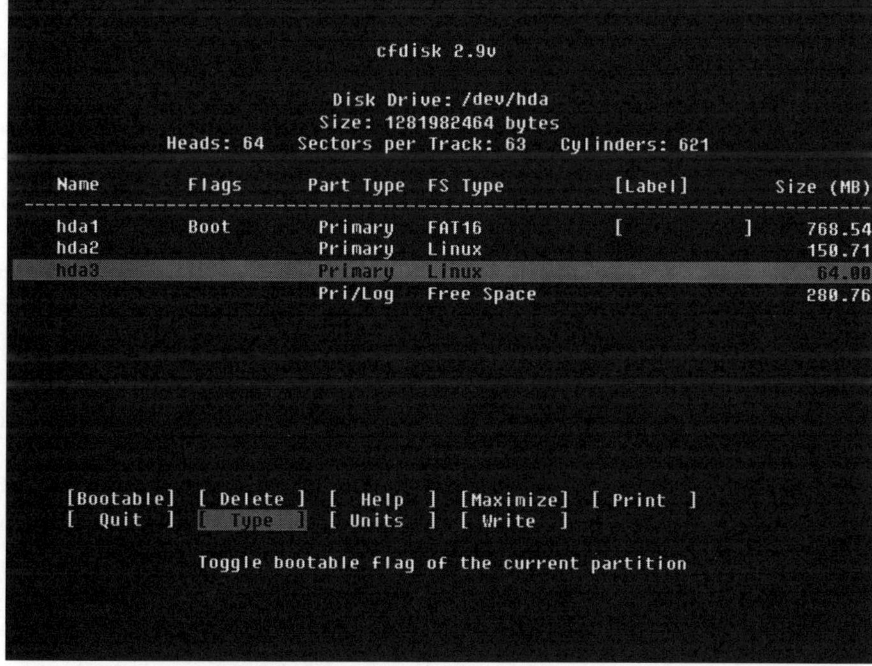

Figure 4-9: cfdisk — ready to change partition type after creating the third partition on the hard drive.

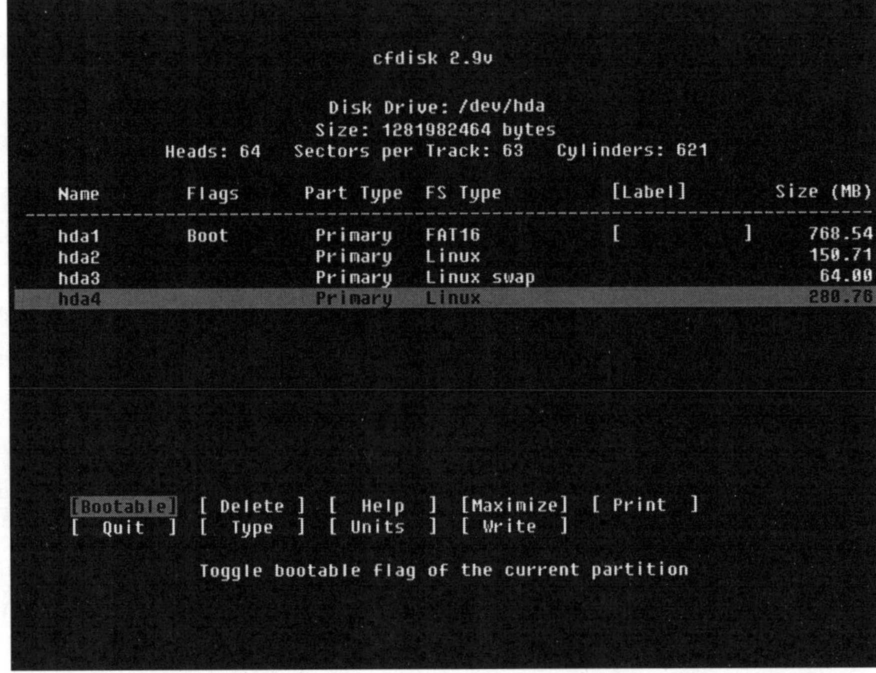

Figure 4-10: cfdisk — after creating all the partitions.

16. **Use your up or down arrow key to highlight the entry containing your old operating system.**

    If you didn't keep your old operating system (or you never had one), skip to Step 18.

17. **Use your right arrow key to highlight the Bootable option and then press Enter.**

18. **Use your up or down arrow key to highlight the entry you created specifically for Slackware.**

    If you followed this list verbatim, the first partition you created is the entry you highlight.

19. **Use your right arrow key to highlight the Bootable option and then press Enter.**

    Your final partition table looks like Figure 4-11 (again, the numbers will differ depending on the sizes you used and the total amount of space your hard drive has).

```
                    cfdisk 2.9v

              Disk Drive: /dev/hda
            Size: 1281982464 bytes
  Heads: 64   Sectors per Track: 63   Cylinders: 621

Name      Flags      Part Type  FS Type        [Label]        Size (MB)
------------------------------------------------------------------------
hda1                 Primary    FAT16          [         ]       768.54
hda2      Boot       Primary    Linux                            150.71
hda3                 Primary    Linux swap                        64.00
hda4                 Primary    Linux                            280.76

[Bootable] [ Delete ] [  Help  ] [Maximize] [ Print  ]
[  Quit  ] [  Type  ] [ Units  ] [ Write  ]

         Toggle bootable flag of the current partition
```

Figure 4-11: cfdisk — ready to write to disk.

20. **Use your right arrow key to highlight the Write option and press Enter.**

    `cfdisk` is somewhat picky at this point — it asks you if you really want to write the partition table to disk.

21. **Type** yes **and press Enter.**

    As a precaution against accidentally overwriting your hard drive, you must actually type **yes** and then press Enter instead of just pressing the *y* key. Otherwise, `cfdisk` just beeps at you noisily.

    `cfdisk` begins writing the table to disk and shows your original options again. On some monitors, the text may be somewhat garbled — don't worry, nothing's broken.

22. **Use your right arrow key to highlight the Quit option and press Enter.**

You have successfully partitioned your hard drive and are ready for the installation of Slackware. If you made it through this section alive, you have no reason to follow the instructions for using `fdisk` in the next section (`cfdisk` and `fdisk` do the same thing), so you can now skip ahead to Chapter 5 and start on the actual Slackware installation. Woo-hoo!

Partitioning with fdisk

After you type **fdisk** at the command prompt (the # prompt) and press Enter, `fdisk` tells you what else to type to partition your disks. If you have IDE hard drives, which are the most common types of drives — see Chapter 2 for info on figuring out what type you have — you use `/dev/hda` or `/dev/hdb` for your drive names (`hda` is the first drive, `hdb` is the second drive). SCSI hard drives use `/dev/sda` or `/dev/sdb` for the drive names. Therefore, if your info from Chapter 2 says that you have SCSI drives, substitute `/dev/sda` for `/dev/hda` in the examples below. Partitions are numbered in the order in which they're created. The first partition of the first IDE drive is named `/dev/hda1`; the second partition of the first IDE drive is `/dev/hda2`, and so on.

If you make a mistake anywhere during these steps, press *q* at the command prompt to quit without doing anything to the disk. Remember that the command prompt is the prompt with the #.

To use `fdisk`, make sure that you've rebooted your computer with your boot and root disks. See the "Rebooting with your Slackware boot disk" section earlier in this chapter for more help on rebooting with your boot disks, and see Chapter 3 if you don't know what the heck boot and root disks are. Type **root** at this login prompt and press Enter.

After you log in to your Slackware system as root, about half a screen of information appears, along with a # command prompt. The important part is at the bottom of the information:

```
To partition your hard drive(s), use cfdisk or fdisk.
To start the main installation, type 'setup'.
```

You need to partition your hard drive before you can run `setup`. To use `fdisk` to partition your hard drive, follow these steps:

1. **Enter** fdisk /dev/hda **at the command prompt.**

   This command tells `fdisk` that you're partitioning the first (or only) IDE hard drive, `/dev/hda`. You get the following prompt in return:

   ```
   Command (m for help):
   ```

2. **Type** p **and press Enter. If you didn't use FIPS described in the "Using FIPS" section earlier in this chapter and have only one partition, skip to Step 5.**

   Your partition table appears, and looks something like this (the numbers differ depending on the size of your hard drive):

```
Disk /dev/hda: 64 heads, 63 sectors, 621 cylinders
Units = cylinders of 4032 * 512 bytes

   Device Boot    Start      End    Blocks   Id  System
/dev/hda1   *         1      381    768064+   6  FAT 16
/dev/hda2           382      620    481824    6  FAT 16
```

The partitions are listed one per line and start with `/dev`, and you should now delete any you don't think you need. If you don't have any partitions to delete you can skip to Step 6.

3. **Type** d **(which stands for *delete partition*) and press Enter.**

   After completing this step, `fdisk` asks you which partition number you want to remove.

4. **Type in the number of the partition you wish to delete and press Enter.**

   To remove the first partition, for example, type **1**.

   The partition is deleted with no questions asked. In fact, `fdisk` doesn't even tell you it has done anything — instead, it returns you to the `Command (m for help):` prompt.

5. **Repeat Steps 3 and 4 for any other partitions that you want to remove.**

   Removing the partition with an operating system on it deletes your operating system or any files from your hard drive!

   Now you need to create a new partition specifically for Slackware.

6. **Type** n **(which stands for *new partition*) at the** `fdisk` **prompt and press Enter.**

   You see the following:

```
Command action
   e   extended
   p   primary partition (1-4)
```

7. **To specify your new partition as a *primary* partition, type** p **and press Enter.**

   A primary partition is a base partition type, as opposed to a secondary or extended partition. You must have a primary partition before you can have any extended partitions because extended partitions are extensions of a primary partition. `fdisk` asks you which partition number you wish to create with the `Partition number (1-4):` prompt.

   You can use fdisk to create a single primary and make the rest *extended partitions*, but it's just easier to remember when they're all primary partition types.

8. **If you have one partition already, type** 2 **and press Enter. If you have no partitions at all, type** 1 **instead.**

`fdisk` prompts you for the cylinder number in which you want to start your new partition and lists a default cylinder number. Accept the default beginning cylinder unless you have a compelling reason to change it. The default starts the next partition immediately following the previous one, or at the partition at the beginning of the drive if no previous partition exists.

Cylinders are the way that the hard drive organizes its information. For example, imagine a hollow tube like an empty toilet paper roll. Now imagine another smaller tube inside the first, and so on. Each tube is a cylinder, and information can be written to those cylinders. The hard drive needs a way to keep track of which cylinder has what data, so it numbers them.

9. **Press Enter.**

   Now you need to tell `fdisk` how much space to give the new partition.

10. **Type in the amount of space you want to allot to the new partition by typing in** +<*amount*>M **and pressing Enter.**

    For example, if you want to give 150MB of space to the new partition, you would type **+150M**. You can give your system any amount of space that you want up to the maximum that you have available.

If you give yourself too little space in your disk partition, you won't be able to install the Slackware software properly. I recommend a minimum of 150 MB and up to 350MB if you have that much space to spare.

You now have a new partition and are now returned to the `Command (m for help):` prompt. You must now create another partition, specifically for use by the system for swapping.

11. **Repeat Steps 6 through 10 to create at least two more partitions (one of which is a swap partition), adding one each time to the number in Step 8. Also, keep in mind the following when you repeat Step 10 for each of the partitions you create:**

    Your second partition should be a swap partition. Swap partitions should use at most three times the amount of physical RAM that you have in your machine. If you have 8MB of RAM, the most swap space you want to have is 24MB. Most systems work well with only double the amount of RAM for swap space, like systems with 64MB of RAM. However, you should not have a swap partition larger than 128MB. Having multiple swap partitions is OK, as is the use of swap files (see sidebar titled "Swap files — going with the alternative").

    Your third partition should be used for the `/usr` directory, which is the location for many system-specific files and applications. This partition should be between 350MB and 800MB, so enter an appropriate amount. If this is your last partition, then just use the number Slackware displays for the default size instead.

    You normally enter a size for your fourth and last partition. This partition is usually used for the `/home` directory, which is where you place personal files. However, because this is the last partition,

Slackware can calculate the remaining space available and use that number instead of your entering in a specific size. Just accept the number that Slackware displays for the default size here.

Once you're done creating partitions, you return to the `Command (m for help):` prompt.

12. **Type** p **and press Enter.**

    Your new partition table appears. In the right column, `fdisk` reports that some partitions are Linux native.

Linux native refers to the type of partition that Slackware recognizes as its own data partition type, as opposed to *FAT 16*, which refers to a DOS or Windows partition.

Now you need to tell `fdisk` that the second partition you made (the one for the swap partition) in Step 11 is the *Linux swap* type, which is how Slackware recognizes that the partition is a swap partition.

13. **Type** t **(for *partition type*) and press Enter.**

    `fdisk` asks you which partition you want to change the type of.

14. **Type in the partition number of the partition you created to be a swap partition in Step 11.**

    `fdisk` offers the following prompt:

    ```
    Hex code (type L to list codes):
    ```

    As you can see from the prompt, you can type **L** if you want to see a list of codes available. Each number is a code used to identify one type of partition. However, since I give you the code you need in the next step, viewing this list is optional.

15. **Type** 82 **and press Enter.**

    82 is the code for a Linux swap partition.

16. **Type** p **and press Enter.**

    Your partition table appears. Notice that the partition listing for `/dev/hdax` (where *x* is the number of the swap partition) now says Linux swap. The partition table should look something like this (the numbers differ depending on the sizes you used earlier and how many partitions you have):

    ```
    Disk /dev/hda: 64 heads, 63 sectors, 621 cylinders
    Units = cylinders of 4032 * 512 bytes

       Device Boot  Start  End   Blocks    Id   System
    /dev/hda1   *       1  381   768064+    6   FAT 16
    /dev/hda2         382  458   155232    83   Linux native
    /dev/hda3         459  491    66528    82   Linux swap
    /dev/hda4         492  621   262080    83   Linux native
    ```

If you have Slackware sharing the hard drive with another operating system, you need to create a dual-boot situation on your hard drive. To do so, you need to change where Slackware is going to look for the boot record (instructions on how to boot the computer) because by default, Slackware looks at the first partition for its boot record. Otherwise, if your first partition isn't Slackware, the computer boots whatever operating system is on that partition and not Slackware.

17. **Type** a **at the** `fdisk` **prompt and press Enter.**

    This tells `fdisk` that you want to change the *bootable flag* on a partition, which is the code that tells the computer to look at this partition first before doing anything else in order to boot the computer.

18. **Type the number of the bootable partition (usually 1) and press Enter.**

    From the example in Step 16, the bootable partition was the one that had an asterisk (*) in the Boot column. This command turns off the bootable flag on that partition. Now you need to turn the bootable flag on for the Slackware partition you created for the / directory.

19. **Type** a **at the** `fdisk` **prompt and press Enter.**

20. **Type the number of the partition you want to make bootable and press Enter.**

21. **Type** p **and press Enter.**

    Your partition table appears and now looks something like this (again, numbers may differ depending on the sizes you used):

```
Disk /dev/hda: 64 heads, 63 sectors, 621 cylinders
Units = cylinders of 4032 * 512 bytes

   Device Boot  Start   End   Blocks    Id   System
/dev/hda1           1   381   768064+    6   FAT 16
/dev/hda2     *   382   458   155232    83   Linux native
/dev/hda3         459   491    66528    82   Linux swap
/dev/hda4         492   621   262080    83   Linux native
```

22. **Type** v **and press Enter.**

    This command verifies the partition table you created by checking to see if all available disk space is allocated. If all the available space is not used, a warning displays on your screen telling you how much space remains.

    If you encounter an error here, redo your partition table. Type **q** and press Enter to quit without saving, then restart these steps starting at Step 1.

23. **Type** w **and press Enter.**

    This command writes the partition table to the hard drive.

Congrats! You are now ready to proceed with setup (see Chapter 5).

Part II

Installing and Configuring Your System

The 5th Wave
By Rich Tennant
IT WAS KEVIN'S FIRST ATTEMPT AT INSTALLING GHOSTSCRIPT. AN ICY CHILL WENT DOWN HIS SPINE AS HIS OUIJA BOARD SUDDENLY FELL FROM THE SHELF CAUSING HIS CANDLE TO FLICKER WILDLY.
"OUIJA"

In this part . . .

Here you walk through the step-by-step process of installing Slackware on your computer. Although technically a complicated process, setting up Slackware is actually easy.

Chapter 5 guides you through the `setup` program and instructs you how to perform the initial configuration of your computer. I will warn you: this is a tough chapter!

In Chapter 6, you will boot your Slackware system for the first time and get a taste of what it's like to have complete control over everything on your computer. You also get to create your own user account.

And in Chapter 7, you will install new packages with the `pkgtool` program, reconfigure your system, and set up a printer.

Chapter 5

Installing Slackware (Finally!)

In This Chapter

- Running through Slackware Linux setup
- Configuring your system

Experienced computer users who have installed a program or operating system can tell you that some installations are easier than others. The ease of installation depends on several key points, including the following:

- The quality of the instructions given with the product
- The amount of work involved in the installation
- How well the new software interacts with the old software
- How the new software interacts with the computer hardware itself

I won't kid you — installing Slackware is a long process. But Slackware has several programs, including the Slackware Linux `setup` program, that make the installation a little easier to deal with than copying files one by one from the CD to the hard drive.

Configuration is another part of installation, although many people skip this step thinking that the software comes preconfigured. (Often it *is* preconfigured, but the preconfiguration is useless for people that want to do real work with their computers because the preconfiguration assumes that you aren't planning on using the computer for much more than home use and doesn't utilize the hardware to its greatest potential.) In this chapter, I show you how to install the Slackware operating system and then perform its basic configuration.

Running Setup

You may have seen or heard other Linux installation programs. Some have fancy bells and whistles, like the Debian/GNU Linux *dbootstrap* program, while others are completely graphical with neat-o icons and arrows, like the Red Hat Linux installation program.

Slackware uses the install program called `setup`. No, it doesn't have fancy graphics, and no cool sounds go off when you type. `setup` is just a simple, effective, menu system, but it gets the job done.

Using the setup main menu

Every good setup program has a main menu that you can return to at any time. Slackware is no exception. The Slackware `setup` main menu is easy to read and understand, and because it's text-based and not graphical, it even works on monochrome (or one-color) monitors.

To begin `setup`, follow these steps:

1. **Boot (or reboot) your computer with the boot and root disks you made in Chapter 3.**

   These disks are the basis for the installation procedure. If you don't have boot or root disks, don't know what they are, or don't know how to reboot your computer, turn to Chapter 3.

   The `login:` prompt appears.

2. **Type** root **and press Enter.**

   Some messages appear on your screen. At the bottom of the text, the following message is displayed:

   ```
   To partition your hard drive(s), use cfdisk or fdisk.
   To start the main installation, type 'setup'.
   ```

   Installation can't begin unless your hard drive is properly partitioned. If your hard drive isn't partitioned, turn to Chapter 4 and follow the instructions there to do so.

3. **At the # command prompt, type** setup **and press Enter.**

   The `setup` menu appears with several options, which are shown in Figure 5-1 and described in the following bullet list.

- **HELP:** Provides detailed information about the `setup` program. It's a good idea to read through the HELP info, even if you don't understand some parts immediately. As you move through the setup process, the information explained in the HELP option becomes clearer. You can always stop at the end of each step in the setup process and go back to the HELP option to get a better picture of the upcoming section and the section that you just completed.

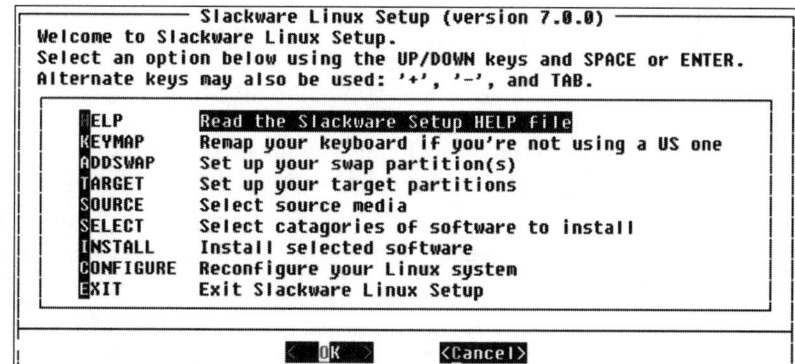

Figure 5-1: The Slackware setup menu.

- **KEYMAP:** This first step in the install process is actually optional. The KEYMAP option enables you to remap your keyboard to a different language. If the U.S. standard keyboard map (which Slackware selects by default) is okay with you, then you can skip the KEYMAP step. See the "Using different keyboards" sidebar in this chapter for more information.

- **ADDSWAP:** Enables you to set up your swap partition. `setup` is programmed to use a swap partition to speed up the installation process. You must have a swap partition in order to install Slackware, as `setup` is programmed to look for a swap partition or exit with an error if one is not found.

Slackware uses a *swap partition* (or a less efficient swap file) to shuffle data in and out of a selected location on the hard drive when conventional memory (RAM) is full. Check out Chapter 4 for more information on swap partitions and swap files.

- **TARGET:** Lets you tell `setup` exactly where you plan on installing Slackware. You must go through this option in order to prepare your hard drive for the Slackware software. `setup` needs to know where it is placing critical system files by determining which partition you use as your root (/) partition and what the other partitions are used for. The root partition is the main partition for the Slackware software, where many of the system's important files are stored.

- **SOURCE:** Tells `setup` where it is getting copies of the software to install from, such as the CD-ROMs included with this book. If you didn't have the CD-ROMs, this option would enable you to install from floppy disks, assuming that you had 23 floppy disks with the A and N series of software programs on them.

- **SELECT:** Enables you to choose which software package you want to have installed on your system. You can install any set of Slackware software packages that you want, provided that you have enough space free on your hard drive to handle them all. The packages appear in menu format with a brief description of each package so that you can choose which packages you wish to install.

- **INSTALL:** Here you perform the actual copying of software from CD (or floppy) to your hard drive.
- **CONFIGURE:** This whopping option is the process by which you give your computer some initial settings to complete the installation. Most of this option is actually optional, as you will be given the chance to skip ahead to the next question while running through this option.

  While configuration is technically a part of the setup process, the process is involved enough that I devote the entire second half of this chapter.

- **EXIT:** If you exit `setup` at any point before performing the INSTALL option, you lose whatever configurations you have done up to that point (except the CONFIGURE option, because that can't be performed until after INSTALL anyway), so choose EXIT only if you have completely finished setting up your system (or if you make a mistake and wish to start over from the beginning). If you want to just stop where you are and go eat dinner or do something else for a while, don't select EXIT — `setup` doesn't mind if you just turn off the monitor and leave the computer running.

Beginning with the next section I walk you through each step in detail, starting with the optional Keymap step.

Setting up Slackware — at last!

Finally it's time to actually install this puppy (Slackware, that is)! Installing Slackware isn't the easiest thing in the world to do, but armed with this sacred tome, you're bound to come out of the process alive! Following are six subsections, one for each of the `setup` options part of the Slackware installation. After completing Step 6: INSTALL, you can move on to configuring Slackware. See the aptly named "Configuring Slackware for the First Time" section later in this chapter for detailed info on configuring Slackware.

Only select the Exit option if you want to start all over or if you have finished installing Slackware! (This doesn't include the CONFIGURE option because you can't run through CONFIGURE until you run through INSTALL.)

During this process, pressing Enter is the same as clicking the OK button on the screen.

Stage 1: KEYMAP

If you're happy with the U.S. standard keyboard map, skip this section and go to Stage 2: ADDSWAP to configure your swap drive. Slackware chooses the U.S. standard keyboard map by default.

When you select the KEYMAP option, a list of keymaps appears. This somewhat confusing list is in order by country code — that is, the country code is the filename and the word "map" is the extension. Ordering the list by country code is the easiest way to differentiate between languages (because you would expect French to be spoken in France, for example). Figure 5-2 shows an example of this keymap listing. There are also keymaps for special keyboards, like the Dvorak keyboard and the emacs keyboard shortcuts. Obviously these listings aren't country codes, just separate listings for yet more keyboard mappings.

A list of country codes and the countries they match are on the Cheat Sheet in the front of this book.

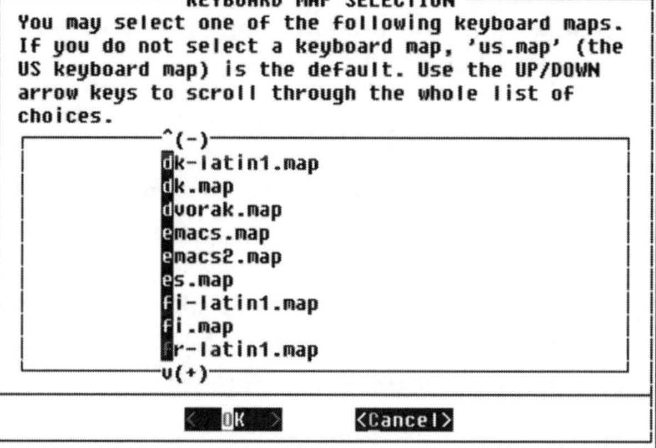

Figure 5-2: The Slackware Keyboard Map Selection dialog box.

To change your keymap, follow these steps:

1. **Select the KEYMAP option from the setup screen.**

   The Keyboard Map Selection screen appears.

2. **Use the arrow keys to scroll up or down through the selections, highlight the keymap of your choice, and press Enter.**

   For example, if you want to change your keyboard language to Finnish, highlight the `fi.map` listing (*fi* is the country code for Finland) and press Enter. Alternatively, if you wanted to change your keyboard map to the Dvorak keymap, you'd highlight the `dvorak.map` listing and press Enter.

   A text-input area appears onscreen for you to test your new keymap.

3. **Type any semi-long phrase into the text-input area and then press Enter.**

   Depending on your keymap, the keys you press correlate to different letters on the keyboard than the normal Qwerty standard. What is then displayed on the screen are the correlated letters. Whether or not this is a recognizable (or legible!) word or phrase depends on your keymap.

4. **If you're not satisfied with what your keymap is doing and want to choose another keymap, type** 2 **at the prompt at the bottom of the dialog box and press Enter to return to the list of available keymaps.**
5. **Repeat Steps 2 through 4 until you're happy with your keymap; then move on to Step 6.**
6. **Once you're satisfied that your keymap does what you want it to, type** 1 **at the prompt at the bottom of the dialog box and press Enter.**

   You return to the Slackware `setup` menu.

Stage 2: ADDSWAP

If you have not created a swap partition, you must do so before continuing with the installation (see Chapter 4).

To set up your swap partition, follow these steps:

1. **Select the ADDSWAP option from the setup menu and press Enter.**

   The Swap Space Detected dialog box appears telling you that `setup` has detected a swap partition, similar to the screen shown in Figure 5-3 (your drive partition names may differ depending on how many partitions you created).

   `setup` asks if you want to install this partition as your swap partition.

```
SWAP SPACE DETECTED

Slackware Setup has detected a swap partition:

   Device Boot    Start       End    Blocks   Id  System
/dev/hda3           459       491     66528   82  Linux swap

Do you wish to install this as your swap partition?

                    < Yes >        <  No  >
```

Figure 5-3: setup finds a swap partition.

2. **Use the left arrow key to select Yes and press Enter.**

   A dialog box appears and tells you that `setup` is formatting the partition and checking for bad blocks. After formatting is done, the Swap Space Configured dialog box appears notifying you that your swap space is configured. `setup` adds to the `/etc/fstab` file (the *filesystem table,* which keeps the master list of file systems and partition types for Slackware), as shown in Figure 5-4.

Using different keyboards

Other languages require extra letters or characters not found in the standard English alphabet, such as á, ø, and _. People needing these letters or characters may have different keyboards, or in some cases, may *remap* the standard U.S. keyboards to fit their needs.

Keymaps affect how you enter data into your computer and how characters look on your screen. In Germany, for example, the obscurely placed *z* key and the prominently placed *y* key are reversed (likely because *z* is used quite often in German whereas *y* is almost never used, which is exactly the reverse of English). If you depend solely on touch-typing (typing without looking at your hands), you may find yourself in a world of hurt if you remap your keyboard to an unfamilar keymap. Even if you do look at your keys, changing your keymap will make it so that what you see on your keys is no longer what you get when you press each one.

Further complicating matters, the creation of files containing plain text is also affected. Newly created files appear distorted to someone who isn't using the same language mapping as the writer, or is unable to read that particular language.

On the plus side, different keymaps enable you to take advantage of keyboards (and software) made specifically for use with other languages.

So be careful when changing your keymapping, and be aware of the limitations that may arise from using something other than plain English. Basically, you're better off sticking with the U.S. standard keyboard map (the default in Slackware) unless you have a compelling reason not to.

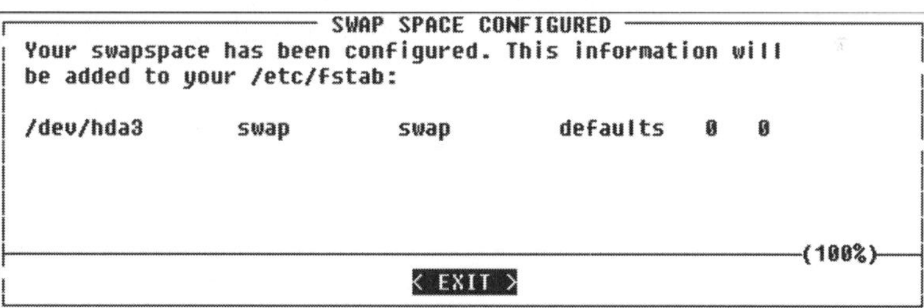

SWAP SPACE CONFIGURED
Your swapspace has been configured. This information will
be added to your /etc/fstab:
/dev/hda3 swap swap defaults 0 0
(100%)
< EXIT >

Figure 5-4: setup has configured your swap partition.

3. **Press Enter.**

   `setup` asks if you want to move on to the next step of the installation process, namely setting up your TARGET drives.

4. **Use the left arrow key to select Yes and press Enter.**

   You are now continuing to the TARGET stage.

Stage 3: TARGET

You can get here to the TARGET option by selecting TARGET from the `setup` main menu, or by finishing the steps in the ADDSWAP option. Either way, the Select Linux Installation Partition dialog box appears, as shown in Figure 5-5.

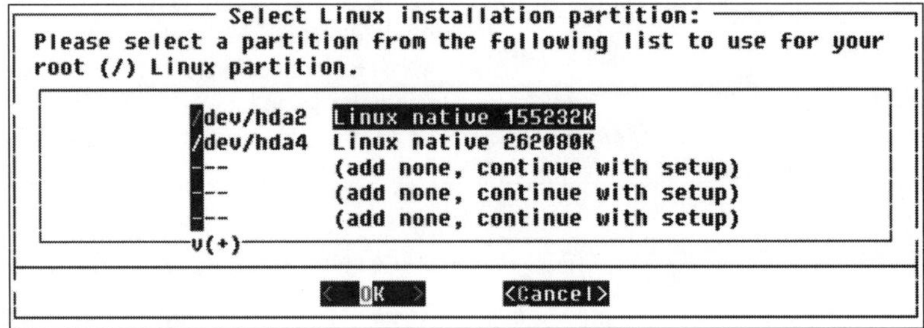

Select Linux installation partition:
Please select a partition from the following list to use for your root (/) Linux partition.
/dev/hda2 Linux native 155232K
/dev/hda4 Linux native 262080K
-- (add none, continue with setup)
-- (add none, continue with setup)
-- (add none, continue with setup)
v(+)
< OK >
<Cancel>

Figure 5-5: setup asks which partition to use as root.

To set up your partitions for Slackware, follow these steps:

1. **In the Select Linux Installation Partition dialog box, use your arrow keys to highlight a partition to use as the root partition and press Enter.**

   `setup` asks if you want to format your partition. A small menu appears below the message with three options: Format, Skip, and Abort. Because this is a new installation, you want to format the partition to get it ready for Slackware.

2. **Use your arrow keys to highlight the Format option and press Enter.**

   `setup` responds with a Format Partition dialog box that asks how you want to format the partition. You are given three options: 4096, 2048, and 1024. The options manage how `setup` organizes files onto your hard drive by formatting the hard drive using larger or smaller blocks of file spaces. A large option like 4096 means that Slackware formats the drive using blocks of space of 4096 bytes.

A large option means that you can place less data on your hard drive, but also that Slackware responds to queries to the hard drive faster because there is less on the disk. Conversely, a small option (like 1024) means that you can place lots of data on your hard drive, but Slackware responds to queries on the hard drive slower because there is more on the disk. Generally, the difference in the amount of data is between 15 to 25 percent more or less, depending on which option you choose.

If you have a small hard drive, you want to maximize the amount of space that you have on the hard drive. Hence, you want to use the smallest number listed.

3. **Use your arrow keys to highlight the size of the blocks you want your hard drive to have and then press Enter.**

   `setup` formats the partition. After formatting is complete, `setup` asks if there are any other partitions that you want to format. A warning about not selecting partitions already in use appears, as shown in Figure 5-6.

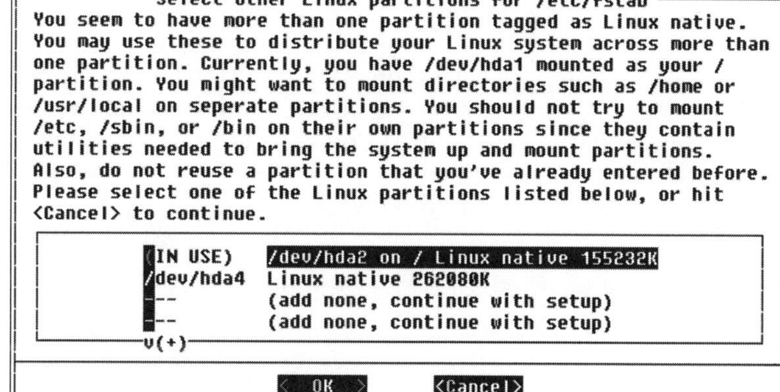

Select other Linux partitions for /etc/fstab
You seem to have more than one partition tagged as Linux native.
You may use these to distribute your Linux system across more than
one partition. Currently, you have /dev/hda1 mounted as your /
partition. You might want to mount directories such as /home or
/usr/local on seperate partitions. You should not try to mount
/etc, /sbin, or /bin on their own partitions since they contain
utilities needed to bring the system up and mount partitions.
Also, do not reuse a partition that you've already entered before.
Please select one of the Linux partitions listed below, or hit
<Cancel> to continue.
(IN USE) /dev/hda2 on / Linux native 155232K
/dev/hda4 Linux native 262080K
--- (add none, continue with setup)
--- (add none, continue with setup)
v(+)
< OK >
<Cancel>

Figure 5-6: Time to select another partition.

4. **Repeat Steps 2 and 3 to format your `/usr` and `/home` partitions, if you created separate partitions for them in Chapter 4. Keep in mind the following:**

   - When `setup` is done, the Select Mount Point dialog box appears asking you where you want the new partition mounted, as shown in Figure 5-7. A *mount point* is a location in the file system where the computer places the partition in order to integrate it into the file system, making it available for use by other programs. In other words, you are asked what directory will be used for that partition.

     The mount point and the name of the directory are one and the same. Note that each mount point begins with a / — this is to signify that the mount point is a direct branch off the main directory (which, incidentally, is denoted as /). See Chapter 9 for more information on the Slackware directory structure.

   - When asked what you want to name the new partition, type in **/usr** or **/home**, depending on which partition you're formatting.

   If you have any partitions left to format after this step, repeat Steps 2 through 4 until you're done. The three partitions covered in the above list are all you really need, though. Having more partitions is outside the scope of this book.

```
SELECT MOUNT POINT FOR /dev/hda4
OK, now you need to specify where you want the new
partition mounted. For example, if you want to put
it under /usr/local, then respond: /usr/local
Where would you like to mount /dev/hda4?

/usr

< OK >      <Cancel>
```

Figure 5-7: Type in the partition mount point.

After you have formatted all partitions, `setup` tells you what information it's adding to the filesystem table (that is, the `/etc/fstab` file, which keeps the master list of filesystems and partition types for Slackware) as shown in Figure 5-8. The `fstab` file is also the list of partitions that are mounted automatically when the computer is booted.

```
DONE ADDING LINUX PARTITIONS TO /etc/fstab

Adding this information to your /etc/fstab:

/dev/hda2       /        ext2       defaults   1   1
/dev/hda4       /usr        ext2       defaults   1   1

(100%)
< EXIT >
```

Figure 5-8: The /etc/fstab filesystem table listing.

If your Slackware installation is not sharing your hard drive with another operating system, you may skip to the next section.

If your Slackware installation is to share your hard drive with a Microsoft operating system such as Windows or DOS, you get a nice message saying that `setup` has detected a DOS or Windows partition. (If you have another Unix or Linux partition, you won't get this message, but you will be able to add your other partition[s] to the `/etc/fstab` by hand using an editor once the installation process is complete.) To add these partitions to `/etc/fstab` so that you can read and write to them while running Slackware (in case you have files or other data that you want to keep and/or have access to while running Slackware), follow these steps:

1. **Use your arrow keys to highlight Yes when setup asks whether you want the DOS or Windows partition added to the `fstab` file and press Enter.**

   `setup` asks which partition you want to add and what you want to call it.

2. **Type a name for the partition in the text field and press Enter.**

   `setup` recommends `/fat-c` or `/fat-d`, in reference to the type of partitions that DOS and Windows use (file allocation tables — FAT), but I like being simple, so I suggest calling it something more obvious, like `/dos` or `/windows`.

After you have added or formatted all the partitions that you're going to use, `setup` asks if you want to go to the SOURCE option. Press Enter to continue to the SOURCE option.

Stage 4: SOURCE

You can get here to the SOURCE option by selecting SOURCE from the `setup` main menu, or by finishing the steps in the TARGET option. Either way, the Source Media Selection dialog box appears, as shown in Figure 5-9.

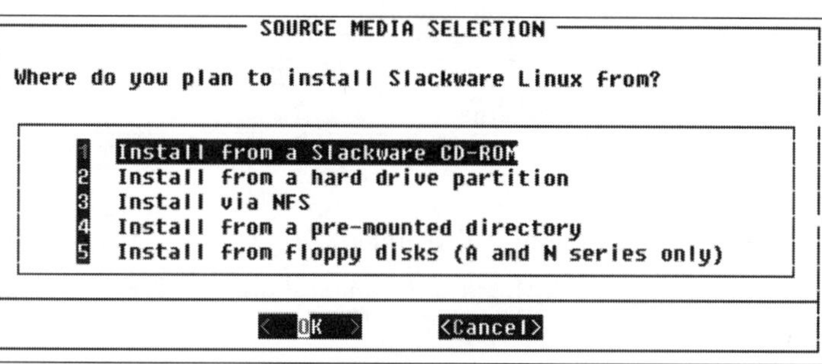

Figure 5-9: Telling Slackware where to find the software to be installed.

Of the options in the Source Media Selection dialog box, options 2 through 4 are for people who downloaded Slackware off the Internet or have another machine running NFS (network file sharing). Option 5 is for those who downloaded or copied Slackware directly to floppy disk. As this book comes with the latest version of Slackware on CD-ROM, I assume you want to use Option 1 and install from the CD.

If there's a newer version of Slackware available other than 7.0, you can always install everything from the CDs included with this book, and then visit the Web page `www.slackware.com/` to download the upgrade packages.

1. **Use your arrow keys to highlight Option 1 and press Enter.**

   `setup` asks if you want to scan your hardware automatically for a CD-ROM drive or manually enter in what kind of CD-ROM drive you have. Even though you may know what kind of CD-ROM drive you have, it's actually easier to let `setup` scan for the CD-ROM drive at this point. (Hey, if the computer wants to do all the work for you, why not let it?)

   Make sure that the Slackware CD is in the CD-ROM drive.

2. **Use your arrow keys to highlight the Auto option and press Enter.**

   If the Slackware CD is not in the CD-ROM drive, `setup` asks you to put it in the drive now.

   When your drive is found, the Choose Installation Type dialog box appears, as shown in Figure 5-10.

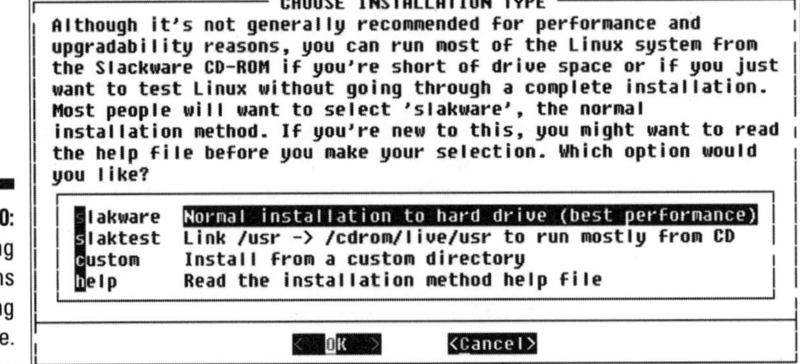
CHOOSE INSTALLATION TYPE
Although it's not generally recommended for performance and upgradability reasons, you can run most of the Linux system from the Slackware CD-ROM if you're short of drive space or if you just want to test Linux without going through a complete installation. Most people will want to select 'slakware', the normal installation method. If you're new to this, you might want to read the help file before you make your selection. Which option would you like?
slakware Normal installation to hard drive (best performance)
slaktest Link /usr -> /cdrom/live/usr to run mostly from CD
custom Install from a custom directory
help Read the installation method help file
< OK >
<Cancel>

Figure 5-10: Checking out options for installing Slackware.

The Choose Installation Type dialog box contains these four options:

- **Slakware:** For the standard installation of Slackware. If you're using the CD that came with this book, choose this option.
- **Slaktest:** For a trial run of Slackware before installing. See the "Testing Slackware with the CD-ROM" sidebar in this section for more details.
- **Custom:** For using a custom copy of Slackware. If you have a CD that someone gave you that's not quite standard (for example, someone made a copy for you but included all sorts of stuff on it besides Slackware), you can select the custom option and enter the location on the CD where the Slackware files can be found.
- **Help:** Check out this option for more detailed information on what the other three options do.

3. **If you're using the CD that came with this book to install Slackware, use your arrow keys to highlight the slakware option and then press Enter.**

   `setup` checks to see if the correct directories actually exist where they're supposed to and reports back whether or not this is so. (If the directories aren't set up correctly, you get a message saying that the directory cannot be found. I can't help you much here if this is the case, except to tell you to check the source to make sure everything is okay. If you're using the CD that came with this book, everything should be fine. If not, see the CD Appendix in the back of this book for customer support info.)

After `setup` has determined that everything is correct, it's time to move on to the next stage of installation, the SELECT option. Press Enter to continue on.

Stage 5: SELECT

You can get here to the SELECT option by selecting SELECT from the `setup` main menu, or by finishing the steps in the SOURCE option. Either way, the Package Series Selection dialog box appears, listing all of the available Slackware software series (or groups of software) on the CD-ROM complete with a short description of the series. For example, the D series contains all of the development software packages. Many of these software series are automatically selected (as denoted by the X in the left column) for you. An example of this dialog box is shown in Figure 5-11.

You must at the very least install the A series of software packages in order to have a working Slackware system! The A series is your Linux operating system (called the Base Linux system), and so this makes perfect sense. In the Package Series Selection dialog box, as shown in Figure 5-11, the A series is automatically checked for you. Do not deselect the A series.

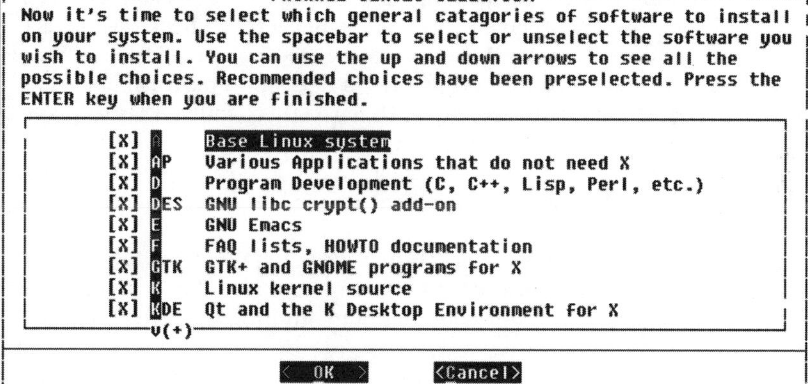

PACKAGE SERIES SELECTION
Now it's time to select which general catagories of software to install on your system. Use the spacebar to select or unselect the software you wish to install. You can use the up and down arrows to see all the possible choices. Recommended choices have been preselected. Press the ENTER key when you are finished.
[X] A Base Linux system
[X] AP Various Applications that do not need X
[X] D Program Development (C, C++, Lisp, Perl, etc.)
[X] DES GNU libc crypt() add-on
[X] E GNU Emacs
[X] F FAQ lists, HOWTO documentation
[X] GTK GTK+ and GNOME programs for X
[X] K Linux kernel source
[X] KDE Qt and the K Desktop Environment for X
v(+)
< OK >
<Cancel>

Figure 5-11: The Package Series Selection dialog box.

Scroll down the list by using your up and down arrow keys and select or deselect a package by highlighting your choice and then pressing the space bar. This toggles the X in the left column on or off (an X in the left column means that series is selected for installation; a blank space means the series is deselected and won't be installed). Don't press Enter (which automatically presses the OK button) until you're certain that you're done with your selections! If you decide to add another series at a later time after installation is completed, you can do so by returning to this stage.

Testing Slackware with the CD-ROM

Slackware is unique in that it enables you to test the operating environment by running most of the base system from the CD. This allows you to see what Slackware will look like after installation, run some of the included software, or even run Slackware from the CD as a normal operation — perhaps as part of a security network or firewall.

If testing Slackware from the CD sounds appealing, select the slaktest option from the Choose Installation Type dialog box and follow all prompts given (you can get to this dialog box by clicking the SOURCE option from the main `setup` menu). Installation from the CD doesn't take up a lot of disk space (40MB at most). On some machines this type of installation may actually be worthwhile due to space limitations on your hard drive or security restrictions on your computer — perhaps you're reading this book while at work and are not allowed to install a new operating system on your workstation.

Table 5-1 shows a list of packages available for install in the Package Series Selection dialog box, as well as whether the package is a good part of a standard. I consider a standard install for users who are just starting out with Slackware to be the following series of software packages: A, AP, F, KDE, N, X, XAP, and Y (gotta have those games in there!). These packages (as shown in Table 5-1) get you the base operating system and all the documentation, plus many of the accessory applications needed to perform just about anything from calculating spreadsheets to listening to music CDs to playing `xbill` (the game). With this set, you also get the KDE desktop, which is great for first-time users, all the networking packages, and the X Windows graphical display system (which KDE is dependent upon).

If you're a developer interested in more high-end applications (such as hacking the Linux kernel source code, for example) then I assume you know who you are and which series to install in addition to those listed in the "Standard Install" column in Table 5-1.

Table 5-1 Software Packages for Slackware

Series Code	*What It Contains*	*Standard Install?*	*Chapter Where Covered*
A	The Base Linux operating system, including everything you need to get Slackware up and running	Yes	—
AP	Applications that don't require the X Windows system to run, but can coexist with X Windows	Yes	—

Series Code	*What It Contains*	*Standard Install?*	*Chapter Where Covered*
D	Programming development applications, including Perl (needed for compiling programs from the source code)	No	—
DES	The `glibc` crypt() add-on, needed to support old-style DES password encryption	No	—
E	The `emacs` editor with a ton of other features included	No	10
F	FAQs, HOW-TO's, and other documentation	Yes	—
GTK	Applications for X that use the GTK+ toolkit, including the GNOME graphical user interface (GUI)	No	12
K	The Linux kernel source code	No	17
KDE	The K desktop environment and Qt libraries	Yes	12
N	Networking utilities, daemons, and other programs	Yes	13
T	The typesetting language TeX. Enables you to format and print high-quality documents to many types of printers	No	—
TCL	TCL/TK (a useful scripting/programming language) and associated utilities	No	—
X	The X Windows System (X) and configuration utilities	Yes	11
XAP	Applications that require X, such as file managers, Netscape Communicator, and image viewers	Yes	11
XD	The X Server development kit, if you're interested in creating your own custom X server	No	—
XV	XView supports the Open Look window manager and enables compiling of XView applications	No	—
Y	Games!	Yes	—

In terms of window managers, if you install just the X series, you only have the fvwm2 and twm window managers. If you install the XAP series as well, your list also includes fvwm95 (which looks remarkably similar to Windows 9*x*). If you install the KDE series, your list includes KDE (most likely at the top of the list as well and already selected for you). An install of the GTK series includes GNOME, and an install of the XV series includes openlook.

You can install both KDE and GNOME, as both are desktops for use with X Windows, but having both installed takes up a lot of room on your hard drive. You should choose one or the other. I recommend KDE because of its ease of use and similarity to certain Microsoft operating systems you've probably used already (and because it takes up less space than GNOME does).

The SELECT option is probably the simplest of all the steps, but it does require prior planning on your part — you need to predetermine what you have room for in your system, what you can install in that amount of space, and what you're likely to use. (See Chapter 4 if you're not sure if you have enough room for the programs you want to install.)

After you finish selecting which software you want to install, `setup` asks you if you want to continue to the next step, the INSTALL option, to copy the software onto disk. Press Enter to move on to the INSTALL option.

Stage 6: INSTALL

You can get here to the INSTALL option by selecting INSTALL from the `setup` main menu, or by finishing the steps in the SELECT option. Either way, the Select Prompting Mode dialog box appears, listing six installation options (not counting help) to choose from, as shown in Figure 5-12. The options are as follows:

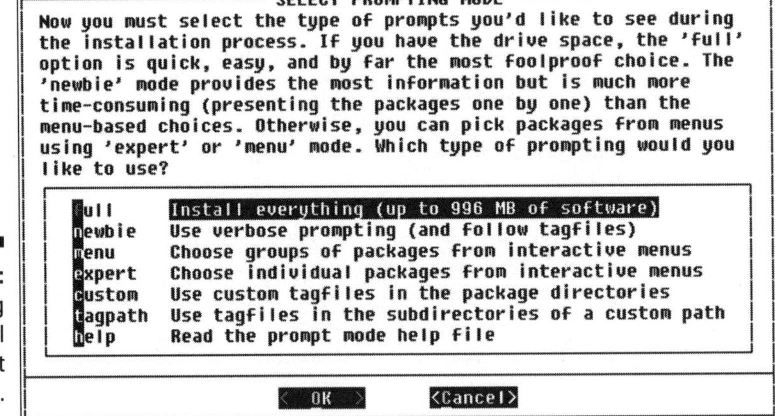

Figure 5-12: Choosing the install option best for you.

- **Full:** This is the safest method of installation because `setup` blindly installs *all* software packages in each series that you chose in the SELECT section. The drawback of this type of install is that you are likely to end up with software that you really don't need, such as X Windows servers for video cards that you don't have.
- **Newbie:** This method takes more time but is the recommended choice if you want to have some kind of control over what is installed. Using this method, `setup` installs only the required packages in each series and prompts you with a Yes or No option for the optional packages.
- **Menu:** If you have a good idea of which packages you want to install, the menu selection may be for you. This option gives you a menu before beginning each series' installation and, similar to the SELECT section, enables you to decide which packages are installed. You are not given a choice concerning the required packages — they are installed for you whether you like it or not.
- **Expert:** The expert option is for those who want complete control over the entire installation. Similar to the menu option, expert shows a list of all packages in a particular series and lets you select which ones you wish to install. Here you actually have a choice on whether or not to install required packages — though it is a good idea to install anything that says REQUIRED next to it.
- **Custom** and **Tagpath:** These options are for those who are hard-core Slackware users who have created their own installation instructions for `setup` to use. The custom option enables you to use different file extensions, while the tagpath option tells `setup` where to look for the custom files or packages.
- **Help:** This option gives a short explanation of each of the other options available, kind of like this bulleted list.

Use your arrow keys to highlight which option you want to use to install Slackware. `setup` then installs the files from the CD to your hard drive at this point (`setup` automatically knows where to place each and every file — practice makes perfect, right?) You see a summary of what each package is called, what it does, as well as its size, as it installs. After the installation completes, you can find where all the files in each package (because some packages contained more than just one file) were installed by examining the contents of the `/var/log/packages` directory. In this directory are files named after each package that was installed. Each file contains the location of each and every file installed as part of the package. You can view these files either with the `more` command (for example, `more /var/log/packages/ppp`) or with an editor (see Chapter 10 for info on the use of editors).

After installing the Slackware package on your system, `setup` asks if you wish to continue on to the CONFIGURE section. Press Enter to continue to the CONFIGURE section.

Exiting setup

If you've performed all the stages up to, but not including, CONFIGURE, you can actually stop the setup process after the INSTALL stage and come back to it later — but don't turn off the computer! The reason is because you don't have the very heart of the Linux operating system installed just yet.

Use this opportunity to lean back away from your monitor (because by now you're probably six inches away from it), get up and stretch, walk the dog, take out the garbage, eat dinner, and maybe take a nap if you've got some extra time. When you're ready to return, just type `setup` and press Enter at the # prompt to go back into the setup process and pick up where you left off.

Configuring Slackware for the First Time

Configuring your system is the last part of the general installation process, and it's a major step. After completing some general configurations, your system is (at last!) going to be up and running. You must go through this configuration if this is a brand-new or first-time installation of Slackware. If you're just adding a new software series — something you can do at any time after the installation is complete — you can skip the rest of this chapter.

Turn to Chapter 19 if you have problems or questions with the configuration process. If this is not your initial install, you can also read more on reconfiguring your system in Chapter 7.

Installing the kernel

You can get to the CONFIGURE option by selecting CONFIGURE from the `setup` main menu, or by finishing the steps in the INSTALL option. Either way, the Install Linux Kernel dialog box appears, as shown in Figure 5-13.

First in the configuration process `setup` installs the Linux *kernel* (the essential software center of a computer), which is basically the core that provides basic services for all other parts of the operating system. `setup` copies the kernel from somewhere safe (for example, the CD or your boot disk) to the hard drive because it isn't designed to create a kernel. `setup` also doesn't ask you to create a kernel from scratch, assuming that you don't have the capabilities to do so.

If you were wondering, no, you haven't copied a kernel already to your hard drive. The K series copies the source code for the kernel to your hard drive, but doesn't give you a working, ready-to-go kernel. You will get that kind of kernel copied to your hard drive presently.

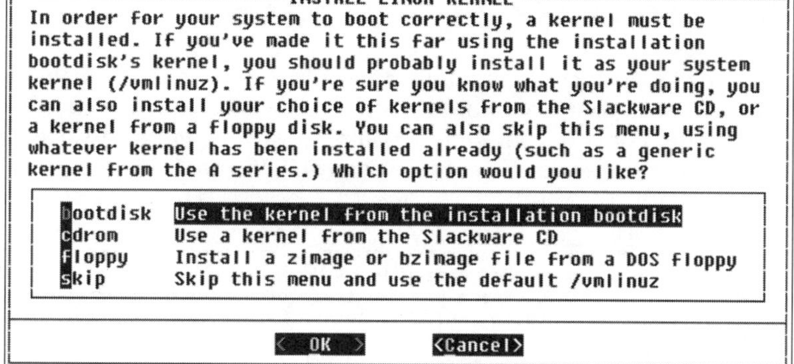

Figure 5-13: The Install Linux Kernel dialog box.

To select an option, use your arrow keys to highlight the desired option and press Enter. You have these four options for your kernel installation:

- **Bootdisk:** The easiest method is the bootdisk option, in which `setup` copies the kernel from your boot disk to the system. (This option is highlighted by default.) You've already booted your system from floppy using this kernel, so why not copy it over to your hard drive?
- **CDROM:** You can choose to install a kernel from the CD. `setup` searches for the `/kernels` directory on the CD and lists all available options. Entries that end in `.i` are for IDE hard drives, and entries that end in `.s` are for SCSI drives. (To find out what type of hard drive you have, turn to Chapter 2.) This is the safest method because there is that very, very small chance that your boot disk kernel has been corrupted in the time between using it to boot your computer and now (floppy disks go bad for any number of reasons, including freak sunspot activity).
- **Floppy:** You can also choose to install a kernel from a floppy disk by selecting the floppy option. Choosing this option makes `setup` look for a DOS disk — not your bootdisk! — in the floppy drive and install a kernel from there.
- **Skip:** You can choose to skip installing the Linux kernel. But if this is your initial installation, I don't recommend it! Skipping this step means you don't have a kernel installed on your computer. That's akin to installing all the Windows programs but not Windows itself on your computer. This step is provided in case you've already got a Slackware system running (with a kernel installed) but just need to reconfigure your system.

Once you select a method for installing a kernel, `setup` copies the kernel from whatever location you specified and moves to the next step in the configuration process, namely backup boot disk creation.

Creating backup bootdisks

The next step in configuring your Slackware system is to create backup bootdisks in case your Slackware system ever fails or you lose your original bootdisk. After copying your kernel, you're presented with the Make Bootdisk dialog box and several options, as shown in Figure 5-14.

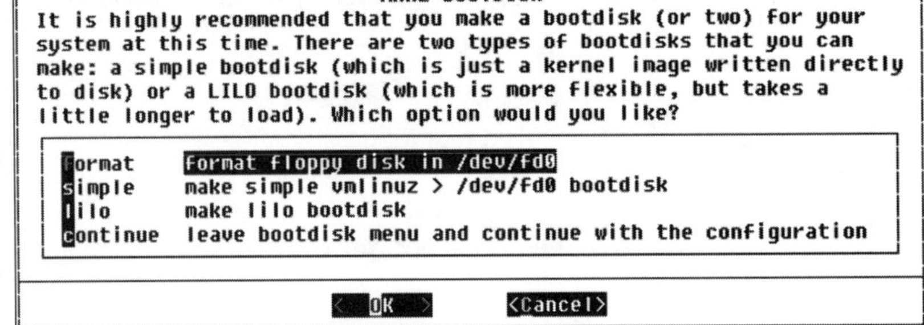

MAKE BOOTDISK
It is highly recommended that you make a bootdisk (or two) for your system at this time. There are two types of bootdisks that you can make: a simple bootdisk (which is just a kernel image written directly to disk) or a LILO bootdisk (which is more flexible, but takes a little longer to load). Which option would you like?
format   Format floppy disk in /dev/fd0
simple   make simple vmlinuz > /dev/fd0 bootdisk
lilo   make lilo bootdisk
continue   leave bootdisk menu and continue with the configuration
< OK >
<Cancel>

Figure 5-14: The Make Bootdisk dialog box.

- **Format:** The format option enables you to format a floppy disk as a Linux-formatted floppy disk (instead of the preformatted DOS/Windows type). To use this option, use your arrow keys to highlight the format option and press Enter. `setup` asks what size floppy disk drive you have, either a 1.44MB or a 1.2MB. The 1.44MB floppy is the standard 3½-inch floppy disk, while the 1.2MB is the 5¼-inch disk.
- **Simple:** Copies the kernel that you just installed on your computer to a formatted floppy disk. This method is similar to the bootdisk that you already have; however, if you have an operating system other than Slackware on your computer, you will not be able to boot that other operating system.
- **Lilo:** Copies the LILO (Linux Loader) boot program to floppy disk and sets up a basic configuration for it. This option is a little more in-depth than the simple option, but well worth it. I suggest using this option if you still have your DOS or Windows partition because it enables you to boot a different operating system (like Windows) instead of Linux in case of a system crash.
- **Continue:** Moves you to the next step of the configuration. After you finish making a bootdisk via one of the preceding choices, or if you decide to not make a backup bootdisk, choose this option to continue with `setup`.

Setting up your modem port

`setup` now attempts to configure your modem if you have one. After leaving the Make Bootdisk dialog box, the Select Modem Device dialog box appears on your screen with five possible choices for the location of your modem's connection to the computer. Each of the first four choices represents one COM (communications) port on your computer, while the fifth choice is "No Modem." Select the COM port that your modem is using by highlighting the proper selection with your arrow keys. If you don't have a modem, then select the No Modem option instead. (If you don't know what COM port your modem is using, turn to Chapter 2.) `setup` then creates a link from the COM port (which is recognized by the computer as the device `/dev/ttyS#`, where # is the number of your COM port) selection you chose to `/dev/modem` so other programs can recognize your modem.

After you set up your modem port (or not if you don't have one), `setup` moves you to the next step: configuring screen fonts.

Establishing your screen font

When you complete your modem configuration, `setup` displays a message asking you if you want to try out some custom screen fonts and gives you two choices underneath the message — Yes or No. You can choose No here, but if you choose Yes, you get a *huge* list, partially shown in Figure 5-15. Use your arrow keys to navigate around the list and press Enter to test out the highlighted font.

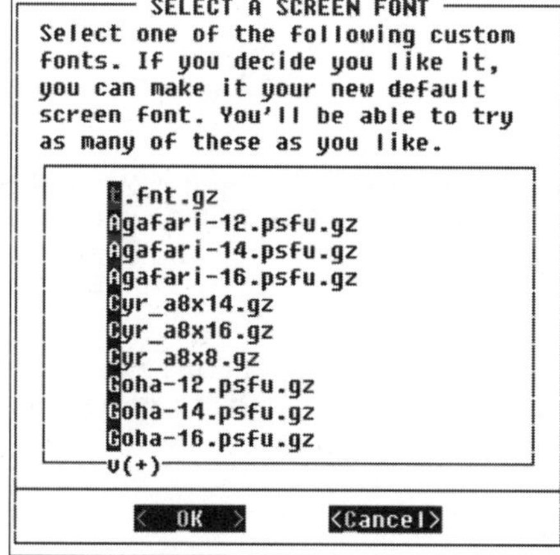
SELECT A SCREEN FONT
Select one of the following custom fonts. If you decide you like it, you can make it your new default screen font. You'll be able to try as many of these as you like.
.fnt.gz
Agafari-12.psfu.gz
Agafari-14.psfu.gz
Agafari-16.psfu.gz
Cyr_a8x14.gz
Cyr_a8x16.gz
Cyr_a8x8.gz
Goha-12.psfu.gz
Goha-14.psfu.gz
Goha-16.psfu.gz
v(+)
OK
<Cancel>

Figure 5-15: The Select a Screen Font dialog box.

`setup` asks if you want to keep the font that you just selected. If you want to return to the original font, choose No and then select default8x16 from the list. (On a whim, I decided to try the gr737-9x16-medieval listing and use that as my default font. I can personally say that medieval European writing does not sit well with the eyes.)

You can change your screen font any time after you finish the installation by typing **fontconfig** at your command prompt and pressing Enter (command prompts are explained in Chapter 8).

Once you have either selected a screen font or bypassed this step, `setup` moves on to install the LILO boot program.

Installing LILO

LILO is the Linux Loader, a boot program that enables you to choose from a list of operating systems upon bootup and boot any operating system available on your hard drive. In order for you to boot your new Slackware system, LILO must be installed and configured, even if Slackware is your only operating system.

After you select (or not) your screen font, the Install LILO dialog box appears, asking how you want to install LILO. You're given three options:

- **Simple**: This option automatically installs LILO for you. Easy, quick, painless — for most users, this is the option to choose.
- **Expert:** This option gives you more control of the LILO configuration process. This option is not recommended for first-time installations because the process is longer, more in-depth, and requires a bit more knowledge of Slackware than the average user typically has. For the technically curious, however, there is an explanation of this process in Chapter 7.
- **Skip:** This skips the LILO installation step completely. If you're reconfiguring your system and already have LILO installed, you can choose this. However, if this is a first-time installation, you should not choose this option!

If you choose skip, you can go back later and rerun this step after you have finished the setup process and rebooted by typing **liloconfig** at your # command prompt and pressing Enter.

To install LILO using the simple option, follow these steps:

1. **Use your arrow keys to highlight the desired option and press Enter.**

   If you installed the X series of Slackware software, LILO gives you a choice of whether or not to use the frame buffer console or the standard

Linux console, as shown in Figure 5-16. The frame buffer console is used to make configuring X easier. The downside is that the frame buffer console makes the X noticeably slow. The standard Linux console is just text, no graphics.

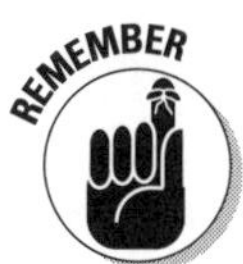

If you did not install X, you won't be given this option.

```
CONFIGURE LILO TO USE FRAME BUFFER CONSOLE?
Looking at /proc/devices, it seems your kernel has support for the
Linux frame buffer console. If we enable this in /etc/lilo.conf, it
will allow more rows and columns of text on the screen, make it
extremely easy to configure X on any VESA video card (with a PS/2
mouse, it should work 'out of the box'), and give you a cool penguin
logo at boot time. However, the frame buffer text console is
noticably slower than a standard text console, and preformance under
X is not as good as with an accelerated X server. Would you like to
use the new frame buffer console, or the standard Linux console?

  standard       Use the standard Linux console (the safe choice)
  1024x768x64k   Frame buffer console, 1024x768x64k  (best for X)
  800x600x64k    Frame buffer console, 800x600x64k
  640x480x64k    Frame buffer console, 640x480x64k
  v(+)

                    <  OK  >        <Cancel>
```

Figure 5-16: The frame buffer console questionnaire.

You can use the arrow keys to scroll down in order to view more selections. The other choices listed are sizes of frame buffer consoles, ranging from 1024 x 768 x 64k (64k is 64,000) to 640 x 480 x 256. The first two numbers are the width and height of the screen; the last number is the number of colors displayed by the video card. The higher the number, the more memory X Windows eats up and the slower your system is on boot time, even if you have a Pentium III 1 GHz processor with 1GB of RAM. (Fast hardware doesn't change the fact that X Windows likes to eat memory by the megabyte.)

If this is the first time that you're going through the `setup` process, the standard console is the best choice. However, if you know your video card and monitor settings and you are confident that you won't burn up your video card, monitor, or both, choose a frame buffer console that matches the minimum settings of your video card and monitor. Please make sure you don't go over what your video card and monitor are capable of, in any case.

2. **Use your arrow keys to highlight the desired setting and press Enter.**

   The Select LILO Destination dialog box appears, as shown in Figure 5-17.

   Choosing the wrong location for LILO renders your disk unbootable! (The Slackware kernel and the LILO boot program must reside on the same partition in order for LILO to boot the machine.)

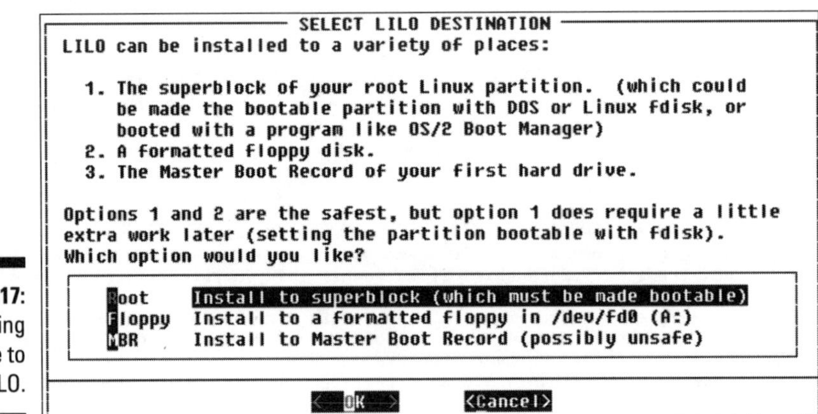
SELECT LILO DESTINATION
LILO can be installed to a variety of places:
1. The superblock of your root Linux partition. (which could be made the bootable partition with DOS or Linux fdisk, or booted with a program like OS/2 Boot Manager)
2. A formatted floppy disk.
3. The Master Boot Record of your first hard drive.
Options 1 and 2 are the safest, but option 1 does require a little extra work later (setting the partition bootable with fdisk).
Which option would you like?
Root Install to superblock (which must be made bootable)
Floppy Install to a formatted floppy in /dev/fd0 (A:)
MBR Install to Master Boot Record (possibly unsafe)
< OK >
<Cancel>

Figure 5-17: Choosing where to install LILO.

- **Root:** The root option installs LILO to the *superblock*, or master location, of your Linux partition. The superblock is usually the partition you chose to be the / (root) partition — in most cases this is the partition named `/dev/hda1`. Select this option if you have more than one operating system on your computer or plan to install multiple operating systems on your computer at a later date.
- **Floppy:** The floppy option installs LILO to a floppy disk, which is the same as making a LILO boot disk. Select this option if you plan to make this computer a secure workstation, bootable only from floppy disk. (This is probably not the choice you want.)
- **MBR:** The MBR option installs LILO to the master boot record of the hard drive. Select this option if Slackware is the only operating system on your hard drive.

3. **Use your arrow keys to highlight the desired option and press Enter.**

   `setup` installs LILO.

Configuring network basics

TECHNICAL STUFF

After you have completed the LILO installation, `setup` asks whether you want to run the networking configuration now. Network configuration determines what your machine is to be named and how your Slackware machine is going to connect to the Internet. Use your arrow keys to highlight Yes only if you know:

- The domain of your Internet Service Provider (ISP) — this is something like `mindspring.com` or `netcom.com`. See Chapter 13 for more information on ISPs.
- The type of IP (Internet Protocol) addressing your ISP uses — static (unchanging) or DHCP (assigned on a need-basis) — and information pertinent to this addressing scheme.

If you do not have this information or have not contacted an ISP, choose No to skip to the next section.

You can redo your network configuration at any time after you have finished the setup process and rebooted by typing **netconfig** at your # command prompt and pressing Enter (command prompts are explained in greater detail in Chapter 8).

If you do have the necessary information and want to go ahead and configure your network settings now, follow these steps:

1. **Answer Yes to setup's question, indicating that you do want to set up your network configuration now.**

   A small text input area appears entitled Enter Hostname, where you need to name your computer. So give your machine a name! And not just Dave or Michelle . . . but don't go overboard like TheGameMasterOfCherryAvenue either! (Slackware won't have a problem if you call your system that, but you may have a hard time explaining it to your friends!)

   I'm naming my machine `slack1`, as you can see in Figure 5-18.

```
                         ENTER HOSTNAME
First, we'll need the name you'd like to give your host. Only
the base hostname is needed right now. (not the domain)

Enter hostname:

slack1

                  <  OK  >          <Cancel>
```

Figure 5-18: Give your computer a name.

2. **In the Enter Hostname field, type the name of your machine and press Enter.**

   Another small text input area appears, asking what the domain of your ISP is. The domain is usually something like `mindspring.com` or `netcom.com`. You can, however, set the domain to an in-home *LAN* (local area network). (See the "Working with in-home LANs" sidebar in this section for more information.)

3. **Type the domain name of your computer into the text field and press Enter.**

   A dialog box appears telling you you're about to set up your Internet Protocol (IP) address. The IP address is the unique address of your machine as it relates to the Internet, kind of like the Zip+4 code that the U.S. Postal Service uses. Three choices appear:

Static: For an assigned, or unchanging, IP address (the IP address is assigned to you by your ISP, kind of like your home address is assigned to you by the subdivision developer or the Post Office). *Static IP addresses* are used on internal networks, either an in-home LAN or a third-party LAN, and are used if you have nameservice (DNS), gateways (accesses to the network), and other assigned IP addresses. Choose this option only if you're planning on connecting to the Internet via a direct network line, or if you're setting up an in-home network.

If you choose static from the three options listed in the dialog box, you are asked for the following information:

- Your IP address
- Your network mask (netmask), which is the way the computer tells what network it belongs to
- Your gateway, which is the route your computer takes to send and receive data to and from the Internet
- Your nameserver, which is the computer that translates machine names to IP addresses

At the end of this list of questions you are asked whether you want the computer to probe for a network card and you are given a Yes or No choice. Use your arrow keys to highlight Yes and press Enter to avoid too many hassles.

DHCP: Stands for Dynamic Host Configuration Protocol, and enables dynamic configuration of IP addresses. This selection is for cable modem users, digital subscriber line (DSL) users, or Ethernet networks using DHCP services. If you select DHCP, a line is added in the boot sequence to have your system check the local DHCP server for your IP address and associated settings.

Loopback: For those with serial modems or laptops using network cards (something not covered in this book, because laptops are a special case altogether). If you select the Loopback option, a line is added in your boot sequence to automatically set up some basic modem configurations.

4. **Use your arrow keys to highlight your IP address type and press Enter.**

   Once you have made your choice, your network configuration is complete.

Getting your mouse set up

Now you need to configure your mouse, which is important if you plan on using X Windows and any desktop environments like KDE and GNOME. Desktop environments depend on your mouse, so you need to have this part set up correctly.

Working with in-home LANs

An in-home local area network (LAN) sounds like it's truly a techie term. Who wants such a thing?

Actually, LANs are not as technical as they sound. More and more people that own multiple computers find that having an in-home LAN actually makes it easier to store and retrieve information, alleviates frustration when the only computer in the house that has Internet access is being used by someone else, and allows for sharing of printers, even if the computers are in different rooms of the house.

All that's necessary for an in-home LAN is that each computer has an *ethernet card* (the standard network technology — your local electronics store keeps plenty of these cards in stock), a small *network hub* (a device that enables several computers to plug into it and talk to each other simultaneously via their network cards), and a spool of *category five* (CAT5) *cable,* which looks suspiciously like actual telephone wire but has a slightly bigger end. (Don't try plugging it into your wall phone jack!)

You also need to read the Linux IP Masquerade HOW-TO (if you install the Slackware F software series, this file is in the `/usr/doc/Linux-HOWTOs/IP-Masquerade` directory) because it covers what's necessary for using Linux in an in-home LAN and answers many frequently asked questions.

When you get to this point, either by configuring your network or by skipping the network configuration, you have a host of choices at your disposal, as shown in Figure 5-19. If you have your manual for your mouse, or if you have the information on your mouse gleaned from Chapter 2, you will now set up your mouse type. Note that selecting the wrong mouse type can *really* cause you headaches because none of the applications that require a mouse will work — some applications are nice and tell you that you have the wrong mouse configured, but others simply won't run at all with nary an error message.

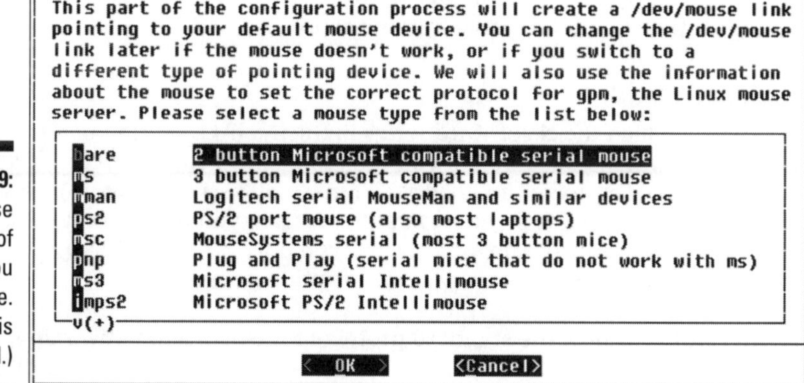

Figure 5-19: Choose what type of mouse you have. (Cheese is optional.)

To set up your mouse, follow these steps:

1. **Use you arrow keys to highlight your mouse type and press Enter.**

   For most computers, choose either bare, ps2, ms3, or imps2. The choices ps2 and imps2 are for PS/2 mice (they have the circular connectors), while the bare and ms3 choices are for serial mice (which have semi-rectangular connectors).

   If you select a serial mouse type, `setup` asks which COM (communications) port your mouse is using. You can easily answer this question if you have your mouse information (if you don't, see Chapter 2). If you need to guess, or don't know, use COM1 for the time being.

   If you installed the X series, you are now asked if you want the `gpm` program to run at boot time. `gpm` (stands for General Purpose Mouse) is a mouse server for the console and for X Windows, which lets applications use the mouse. Yes and No options appear underneath the `gpm` question.

2. **Use your arrow keys to highlight either Yes or No and press Enter.**

   You have completed your mouse configuration! If you made a mistake and want to change it, you can redo the mouse setup later after you have finished the setup process and rebooted by typing the following at the # command prompt:

   ```
   rm /dev/mouse ; ln -s /dev/ttyS# /dev/mouse
   ```

   where # is the number of the COM port needed. Remember, computers count from 0, not 1, so COM1 is S0, COM2 is S1, and so on.

Finalizing miscellaneous configurations

Leftover configurations appear at the end of the setup process. They're small, quick, and easy to miss, but try not to overlook them. I call them "leftover" because they don't quite fit anywhere else, which is probably why they're here at the end of the configuration section.

Sending mail

If you installed the N software series in the INSTALL section of the setup process (which you should if you wish to connect to the Internet), `setup` asks if you want to set up `sendmail` (an e-mail server program) via SMTP/BIND or UUCP. If you're an at-home user, you really don't want to have an e-mail server program anyway, but you only get SMTP/BIND and UUCP as choices — there's no skip or continue option here.

SMTP/BIND is now the standard protocol for e-mail and networking, whereas UUCP is an older protocol, usually reserved for backwards compatibility or connections over serial lines (old gray cables connected to your computer) instead of over modem or Ethernet lines. I strongly recommend using your arrow keys to highlight SMTP/BIND and press Enter.

Selecting a time zone

After you make a selection regarding `sendmail` (you chose SMTP/BIND, right? hint, hint . . .), a message appears asking you which time zone you're in, as shown in Figure 5-20. (All U.S. time zones available are listed, but more choices exist if you scroll down the screen.) Note that there are choices for areas like Arizona and Indiana that don't use (or need!) Daylight Savings Time. Just scroll up or down with your arrow keys and press Enter when your time zone is highlighted.

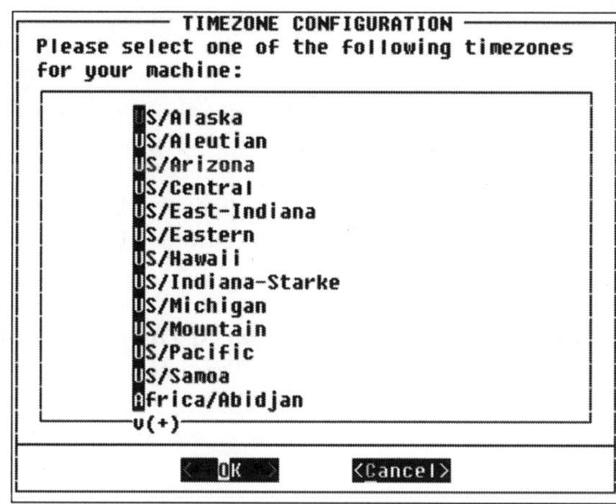

Figure 5-20: Selecting your time zone.

Choosing your window manager

Once you make your time zone selection, a new dialog box appears asking which window manager for X Windows you want to use as your default, as shown in Figure 5-21. In the dialog box, you see a listing of all window managers that were installed when you went through the INSTALL section of the setup process. If you installed just the X series, you will only have fvwm2 and twm listed. If you install the XAP series as well, your list also includes fvwm95 (which looks remarkably similar to Windows 9*x*). If you install the KDE series, your list includes KDE (most likely at the top of the list as well and already selected for you). An install of the GTK series includes GNOME, and an install of the XV series includes openlook. See the "Stage 5: SELECT" section in this chapter for more info on the different window managers.

You can only select one window manager, so use your arrow keys to scroll up or down and press the space bar to make or remove your selection. Press Enter to accept your selection.

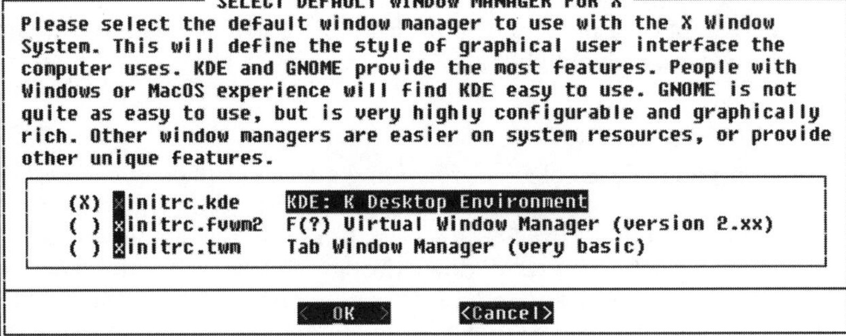

Figure 5-21: Choosing your window manager. Decisions, decisions!

Giving root a password

The final setup question appears on the screen, asking if you want to give the super user (root) account a password. Use your arrow keys to highlight No and press Enter. You change the root password in Chapter 6. After you make your selection you are returned to the `setup` main menu.

Congratulations! You have completed the setup process! Use your arrow keys to highlight the EXIT option from the Slackware Linux `setup` main menu and press Enter.

Take a break, go grab something to drink, and relax! Then mosey on over to Chapter 6 to boot your new Slackware system! Woo-hoo!

Chapter 6

Giving Slackware the Boot

In This Chapter

- Rebooting with more options
- Starting up Slackware
- Meeting the super user (root)
- Creating a new account and changing passwords
- Playing with virtual consoles
- Logging off

Your first reboot after any installation is cause for worry — and your first reboot of Slackware will be no different, but you can master your fears with a little help. Slackware is multiple-user capable, which means that more than one person can use the computer at a time. Multiple user accounts come in handy when you have to work on several projects at the same time. In this chapter, I show you how to create a user account, which protects you as well as the computer.

This chapter also introduces you to the super user account, which is the account used to install Slackware. The super user account is extremely powerful but vital to the system. In this chapter, I discuss some of the important do's and don'ts of using the super user account.

Finally, I cover the steps of logging out of your accounts when you're done working. You never know what gremlins may do to your computer if you leave yourself logged in.

Rebooting with Flags

You're finally done with setup. (Woo-hoo!) You've installed all the software packages that you're going to install for now and you're ready to play. Now you have to shut down the computer and reboot so that all your changes take effect.

Rebooting is very simple. After you've exited setup, or at any other time after installation is completed, at the # command prompt, type **shutdown -r now** and press Enter. This command shuts down the computer and reboots it (the -r in the above command stands for reboot). You receive messages that say `Sending processes the TERM signal...` among other gibberish, and your computer reboots.

If you want to power off the computer now instead of rebooting, at the # command prompt, type **shutdown -h now** and press Enter. The -h in the command causes the system to halt after it finishes, allowing you to turn off the computer. (You can turn off your computer when the screen says Power Down.)

The -r and -h parameters are called *flags*. Slackware uses flags to pass extra information to the programs in case other options are available, like the -r and -h flags for the shutdown command. Flags are used more often in later chapters of this book.

If you want to shut down your system at a specific time, change the word *now* in the `shutdown now` command to a military time (13:00 is 1 p.m., 14:00 is 2 p.m., 0:00 is 12 a.m., and so on). For example, say you want to shut the system down at 8:30 p.m. At the # command prompt, you type the command **shutdown -h 20:30**, and the computer halts itself at 8:30 p.m. This is useful if you are running a process that you know will complete by a certain time, but you don't want or need to be around when it finishes just to shut the machine off. (If you were wondering how the computer knew what time it was, the time is set automatically the moment you turn on your machine before anything starts running.) Just remember that the correct time zone needs to be set (you did this in the `setup` program back in Chapter 5) for times to appear accurately.

If you want to shut down your system in a specific number of minutes instead of a specific time, change the word "now" in the `shutdown now` command to +#, where the # is any number greater than 1. ("Now" is equal to +0, so if you entered `shutdown -h +0`, the computer would shut down, well, now.) For example, if you want to reboot your machine in 12 minutes, you type **shutdown -r +12** at the command prompt and your computer reboots in 12 minutes. This technique is often used by system administrators who perform maintenance on the machine in the middle of a workday, while people are using the machine. By using this form of shutdown, users have a set number of minutes before the machine is shut off to finish up what they're doing and log out.

In any case, now is a good time to shut down and reboot. If you decide not to reboot and use an `-h` flag instead, you can turn off your computer when it's finished shutting down. (By the way, turning off your computer without shutting down runs the same risk of corrupting data that was possible in Windows 9x. It's never a good idea to just turn the computer off without shutting down first.)

Booting Slackware for the First Time

Your first boot of Slackware can tell you a great deal about how your computer is going to run. If you installed the Slackware software correctly and arranged your configurations right, Slackware boots very quickly.

If you chose not to reboot your computer immediately after completing the Slackware installation (see Chapter 5 for info on the Slackware installation process), then you need to reboot it now. To reboot your computer, follow these steps:

1. **Turn on any devices that you have attached to your computer, like a scanner, a printer, and a monitor.**
2. **Turn on your computer.**

   LILO, the Linux Loader software that boots Slackware, waits for approximately 12 seconds as you decide which operating system to boot. But if you wait too long, LILO boots the first partition listed — in this case DOS or Windows.
3. **To boot Slackware, type** linux **at the** `boot:` **prompt and press Enter. (Similarly, you can type** dos **and press Enter to boot your old DOS or Windows operating system.)**

If you used FIPS (see Chapter 3 for information on FIPS) and kept your old operating system, and Slackware was installed correctly, the following code appears:

```
LILO

Welcome to the LILO Boot Loader!

Please enter the name of the partition you would like to boot
at the prompt below. The choices are:

DOS     - DOS or Windows (FAT/FAT32 partition)
Linux   - Linux (ext2fs partition)

boot:
```

If you got rid of your old operating system and only have Slackware installed on your computer, you're presented with one choice, `Linux`, after the LILO welcome message. Press Enter to boot Slackware.

If Slackware was not installed correctly, only the letters `L` or `LI` appear on your screen. This means that an error exists with LILO. Reboot using your Slackware boot and root disks and reinstall LILO (see Chapter 5 for more information on booting with boot and root disks and configuring LILO for the first time).

Assuming Slackware is installed correctly, lots of information is displayed on the screen during the boot process — this is Slackware's way of finding out more information (called *probing*) about your computer. When all is said and done, a `login:` prompt appears. You have just completed your boot to Slackware!

Confronting the Power of Root

Super user — the idea seems weird. How can there be one person who is a "super" user for your computer? As unusual as it sounds, your system needs a super user to control the general system functions — things that you may not see running but are necessary for the system to work right. The super user also does things like adding drives to the system, moving files around, installing new programs, and rebooting the system. The super user can do almost anything, at any time, anywhere on your system.

The super user can also do bad things to the system, like moving other people's files, damaging partitions, and removing necessary programs that the system needs to run correctly. The super user holds all the power of the system, good and bad.

In the Slackware world, the super user is called *root.*

Anytime you see the `login:` prompt, type **root** and press Enter. You are now logged in, or allowed access, to your system as the super user! You command prompt looks like this:

```
slack1:~#
```

(The name of your machine appears where `slack1` appears in the prompt. You named your machine as part of the installation process shown in Chapter 5.)

The system is now waiting for you to tell it what to do. The # (pound sign) at the end of the prompt means that you're the `root` (super) user and have complete control of the machine. From now on, the phrase # command prompt means that you are logged in as `root`, and are ready to type commands at that prompt.

Understanding roles

The `root` account is very powerful — I can't stress this enough. No restrictions exist for `root`, which makes it easy to commit errors that have disastrous consequences, such as removing hard drives from the system while the system is in operation.

The best way to prevent problems is to avoid being logged in as `root` for normal tasks. Instead, you should log in to your own personal account. (For more info on creating your own personal account, see the section later in this chapter titled "Managing Accounts.") If you must be `root`, make sure that you double-check your typing before pressing Enter. Also, log in as `root` only when absolutely necessary, like when you have to install a new program or fix a disk. When you finish with your task as `root`, log out. See the "Getting Out of the System" section later in this chapter for instructions on logging out.

Finally, make sure that you understand the different prompts for personal accounts and `root`. By prompt, I mean the symbol at the end of the command line, like `slack1:~#`. Table 6-1 lists the typical prompts for user accounts on a Slackware system:

Table 6-1 Command Prompts for User Accounts

Command Line Ends With	*Signifies Account*
#	root (super user)
$	personal account (bash shell user)
%	personal account (csh shell user)
>	personal account (tcsh shell user)

(Shells, like `bash`, `csh`, and `tcsh`, are discussed in greater detail in Chapter 8.)

Abiding by the rules

Now that you have Slackware installed and have access to the root account, you're your own systems administrator! This role calls for maturity and self-control because the ideas you practice at home tend to stay with you as you go to work, school, the doctor's office, and anyplace else.

Some people have a tendency to be overwhelmed with a feeling of control when they first log in as `root`. Because `root` is so powerful, those people use their newfound privileges in a not-so-nice manner, like reading other people's e-mail if it's stored on the machine, deleting files, and generally behaving like a child with a new toy. The `root` account is a cross-platform problem that exists in other operating systems, not just Slackware. However super user powers are limited to the particular machine the access works on — having super user access on one machine doesn't mean that the access works on another machine. Table 6-2 highlights some of the do's and don'ts of using root.

Table 6-2 Super User Account Do's and Don'ts

Do	*Don't*
Keep the password secret	Give out the password
Install system software	Install personal software as root
Upgrade system software	Keep multiple versions of software apps
Read the `man` pages	Type commands to see what will happen
Check system logs daily	Remove system logs without reading them

Managing Accounts

Slackware enables you to create a new user account only when you're logged in as `root`. You should have a separate account — an account other than `root` — for yourself, even if you're the only user on the system. You never want accounts to be shared because accounts are what Slackware uses to uniquely identify users to the system. Accounts are like your ATM PIN number, which you'd never share with anyone else!

Slackware keeps track of several pieces of information about each user, including the following:

- The username, which is the unique identifier for each user.
- The user ID, or UID, which is a unique number for each user.
- The group ID, or GID, which is another unique number denoting what group on the computer the user belongs to.
- The password of the user.
- The home directory of the user, which is where the user is placed upon logging in to the system. (See Chapter 9 for more on directories.)
- The login shell, which is the subsystem that the user works in. (See Chapter 8 for more on the login shell.)

These bits of information are important because they can quickly tell you what the account is capable of doing on the system — what group the account belongs to (whether the group is a users group or an administrators group), and where the account's home directory is located on the system (the location the account starts from upon login). You can find this information (except for the password) in the `/etc/passwd` file. The password itself is found (encrypted as a string of nonsense garbage) in the file `/etc/shadow`.

Creating a new account

At the # command prompt, type **more /etc/passwd** and press Enter. You see several accounts already in this file by default. Slackware creates these default accounts for various functions ranging from network functionality to system operation. For example, the `bin` account is used to run the program `portmap`, which is used for network services. No person ever uses the `bin` account; it's there to run system functions.

You can add users to the `/etc/passwd` file by using the `adduser` program. By adding users to the file, you're actually creating new accounts.

To create a new account, make sure that you're the `root` user (meaning you've logged in with the `root` account) and follow these steps:

1. **At the command prompt (#), type** adduser **and press Enter.**

   The following prompt appears:

   ```
   Login name for new user (8 characters or less) []:
   ```

   The new login name must be a total of eight characters (letters and numbers only) or less.

   For example, my first name is only four letters long, so I type **paul** and press Enter. In the rest of these instructions, substitute your own user name for `paul`. Through the rest of the `adduser` program, enter your information after the colon (:) in each prompt.

   Throughout these instructions, make sure that you use only lowercase letters, not CAPITAL LETTERS! Capital letters in account creation can wreak havoc with system software.

2. **Type your new login name and press Enter.**

   The following prompt appears:

   ```
   User id for paul [defaults to next available]:
   ```

   This prompt is actually asking for a user ID number to associate with the user name `paul`. The system automatically chooses the next available user ID number, unless you give it one. To save time, let the system choose.

3. **Press Enter.**

   The following prompt appears:

   ```
   Initial group for paul [users]:
   ```

`users` is the default group for every newly created user account on the system. This is the most basic group on the system. If you don't want this account to be in the `users` group, you can type another group name here — however, the group name must be a name listed in the file `/etc/group`. (Press Ctrl+C to quit `adduser` and then at the # command prompt, type **more /etc/group** and press Enter to see the list of known groups on the system. Of course, this means you must restart `adduser` from Step 1.)

Using the default group listed (`users`) is standard for new user accounts.

4. **Press Enter.**

The following prompt appears:

```
Additional groups [enter for none]:
```

This prompt enables you to specify other groups besides `users` for the account `paul` to belong to by typing another group name. This prompt is really for advanced system administrators who need to tailor new accounts for workstations and workgroups. Unless you're really creative with your account management, you should just accept the default (none, or no more) here.

5. **Press Enter.**

The following prompt appears:

```
paul's home directory [/home/paul]:
```

The *home directory* is the starting point for an account after the account is logged in to a system. Selecting the default is a good choice because the system automatically chooses the `/home` partition for user directories.

6. **Press Enter.**

The following prompt appears:

```
paul's shell [/bin/bash]:
```

Shells are working areas for accounts, which let you navigate around the system. In other words, the shell is the interpreter between you and the system that passes your commands to the system in a form that it can easily recognize. For more information on shells, check out Chapter 8.

The default shell listed (`/bin/bash`) is okay, but a better one is `/bin/csh`, and that's what you want to use. `/bin/bash` is better for experienced users, while `/bin/csh` is easier for first-time users. The reason that the `/bin/bash` shell is the default is because Slackware assumes you're an experienced user.

7. **Type** /bin/csh **and press Enter.**

   The following prompt appears:

   ```
   paul's account expire date (MM/DD/YY) []:
   ```

   This prompt asks you when you want this account to expire. The idea here is for system administrators to have some way to keep track of employees who are working on temporary assignments. You don't want it to expire, so leave this blank.

8. **Press Enter.**

   A summary of everything that you've done up to this point appears on the screen. The summary lists all the choices you've made so far, such as login name, user ID number, and groups that the account belongs to. At the end of the summary, Slackware gives you the choice of bailing out if you made a mistake by pressing Ctrl+C. If, however, you made no mistakes, then move on to Step 9.

9. **Press Enter.**

   The message Making new account . . . appears on your screen. Cool!

The `adduser` program now asks you to provide a bunch of information, such as your full name, your room number, and your work and home telephone numbers. For each piece of information requested on the screen, just press Enter. `adduser` provides these prompts for those people that are using Slackware in a work environment and need to keep track of their employees.

Finally, the `adduser` program presents the following message:

```
New password:
```

`adduser` wants you to give the account a password. Your password can be any length between 5 and 127 characters long.

Try to use letters and numbers for your password. Don't just use your name, your significant other's name, your pet's name, your phone number, or anything that can be easily connected with you. Instead, try making up words by using a combination of letters and numbers and punctuation, like 2b0r!2b (To be, or not to be) for example.

If you know any foreign languages, another good way to choose passwords is to use words in another language and add some numbers with it. For example, if you know Spanish, you can use the password 1palabra (one word in English).

`adduser` does not echo, or display, the password you type on the screen. This is a security measure to prevent prying eyes from looking over your shoulder at your screen when you type your password.

Providing friends with access

One of the nice things about Slackware is the fact that you can create accounts for your friends on the same machine. When you've got Dominic or Keith or Katy visiting, and that person wants to get online, they can do so with their own private account.

Establishing separate accounts means that you don't have to worry about your friends rummaging through your private folders or seeing your e-mail. Your friends can have online access, but to their accounts only.

Of course, if you have the root password, you must remember to control your own desire to rummage through their stuff as well. After all, snooping isn't nice, even if you do have the power to do so.

To set the password for the new account, follow these steps:

1. **Type your new password after the colon (:) and press Enter.**

   The following message appears on screen:

   ```
   Re-enter new password:
   ```

   `adduser` asks you to reenter your password in case you made any typos or mistakes.

2. **Type your new password again and press Enter.**

   If you type your new password exactly the same twice in a row, `adduser` shows the following message:

   ```
   Password changed.
   Done...
   ```

   After this message appears, you're returned to your command prompt (the prompt with the # at the end).

You've just created your new account!

Changing passwords

Passwords are the keys to the Slackware system. Only people (like you) who hold the keys can complete certain tasks, like shutting down the machine. You can keep up your system's security by occasionally changing your password.

When you first booted your newly installed Slackware system, the `root` account didn't have a password set. To give your `root` account a password, follow these steps:

1. **At the** `login:` **prompt, type** root **and press Enter.**

   You're now logged in as the root user.

2. **At the command prompt (#), type** passwd **and press Enter.**

   By typing **passwd,** you change the password for the account that you're currently using. If you were using an account other than `root`, Slackware would prompt you for the old password (if one exists) before being able to change the password.

   `root`, however, has the ability to change another account's password. To change another account's password, you would type **passwd [account]**, where `[account]` is another login account. For example, if you want to change the password for the account `paul`, you can type **passwd paul** and repeat Steps 1 through 3 for changing a password.

   The message `Changing password for root` appears on the screen.

3. **At the** `New password:` **prompt, type the new password and press Enter.**

   Slackware doesn't display your new password on the screen. When you press Enter, the system tells you to reenter the new password.

4. **Type your new password again and press Enter.**

   If you type in the new password exactly the same twice in a row, the message `Password changed` appears.

As long as you know the root password, you can always change the password for an account by following these steps.

Understanding Virtual Consoles

A *console* is the monitor and keyboard connected directly to your computer — it's where you get most of your work done. *Virtual consoles* enable users to have simultaneously multiple work sessions on a single console. Some Slackware users feel that virtual consoles are unnecessary, especially if you install X Windows, which is the graphical display system for Slackware (for more on X Windows, see Chapter 11). Understanding how virtual consoles work, however, is important, and you may have use for them in the future.

To see how virtual consoles work, follow these steps:

1. **Make sure that you're logged in to your Slackware system, as root or as another account that you've created.**

   You should be at the `#` or `%` prompt, depending on which account you logged in to. (Remember, these symbols represent your command prompt.)

2. **Press Alt+F2.**

   You are now at the `login:` prompt.

3. **Press Alt+F1.**

   You are now back at the # or % prompt again.

What you just did is switch your console from console 1 — where you were at your command prompt — to console 2 — which wasn't logged in yet, and was sitting at a `login:` prompt. Using virtual consoles, you can run a program in console 1, switch to console 2 to run another program, and monitor both programs from console 3.

Slackware allows you to have up to six virtual consoles. To switch among any of the six, press the Alt key and any function key from F1 through F6. F1 represents console 1, F2 represents console 2, and so on.

Virtual consoles are a little restrictive because you can only work in one virtual console at a time. But virtual consoles provide a good way to execute multiple programs in more than one work session at the same time.

Getting Out of the System

You wouldn't believe how many people forget to log off when they're done working on their systems — it's just like forgetting to do the Start⇨Shutdown sequence in Windows before turning off your computer.

Logging off is also a security measure — after you're logged off, no one can run programs as you (under your account's user ID) or as `root`, unless they have the password to those accounts. But forgetting to log off is like leaving the front door to your house wide open with a sign saying, "Please come in and take anything you find."

To log off of an account, type **exit** at the command prompt and press Enter. When you do, the word `logout` appears. You're then taken back to the `login:` prompt.

Logging off is not the same as shutting down. If you plan to shut down your computer, you must first log in as root, and then type **shutdown -h now** before you turn off the power. (See the beginning of this chapter for more information on the shutdown command.)

You can't shut down your computer if you're not using the `root` account. Personal accounts don't have the ability to use the `shutdown` command. You can, however, restart your computer as any account if you press Ctrl+Alt+Del at any time. This sends the equivalent of a `shutdown -r now` command to the computer.

Chapter 7

Reconfiguring Your System

In This Chapter

- Understanding the pkgtool program
- Manipulating tools for configurations
- Configuring a printer

Somewhere down the road, you may decide that you don't like the way your system is set up. Or you may want to add a modem if you don't have one already, and connect to the Internet. In Windows, whenever you add a piece of hardware or change some internal software, you must modify the system settings. In fact, anyone who sits down at a Windows machine can change its settings. Slackware enables you to change or modify both hardware and software settings without having to repeat the entire setup process. For example, you can change your screen fonts without having to reset your network and mouse configuration; you can install the newest gizmo-producing program without any problem; or you can set up a printer. In this chapter, I show you how to use Slackware's package installation and removal programs to install and remove new applications.

However, you need administrative privileges to change settings. To reconfigure your system or install new packages, you must log in to your system using the `root` account. (For help on logging in and logging off, see Chapter 6.) In this chapter, I show you how to reconfigure your system quickly and easily.

Installing and Removing Programs with pkgtool

Installing new software is a major pain, especially if the software developers don't tell you exactly where to install a new program on your system. Slackware provides a well-developed tool called *pkgtool* to help you install or remove programs. pkgtool has several features, including a main menu similar to the setup program (see Chapter 5 for more information on the setup program). pkgtool uses *packages*, which are containers that house installation programs, help files if applicable, and actual applications and associate files.

After completing the Slackware installation and rebooting your system (see Chapter 5), you can access pkgtool in two ways: from the `setup` main menu or from the # command prompt. Both procedures run the pkgtool program, but running pkgtool from the setup menu enables you to configure other parts of the system. For now, you want to run pkgtool from the command prompt.

At the # command prompt, type **pkgtool** and press Enter. The pkgtool main menu appears with six choices: Current, Other, Floppy, Remove, View, and Exit, as shown in Figure 7-1.

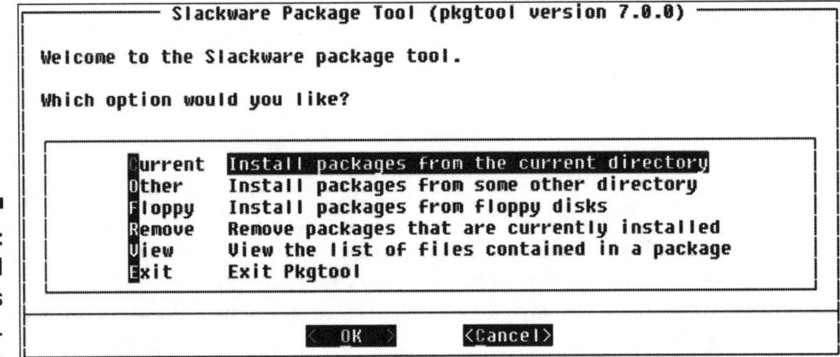

Figure 7-1: The pkgtool menu lists six choices.

You can navigate the pkgtool main menu by using your up- and down-arrow keys to highlight choices. Then press Enter to make your selection.

The last menu option is Exit. Highlighting Exit and pressing Enter closes pkgtool and returns you to your command prompt.

Installing packages from the current directory

pkgtool enables you to install packages from the current directory or folder if you copied the package from the CD-ROM, a floppy disk, or the Web. The *current directory* is the location on the hard drive from which you run pkgtool. (See Chapter 9 for more information on directories, files, and the file system.) For example, if you have a prompt that says `slack1:/var/tmp#`, your current directory is /var/tmp. If Windows had similar directories, it would be `C:\var\tmp`.

To install new packages from the current directory, follow these steps:

1. **Type** pkgtool **at the # command prompt and press Enter.**

   The pkgtool main menu appears.

2. **Select the Current option by using the arrow keys to highlight it, and then press Enter.**

   pkgtool lists any available Slackware packages (those ending in.tgz). pkgtool can use a package if it resides in the same directory you're running pkgtool from (the current directory).

3. **Use the arrow keys to scroll up and down and press the space bar to highlight and select a package.**

   An X appears next to packages you select. You can select multiple packages.

   Select packages based on their file names. For example, in your list you may have the packages lilo.tgz, netscape.tgz, and sysklogd.tgz listed. The lilo.tgz package contains the LILO boot loader, the netscape.tgz package contains Netscape, and the sysklogd.tgz package contains the syslog-logging daemon (for keeping track of things happening on your system).

4. **Press Enter to install the selected packages.**

   Each package contains instructions telling pkgtool where on your hard drive to install the programs and associate files. pkgtool follows these instructions automatically.

pkgtool displays a message for each package it installs that gives some information about the package: for example, how big the files are and the approximate time required to install the package. After the packages are installed, pkgtool exits back to your command prompt immediately.

Installing packages from another location

Sometimes you may accidentally run pkgtool but the packages reside elsewhere on your hard drive than the current directory. In this case, pkgtool gives you the option to install packages from a different location, such as a CD-ROM, rather than the current directory. The most common reason for packages to reside elsewhere on the system is due to archiving — all the packages for the system may reside in one particular location, like another partition or a CD-ROM, for the specific purpose of keeping everything together.

To install packages from a different location, follow these steps:

1. **Type** pkgtool **at the # command prompt and press Enter.**

   The pkgtool main menu appears.

2. **Select the Other option by using arrow keys to highlight it, and then press Enter.**

   A dialog box appears with a text-input area, asking you what directory your new packages are stored in.

3. **Type the full path of the directory in the text-input area and press Enter. The full path is the exact location of the directory, starting with a slash (/).**

   For example, if you want to install the packages on the Slackware CD-ROM from the XAP series, type **/cdrom/slakware/xap** and press Enter.

   If any Slackware packages are available (packages ending in.tgz), pkgtool lists them.

4. **Use your arrow keys to scroll up and down and press the space bar to highlight and select a package.**

   An X appears next to packages you select. You can select multiple packages.

   Select packages based on their file names. For example, packages in your list may include lilo.tgz, netscape.tgz, and sysklogd.tgz. The lilo.tgz package contains the LILO boot loader, the netscape.tgz package contains Netscape, and the sysklogd.tgz package contains the syslog-logging daemon (for keeping track of things happening on your system).

5. **Press Enter to install the selected packages.**

   Each package contains instructions telling pkgtool where on your hard drive to install the programs and associate files. pkgtool follows these instructions automatically.

pkgtool displays a message for each package it installs that gives some information about the package, such as how big the files are and how much time is needed for package installation. After the packages are installed, pkgtool exits back to your command prompt immediately.

Installing packages from a floppy disk

At times, you may receive floppy disks from friends who want you to try the programs. The use of floppy disks for saving packages is a good idea because floppy disks themselves are *removable media* (meaning you can take the disk out of the floppy drive and go somewhere else with it). This gives you and your friends the added benefit of being able to exchange programs and packages without a lot of hassle. And pkgtool can install packages from a floppy disk, so you don't have to copy packages to your hard drive first, thus saving you disk space.

Note that some packages, like netscape.tgz, won't fit on a single floppy disk. However, other packages like workbone.tgz (a text-based CD-ROM music player) or vim.tgz (a very cool editor) will easily fit on a floppy disk.

To install packages from a floppy disk, follow these steps:

1. **Type** pkgtool **at your # command prompt and press Enter.**

   The pkgtool main menu appears.

2. **Select Floppy by using the arrow keys to highlight it, and then press Enter.**

   The Select Floppy Drive dialog box appears, as shown in Figure 7-2. If you have only one 3½-inch floppy drive, use the first option. If you have more than one 3½-inch floppy drive, the first option is your A: drive, and the second is your B: drive. The same holds true for 5¼-inch floppy drives — use the third and fourth options instead of the first and second.

```
SELECT FLOPPY DRIVE
Which floppy drive would you like to install from?

/dev/fd0u1440   1.44 MB first floppy drive
/dev/fd1u1440   1.44 MB second floppy drive
/dev/fd0h1200   1.2 MB first floppy drive
/dev/fd1h1200   1.2 MB second floppy drive

< OK >     <Cancel>
```

Figure 7-2: Select a floppy drive.

3. **Select a floppy drive letter by using your arrow keys to highlight it and then press Enter.**

   The Software Selection dialog box appears, as shown in Figure 7-3.

   This part is somewhat confusing because pkgtool still has the ability to install an entire disk set of packages. In the older versions of Slackware, a *disk set* was a software series of packages, like the A series or N series of Slackware software, but entire software series no longer fit on floppy disks. Hence this option is maintained for backwards compatibility.

   The likely scenario is that you have a couple of program packages on a floppy disk. To install packages from a floppy disk, leave the text area blank. However, if you happen to have a disk set on floppy disks, in the text input area, enter the names of the disk set that you want to install, like D or XAP. (See Chapter 5 for a list of Slackware software series.)

```
SOFTWARE SELECTION

Enter the names of any disk sets you would like to install.
Seperate the sets with a space, like this: a b oi x

To install packages from one disk, hit [enter] without typing
anything.

<  OK  >      <Cancel>
```

Figure 7-3: Prompting for disk sets (Slackware software series) to install.

4. **Leave the text area blank and press Enter.**

   A message appears, telling you to insert the floppy disk that contains the package(s) for installation on the floppy drive. Two choices appear underneath the message — Quit and OK. Choose OK by clicking it with your mouse or by using your arrow keys to highlight OK and pressing Enter to continue.

   Do not use Linux-formatted floppy disks with this option! pkgtool exits immediately without any warning if it finds a Linux floppy disk in the floppy drive. To install a package from floppy disk, pkgtool expects the package on DOS or Windows floppy disk; using another type of floppy disk causes errors in pkgtool. Use DOS- or Windows-formatted disks instead.

5. **Insert the floppy disk containing the package or packages to install into your floppy drive and press Enter.**
6. **Use your arrow keys to scroll up and down and press the space bar to select a package.**

   You can select multiple packages, if multiple packages exist on the floppy disk. An X appears next to a package you select. Select your package based on the name of the package.

   For example, your list may contain the packages lilo.tgz, netscape.tgz, and sysklogd.tgz. The lilo.tgz package contains the LILO boot loader, the netscape.tgz package contains Netscape, and the sysklogd.tgz package contains the syslog-logging daemon (for keeping track of things happening on your system).

7. **Press Enter to install your selected packages.**

Within each package are instructions telling pkgtool where on your hard drive to install the programs and associate files. pkgtool automatically follows these instructions.

After the packages are installed, pkgtool exits and the command prompt returns.

Removing installed packages

You may decide that you no longer want a specific package installed. In other operating systems, such as Windows or DOS, you have to search through the system to remove the package and all its associated files. In Slackware, however, pkgtool removes installed packages and their related files without your having to search for all the parts of the program.

To remove installed packages, follow these steps:

1. **Type** pkgtool **at the # command prompt and press Enter.**

   The pkgtool main menu appears.

2. **Select the Remove option by using the arrow keys to highlight it, and then press Enter.**

   A small window appears, telling you that pkgtool is searching. The program then displays a list of all packages installed on the system (as shown in Figure 7-4). This list differs depending on the packages you have installed on your system.

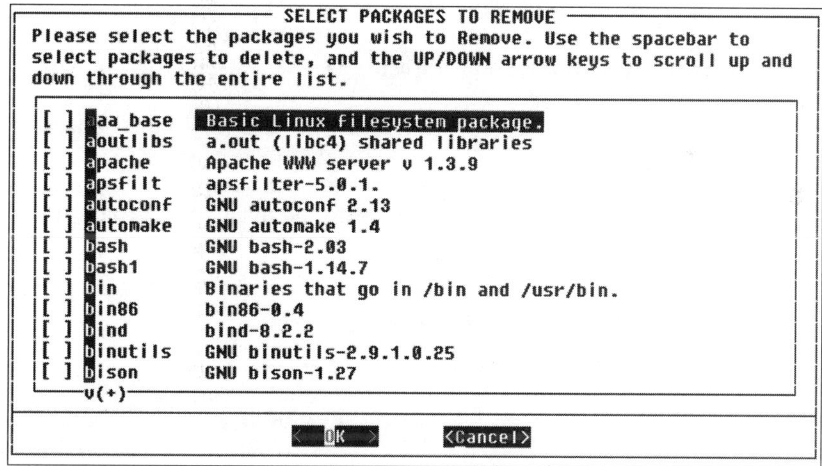

Figure 7-4: The list of packages available for removal.

3. **Use your arrow keys to highlight a package and then press the space bar to select.**

   An X appears next to the package that you selected.

   You may select multiple packages by highlighting another package and pressing the space bar.

4. **Press Enter to remove the selected packages.**

   A message appears telling you that pkgtool is removing the packages that you selected. After the selected packages are removed, pkgtool tells you that the list of packages removed is stored in the `/tmp` directory in a file called `PKGTOOL.REMOVED`. You can browse the contents of this file by typing **more /tmp/PKGTOOL.REMOVED** at your command prompt and pressing Enter.

5. **Press Enter to exit pkgtool.**

   pkgtool exits, returning you to the command prompt.

Viewing software package contents

You may want to view the contents of a software package to see whether a certain file, program, or directory is included in that package. You may also want to check a package to see whether it includes the latest version of a file or program. pkgtool enables you to list what's inside software packages to satisfy your curiosity. pkgtool also discloses how large a compressed software package is, and how much space the packages will take up on your system after installing.

To view the contents of a software package, follow these steps:

1. **Type** pkgtool **at the # command prompt and press Enter.**

   The pkgtool main menu appears.

2. **Select the View option by using the arrow keys to highlight it, and then press Enter.**

   pkgtool prompts you with a list of software packages currently installed on the system, as shown in Figure 7-5.

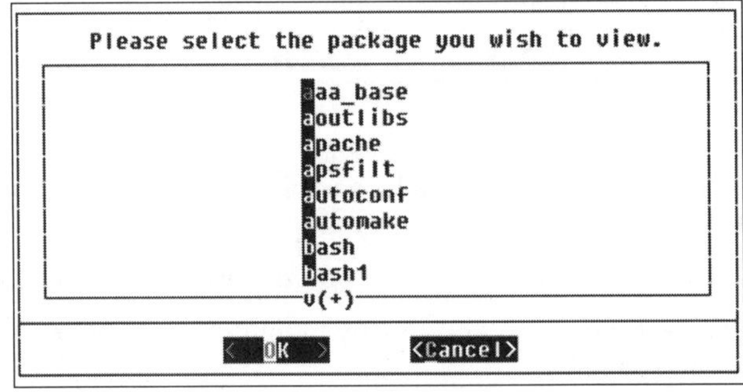

Figure 7-5: Select a package that you want to view.

3. **Use the arrow keys to highlight a software package to view and press Enter to select it.**

   An example of a package is shown in Figure 7-6.

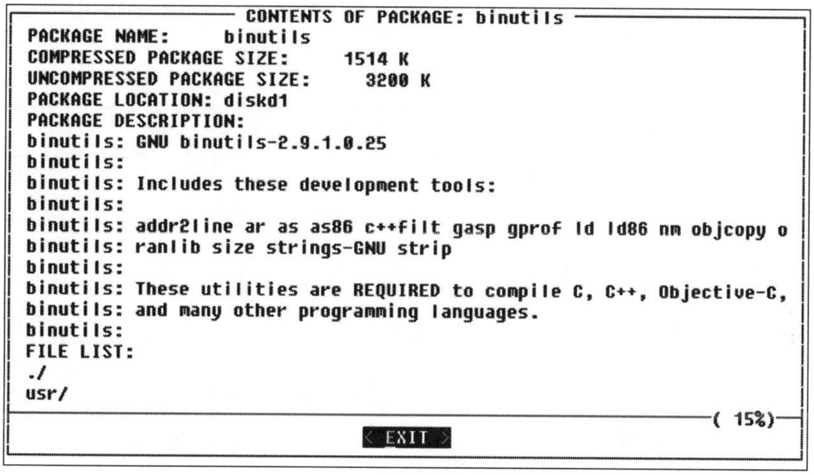

```
──────────── CONTENTS OF PACKAGE: binutils ────────────
PACKAGE NAME:     binutils
COMPRESSED PACKAGE SIZE:     1514 K
UNCOMPRESSED PACKAGE SIZE:     3200 K
PACKAGE LOCATION: diskd1
PACKAGE DESCRIPTION:
binutils: GNU binutils-2.9.1.0.25
binutils:
binutils: Includes these development tools:
binutils:
binutils: addr2line ar as as86 c++filt gasp gprof ld ld86 nm objcopy o
binutils: ranlib size strings-GNU strip
binutils:
binutils: These utilities are REQUIRED to compile C, C++, Objective-C,
binutils: and many other programming languages.
binutils:
FILE LIST:
./
usr/
──────────────────────────────────────────( 15%)─
                    < EXIT >
```

Figure 7-6: Viewing the contents of the binutils.tgz package.

Every viewing has the same format. The name of the package is listed along with its compressed size — the size of the package on the CD-ROM — and its uncompressed size, which is the amount of disk space the package currently occupies on your system. Then, package location tells you which Slackware software series the package is found in (in the example from Figure 7-6, this package is in the D series), and lastly, a brief description is given of the package.

4. **Press Enter to exit the view.**

   You can now select another package to view by using the arrow keys. Press Enter to see the package contents.

5. **Press *c* to cancel and leave the pkgtool view menu.**

   You return to the pkgtool main menu.

Piecing Together pkgtool

Some people don't like to use menu interfaces and dialog boxes when they install software packages, finding such interfaces clumsy or overrated. Instead, they want to get their hands dirty — they want to see what's going on behind the scenes of programs like `setup` and `pkgtool`. To feed this demand, the folks at The Slackware Project broke down parts of pkgtool into separate programs so that you can run individual programs instead of the all-in-one pkgtool program. This doesn't mean that pkgtool is slow or that the individual programs are faster; it just means that there are other alternatives available than using pkgtool.

Table 7-1 lists the separate programs that make up some of pkgtool's core task.

Table 7-1 The Parts of Pkgtool

Program	*Function*
`installpkg`	Installs packages to the system
`removepkg`	Removes packages from the system
`upgradepkg`	Upgrades older versions of packages on the system

Not to be forgotten, Slackware also has a utility to convert another popular package format (.rpm packages) to the Slackware-friendly package format. This utility, rpm2tgz, has become popular in recent years, as users are no longer forced to wait for program developers to package applications in .tgz format in addition to .rpm format.

To accomplish any kind of package installation or removal, log in to the super user account. The super user account is the only account that can make system-wide changes, such as upgrading packages. See Chapter 6 for more information on the super user (`root`) account.

Installing, removing, and upgrading software packages

The three most common tasks associated with software packages are installing them, removing them, and upgrading them. A *version* is a release of a software program that performs some function, but also fixes problems with an older model of the program. A good example is Slackware itself. The CD-ROMs in the back of the book contain version 7.0 of Slackware, but the previous version of Slackware is 4.0. The higher the version number, the more recent the program version.

Suppose you decide to install Netscape from the CD-ROM because you didn't install it when you installed the rest of the Slackware system. Netscape is contained in the package appropriately named netscape.tgz, which is found in the directory `/cdrom/slakware/xap1`. To install Netscape, do the following steps:

1. **At the # command prompt, type** cd /cdrom/slakware/xap1 **and press Enter.**

   Your command prompt now says `slack1:/cdrom/slakware/xap1#`. (The name of your machine will differ from `slack1`.) This means you are now in the `/cdrom/slakware/xap1` directory on the CD-ROM.

2. **At the # command prompt, type** installpkg netscape.tgz **and press Enter.**

   Slackware reads the `netscape.tgz` package and then executes the instructions within the package that tell Slackware where to install the files. The files appear in their proper locations in the system automatically. When Slackware is finished installing, a text file called `netscape` is placed in the directory `/var/log/packages`. This file contains a summary of everything Slackware did to install the `netscape.tgz` package.

Suppose, for example, you tried Netscape and didn't like it. Because you didn't like it, you decided to remove it from the system because there are better things to do with the space on your hard drive than store a program you don't like. Here's what you do to remove Netscape:

1. **At the # command prompt, type** ls /var/log/packages/netscape **and press Enter.**

   The following line appears:

   ```
   /var/log/packages/netscape
   ```

   This ensures that the Netscape package summary exists in the package summary directory. The system cannot automatically remove packages without knowing what files to remove, and the package summary lists this information.

   If this file is missing, or if you get a No Such File or Directory Error, either the package has been removed, it was never installed, or it was installed in a nonstandard way. If the third scenario is true, you may want to seek out a computer guru to get rid of the program for you.

   After you know the package summary exists, you can remove the package.

2. **At the # command prompt, type** removepkg netscape **and press Enter.**

   Slackware removes the Netscape package from the system and returns you to the command prompt.

If you want to see what's been installed or removed without actually installing or removing the package, type `-warn` in between installpkg or removepkg and the package name (like netscape) to get a list of what will be done. For example, `installpkg -warn netscape.tgz` lists all the installation files for package `netscape`, but doesn't actually do the installation.

Differentiating between Red Hat Linux and Slackware

Perhaps the only real difference between Red Hat Linux and Slackware is the way the system is laid out on the computer. Then again, it could be the fact that Red Hat is a multimillion dollar company employing hundreds of developers, while Slackware is still a party of one (but growing steadily).

One of the innovations that the folks at Red Hat came up with is the idea of the Red Hat Package Manager (rpm) program , which takes packages with the `.rpm` extension and automatically installs them on a Red Hat Linux system. This was arguably the turning point in Red Hat's existence because this kind of package management system enabled Red Hat to control how programs were installed on the system instead of a program developer in Australia, for example, controlling the installation.

Nonetheless, Slackware's package management system (pkgtool) is as robust and manageable as the Red Hat rpm system. The difference between the two methodologies is that you cannot place .rpm packages on a Slackware system without undergoing a conversion process first, but a Slackware package is installable on a Red Hat Linux system by using the `tar -xzf` command.

In fact, Slackware packages can be installed on any Linux distribution, regardless if that system uses pkgtool, or a proprietary package management tool (like rpm). What a great system!

Suppose, for example, that Netscape upgrades from version 4.61 to version 5.0 (it's been a long time in the making). You obviously want to use the latest version of Netscape because later versions fix problems in earlier versions., After downloading the new version of Netscape, type **upgradepkg netscape.tgz** at the # command prompt to upgrade Netscape to version 5.0.

Converting .rpm to .tgz

Slackware packages come with `.tgz` or `.tar.gz` extensions. However, not all Linux packages have these extensions. Some have the `.rpm` extension, which denotes a package for use with Red Hat Linux (a different Linux distribution). This doesn't mean that you can't use `.rpm` packages; you just need to convert the package into a Slackware-friendly format.

Slackware has a program called `rpm2tgz` that converts `.rpm` packages into `.tgz` packages. This conversion enables programs like pkgtool and installpkg to install the software packages. Without doing this conversion, you cannot unpack or install `.rpm`.

The reason for occasionally using `.rpm` packages instead of `.tgz` packages is that sometimes someone who only runs Red Hat Linux, not Slackware Linux, packages the program you want to run. Because that person only uses Red Hat Linux, he only packages his software using the `.rpm` package format.

Suppose, for example, that you want to use AOL Instant Messenger (AIM) to talk to your buddy over the Internet. Slackware doesn't come with an AIM client, but your buddy e-mailed you a program called `gaim` that does the same thing. One problem — the program is packaged as a `.rpm` package. To use it, you need to type the following at a command prompt:

```
rpm2tgz gaim.rpm
```

The `gaim.rpm` package converts to `gaim.tgz`. You can use installpkg or pkgtool to install the `gaim` program.

Exploring Other Configuration Tools

`setup` and `pkgtool` aren't the only configuration utilities that Slackware offers. The previous section covers the package management utilities that complement `pkgtool`, such as `installpkg`, `removepkg`, and `upgradegpkg`. In this section, you explore the utilities that complement the `setup` program:

- fontconfig — for changing the fonts on your screen
- liloconfig — for changing how LILO boots your computer
- netconfig — for changing how your network is set up

For example, suppose that you want to change the font or typeface that the computer is currently using. fontconfig is the program you want to use to accomplish that. Maybe you recompiled a kernel and want to try it out at your next reboot. Use liloconfig to switch kernels. Or, maybe you just changed ISPs and need to set up your system to use the new ISP. netconfig can help you make the necessary changes to your system.

To use any of the configuration utilities discussed in the next three sections, you must log in as the root user.

Changing fonts on your system

The `fontconfig` program enables you to change the font that displays on your text console. Changing the typeface alters the appearance of your command prompt, text on your monitor, and every single character that displays on your monitor. One of the benefits of using fontconfig is that it makes the text more readable — perhaps the font that the system uses by default is too small, or appears fuzzy on your monitor. Obviously, you need to see what you're doing in order to work effectively!

To change your computer's font, follow these steps:

1. **At the # command prompt, type** fontconfig **and press Enter.**

   The Screen Font Configuration dialog box appears, asking you if you want to try out some screen fonts. You have two options — Yes or No.

2. **Select Yes by using the arrow keys to highlight it, and then press Enter.**

   A list of available fonts appears, as shown in Figure 7-7. Press the up- and down-arrow keys to scroll the list. Unfortunately, you won't find examples of each font. You have to try out several fonts to see which works best for you.

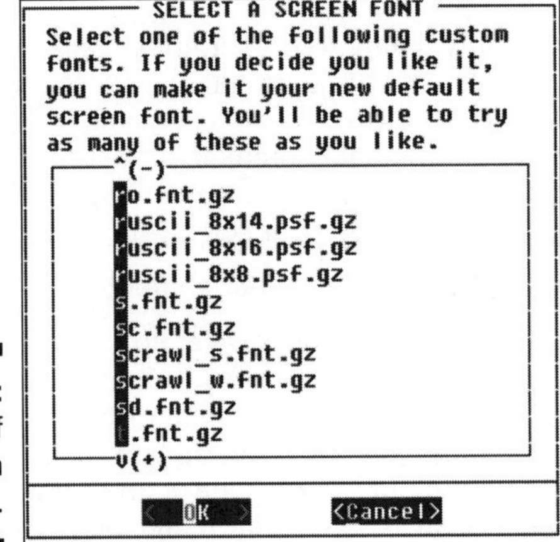

SELECT A SCREEN FONT
Select one of the following custom fonts. If you decide you like it, you can make it your new default screen font. You'll be able to try as many of these as you like.
^(-)
o.fnt.gz
ruscii_8x14.psf.gz
ruscii_8x16.psf.gz
ruscii_8x8.psf.gz
s.fnt.gz
sc.fnt.gz
scrawl_s.fnt.gz
scrawl_w.fnt.gz
sd.fnt.gz
.fnt.gz
v(+)
OK
<Cancel>

Figure 7-7: The list of fonts from fontconfig.

3. **Use your arrow keys to highlight a font choice and Press Enter.**

   The Set As Default Font dialog box appears with Yes and No options at the bottom. The text in this dialog box displays in the new font. If you don't like that font, use your arrow keys to highlight No and press Enter to return to the list of fonts. Repeat this step until you find a font that you like.

4. **Use your arrow keys to highlight Yes and press Enter when you find a font you like.**

   fontconfig exits, returning you to the command prompt.

Your new screen font appears. Whether or not this is a good thing or bad thing depends completely on the font you chose.

Reinstalling your boot program

You need to reinstall your boot program when you make major changes to your computer. Major changes to your system include compiling your own *kernel* (the core of the operating system) or copying a preconfigured kernel onto your system, changing which hard drive partition is bootable, or even adding a second hard drive to your computer. Such system-wide changes affect how the Slackware acts, but your changes are not seen until the system is rebooted.

If you make a change to the system that affects how Slackware works (such as creating a new kernel), you need to reinstall LILO (the Linux Loader — the boot program for Slackware) so that your system recognizes the new changes upon boot. (See Chapter 5 for additional information on LILO.)

To reinstall LILO on your system, follow these steps:

1. The Install LILO dialog box appears, as shown in Figure 7-8. Three options are available: simple, expert, and skip.

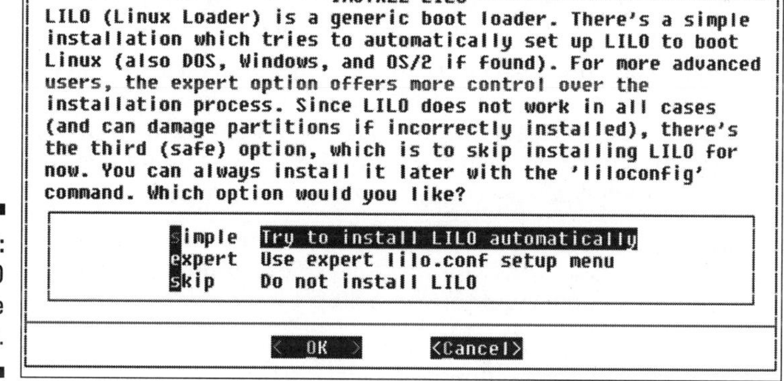

INSTALL LILO
LILO (Linux Loader) is a generic boot loader. There's a simple installation which tries to automatically set up LILO to boot Linux (also DOS, Windows, and OS/2 if found). For more advanced users, the expert option offers more control over the installation process. Since LILO does not work in all cases (and can damage partitions if incorrectly installed), there's the third (safe) option, which is to skip installing LILO for now. You can always install it later with the 'liloconfig' command. Which option would you like?
simple Try to install LILO automatically
expert Use expert lilo.conf setup menu
skip Do not install LILO
< OK >
<Cancel>

Figure 7-8: The LILO welcome screen.

If you're really into technical stuff, check out the sidebar, "Playing with /etc/lilo.conf," later in this chapter to discover more about what LILO really does.

2. **Select Expert by using the arrow keys to highlight it, and then press Enter.**

   The Expert LILO Installation dialog box appears, giving you nine choices; for now, you only want to proceed with the following five steps:

   - Begin
   - Linux
   - DOS (if you have a DOS or Windows partition)
   - View
   - Install

   You can choose `skip` to return to the LILO Installation dialog box. Otherwise, I recommend reading Help almost immediately. To do so, use your arrow keys to highlight Help and press Enter.

3. **Select Begin by using the arrow keys to highlight it, and then press Enter.**

   The Optional append= Line dialog box appears, which asks you for any extra parameters you may need to pass along to LILO at boot time. Parameters include what the CD-ROM drive is called, how much memory you have, and additional swap partitions you may want enabled. Unless you have a specific need, you can just skip this.

4. **Press Enter again to skip the addition of an append= line.**

   The Configure LILO To Use Frame Buffer Console? dialog box appears, but only if you installed X Windows. (If not, skip to Step 5.)

   This dialog box also contains several options which list common video settings for use with the frame buffer console. At this point, you should know what kind of video settings your video card and monitor can handle from your walkthrough of the steps in Chapter 2. (You can even get this information from your video card's manual if you still have it.)

   Alternatively, you can stop the program here by pressing Ctrl+C and turning to Chapter 11 for an in-depth exploration of your video card and monitor. (You can restart from Step 1 later.)

   The standard console shows text upon boot-up. The other choices listed are sizes of frame buffer consoles, ranging from 1024x768x64K to 640x480x256. (The first two numbers are the width and height of the screen; the last number is the number of colors displayed by the video card from 64,000 to 256.) The higher the numbers, the more memory that is used, and the slower your system is on boot time.

WARNING!

Unless you know which video settings your video card can handle, choose the `standard` option from the list of video setting options.

5. **Select Standard by using the arrow keys to highlight it (or the correct video setting for your card) and then press Enter.**

   The Select LILO Target Location dialog box appears, giving you three options, as shown in Figure 7-9.

   Two of the three options are significant:

   - **Root:** The root option installs LILO to the *superblock*, or master location, of your Linux partition. The superblock is usually the partition you chose to be the / (root) partition — in most cases this is the partition named /dev/hda1.
   - **MBR:** The MBR option installs LILO to the master boot record of the hard drive — use this option if you didn't use FIPS and instead wiped your old operating system off your hard drive. (See Chapter 3 for information on using FIPS.)

   In almost every case, LILO users use the root option because it gives them the most control over the system. However, if Slackware is the only operating system on your hard drive, the MBR option is actually a better choice.

WARNING!

Choosing the wrong location for LILO renders your hard drive unbootable!

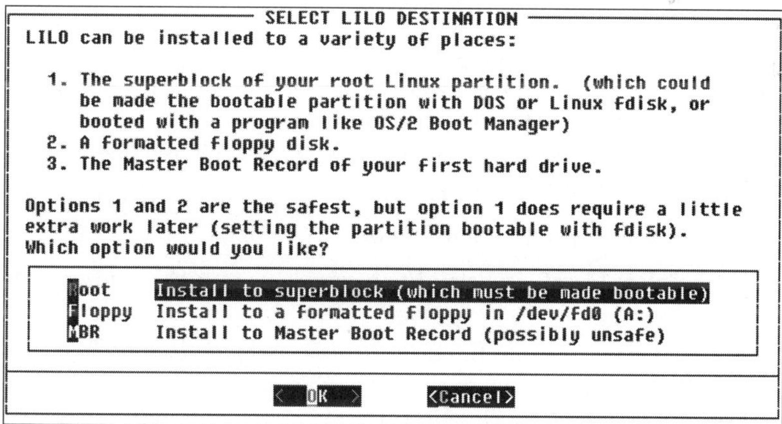
SELECT LILO DESTINATION
LILO can be installed to a variety of places:
1. The superblock of your root Linux partition. (which could be made the bootable partition with DOS or Linux fdisk, or booted with a program like OS/2 Boot Manager)
2. A formatted floppy disk.
3. The Master Boot Record of your first hard drive.
Options 1 and 2 are the safest, but option 1 does require a little extra work later (setting the partition bootable with fdisk).
Which option would you like?
Root Install to superblock (which must be made bootable)
Floppy Install to a formatted floppy in /dev/fd0 (A:)
MBR Install to Master Boot Record (possibly unsafe)
< OK >
<Cancel>

Figure 7-9: Select a location for LILO.

6. **Use your arrow keys to highlight your LILO target selection and press Enter.**

   The Choose LILO Delay dialog box appears with four options: none (no wait), 5 (five seconds), 30 (30 seconds), or forever (until you type something on the keyboard).

7. **Use your arrow keys to highlight the amount of delay time you wish to have before booting and press Enter.**

   You return to the Expert LILO Installation dialog box to select what kind of partition to add to LILO as a bootable partition.

8. **Select the Linux option by using the arrow keys to highlight it, and then press Enter.**

   LILO displays the Select Linux Partition dialog box, which lists available hard drive partitions. In the text input area box, you must type in the name of the bootable partition. In most cases, this is /dev/hda1, because that's the first partition available on your hard drive.

   If you have multiple operating systems on your computer, you may select DOS from the Expert LILO Installation dialog box and tell LILO that a DOS partition is bootable also.

9. Type the name of the bootable partition in the text-input area and press Enter.

   You return to the Expert LILO Installation dialog box.

10. **Select View by using the arrow keys to highlight it, and then press Enter.**

    Selecting this option previews your LILO configuration file. If you see something that's not to your liking (perhaps you changed your mind and want a longer or shorter delay before booting), you can change it when you return to the Expert LILO menu in the next step.

11. **Press Enter.**

    The Expert LILO menu returns.

12. **Select Install by using the arrow keys to highlight it, and then press Enter.**

    LILO installs into the location you specified in Step 6.

At this point, LILO reinstallation is complete and returns you to the command prompt.

Playing with /etc/lilo.conf

Occasionally, you may have to make a change to how LILO works, and you don't want to go through the hassle of using liloconfig. That's okay — Slackware encourages people to get their hands dirty and figure out where the configuration files are on the system.

Most, but not all, configuration files are kept in the /etc directory. (Directories in Slackware are akin to folders in Windows. See Chapter 9.) To reach the `/etc` directory, at your command prompt type **cd /etc** and press Enter. The LILO configuration file is `/etc/lilo.conf`.

Starting at the top of the file, any lines that begin with a # are comments and are ignored by the system. This is because comments are reminders for the programmer or user to help remember why the line or entry was written a particular way. Next, the line that says `boot = /dev/hda` tells LILO on which hard drive it's supposed to look for the boot program.

The next line, `message = /boot/boot_message.txt`, tells LILO where to find the welcome message to display upon boot-up. The welcome message is the greeting you see on the screen when you turn on your computer that asks you to choose your operating system.

The next line is the `prompt` line, which tells LILO to display a prompt on the screen for a command. This prompt is usually `boot:`, but advanced users have been known to customize it.

Following that, the `timeout = 1200` line tells LILO to delay booting for 120 seconds. You can specify any number here for the timeout line, but remember that LILO counts in tenths of a second — in this example, 1200 is 120 seconds, which is two minutes. The existence of this line at all means that you want LILO to wait until you enter which operating system to boot at the `boot:` prompt.

The next line, `vga = normal`, tells LILO that you're using the standard text-based console, rather than a frame buffer console. You can see other options listed below this line that are preceded by #, thus making the system ignore them because the system sees any line beginning with a # as a comment.

After all the comments, the next line, `image = /vmlinuz`, tells LILO where the kernel is found and what the kernel is named. In this case, `vmlinuz` is the name of the kernel, and it is found in the / (root) directory.

The line under that is `root = /dev/hda1`, which tells LILO which hard drive partition is the root partition.

The next line, `label = Linux`, is the name of this Slackware system to boot. You can call this anything you want; the label you give it is later displayed upon turning on your computer as one of the options to boot. Remember to give your system a name that is easily recognized, otherwise others using your computer may not know what system to boot. You can also specify multiple `images` and `labels` in `lilo.conf` in case you want to run a specific version of Slackware on a given day.

The last line, `read-only`, tells Linux to boot the root partition (/dev/hda1) as read-only and do some error-checking on it before it's ready to run. This ensures that if errors do exist on your disk partitions, they can be fixed before you ever get to work on them.

Now, knowing what each line does, you have more power over your Slackware system!

Networking configuration

You may decide to change Internet Service Providers (ISP) at some point (for lower prices, better service, or even friendlier customer service). When you change ISPs, you need to change your networking configuration to match your new ISP. Slackware makes this change smoother.

You must have the necessary information from your ISP for the networking change to work. You need the domain name of the ISP (like `aol.com`) and the Internet Protocol (IP) type your ISP uses. If you don't have this information, you need to contact your ISP and get it.

To change your network configuration, follow these steps:

1. **At the # command prompt, type** netconfig **and press Enter.**

   The Network Configuration dialog box appears telling you that you are about to configure your network.

2. **Press Enter.**

   The Enter Hostname dialog box appears with a text-input area. You are asked to give your machine a name. You already named your machine when you went through the INSTALL section of the `setup` program. (See Chapter 5 for info on `setup`.) However, by running the netconfig program, you have the opportunity to change your machine's name now, so give your machine a name, even if it's just "computer."

3. **Type the name of your machine in the text-input area and press Enter.**

   The Enter Domain name dialog box appears with a text input area. You are asked for the domain name of your computer. This is the new ISPs domain name, like `aol.com`.

4. **Type the domain name of your computer in the text-input area and press Enter.**

   The Setup IP dialog box appears with three options. You are asked for your Internet Protocol (IP) address type, as shown in Figure 7-10. The IP address is the unique address of your machine as it relates to the Internet, kind of like the Zip+4 code that the U.S. Postal Service uses.

   Of the three options, DHCP and Loopback are the most likely ones to choose, depending on how you're connecting to your ISP:

   - **DHCP:** This stands for Dynamic Host Configuration Protocol. DHCP enables dynamic configuration of IP addresses. This selection is for cable modem users and digital subscriber line (DSL) users.

   - **Loopback:** Loopback is for normal modems, serial modems set up for SLIP or PPP connections, or laptops using network cards.

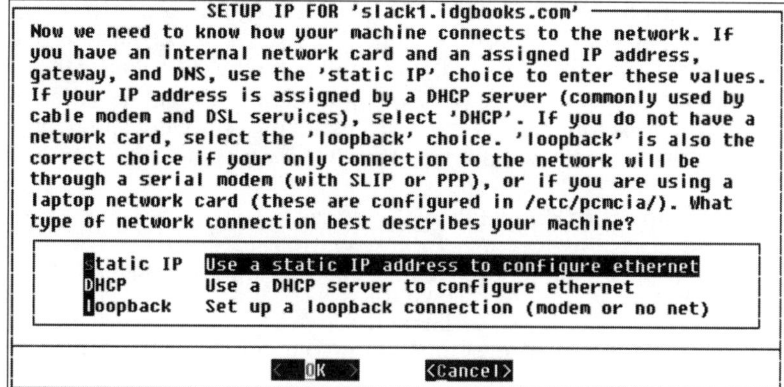

SETUP IP FOR 'slack1.idgbooks.com'
Now we need to know how your machine connects to the network. If you have an internal network card and an assigned IP address, gateway, and DNS, use the 'static IP' choice to enter these values. If your IP address is assigned by a DHCP server (commonly used by cable modem and DSL services), select 'DHCP'. If you do not have a network card, select the 'loopback' choice. 'loopback' is also the correct choice if your only connection to the network will be through a serial modem (with SLIP or PPP), or if you are using a laptop network card (these are configured in /etc/pcmcia/). What type of network connection best describes your machine?
static IP Use a static IP address to configure ethernet
DHCP Use a DHCP server to configure ethernet
loopback Set up a loopback connection (modem or no net)
< OK >
<Cancel>

Figure 7-10: Select an IP type.

5. **Use your arrow keys to highlight your IP address type and press Enter.**

   Netconfig exits.

Your network reconfiguration is complete.

Setting Up Your Printer

A printer is a major part of any computer purchase. After all, you need something to print out those school reports, stock quotes, game cheat codes, and song lyrics.

A printer in Slackware consists of the printer hardware and a location on the file system called the print queue, where files go that are waiting to be printed. The print queue enables Slackware to print files without having to wait for the printer to finish the previous print job. By default, Slackware prints files in the queue on a first-come first-served basis, thus avoiding interruptions in the printing process.

Slackware uses the program apsfilter to set up printers and print queues. This program comes with its own menu system and is very easy to use.

You need to know the make and model of your printer (like HP DeskJet 500) and what kind of printer it is (parallel or serial, which determines what port the printer connects to) before attempting to set up your printer. Any other information about your printer, like the printer manual or info you wrote down while walking through the steps in Chapter 2, is also helpful.

You must have installed the following packages in order to set up your printer: `apsfilt.tgz` (AP series) `ghostscr.tgz` (AP series), and `gsfonts.tgz` (AP series). If you don't have these packages installed, or skipped them for any reason, you should install them now. Use the installpkg instructions found in the section "Installing, removing and upgrading packages" earlier in this chapter to install these packages quickly.

To set up your printer, follow these steps:

1. **At the # command prompt, type** /usr/lib/apsfilter/SETUP **and press Enter.**

   Some information scrolls down your screen, then apsfilter shows a welcome message.

2. **Press Enter.**

   apsfilter shows some general information about what the SETUP script does, like setting up printers and print queues and creating print filter configuration files.

3. **Press Enter again.**

   The apsfilter main menu appears, as shown in Figure 7-11. At the bottom of the screen is the phrase `Your choice ?`, after which is a small text input area. Several choices appear.

```
=================================================================
  A P S F I L T E R   S E T U P                  -- MAIN MENUE --
=================================================================

                                               currently selected
-----------------------------------------------------------------
(D)     Available Device Drivers in your gs binary   (gs -h)
(R)     Read ghostscript's docu about device drivers (devices.txt)
(1)     Printer Driver Selection                [ ]
(2)     Interface Setup                         [ ]

For printing the test page:
(3)     Print Resolution in "dots per inch"     [ ]
(4)     Toggle Monochrom/Color (1bpp=b&w)       [ ]
(5)     Paper Format                            [ ]
(T)     Print Test Page (after step 1-5)

(C)     ==> Continue printer setup with values shown above

(Q)     Quit Setup

Your choice ? █
```

Figure 7-11: The apsfilter main menu.

If you want to read documentation about device drivers, type **r** in the text input area and press Enter.

4. **Type** 1 **and press Enter.**

   The Printer Driver Selection screen appears, as shown in Figure 7-12. Again, another text-input area is at the bottom of the screen.

   Seven major printer manufacturers and models are listed in Figure 7-12 (like Apple, Canon, HP, Okidata, and so on). If your printer make and model is not one of the first seven, two other options are available. Option 8, printers that don't support Postscript (a programming language that describes the appearance of a printed page), is for dot matrix printers manufactured around the late 1980s. Option 9 is for printers that support Postscript but don't fall into the first seven options.

5. **Type the number corresponding to the maker of your printer in the text-input area and press Enter.**

   A list of printers for that manufacturer appears. Your printer may not be listed here. If not, press Enter to go back to the Printer Driver Selection screen and select another manufacturer and model.

If you can't find your printer in the list, Press Enter to go back to the Printer Driver Selection screen and try using selection number 9.

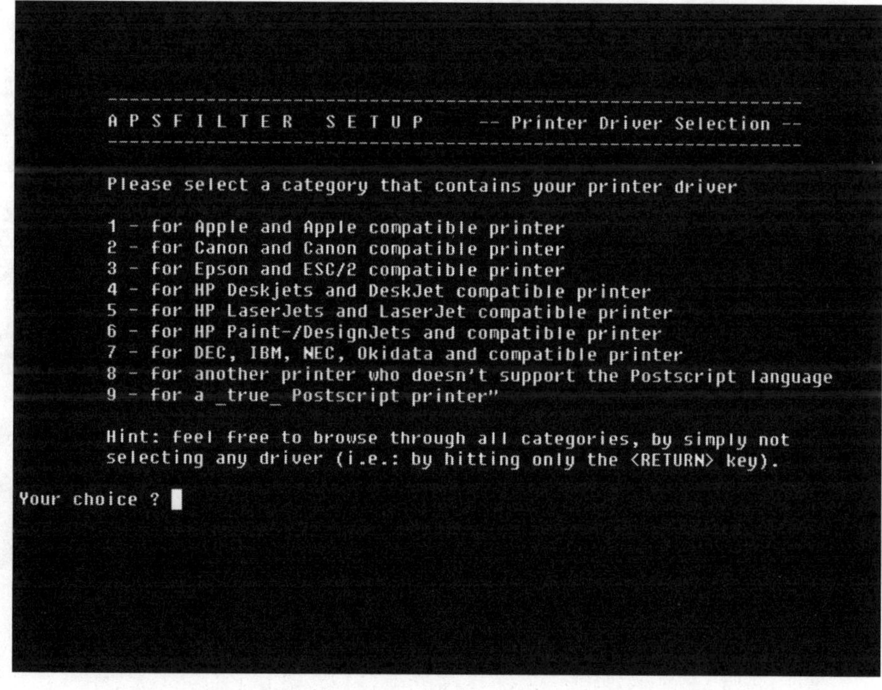

Figure 7-12: The apsfilter driver selection menu.

6. **Type the number corresponding to your printer model in the text-input area and press Enter.**

   A message from apsfilter appears asking you to confirm your selection.

7. **Type** y **in the text input area and press Enter.**

   The apsfilter main menu appears again.

8. **Type** 2 **in the text input area and press Enter.**

   The apsfilter Interface Setup screen appears, as shown in Figure 7-13. If you have a parallel printer choose option 1, otherwise choose option 2.

9. **Type the number corresponding to your printer type in the text-input area and press Enter.**

   apsfilter tells you it needs to find which port your printer is using, shown in Figure 7-13. You should know which LPT port your printer is connected to, but if not, or if this is a new installation of a printer, choose LPT1 as your parallel printer port. Remember, the computer counts from 0, so LPT1 is /dev/lp0 and LPT2 is /dev/lp1.

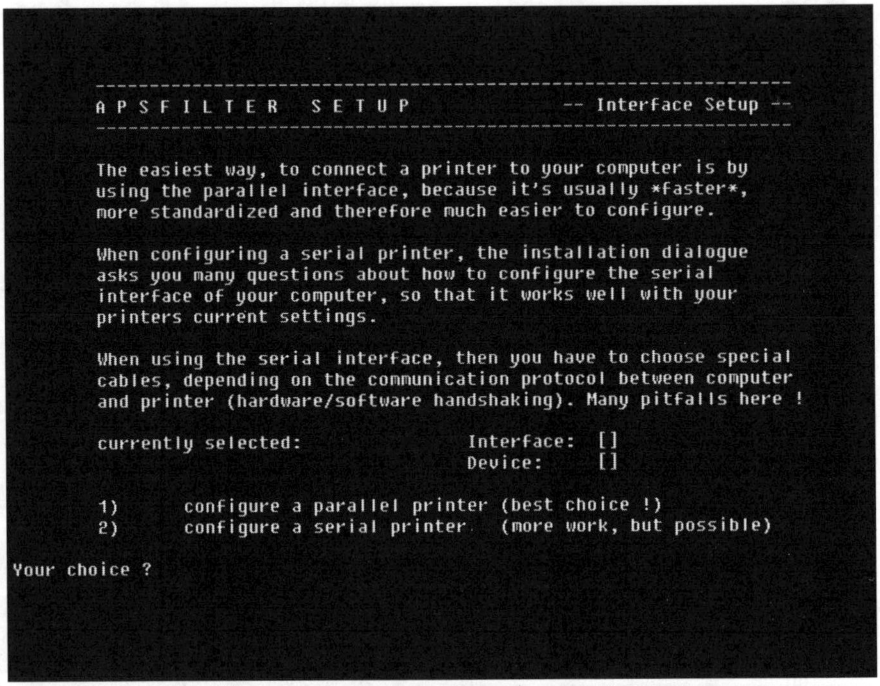

```
-----------------------------------------------------------------
A P S F I L T E R   S E T U P              -- Interface Setup --
-----------------------------------------------------------------

The easiest way, to connect a printer to your computer is by
using the parallel interface, because it's usually *faster*,
more standardized and therefore much easier to configure.

When configuring a serial printer, the installation dialogue
asks you many questions about how to configure the serial
interface of your computer, so that it works well with your
printers current settings.

When using the serial interface, then you have to choose special
cables, depending on the communication protocol between computer
and printer (hardware/software handshaking). Many pitfalls here !

currently selected:                Interface:  []
                                   Device:     []

1)      configure a parallel printer (best choice !)
2)      configure a serial printer  (more work, but possible)

Your choice ?
```

Figure 7-13: The apsfilter Interface Setup screen.

10. **Type** /dev/lp0 **(or** /dev/lp1**, depending on your printer info) in the text-input area and press Enter.**

    The apsfilter main menu appears. You can now attempt to print a test page. If you would rather just continue with the printer setup, skip to Step 21.

11. **Type** 3 **in the text-input area and press Enter.**

    The Print Resolution screen appears, as shown in Figure 7-14. Note that apsfilter tells you that the changes you make here only affect the print resolution of the test page.

    Any program that uses the printer on your Slackware system has its own print settings — like resolution, color, and font. The only common denominator is that all the programs use the print queue to print files. Hence, setting any kind of print settings in the apsfilter SETUP program only affects the test page you're about to create.

12. **Type** d **in the text-input area to use the predetermined default resolution and press Enter.**

    The apsfilter main menu appears.

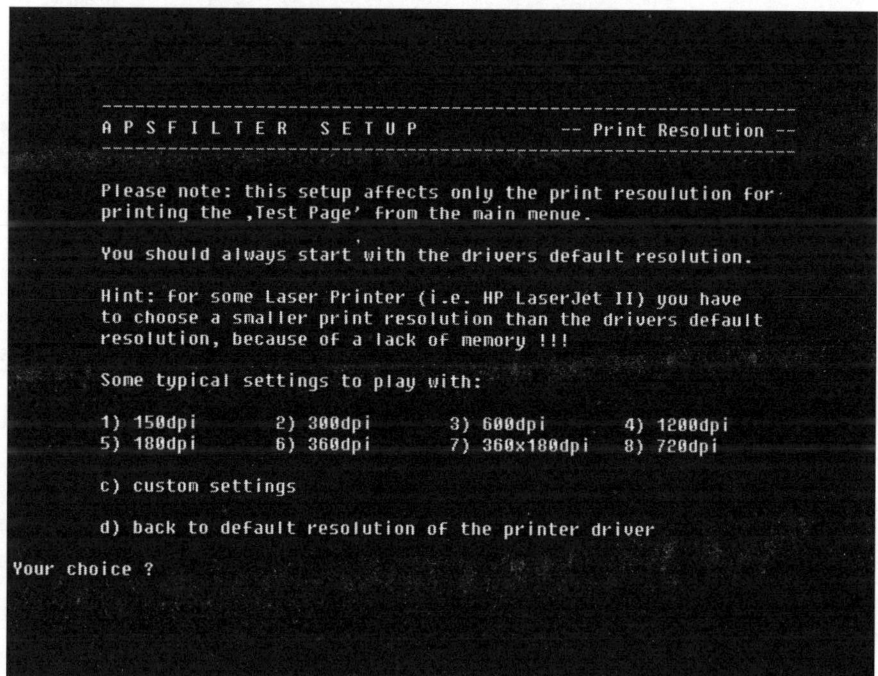

A P S F I L T E R   S E T U P   -- Print Resolution --
Please note: this setup affects only the print resoulution for printing the ,Test Page' from the main menue.
You should always start with the drivers default resolution.
Hint: for some Laser Printer (i.e. HP LaserJet II) you have to choose a smaller print resolution than the drivers default resolution, because of a lack of memory !!!
Some typical settings to play with:
1) 150dpi   2) 300dpi   3) 600dpi   4) 1200dpi
5) 180dpi   6) 360dpi   7) 360x180dpi   8) 720dpi
c) custom settings
d) back to default resolution of the printer driver
Your choice ?

Figure 7-14: The apsfilter print resolution screen.

13. **Type** 4 **in the text-input area and press Enter.**

    The Monochrome/Color Setup screen appears. Note again that this only affects the test page.

14. **Type** d **in the text-input area to use the predetermined defaults and press Enter.**

    The apsfilter main menu appears again.

15. **Type** 5 **in the text-input area and press Enter.**

    You are taken to the Paper Size screen. In this screen is a list of common sizes of printer paper. Because you're just printing a test page, use the letter size, which is option 2.

16. **Type** 2 **in the text-input area and press Enter.**

    The apsfilter main menu appears again. Now you're ready to print a test page.

17. **Type** t **in the text-input area and press Enter.**

    The apsfilter Test Page screen appears, as shown in Figure 7-15. The message on the screen tells you what to do in case your test page does not come out correctly. If the test page does not come out correctly, you must repeat Steps 4 through 7 again, but choose a different printer model or manufacturer.

18. **Type** t **in the text-input area and press Enter.**

    The command that apsfilter uses to print the test page appears. This command differs depending on the printer you selected and the resolution, color, and font settings. For example, if you set up an HP LaserJet, the command that is used to print the test page is:

    ```
    cat /usr/lib/apsfilter/setup/tiger.ps | gs -q -
           sDEVICE=/dev/lp0 -sPAPERSIZE=letter -dNOPAUSE -
           dSAFER -sOutputFile=/tmp/tiger.out -
    ```

    After this command displays, a small confirmation message appears underneath asking if you are ready to print the test page.

19. **Type** y **next to the [y/n] question and press Enter.**

    If any error messages appear on the screen, such as No Such Device or Unrecognized Format, you must repeat Steps 4 through 7 again and choose another printer type to see if that fixes the problem. If that still doesn't fix your problem, turn to Chapter 19 for some helpful hints.

    If everything went smoothly, a brand-new test page prints out on your printer.

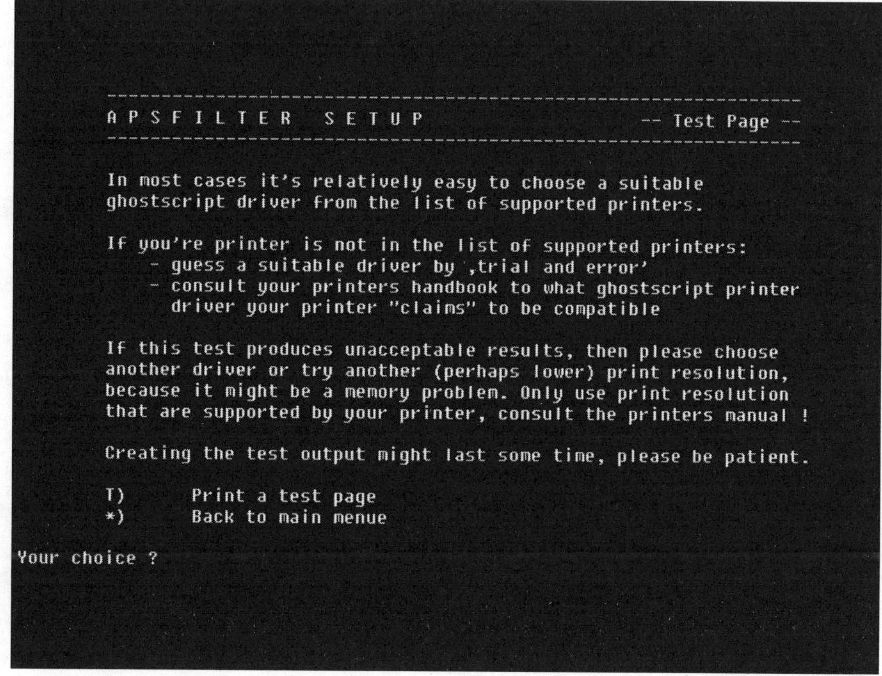

A P S F I L T E R   S E T U P   -- Test Page --
In most cases it's relatively easy to choose a suitable
ghostscript driver from the list of supported printers.
If you're printer is not in the list of supported printers:
- guess a suitable driver by ,trial and error'
- consult your printers handbook to what ghostscript printer
driver your printer "claims" to be compatible
If this test produces unacceptable results, then please choose
another driver or try another (perhaps lower) print resolution,
because it might be a memory problem. Only use print resolution
that are supported by your printer, consult the printers manual !
Creating the test output might last some time, please be patient.
T) Print a test page
*) Back to main menue
Your choice ?

Figure 7-15: The apsfilter Test Page screen.

20. **Press Enter.**

    The apsfilter main menu appears.

21. **Type** c **in the text-input area and press Enter.**

    The system displays a number of messages as it checks for certain items on the system, as shown in Figure 7-16.

    apsfilter then lists two options and asks you if your printer is color or black and white (monochrome).

22. **Type the letter corresponding to your printer (either** c **for color or** m **for monochrome) in the text-input area and press Enter.**

    The system displays a message showing what it thinks is the owner and group of the print queue (apsfilter calls it the spooldir) and asks you to confirm this information.

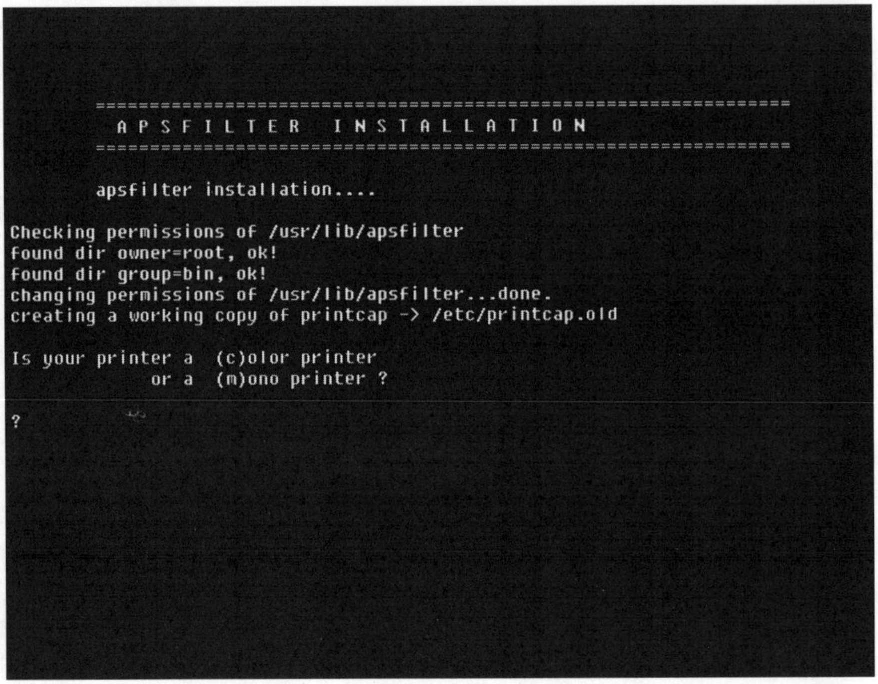

```
=================================================================
  A P S F I L T E R   I N S T A L L A T I O N
=================================================================

    apsfilter installation....

Checking permissions of /usr/lib/apsfilter
found dir owner=root, ok!
found dir group=bin, ok!
changing permissions of /usr/lib/apsfilter...done.
creating a working copy of printcap -> /etc/printcap.old

Is your printer a  (c)olor printer
             or a  (m)ono printer ?

?
```

Figure 7-16: Installing apsfilter parameters.

23. **Type** y **in the text-input area and press Enter.**

    apsfilter displays some information about a customizable apsfilter file in the /etc directory.

24. **Press Enter three times.**

    Each time you press Enter, a new informational message appears. apsfilter's work is now complete. (It even says that its job is done.) The command prompt returns.

Your printer is now set up. If you encounter problems not listed in the steps above, see Chapter 19 for more help.

Printing remotely with apsfilter

If you have a printer hooked up to another computer that is on a network and you want to print a file, you can use apsfilter to set up remote printing capabilities on your PC. The following instructions show you how.

You must edit the file `/etc/printcap` and change all the occurrences of `/dev/lp0` to `/dev/null`. See Chapter 10 for help with editors. Remember, `/etc/printcap` means that the file printcap is found in the /etc directory.

Make sure that the line `:mx#0:\` exists in your printer's entry in the `/etc/printcap` file, otherwise you'll have to add it. Then you must change the line `sh:` to `:sf:sh=false:rm={remote IP address of your printer}:`. The remote IP address is the unique Internet Protocol address, usually of the form x.x.x.x, assigned to that printer.

Type the command `lp -Praw {filename}` to print Postscript or graphic files, or `lp -Pascii {filename}` to send text files. Remember that uppercase and lowercase letters in the filename and the commands make a difference as to what gets printed!

Part III
Utilizing Slackware Basics

"Drive carefully, remember your lunch, and always make a backup of your directory tree before modifying your hard disk partition file."

In this part . . .

Here you discover the basics of the Slackware operating system, such as how to navigate within Slackware, how Slackware organizes itself, how to edit text, and how to set up your desktop with X Windows.

Chapter 8 introduces you to the concept of shells, which is how users get around within Slackware. You also get an explanation of how the command line works — something you need if you plan to do anything with your new Slackware system.

Chapter 9 runs through the concepts of files and directories within Slackware. You learn how to archive files and directories and compress them to save space.

In Chapter 10, you get familiar with three different types of text editors. Editors are extremely useful for changing something here or adding something there. Plus, you can't do any heavy-duty configurating without one.

Chapters 11 and 12 cover setting up your desktop. The X Windows system dominates Chapter 11. Installing X Windows is the toughest part of setting up your machine. Make sure you follow the directions or you may end up with a smoking monitor. Chapter 12 involves the KDE and GNOME desktops — this is where you get a taste of what your Slackware machine can *really* do for you.

Chapter 8

Shells as Interpreters

In This Chapter

- Familiarizing yourself with csh
- Characterizing metacharacters
- Redoing commands
- Finishing what you type
- Scripting a shell script

Computers do exactly what you tell them to do and nothing more. The challenge is finding a way to get those finicky computers to do exactly what you want them to do. You can't talk to a computer like you talk to another person (though a computer acts as stubborn as one sometimes), even if the computer has voice recognition. This is because computers don't understand implications, only statements and directives. Of course, this doesn't mean that all computers understand perfect English grammar, either.

Because of these drawbacks, you need something built into your system that takes your commands and puts them in a recognizable format for the computer to work with. In other words, you need an *interpreter.* In the Linux world, interpreters are commonly called *shells*. And like any ocean, Slackware comes with a variety of shells.

The Bourne shell, abbreviated as `sh`, is considered the first shell for Unix, but programmers who wanted different functionality in a shell have created several others. One group of programmers at the University of California at Berkeley used the powerful C programming language as a model for a shell and created what is known as the C shell, abbreviated as `csh`. Not to be outdone, the good people at the GNU Project created a shell from scratch that is similar in many respects to the Bourne shell. They called it the Bourne-again Shell (`bash`).

Because Linux was designed from the beginning to be Unix-like, Linux also uses these three along with many other shells for interpreting commands between the user and the computer. In this chapter, I show you some basic `csh` commands. You also unearth interesting shell commands that help you perform tasks such as command repetition, command completion, metacharacters (otherwise known as wildcards), and shell scripting to perform multiple commands at once.

Becoming Familiar with csh

You need to be familiar with the phrase "in the shell." When you log in to your Slackware machine, you tell the computer to use a predetermined shell as your command interpreter. A command prompt that looks something like this appears on your screen (the hostname will differ depending on the name of your machine):

```
hostname:~>
```

The > represents the command prompt. (Other shells use a % instead of a > for their prompt.) If you're logged in as root, you have a # as your command prompt instead. This is the easiest way to tell which account you're using. All your commands are typed at this command prompt, so consider it an always-on text input area. When you have a command prompt ready for you to type at, you are "in the shell."

If you're logged in as the root user, log out and log back in to your own personal account (if you haven't created your own account, see Chapter 6 for instructions on how to do so). Typos can be dangerous, and you want to limit the amount of potential damage for now.

In the following examples, any characters, letters, or words within `[square brackets]` are optional, meaning that you can omit them if you want. Anything within `{curly braces}`, however, is mandatory, meaning that you must type in the character, word, or phrase specified within the `{}`; otherwise, the command doesn't work. For example, the command `more {filename}` means that you have to tell the command `more` to use the file called `filename` for the command to work.

Using the command prompt

The command prompt is where you enter all your commands. Slackware expects commands to have the same format: command, options, redirection, input/output. The options, redirection, and input/output file are optional, meaning that you can just type the command and press Enter, and Slackware executes the command that you typed. Throughout this book, anything enclosed in square brackets [like this] is optional and can be omitted.

Flagging commands

Options are also called *flags* and are usually preceded by a minus sign or dash (-). This is for your own good because the options for most commands are pretty puzzling. You can run together as many options as are available for a command if the whole list of options is preceded by a dash. An easy example is the command `ls`, which lists all files in the current directory. A typical use of the `ls` command is

```
ls -la /
```

This command lists all the contents of the root (/) directory. Nothing fancy there. You can also type **ls -l -a** / to accomplish the same thing. No rule exists that says you have to run flags together — you can separate them if you feel the need, it's just easier to remember if you keep the flags together.

Redirecting commands and taking input/ouput

Redirecting means telling the command to do something with its output, or to take input from another source. The common redirection characters are | (the pipe), > (the greater than sign), >> (a double greater than sign), and < (the less than sign — remember, we're reading from left to right here).The | character tells the command to take the output and send it to the next command | like

```
ls -la /bin | grep name
```

This tells Slackware to list all files in the `/bin` directory and then search the list for the word `name`, as shown in Figure 8-1.

```
slack1:~> ls -la /bin | grep name
lrwxrwxrwx   1 root     root            8 Nov 14 07:10 dnsdomainname -> hostname
*
lrwxrwxrwx   1 root     root            8 Nov 14 06:55 domainname -> hostname*
-rwxr-xr-x   1 root     bin          8920 Oct 21 22:36 hostname*
lrwxrwxrwx   1 root     root            8 Nov 14 07:10 nisdomainname -> hostname
*
-rwxr-xr-x   1 root     bin          5836 Jul 30 19:41 uname*
lrwxrwxrwx   1 root     root            8 Nov 14 07:10 ypdomainname -> hostname*
slack1:~> █
```

Figure 8-1: Listing files in the /bin directory and searching for the word name.

Right away, you should notice that several files exist with the word `name` in them, and that the text wraps around the screen because it ran out of room. This is normal in Slackware — occasionally files or directories have names that are longer than 16 or 20 characters. Slackware takes the opportunity to wrap your text for you so you can read everything.

You can also tell the command to send its output to a file like

```
ls -la /bin > mylist
```

This tells the `ls` command to list all the files in the `/bin` directory and put that list in another file called `mylist`.

Hey, but maybe you want to add something to the file `mylist`. Use the double greater than sign:

```
echo "Date: 2/20/2000." >> mylist
```

This tells the `echo` command to repeat (echo) the line `Date: 2/20/2000` and add it the file `mylist` as the very last line.

Finally, you can tell a command to take input from another location like

```
mail mom@momshouse.somewhere.com < myletter
```

This tells the `mail` command to send the file `myletter` to `mom@momshouse.somewhere.com`. Pretty neat, especially if you have e-mail already typed and ready to go.

Commanding the basics

Every Slackware user must know the five basic commands to navigate around the shell. Hundreds of commands are built in to every shell for each operating system, but these five are the same for every Unix or Unix-like system, such as Slackware. The following list describes the five basic commands:

- `ls` — The `ls` command lists files in a directory that you specify. If you don't specify what directory's files to list, `ls` assumes that you mean for it to list the files in the current directory. The basic format is `ls` [directory].
- `rm` — The `rm` command removes files. You must specify what file or files to remove, otherwise `rm` replies with an error message stating that it can't remove something that isn't there. The basic format is `rm` {filename}.
- `cd` — The `cd` command changes directories from your current directory to another directory that you specify. If you omit the directory name to change to, `cd` changes directories from your current directory to your home directory. The format for this command is `cd` [directory].

- cat — The cat command causes the contents of a file or multiple files to appear. The format for this command is cat {filename}.
- mv — The mv command moves a file or directory from one place to another. The mv command lends itself to being used for renaming things. mv differs from cd in that mv must always have two components: the original file or directory and the new location or name. mv also differs from cd in that using mv does not change the directory you are currently working in. The format is mv {oldfile} {newfile or destination}.

Two other commands that you must know in case of emergencies, are the Interrupt command and the Suspend command.

Getting answers from the Slackware electronic manual

In Slackware, you often need to perform some kind of action for which you may not know the command; or you know the command, but you're not sure which flags apply. Surely this information is contained in a manual or help file somewhere, right?

Slackware includes all the manual pages you could possibly ask for and more on the CD-ROMs included with this book. You must install the Slackware F series in order to have access to this information, though, because the F series contains the Slackware manual pages and the Linux HOW-TO documentation for accomplishing more advanced tasks.

Manual pages, or *man pages*, are your digital information source for almost every command or program that Slackware has. To access this information, type **man {command}** and press Enter. Your screen clears for a moment, then the beginning of the manual page is displayed. Press the space bar to scroll through the pages of information. Start using the man command by typing **man man** at the command prompt and press Enter (to get help on the man command itself).

If you need to accomplish a task, but you're not sure which command to use, you can try searching the man pages. Use the command man -k {task} to make Slackware try to find a command that matches the task you're trying to accomplish. Or, if you remember the command that you need but can't remember how it's spelled, try typing **man -K {word}** (note the uppercase K in this instance). Remember, Slackware is case-sensitive, so uppercase and lowercase letters make a difference when you type in a command.

Sometimes a command doesn't have a man page. In these unusual cases, the developer didn't have time to create a man page for the command. Instead, the developer places a back door on the command in case you need help. To use this back door, type either **-h** or **—help** flags after the command that you're using, like cat —help. A small help file appears, listing the flags available and a brief description of what each flag does when used with the command. From the descriptions of the flags, you can generally figure out what the command is capable of.

You can execute the Interrupt command by typing **Ctrl+C**. No text-input area exists for you to type this command. Anytime you want to use the Interrupt command, you just hold down the CTRL key and press the C key at the same time. When you use the Interrupt command to interrupt another command or program, you see a `^C` displayed on the first available blank line near the bottom of your screen. This means that the program or command that you were just running was interrupted or killed. You will also be taken back to a command prompt. An interrupted program or command must be restarted — it cannot continue where it left off if run again.

You can execute the Suspend command by typing **Ctrl+Z**. Like the Interrupt command, you run the Suspend command at any time — no text-input area needed — by holding down the CTRL key and pressing the Z key simultaneously. If you suspend a process or program, you see either the message `Suspended` displayed near the bottom of your screen or you see a `^Z` displayed. You are then taken to a command prompt. A suspended process or program can be picked up where it left off by typing **fg** at the command prompt and pressing Enter.

Working with Metacharacters

Suppose, for example, you have a directory with 100 files inside it (which isn't uncommon). What happens if you want to selectively list the files in this directory, like those that start with the letter m? Or, what if you had to move all the files that started with the letter g to another location for archiving purposes? That's a lot of typing, even if only one-quarter of the filenames start with the letter g.

Slackware can do all this typing for you in short order. *Metacharacters,* or *wildcards,* are used to replace a character or group (string) of characters in your filenames or directory names. The two wildcard characters commonly used are the asterisk `(*)` and the question mark `(?)`.

The * metacharacter matches any character in its place or any number of characters to the right of the *. For example, the command `ls my*` causes any files that begin with `my`, including `my`, `myq`, `mydog`, `mycar`, and `mythisisaverylongfilename`, to appear. This also means that if you type `ls *`, everything in the directory appears — not a good idea if the directory contains a ton of files.

The ? metacharacter matches any single character in its place. For example, the command `ls my?` causes any filenames that begin with `my` and are exactly three characters long, like `mya`, `myc`, and `myz`, but not `my` or `mydog`, to appear.

What if the filename has a * or ? in it? Slackware conveniently comes with a character to change those wildcard characters into normal characters (this is called *escaping* the character) — the backslash (\) character. For example, to remove the file I mistakenly named myem*il, I type **rm myem*il** at the command prompt, and press Enter. Escaping the character also works for filenames that have a \ in them, like myback\slash. In this case, I would type **rm myback\\slash** to remove the file.

You can also use the \ to rename files with the mv command. For example, instead of removing the myem*il file, you may want to rename it to myemail. At the command prompt, type **mv myem*il myemail** and press Enter.

Typing Repeated Commands

Slackware makes it easier for you if you have to repeat commands or run commands multiple times by keeping a list of all the commands you type when you first log in. Using that list sure beats typing an 80-character command again and again.

Slackware's command list is limited to about 100 commands. To access the list, type **history** at the command prompt and press Enter. Your recent commands appear in the order that they were typed with a number preceding each one. The number marks the order in which commands were typed, starting with 1 for the first command you typed after logging in.

Suppose, for example, that you typed **echo hi > myfile** a while ago but you removed the myfile file. In the history list, you see that the command is listed as the fourteenth command that you typed. You can repeat this command by typing **!14** and pressing Enter, which tells Slackware to repeat the fourteenth command in your list.

If you want to repeat that echo command immediately, type **!!** at the command prompt and press Enter. The !! executes the very last command that you typed.

Suppose that you typed in the following command three or four commands ago:

```
cat /etc/inetd.conf | grep nobody | sed -e 's/tcp/WHEE/' >!
        /tmp/newconf
```

Now you realize that you need to do it again, but don't want to type the full command. If you haven't run a cat command since that long one, you can, at the command prompt, type **!cat** to rerun your extremely long cat command. The !cat command repeats the very last cat command you typed. This means that if you type **cat /etc/inetd.conf** and then type **cat /etc/motd**, when you type **!cat**, you are executing the cat /etc/motd command, because that was the last cat command you typed.

Searching your command history

Slackware offers another way to retrieve long commands if you forget them. Instead of displaying your entire file history on the screen, Slackware backs up within your file history, displaying previous commands one at a time. This is similar to the Undo process. Type **Ctrl+P**, and the last command that you typed reappears. Type it again, and Slackware shows the next-to-last command you typed, and so on. When you find what you're looking for, press Enter or use the Backspace key to delete characters in the command, thus changing the command.

Changing previous commands

If you make a mistake while typing a command, Slackware lets you correct your mistake without having to retype an entire line. Consider the following command:

```
cat /etc/inetd.conf | grep nobody | sed -e 's/tcp/WHEE/g' >!
        /tmp/newconf
```

This command lists the contents of the file `/etc/inetd.conf`, then looks specifically for lines that have the word `nobody` in them. Then it changes the word `tcp` to `WHEE` in those lines and dumps the changed lines in the file `/tmp/newconf`.

If you find that you need to change the word `udp` instead of `tcp`, you can either retype the entire command again (no thanks!) or redo the command with your correct word (called *substituting*) by typing **^tcp^udp** at the command prompt and pressing Enter. The ^ (carat) mark tells Slackware to find the word or string immediately following it and change that word or string to the word or string following the next ^ mark. This only works for the command you just typed, as shown in Figure 8-2.

Suppose that you want to change tcp to udp as in the previous example, but you ran the `cat` command three commands ago, so the ^ substitution method won't work. You can bring that `cat` command to the front of your history list and make it the last command executed by typing **!cat:p** at the command prompt and pressing Enter. (Note the :p after the !cat — the :p stands for "print only.") The `cat` command appears but does not run. Now you can make your substitution with the ^ marks by typing **^tcp^udp** at the command prompt and pressing Enter. (See Figure 8-3.)

```
slack1:~> cat /etc/inetd.conf | grep nobody | sed -e 's/tcp/WHEE/g' > ! /tmp/new
conf
slack1:~> ^tcp^udp
cat /etc/inetd.conf | grep nobody | sed -e 's/udp/WHEE/g' > ! /tmp/newconf
slack1:~> more /tmp/newconf
# tftp  dgram   WHEE    wait    nobody  /usr/sbin/tcpd  in.tftpd
finger  stream  tcp     nowait  nobody  /usr/sbin/tcpd  in.fingerd -u
# systat        stream  tcp     nowait  nobody  /usr/sbin/tcpd  /bin/ps -auwwx
auth    stream  tcp     wait    nobody  /usr/sbin/in.identd     in.identd -w -t1
20 -l
slack1:~> █
```

Figure 8-2: Modifying the last command to change udp to WHEE instead of tcp to WHEE.

```
slack1:~> cat /etc/inetd.conf | grep nobody | sed -e 's/tcp/WHEE/g' > ! /tmp/new
conf
slack1:~> more /tmp/newconf
# tftp  dgram   udp     wait    nobody  /usr/sbin/WHEEd in.tftpd
finger  stream  WHEE    nowait  nobody  /usr/sbin/WHEEd in.fingerd -u
# systat        stream  WHEE    nowait  nobody  /usr/sbin/WHEEd /bin/ps -auwwx
auth    stream  WHEE    wait    nobody  /usr/sbin/in.identd     in.identd -w -t1
20 -l
slack1:~> !cat:p
cat /etc/inetd.conf | grep nobody | sed -e 's/tcp/WHEE/g' > ! /tmp/newconf
slack1:~> ^tcp^udp
cat /etc/inetd.conf | grep nobody | sed -e 's/udp/WHEE/g' > ! /tmp/newconf
slack1:~> !more
more /tmp/newconf
# tftp  dgram   WHEE    wait    nobody  /usr/sbin/tcpd  in.tftpd
finger  stream  tcp     nowait  nobody  /usr/sbin/tcpd  in.fingerd -u
# systat        stream  tcp     nowait  nobody  /usr/sbin/tcpd  /bin/ps -auwwx
auth    stream  tcp     wait    nobody  /usr/sbin/in.identd     in.identd -w -t1
20 -l
slack1:~> █
```

Figure 8-3: Changing your last command in conjunction with !cat:p.

Using Command Completion

Another way to avoid retyping long filenames or command names is by using *command completion*, or letting Slackware fill in the blank for the rest of the word, filename, or command. Command completion helps tremendously in situations where repetitive typing would take a long time, or in situations where you already know what you need to accomplish, but your fingers don't type as fast as your brain.

Suppose that you have a file named `wdchgtyimzsw3pghiu` in your directory. You want to rename it `myfile`, but having to type **wdchgtyimzsw3pghiu** is hard on your fingers, not to mention having to hunt through all the keys on the keyboard to put all the characters in `wdchgtyimzsw3pghiu` in the correct order. Instead of going through all that hassle, you can do this:

```
mv wd<TAB> myfile
```

The moment that you hit the Tab key, the rest of the filename appears!

Command completion also works for commands as well as filenames. Suppose that you want to use the network card setup utility for Slackware, but you can't remember the exact spelling for the command other than it begins with `ifc`. At the command prompt, type **ifc<TAB>** and the rest of the command (ifconfig) appears on the command prompt. What a great tool!

If you don't put in enough letters on the command prompt to make the command or filename unique enough for `csh` to find it, the system beeps at you and doesn't complete the command or name. Make sure that you have enough letters to ensure the uniqueness of the command or filename that you're looking for.

Creating a Shell Script

You may find that you have to repeat a 15-step process because there's no better way to apply that process. That's where Slackware comes in. Slackware's shells enable you to write *shell scripts*, which are methods you use to run redundant processes without typing the same steps over and over. All of the commands you want to run are contained within the shell script, and the script is executed. This is kind of like buying two dozen eggs at the store but having to carry them all home without egg cartons to store them in. Shell scripts represent the egg cartons; they enable you to carry more groceries instead of worrying which egg is about to fall to the ground. Shell scripts enable you to get all the work done you would otherwise have to do one command at a time so you can focus on more important things (like if the milk is on top of the bread again).

Suppose, for example, that you run the following five commands each time you log in:

date — to see the current time and date

pwd — to see what your current directory is

who | grep keith — to see if your friend Keith is on the computer

fortune — to read the fortune of the day

uptime — to see how long the computer has been running.

Typing these commands at the command prompt every time you log in gets boring after a while. Not only that, but sometimes you make mistakes, so you have to retype the command, or maybe your mind blanks for a second on what command does what and you need to look up a manual page to refresh your memory. You know there has to be a way to make this process easier.

Follow these steps to formulate a shell script to run whenever you log in:

1. **At the command prompt, type** echo "#\!/bin/csh" > inscript **and press Enter.**

   You are returned to another command prompt. This command places the line `#!/bin/csh` as the first line in the file `inscript`. You can see the results at the top of Figure 8-4. The \ (backslash) is in front of the ! (exclamation point) because the `echo` command doesn't recognize the ! as a normal character without it. Notice that when the `more` command is issued to look at the contents of `inscript`, the \ is not there.

   A shell script needs the #!/bin/csh line in order to run because the script needs to know what shell or interpreter to use. In this case, you're telling the system that when it runs `inscript`, it's supposed to use `csh` as its shell.

   Use the command `more inscript` after completing each step to ensure you haven't made any typos.

2. **At the command prompt, type** echo "date" > inscript **and press Enter.**

   You return to another command prompt. This command puts `date` as the second line of inscript. If you type **date** by itself and press Enter, Slackware displays the current time and date.

3. **At the command prompt, type** echo "pwd" > inscript **and press Enter.**

   You return to another command prompt. This command puts `pwd` as the next line of inscript. Typing **pwd** by itself at the command prompt and pressing Enter causes Slackware to display your current directory on the screen.

```
slack1:~> echo "#\!/bin/csh" > inscript
slack1:~> more inscript
#!/bin/csh
slack1:~> echo "date" >> inscript
slack1:~> more inscript
#!/bin/csh
date
slack1:~> echo "ppp-go" >> inscript
slack1:~> more inscript
#!/bin/csh
date
ppp-go
slack1:~>
```

Figure 8-4: Creating a shell script — adding the date and the current working directory commands to your shell script one at a time.

4. **At the command prompt, type** echo "who | grep keith" > inscript **and press Enter.**

   You return to another command prompt. This command puts `who | grep keith` as the next line of inscript, as shown in Figure 8-5. When you type **who | grep keith** at the command prompt and press Enter, Slackware searches the computer's list of current users and looks for the username `keith`. If Slackware finds `keith`, it shows `keith` as being logged in; otherwise, nothing happens.

5. **At the command prompt, type** echo "fortune" > inscript **and press Enter.**

   You return to another command prompt. This command puts `fortune` as the next line of inscript, as shown in Figure 8-5. Typing `fortune` at the command prompt and pressing Enter causes the fortune program to display a random witty quote on your screen.

6. **At the command prompt, type** echo "uptime" > inscript **and press Enter.**

   You return to the command prompt. This command puts `uptime` as the next line of inscript, as shown in Figure 8-5. Typing **uptime** on the command line and pressing Enter shows, in columnar format, the current time, how long the computer has been running, how many users are currently logged in, and the load average (the number of seconds required to execute a command) on your screen.

```
slack1:~> echo "who | grep keith" >> inscript
slack1:~> more inscript
#!/bin/csh
date
ppp-go
who | grep keith
slack1:~> echo "fortune" >> inscript
slack1:~> more inscript
#!/bin/csh
date
ppp-go
who | grep keith
fortune
slack1:~> echo "uptime" >> inscript
slack1:~> more inscript
#!/bin/csh
date
ppp-go
who | grep keith
fortune
uptime
slack1:~> █
```

Figure 8-5: Creating a shell script — adding a user lookup, the fortune of the day program, and a system description to your shell script.

7. **Type** chmod 700 inscript **and press Enter.**

   You return to the command prompt. The `chmod` 700 inscript command tells Slackware that the file inscript is now an executable file, as shown in Figure 8-6. The asterisk at the end of the filename denotes that the file is executable. The green color also denotes that the file is executable.

   When you create a file, the default *permissions* (attributes) for the file does not include execute permissions. In other words, a newly created file is assumed to be a text file, not a shell script. You must explicitly tell Slackware (via the `chmod` command) that your file is a shell script by adding the execute permission to the file. See Chapter 16 for more info on permissions.

Now, at your command prompt, type **inscript** and press Enter. All the commands you typed are run, one after the other, without your having to type a single key more, as shown in Figure 8-7. Isn't that great? Note that the only command not returning any information was the search for the user `keith`, which means that Keith is not online. The `grep` command in the command `who | grep keith` doesn't return any information if the search string (in this case, the word `keith`) is not found.

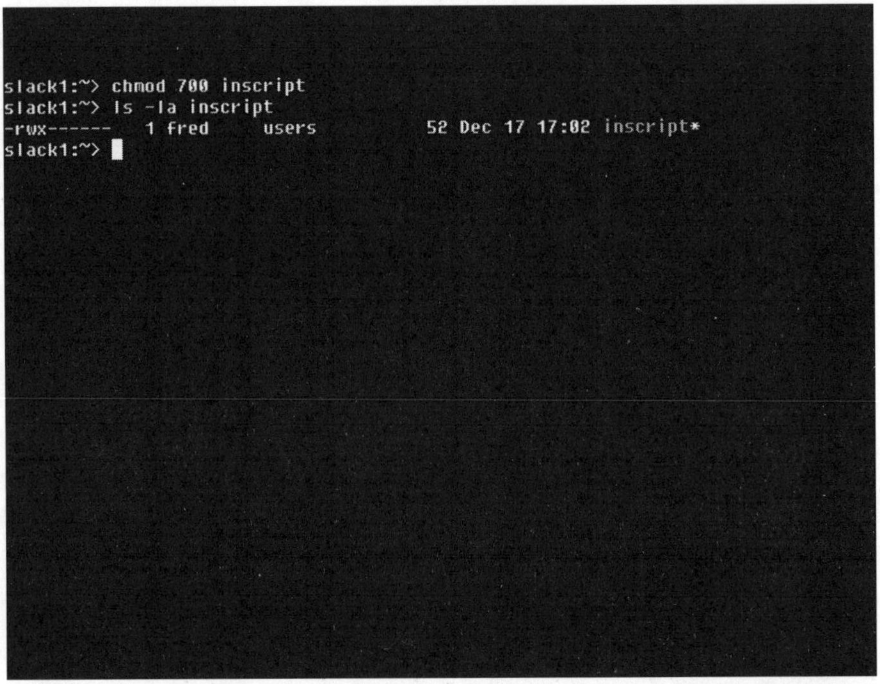

```
slack1:~> chmod 700 inscript
slack1:~> ls -la inscript
-rwx------   1 fred     users          52 Dec 17 17:02 inscript*
slack1:~>
```

Figure 8-6: Results of the chmod command.

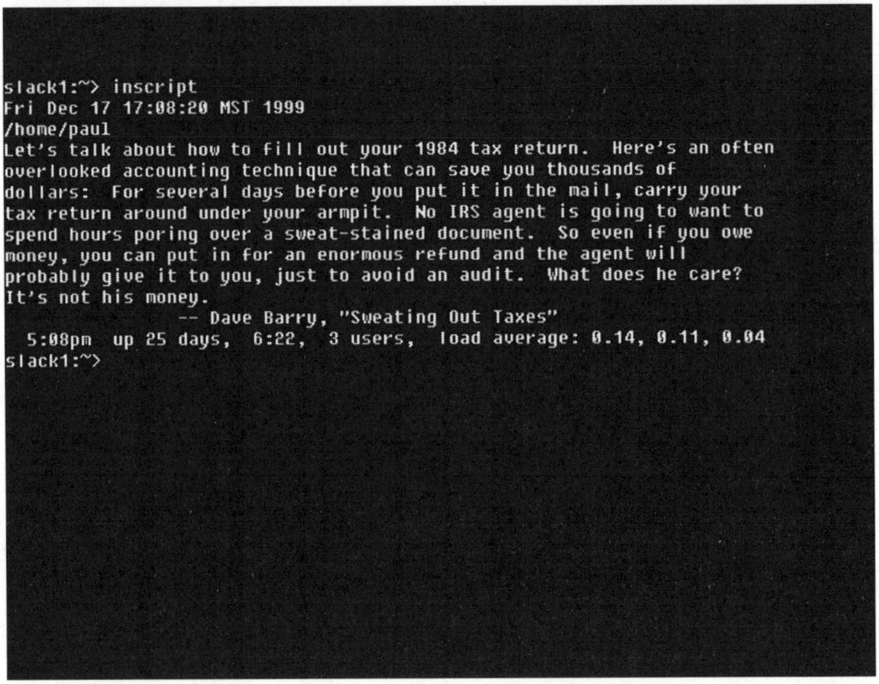

```
slack1:~> inscript
Fri Dec 17 17:08:20 MST 1999
/home/paul
Let's talk about how to fill out your 1984 tax return.  Here's an often
overlooked accounting technique that can save you thousands of
dollars:  For several days before you put it in the mail, carry your
tax return around under your armpit.  No IRS agent is going to want to
spend hours poring over a sweat-stained document.  So even if you owe
money, you can put in for an enormous refund and the agent will
probably give it to you, just to avoid an audit.  What does he care?
It's not his money.
                -- Dave Barry, "Sweating Out Taxes"
  5:08pm  up 25 days,  6:22,  3 users,  load average: 0.14, 0.11, 0.04
slack1:~>
```

Figure 8-7: Results of running your shell script.

Shell scripts are as long or as short as you need them to be. Some hold only one command while others hold hundreds of commands. Shell scripts use simple programming syntax including if-then, for, while, and *goto*. Allowing for programming syntax makes shell scripting a powerful tool at your disposal.

You also find that several automated tasks within your Slackware computer are actually shell scripts written by the programmers eons ago, like your boot programs, for example. Look at the file `/etc/rc.d/rc.M` by typing **more /etc/rc.d/rc.M** at the command prompt and pressing Enter. Use the space bar to move to the next screen of text. This is a shell script in action.

Shell scripting is complicated, granted, but it doesn't have to be the domain of computer wizards either. All you need are a few commands you want to automate and you've got yourself a shell script.

Making mistakes

Slackware commands may seem cryptic at first, until you realize that each command is most likely an abbreviation for a longer word or meaning. Sometimes the command name is even a joke for the programmer or developer (like the command `less` does exactly what the command `more` does with some extra functionality added).

You get used to how commands work and interact by using them, and by doing so, you open up a whole new realm of possibilities for you and your computer. Just remember not to be logged in as root too often to limit the number of bad things that happen. And if you're not sure of what you're typing, use your trusty Backspace key to erase your command before you press Enter.

Also, remember that man pages are the savior of Slackware users. Because man pages are already on your computer, they become instant sources of information at your fingertips. With man pages, you avoid using the wrong command to accomplish a given task by looking up what a command does. However, even after you read through the man page and think you're using the correct command, mistakes still happen. So don't be afraid to make mistakes, even if during your last one you accidentally deleted everything on your computer. (Okay, so maybe I'm the only person who's ever done that. Oops.)

Chapter 9

Directing Files and Filing Directories

In This Chapter

- Mastering files and directories
- Cataloging file contents
- Managing the file system
- Fabricating and packing files and directories

Trees are green leafy things that adorn our parks and drop leaves all over our front lawns. They grow tall, nest birds, and attract lightning in a rainstorm. (But if you're like me and live in Arizona, then you just have cactus and no such things as trees with leaves . . . or rain for that matter.)

Slackware users should be familiar with a different kind of tree — the upside-down tree that forms the Slackware directory structure. On each branch of this upside-down tree are the leaves, which represent the files in your computer, while the branches themselves are the directories that hold the files. Understanding the directory structure is an important step toward being able to use Slackware efficiently. In this chapter, I show you how Slackware organizes its files and directories and how files and directories relate to each other.

Getting to Know Files and Directories

Files and directories in Slackware are generally the same as files and directories in Windows or DOS. In Slackware, you may have a file called `myfile` in a directory called `mydirectory`. A Slackware file is information stored in a specific place on the hard drive. Slackware determines where this place on the hard drive is located by the name of the file (the filename) and directory. In Slackware, a directory is a file that contains other files (what Windows calls a folder). Directories and filenames can be up to 256 characters long and can use a variety of characters from the alphabet, as well as other characters like ^, #, (, _, and -. Directories and filenames can even contain periods (.) and commas (,) if you desire.

An important difference between Windows and Slackware is that Slackware is *case-sensitive,* which means that you type a filename as it appears. For example, `MYFILE` and `myfile` are completely different.

Case-sensitivity doesn't just extend to files and directories — your password is case-sensitive, as is your login name or account!

Location of a file makes a difference, too. If the `myfile` file is in the `mydirectory` directory, the *full path* of the file is `/mydirectory/myfile`. The full path is the complete location of where a file is located.

You can have as many files as you want in a directory, as long as none of the files have the same filename. You can, however, have the same filename in a different directory. Confused? Here's an example: Suppose that you have a file called `funfunfun` in `mydirectory`. Your friend Keith creates another file called `funfunfun` in his own directory called `kethsdirectory`. Slackware allows this because the full path for your file is `/mydirectory/funfunfun` while the full path for Keith's file is `/kethsdirectory/funfunfun`. The full path of each file is different and therefore acceptable on the system. If Keith tries to move his file called `funfunfun` into `mydirectory`, Slackware tells him that the file already exists there.

You can always tell what directory you're currently in by typing **pwd** at the command prompt.

Typecasting files

Slackware understands and utilizes several different file types. You must know these types because you're bound to encounter them all at one point or another.

- **Text files:** Files that contain straight ASCII text.
- **Binary files:** Files that are either compiled programs (and therefore executable) or contain binary data only readable by another program.
- **Device files:** Special files that represent specific pieces of hardware in your machine. The `/dev` (which stands for device) directory is where Slackware expects device files to reside.

- **System files:** Files that are real-time representations of your computer's status. Real-time means that the contents of each file change every nanosecond, and that looking at a system file is like looking at a snapshot of your current system. These files are found in the `/proc` directory (which stands for processes).
- **Directories:** Slackware treats Directories as files because they contain a list of the files within them.

Nesting in the directory tree

Directories can contain other directories, which is where the concept of the upside-down tree comes from — the branching of directories from the main (trunk) directory. A directory contained within another directory is called a subdirectory. Having multiple subdirectories is *nesting*.

The main (trunk) directory is called the *root* directory and is always represented by / (a slash). All directories are subdirectories of /. Because all directories branch off the root directory, you can tell where a directory or file is, given the full path of the file. Suppose that you were told to look at the `groups` file in the `etc` directory. The full path of this file is `/etc/groups`, which means that you must look in the root directory (/) for the subdirectory called `etc` (`/etc`). Within the `etc` subdirectory is a file called `groups` (`/etc/groups`).

Every directory has a minimum of two entries: the single dot (.), which stands for the directory that you're currently in, and the double dot (..), which stands for the directory directly above the one that you're currently in. Using the example in the preceding paragraph, if you are in the `/etc` directory and type the command **ls ..** at the command prompt, you would see the directory listing of /.

You cannot name any files or directories `.` or `..` because those filenames are reserved. Similarly, you cannot name any file or directory / because it's a reserved name.

Organizing Your Files and Directories

Listing the contents of a directory is crucial to working with Slackware. Unless you have a photographic memory, you probably won't remember where every file on your system is stored, much less how to spell each one. You must also master changing directories from your current directory to another directory. The commands for creating new directories and files and moving files and directories around your Slackware system are also necessary for working with Slackware.

Listing directory contents

To get a listing of your directory's contents, you use the `ls` command. The `ls` command returns the content listing of the specified directory (or the current directory if no directory is specified), as shown in the following example:

```
slack1:~> ls
funfile inscript* wheefile
slack1:~>
```

In this example, you issue the `ls` command. Because no directory is listed after the `ls` command, Slackware lists the contents of the current directory which has a total of three files — `funfile`, `inscript`, and `wheefile`.

When running the `ls` command, if you see entries ending in an asterisk (*), that means the entry is an executable file or program, which is a file or program that is executed like a command. If the entry ends in a slash (/), then the entry is a subdirectory.

Changing directories

You can change from one directory to another by using the `cd` command. When you use the `cd` command, you're telling Slackware to change your directory from the current directory to the one specified after the `cd` command. If you don't specify a directory to change to, Slackware assumes that you want to go to your home directory, which is your personal account's starting directory. This directory is named after your login name. So if, for example, your login name is `paul`, then your home directory is `/home/paul`. Note that typing **cd ..** takes you back up one directory in the tree because the `..` represents one directory level higher than your current position.

When you change directories, your command prompt also changes to list the current directory that you're working in.

Here's an example of how to use the `cd` command:

```
slack1:~> cd /etc
slack1:/etc> cd /usr/local/bin
slack1:/usr/local/bin> cd
slack1:~>
```

In this example, you issue the `cd` command from the home directory of the account, as evidenced by the ~ (tilde) in the command prompt. The first line changes the current directory to `/etc`. The second line changes the current directory to `/usr/local/bin`, and the third line changes the current directory back to the home directory of the account.

Creating and removing directories

Creating new directories is a skill necessary for organizing your files. You can create new directories with the `mkdir` command. The format for this command is `mkdir {directory name}`. After you create a directory, you can list its contents by using the `ls` command. But remember, using the `ls` command on a newly created directory doesn't produce a directory listing because no files exist yet.

Removing directories is equally easy. The format for this command is `rmdir {directory name}`. The caveat with `rmdir` is that the directory must be empty, meaning that you have to remove all the files in the directory first!

The following is an example of creating and removing directories:

```
slack1:~> mkdir mydirectory
slack1:~> ls
funfile inscript* mydirectory/ wheefile
slack1:~> cd mydirectory
slack1:~/mydirectory> ls
slack1:~/mydirectory> cd ..
slack1:~> rmdir mydirectory
slack1:~> ls
funfile inscript* wheefile
slack1:~>
```

In the previous example, the command `mkdir mydirectory` creates a new directory called `mydirectory`. The output from the `ls` command then verifies that `mydirectory` has indeed been created. The next command, `cd mydirectory`, changes the directory to the newly created `mydirectory`. There is no output from the next `ls` command since there are no files in the directory. Finally, the `cd ..` command changes the directory to the directory to the one above the current one (which is the home directory of the account, signified by the ~), and then the directory is removed via the `rmdir mydirectory` command. A final `ls` output verifies that the directory has been removed.

Notice that throughout the example, the current working directory is shown in the prompt.

Creating files

Creating files is another easy task. If you want to create a file that contains absolutely nothing and is just an entry in a directory listing, you can do so via the command `touch {filename}`. Creating empty files is useful if you need to remind yourself of something (like a warning not to remove files from the directory), or if you've created a shell script that looks for the existence of certain file names. Another way to create a file is to use the `echo` command. For example, the command `echo "whatever" > myfilename` creates a file containing the word "whatever" in the file `myfilename`. (By itself, `echo` will simply display [echo] whatever follows the echo command back to the screen.)

A third method of creating files is by combining the contents of two or more other files. Suppose that you have two files named `file1` and `file2`. You can create a third file, called `file3`, by typing **cat file1 file2 > file3** at the command prompt and pressing Enter. The following examples show the three ways of creating files:

```
slack1:~> touch myfile
slack1:~> ls
funfile inscript* myfile wheefile
slack1:~> echo "whatever" > file1
slack1:~> ls
file1 funfile inscript* myfile wheefile
slack1:~> echo "dude" > file2
slack1:~> ls
file1 file2 funfile inscript* myfile wheefile
slack1:~> cat file1 file2 > file3
slack1:~> ls
file1 file2 file3 funfile inscript* myfile wheefile
slack1:~>
```

In this example, the `touch myfile` command creates an empty file called `myfile`. The output of the `ls` command verifies that the file is created.

The `echo "whatever" > file1` command creates a file named `file1` that contains the word "whatever." Again, the output of `ls` verifies this file's creation. The file `file2` is also created in the same way.

The `cat file1 file2 > file3` command creates the file named `file3` using the contents of `file1` and `file2`. Note that the output from `ls` shows that `file3` is indeed there.

Removing and renaming files

Because you're able to create files, you must also have a way to remove files. You can accomplish this task by using the `rm` command. To remove a file, type **rm {filename}**. If you want to remove multiple files at the same time, type **rm {filename} {filename}** at the command prompt.

You may also need to rename a file at a later time. To do so, you use the `mv` command. The format for this command is `mv {oldfilename} {newfilename}`.

You can rename directories the same way you rename files by using the `mv` command. You would type **mv {old directory name} {new directory name}** at the command prompt.

The following is an example of removing and renaming files:

```
slack1:~> ls
file1 file2 file3 funfile inscript* myfile wheefile
slack1:~> rm file1
file2 file3 funfile inscript* myfile wheefile
slack1:~> rm file2 file3
slack1:~> ls
funfile inscript* myfile wheefile
slack1:~> my myfile AnewFileName
slack1:~> ls
AnewFileName funfile inscript* wheefile
slack1:~>
```

In this example, the `rm file1` command removes the file `file1` from the system. `rm file2 file3` removes the files `file2` and `file3` from the system as well. The output of the `ls` command shows the results of both `rm` commands. Lastly, the `mv myfile AnewFileName` command renames the file `myfile` to `AnewFileName`.

Looking at the contents of a file

You may at times have to look at the contents of a file. For example, say you need to know what user groups are defined on the system. That information is held in the file `/etc/group`. When that is the case, you can use the `cat` and `more` commands. Each causes the contents of a file to display on your screen; however, the `more` command actually causes the contents of the file to display a screenful at a time. Use the space bar to move to the next page (screenful) of output.

Suppose that you want to look at the file, `wheefile`, in the home directory. If the file is not a large file, then at the command prompt, you type **cat wheefile** and press Enter. If the file is a large file, however, the contents zip quickly past your screen. In this case, you want to use the `more` command. The format for this command is `more {filename}`. Now you can easily read the file's contents by pressing the space bar to move forward to the next page of output, as shown in Figure 9-1. You can also press the `b` key to move backward a page at a time. As a general rule, anytime you want to view the contents of a file one page at a time, use `more` instead of `cat`.

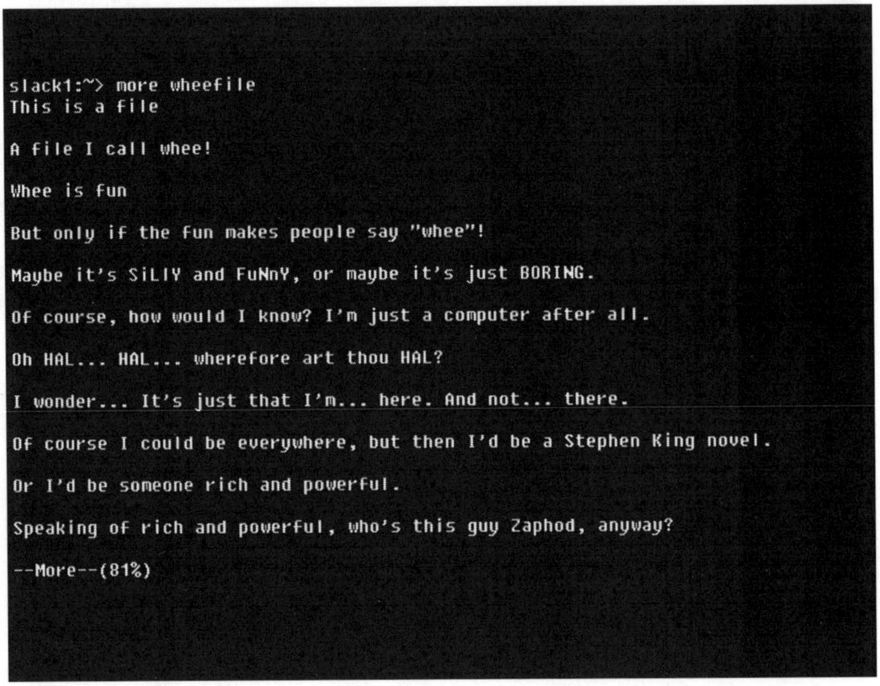

```
slack1:~> more wheefile
This is a file

A file I call whee!

Whee is fun

But only if the fun makes people say "whee"!

Maybe it's SiLlY and FuNnY, or maybe it's just BORING.

Of course, how would I know? I'm just a computer after all.

Oh HAL... HAL... wherefore art thou HAL?

I wonder... It's just that I'm... here. And not... there.

Of course I could be everywhere, but then I'd be a Stephen King novel.

Or I'd be someone rich and powerful.

Speaking of rich and powerful, who's this guy Zaphod, anyway?

--More--(81%)
```

Figure 9-1: Results of using the more command.

You can use either the `more` or `cat` command in conjunction with another command by placing the | (pipe) at the end of the command. Suppose you've got two files, `wheefile` and `funfile`, and you want to look at both back-to-back. At the command prompt type:

```
cat wheefile funfile | more
```

The contents of first `wheefile` and then `funfile` are displayed a page at a time on your screen. The contents of `funfile` will not appear until all the contents of `wheefile` have been displayed. You can also type **more wheefile funfile**, which does the same thing. Using the `more` command in this fashion to view multiple files in a row, however, doesn't allow you to use the `b` key to move backward in the file.

Organizing the File System

Slackware follows the Linux Filesystem Hierarchy Standard (FHS), which means that on every Slackware machine, the directory structure complies with the one the FHS has set as the standard. In other words, the directory structure between two different Slackware machines is identical upon installation. As shown in Figure 9-2, the standard Slackware file system really does look like an upside-down tree, with directories branching out from the root (/) directory.

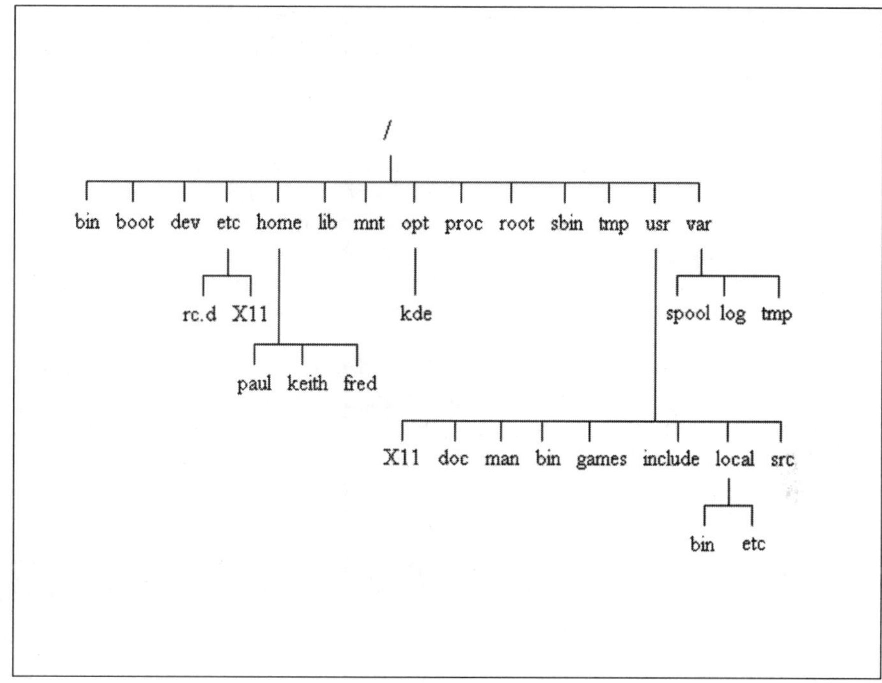

Figure 9-2: A partial Slackware directory structure.

Programmers and developers can easily navigate Slackware by using the FHS in order to compile or install programs. In other operating systems, like Windows, all the system files are in one directory, making for a huge jumbled mess. If you accidentally delete that directory, then you're out of luck. Slackware, on the other hand, uses multiple directories to store its system files, making organization easier on a system-wide level.

The FHS states that several directories for system files exist, thus minimizing the amount of damage that you can do by accidentally erasing one of these directories. The FHS is also intended to support interoperability of applications, system administration tools, development tools, and scripts, as well as keeping greater uniformity of documentation.

Rooting around in /

The base of the file system is the root directory. If you take a look at the contents of the root directory by typing **ls -la /** at your command prompt and pressing Enter, you see several subdirectories listed in the / (root) directory. Most of these subdirectories are critical to the continuing operation of Slackware. If you accidentally delete one — as long as you don't turn off your computer — you can recreate it by using the CD-ROM and reinstalling the A series of Slackware software packages (descriptions of the Slackware software series of packages are in Chapter 5).

The / (root) directory organizes the subdirectories according to the files that they contain. This logic also works in reverse — files that are necessary for a specific function are placed in directories depending on what the function is. For example, if the files are necessary for system-specific functions, then the files are placed in the /usr directory. However, if the files are necessary for general configurations, then the files are placed in the /etc directory. The following sections examine each of the subdirectories in / in greater detail.

To change from your current directory to each of the following directories, type **cd {directory name}** at your command prompt and press Enter. For example, to change to the /bin directory, type **cd /bin**. To list the contents of a directory after you change directories, type **ls** at your command prompt and press Enter.

/bin — The essentials

The /bin directory contains all the binaries (applications and programs or commands) for use by users — regular users and the system administrator (root) — on the system. The /bin directory has no subdirectories.

Some of the commands found within /bin are

- cat: Used to display the contents of a file
- echo: Used to display a line or phrase of text
- more: Used to display the contents of a file one screenful at a time
- mv: Used to move or rename files or directories
- rm: Used to remove files from the system

All shells are located in /bin, including csh and bash. Remember, shells are the interpreters between you and the computer for all your commands. (For more info on shells, turn to Chapter 8.)

/boot — For booting your computer

The /boot directory contains everything your system needs to boot except for configuration files. (Configuration files reside in the /etc directory. See the section, "/etc — Configuration for the masses," later in this chapter.) The kernel itself can reside either in / or in /boot.

Examples of the files found in /boot are

- boot_message.txt: The message displayed by LILO upon boot
- map: Contains the name and location of the kernel for LILO to boot
- System.map: The data map of the system

These are system-specific files, which are necessary for booting your computer. All files in the /boot directory should not be edited by you or anyone else.

/dev — Devices and other assorted devs

The /dev directory contains all the device files (see the "Typecasting files" section earlier in this chapter). These include files that represent partitions of your hard drive, your sound card, your video card, or any other hardware pieces that you may have.

Commonly used device files in /dev are:

- dsp: Represents the partition for your sound card
- fd0: Represents the partition for your floppy drive
- lp0: Represents the partition for your parallel port (usually connected to a printer)
- console: Represents the partition for sending output to the console

The /dev directory also contains the usable locations for virtual consoles (see Chapter 6) and remote consoles. *Remote consoles* are consoles for users who log in from a remote location by using a direct Internet connection — like from a place of employment or a school that has Internet access — or a modem connection instead of logging in from the computer's physical site. Each remote console location is called a *tty*. tty actually stands for teletypewriter, which is a nod back to the early days of the Internet when computers used special consoles that consisted of a keyboard and dot matrix printer. The more tty's that you have, the more people can log in at the same time. You can run out of tty's — the number of tty's on your system is a finite number — but it isn't likely because you would require upwards of 300 users on your computer at the same time.

/etc — Configuration for the masses

The /etc directory contains the configuration files for your Slackware system. The /etc directory can also include subdirectories relevant to certain programs on the system. In no instance should programs themselves be found in /etc. In other words, /etc is for files and directories but not programs.

Some of the files found in /etc are:

- lilo.conf: The configuration file for LILO
- syslog.conf: The configuration file for the system logger, which is the utility that keeps track of everything that happens on your system
- sendmail.cf: The configuration file for sendmail, an e-mail server program
- passwd: The password file

Sending flames to /dev/null

`/dev/null` is the black hole of your operating system. `/dev/null` is a special file that sends an end of file (EOF) character to any program that uses it. (The EOF character denotes the end of the file, hence its name.) Moving files to `/dev/null` is like throwing them in the trash — the system automatically deletes the file or files that you're moving to `/dev/null`.

Copying `/dev/null` to a file effectively removes the contents of the file because you overwrite the file with the EOF character. After you remove a file, it cannot be restored (not even by a wish, for those that are avid role-playing gamers).

Flaming refers to the practice of sending not-very-nice e-mails to people, telling them where to go, what their mother does for a living, and making remarks about the family tree not forking. The counter for flaming is usually to tell the originators of the flames to send their nasty e-mails to `/dev/null`. Of course, you can't *really* make people send e-mail to `/dev/null`. But informing the people sending the flames that their messages are being sent to `/dev/null` is equal to telling them that their messages are being automatically deleted without ever being read. Telling someone to send their flames to `/dev/null` is akin to telling them to "talk to the hand."

However, if you get a flame in a text file (say it's called `flame.txt`), send it to `/dev/null` by typing **mv flame.txt /dev/null** at your command prompt:. Voilà! The flame is snuffed out.

You can also find files specific to networking, like `hosts.allow` (the list of hosts allowed to connect to the system), `hosts.deny` (the list of hosts denied from connecting to the system), and `inetd.conf` (the configuration for all networking programs).

Slackware also contains the subdirectories `rc.d` and `X11` in the `/etc` directory. `rc.d` is where all the system initialization scripts are kept — these are run after the machine is booted. `X11` is where all the configuration files for the X Windows system are found. (See Chapter 11 for more information on X Windows.)

/home — The place to go

`/home`, which is an optional directory, contains the user (personal) directories. If you log in as your personal account (not as the root user), you start in `/home/your-login-name`.

`/home` directories, by default, aren't secure, which means that another user can look and see what you've got stored in your home directory. You can change that by altering the permissions on the directory — a topic I cover in greater detail in Chapter 16.

/lib — The great library of Slackware

The `/lib` directory contains all the system's program library files, which are the common routines that programs need to run correctly. These common routines are saved in binary data format — unreadable to the casual observer. `/lib` doesn't contain program libraries for nonessential system programs. For example, common system commands like `ps` and even the kernel itself depend on the routines in `/lib` to function correctly. However, the GNOME desktop depends on library routines found in `/usr/lib`, which are library routines specific to that program.

/mnt — A temporary place to rest

A *mount point* is where a / (root) directory places a file system so that its contents can be accessed. `/mnt` — short for mount — is a directory that the system administrator uses to temporarily mount file systems as needed. The contents of this directory can change at any time, depending on what file systems are mounted by the system administrator.

/opt — An optional locale

You can install custom applications, like the KDE desktop, in the `/opt` directory. Although this directory is optional, new application developers and programmers are using `/opt` more and more frequently. By placing their work in the `opt` directory, new developers and programmers can differentiate their work from older Slackware programs. Using `/opt` also means that these new developers don't have to worry as much about where their program fits in to the FHS because the `/opt` directory is, well, optional.

/root — The home of the gods

`/root` is the home directory of the super user account. (Hardcore Linux users call the super user or system administrator account — root — "god" because it has no restrictions whatsoever.) You shouldn't confuse `root`, `/root`, and /. The super user account is `root`; `/root` is the home directory of the `root` account; and / is the main trunk (root) of the entire file system tree. Other user accounts should never see the contents of `/root` because even the super user needs a place to store personal files or files relating to the critical operation of the system.

/sbin — The storage for system binaries

The `/sbin` directory contains system-specific programs reserved for the system administrator. The programs in the `/sbin` directory, in addition to those stored in the `/bin` directory, are essential for booting the system.

Some of the programs necessary for system operation that are found in /sbin are:

- swapon: Used to turn on your swap partition
- reboot: Used to reboot the system (only usable by the system administrator)
- fdisk: Used to (re)partition your hard drive(s)
- ifconfig: Used to set up your network card (and your network)

What's the difference between /bin and /sbin? /bin is the place for programs that everyone uses, while /sbin houses programs of administrative use. This is to keep regular users from running administrative commands.

/tmp — The place for temporary files

The /tmp directory is just a temporary directory. If a file is left in the /tmp directory, the system can come by on a routine maintenance check and remove it. (Normal operation for Slackware includes removing the contents of the /tmp directory nightly.)

Users and the system administrator both use the /tmp directory as a place to temporarily store files or data. Users and system administrators most commonly use /tmp to download software packages from the Internet and examine the packages in the /tmp directory. Programs that require temporary storage space while running, in order to calculate and sort data and write output files, also use this directory.

/var — Constantly changing

The /var directory (/var stands for variable) contains any and all system information that changes during the course of the computer's run, such as system logs, outgoing and incoming e-mail, and print queues. Any program that needs to dynamically take or remove information or data from the system uses the /var directory.

For example, you can find the system logs in the /var/log subdirectory. (To get there, at your command prompt type **cd /var/log** and press Enter.) You use system logs to see what's happening with your system. System logs serve as points of reference in case something goes wrong with your system — the system makes a note in the files of /var/log of every system error. Another example is the /var/spool/lpd subdirectory, where the system sends files to be printed and stores printer queues. If you have a printer hooked up to your Slackware machine, you will become very familiar with the /var/spool/lpd directory. Lastly, editors, such as vi and pico (used for changing the contents of files), use /var/tmp for their editing space (see Chapter 10 for information on editors).

`/var` is also important because upon boot-up, `/var` checks the `/usr` directory (see the next section) for errors. If `/usr` has errors, or cannot be mounted, you can use `/var` as a small temporary `/usr` partition.

Leading the charge — /usr

The `/usr` directory is the most important directory on the system. `/usr` contains a wealth of subdirectories, almost all of which are necessary for the operation of the system. While having the / directory is enough to boot the machine, without the `/usr` directory the machine cannot continue to function properly because several system-dependent programs reside in /usr. For example, almost all the system's daemons (programs that run automatically in the background upon power up), are housed in the `/usr/sbin` directory.

`/usr` contains the follow subdirectories:

- `X11R6`: The X Windows System
- `doc`: Slackware and Linux manuals and online information
- `man`: The manual pages
- `bin`: Most user commands not found in `/bin`
- `games`: Games!
- `include`: Files needed for compiling programs
- `local`: Programs and configuration files specific only to your computer
- `src`: The source code for the Linux kernel

The `/usr` directory itself shouldn't contain any programs; programs and assorted files should reside in the subdirectories below `/usr`. For example, the `/usr/local` directory contains files and subdirectories native to the particular machine. (The contents of `/usr/local` vary from computer to computer.)

Processing it all — /proc

Although not necessarily a part of the FHS, `/proc` has its place in Slackware because it contains every single piece of information currently running on your system.

Commands like `ps` and `uptime` pull up information about the system — like currently running processes, system load, and RAM usage — from this directory. Every process currently running on your system has an entry in `/proc`. `/proc` is also *real time*, which means that changes to files in `/proc` are immediately seen by the system. A sample listing of the entries in `/proc` is shown in Figure 9-3. Note that entries with a slash (/) after them are subdirectories.

```
slack1:~> ls /proc
1/      17391/  22024/  69/  bus/          ioports  mounts      stat
112/    17392/  3/      73/  cmdline       kcore    net/        swaps
114/    17393/  4/      76/  cpuinfo       kmsg     parport/    sys/
115/    17400/  5/      78/  devices       ksyms    partitions  tty/
17353/  17401/  5070/   80/  dma           loadavg  pci         uptime
17354/  17403/  5071/   82/  fb            locks    rtc         version
17363/  2/      5120/   85/  filesystems   mdstat   scsi/
17388/  20381/  5284/   87/  fs/           meminfo  self@
17389/  20382/  5296/   89/  ide/          misc     slabinfo
17390/  22023/  67/     96/  interrupts    modules  sound
slack1:~>
```

Figure 9-3: A sample listing of the files in /proc.

Each number listed in Figure 9-3 is actually the ID number of a currently running process on the machine. (Yes, Figure 9-3 shows many numbers, which means there are a lot of processes running on the computer.) The remaining files listed contain current system hardware settings. The `cpuinfo` file contains information on the CPU, and the `partitions` file contains information on the hard drive partitions in use.

Packing Files by Using Compression

Before the advent of 10GB hard drives, drive space was at a premium — you didn't want to have a lot of files on your hard drive in case you needed the space for something else. To solve this problem, archival and compression programs were created in order to shrink the size of files and archive them. Today, hard drive space isn't much of a problem, but you still may find you need to pack a directory and all its files into a nice, neat archive.

tarring and feathering

You can package programs and files together by using the `tar` command. `tar` preserves ownership, permissions, and order of everything that is archived.

Some archival programs change the ownership and permissions of the files in the archive to whoever unpacks the archive. `tar` stands for tape archive, but only twice in the last decade have I seen anyone actually use the command to write information to a tape for archiving. You typically see `tar` used with the `-f` flag, which tells `tar` to create an archive file (a tar file) instead of an archive on a tape.

The presence of the .tar extension at the end of a filename indicates a tar file.

To create an archive of several files in your directory, at the command prompt type:

```
tar -cf archive.tar file1 file2 file3
```

The `-c` flag tells `tar` to create a file (file creation is indicated with the `-f` flag) called `archive.tar` and to use the files named `file1`, `file2`, and `file3` as the contents of the `archive.tar` file. Suppose that you have a directory called `mydir`. Inside `mydir` are 50 files that you want to archive. To pack the contents of the `mydir` directory in one shot, without having to specify all the files on one line, at the command prompt type:

```
tar -cf archive.tar mydir/
```

`tar` attempts to archive `mydir` as if it were another file. But when `tar` sees that `mydir` is a directory, `tar` archives all the files stored in the `mydir` directory.

To unpackage a tar file, use the `-x` flag instead of the `-c` flag (`-x` stands for extract). To unpack the archive file `archive.tar`, at the command prompt type:

```
tar -xf archive.tar.
```

The contents of `archive.tar` unpack into the current directory. If the archive just contains files, these files are placed in the current directory. If the archive is a subdirectory, the subdirectory is created in your current directory, and all the files extract into that newly created subdirectory.

gzipping around the system

`gzip` is one of the most frequently used compression programs in Slackware. `gzip` compresses files into smaller files (similar to the `pkzip` program for DOS/Windows, only better) so that they take up less disk space without ruining the integrity of the file's data.

`gzip` files are identified by the .gz extension at the end of a filename.

To compress a file, at the command prompt type:

```
gzip {filename}
```

gzip runs differently depending on the flag used, usually a number flag between 1 and 9. The higher the number, the better the compression. The drawback is that the higher the number, the more time it takes for gzip to compress. The reverse is also true — the lower the number, the worse the compression, but gzip compresses in less time.

If you want to compress a file right this second, at the command prompt type:

```
gzip -1 {filename}
```

If you want to make the file as small as possible, at the command prompt type:

```
gzip -9 {filename}
```

gzip checks to see if files have already been compressed by checking the file's extension. If the file already has a .gz extension, gzip ignores it and moves on.

Don't try to fool gzip by compressing a file, renaming it to get rid of the .gz extension, and compressing it again. You can ruin the data in your file.

To uncompress files, use gunzip. The format for gunzip is gunzip {file.gz}. If the file doesn't have a .gz extension, gunzip cannot uncompress it. gunzip also decompresses files compressed with other compression utilities, such as compress. The use of compress is outdated, however; gunzip contains support for compress files in order to maintain compatibility with older archives.

Here are some examples of uncompressing files by using gunzip:

```
slack1:~> gunzip -v file1.gz
file1.gz:   78.7% - replaced with file1
slack1:~> gunzip -v file2.Z
file2.Z:    26.8% - replaced with file2
```

(file.gz is a gzipped file, and file.Z is a compress file.) The -v flag tells gunzip to go into *verbose* mode, which means that whatever gunzip is doing, it is going to tell you what it's doing while it's doing it. Verbose mode for many programs is kind of like having a running account of what's going on while the program is running. The drawback is that the amount of information the program spits back at you might be more than you wanted to know.

gzipping the tar out of it

This chapter isn't complete without telling you that using `gzip` and `tar` together makes for a superb archival process. `tar` can combine several files and directories together into one archive while `gzip` can compress it to the smallest point possible.

The process is quite simple — use `tar` to create your archive first (see the section "tarring and feathering" earlier in this chapter), and then use `gzip` on your newly created `tar` archive (see the preceding section "gzipping around the system") to create an archive that has a .tar.gz extension. These archive files are commonly called *tar-gzipped* archives.

Suppose that you have a directory called `mydir`. To archive that directory, follow these steps:

1. **At your command prompt, type** tar -cf archive.tar mydir/ **and press Enter.**

   Slackware archives the directory `mydir` and its contents into the file `archive.tar`.

2. **At your command prompt, type** gzip -9 archive.tar **and press Enter.**

   `gzip` compresses the `archive.tar` file. The `-9` flag forces `gzip` to use its best compression method on the `archive.tar` file. This results in a tar-gzipped file called `archive.tar.gz` that contains the contents of `mydir`.

You can use tar-gzipped archives on any Linux system in existence, regardless of computer type or Linux version. The `tar` and `gzip` commands are standard commands in any version of Linux, including Slackware. Because tar-gzipped archives take up less space than a normal tar archive, saving these archives to floppy disks or Zip disks (assuming you have a Zip drive) is easier. You can now trade copies of your archives with fellow Linux users.

Chapter 10

Editing Away

In This Chapter

- Getting to know your editors
- Working with `vi`
- Peeking at `pico`
- Enjoying `emacs`

Word processing programs are indispensable computing tools. These programs enable you to alter the presentation of documents in numerous ways, including formatting text and altering fonts. The drawback with word processors is that they take up a lot of hard drive space and require your computer to have a decent amount of speed and memory. Enter *editors* — small, quick programs (with the exception of `emacs`) that enable you to perform a range of functions, from writing yourself little notes to sending e-mail to even composing a master's thesis. (Don't laugh, I knew graduate students at the University of Arizona that did this.) What makes editors more desirable than word processors is that word processors depend on a graphical interface, while editors do not — hence you can use an editor with or without X Windows in Slackware. Various types of editors exist — some created for specific functions. In this chapter, I cover the text editors that you're most likely to use.

Introducing Editors

Editors are text manipulators in the basest sense — that is, the primary function of an editor is to create, change, or delete text. Editors come in handy for almost any job, from creating long text files to editing Web pages to even taking notes in class on your laptop — though experience shows editors end up used more for sending and receiving e-mail than anything else. This is because all e-mail programs need some way to have the user create a message for sending or replying — there's no reason to try and duplicate effort when editors already exist to do the job for them. Editors don't care if the file is going to be a text file, source code for a program, a shell script, or even a compiled executable program, because editors do exactly what they're told (just like computers) — if you tell an editor to edit file A, and file A is an executable program, the editor is going to open it anyway because you told it to. (Only Linux gurus actually edit compiled programs, because compiled programs are now in machine language code and not readily legible to the rest of us.)

Because Slackware treats everything as a file, editors give you the power to change any file on the system with a touch of a key. However, just like word processors, editors need a way of executing commands or navigating in and around the file when you're not entering text. Some editors, like `vi`, call this navigation *command mode* in order to designate a mode when text is not entered, with *insert mode* being the mode when text is entered. Other editors, like `pico`, only have one mode (insert mode) and use Control keys (functions executed by holding down the Ctrl key and pressing another key at the same time) to execute commands.

Control keys in Unix are usually prefixed by the carat (^), though this book uses Ctrl to indicate when you are supposed to press the Control key. For example, you may see ^Z which is the same as Ctrl+Z.

Editors need a place to store the changes to the file as you make them. This place is called a *text buffer*, which is a location on the hard drive or in memory used as storage for the file's changes or modifications. When you make changes to your file, your changes are not made to the file until you save the file, causing the text buffer to *flush* or write all changes to the hard drive. If you quit your editor without saving your changes, the text buffer is then erased instead of flushed and no changes are written to the file.

Vi-ing, not vying

`vi` is one of the most widely used and most powerful editors available. `vi` is a visual editor (most editors or word processors are), which means that you can see what you're editing as you edit. `vi` is also somewhat complex, so you should try it out a couple of times to test its capabilities. Using `vi` to edit files becomes second nature after your first couple of uses.

In the following directions, the *current line* is the line that your cursor is on. The *current word* is any string of characters separated by spaces that your cursor is on — the string starts and ends with a space, but does not include the space. For example, if your cursor was on the word "example" in "for example," "example" would be the current word. Finally, the *current character* is the character your cursor is on.

One thing to note — the `vi` editor in Slackware is not actually `vi` but `elvis`, which is a replacement for `vi` with several additions. While the original `vi` is a powerful editor, the `elvis` editor has all the functionality of the original `vi` plus some enhancements. Hence, the good folks at The Slackware Project have made the command `vi` actually run `elvis`, so if you type the command **vi**, it's the same as typing the command **elvis**. The reason for this is that many people around the world are used to typing `vi` to get an editor, and since `elvis` is an enhanced `vi`, having the command `vi` run `elvis` makes more sense than having to inform people that `vi` is no longer available and they are to use `elvis` instead. The commands shown for `vi` in this chapter work for any version of `vi`, whether it be the original `vi`, `elvis`, or other `vi` clones. Throughout this section, I make notes on commands specifically for `elvis` that are not available in the original `vi`.

To start `vi`, follow these steps:

1. **At the command prompt, type** vi **and press Enter.**

   Alternatively, you can edit a specific file by typing **vi {filename}** and pressing Enter. `vi` runs and brings you to a blank screen with tildes (~) down the left column. You are now within the `vi` editor.

2. **Type** :set all **and press Enter.**

   Your current settings for `vi` are shown.

The following sections assume you're already running `vi`. Any commands that begin with a colon are typed at the bottom of your screen, regardless of where your cursor is at the time.

You must press Enter at the end of a command that begins with a colon (:) or at the end of a search string in order for the command to execute. For example, if you want the `set all` command to function correctly, you must type **:set all** and then press Enter. If you want to search for the word "fun" in your file, you would type **/fun** and press Enter

Operating modes of vi

`vi` has two *modes* or uses: command and insert. When you start `vi` , you are automatically placed in command mode. In insert mode, the keys on the keyboard represent the actual characters (letters, numbers, punctionation characters, and so on); while in command mode, however, the keys represent `vi` commands. So, if you're in insert mode in `vi` and type **/whee**, that would be exactly what you see entered. If you're in command mode, however, and type **/whee**, `/whee` will appear at the bottom of your screen because the / character is actually the character used to search the file for a string (in this case the word "whee"). The Enter key in insert mode is the same as a carriage return on a typewriter or a word processor — it moves the cursor to the beginning of a new line — while in command mode, Enter is only used to end a command that begins with a colon (:) or to submit a search command.

Once `vi` is running, to change to insert mode from command mode, press *i* (but do not press Enter). It doesn't matter where in the file you are when you press *i*. Now start typing. The `i` key tells `vi` to insert text at the cursor. The starting point for text to be inserted is wherever the cursor is when you press *i*. To go back to command mode, press the Esc key. You can press the Esc key at any time and be switched directly into command mode — the same goes for the `i` key to switch to insert mode. You don't see any change on your screen when you switch modes, though you do hear a beep if you press Esc more than once. (I have a habit of hitting it twice just to make sure I'm in command mode because I type too fast for my own good.)

Note that `vi` doesn't have any command prompts — it assumes that the commands you wish to execute are to be run immediately.

In `elvis`, you can see what mode you are in by typing **:set showmode** and pressing Enter. (This command is not available in the original `vi`.) This activates a little notifier in the bottom-right corner of your screen, which lets you know what mode you are in. You also have several other keys at your disposal to change from command to insert mode, as shown in Table 10-1.

Table 10-1 Mode Change Commands in vi

Key	*Description*
A	Insert text after the cursor
O	Open a new line after the current line and add text
Shift+O	Open a new line before the current line and add text
Shift+I	Insert text at the beginning of the current line
Shift+A	Insert text at the end of the current line

You don't need to press Enter after any of these commands because they are automatically executed the moment you press the command's key.

For an example of `vi`'s insert mode, use the following steps (if you're already running `vi`, skip to Step 2):

1. **At your command prompt, type** vi *myfile* **and press Enter.**

   Replace *myfile* with whatever you want to name the file, if you wish. I assume you keep the moniker myfile throughout this chapter. If you don't, just remember to adjust the directions in this chapter accordingly. `vi` runs and brings you to a blank screen with tildes (~) down the left column. You are now within the `vi` editor.

2. **Type** :set showmode **and press Enter.**

   The message `Command` appears in the bottom right corner. You are in command mode.

3. **Press *i*.**

   The message in the bottom right corner changes to `Input`. You are now in insert mode.

4. **Type the following, making sure you press Enter at the end of each line:**

```
Hi there. I am your computer!
Four score and seven years ago
Would you like to play a game?
```

   What you type is displayed on the screen.

5. **Press the Esc key.**

   The message in the bottom right corner changes to `Command`. You are now in command mode.

6. **Type** :wq **and press Enter.**

   Your file is saved and is called `myfile`. `vi` exits.

Navigating vi

Editing files is difficult without the power to change lines or move text around. Slackware's version of `vi` lets you use the arrow keys to move within the file, although some earlier versions of `vi` do not (Slackware or other Unix or Linux variants included). You can use other keys to navigate inside your file in case your arrow keys do not work. Table 10-2 shows the list of keys that are equivalent to your arrow keys.

Navigational commands require you to be in command mode for the commands to work. To get to command mode, press the Esc key. If you're not sure which mode you're in, press Esc anyway — the computer just beeps if you're already in command mode.

Table 10-2 Directing vi

Key	*Description*
H	Move the cursor one character to the left
J	Move the cursor one line up
K	Move the cursor one line down
L	Move the cursor one character to the right

Other navigational keys that are useful for moving by word or by line are shown in Table 10-3.

Table 10-3 More Navigation in vi

Key	Description
B	Move cursor backward to the beginning of the word
E	Move cursor forward to the end of the word
W	Move cursor forward to the beginning of the next word
Ctrl-F	Move forward one screen
Ctrl-B	Move backward one screen
1+Shift+G	Go to the beginning of the file
Shift+G	Go to the end of the file
0	Go to the beginning of the line
$	Go to the end of the line

The `G` command enables you to move to a specific line number. Type the line number and then press Shift+G. The command `14G`, for example, moves the cursor to the 14th line of the file. The `G` command by itself takes you to the end of the file.

Again, none of these commands require you to press Enter. The commands automatically move through the file as soon as you type the key command sequence.

For an example of `vi`'s navigational capabilities, use the following steps (if you're already running `vi`, skip to Step 2):

1. **At your command prompt, type** vi myfile **and press Enter.**

   `vi` runs and brings you to a blank screen with tildes (~) down the left column. You are now within the `vi` editor.

2. **Type** :set showmode **and press Enter.**

   The message `Command` appears in the bottom right corner. You are in command mode. The cursor is over the H in `Hi there`.

3. **Press *l* twice.**

   The cursor moves to the space between `Hi` and `there`.

4. **Press *j* twice.**

   The cursor moves two lines down, with the cursor over the u in `Would`.

5. **Press *w* twice.**

   The cursor moves to the beginning of the word `like`.

6. **Press *0*.**

   The cursor moves to the beginning of the line.

7. **Press *$* (Shift+4).**

   The cursor moves to the end of the line.

8. **Type** :wq **and press Enter.**

   Your file is saved. `vi` exits.

Deleting text

Part of the function of an editor is to remove unwanted text from a file. `vi` has many commands for deleting text, as shown in Table 10-4.

Table 10-4 Removing Text in vi

Key	Description
DD	Delete the current line
X	Delete the current character
DW	Delete the current word
Shift+D	Delete everything from the cursor to the end of the line

You can specify the number of lines, characters, or words that you want to delete by typing a number before the command. The format for the command is `#{command}`, where # is any number greater than 1. For example, the command `3dd` deletes the current line, plus the next two lines under it. The command `3dw` deletes the word that the cursor is on (the current word) plus the next two words after it.

Deletion commands require that you're in command mode for them to work. To get to command mode, press Esc. If you're not sure if you're in command mode, press Esc anyway.

One of the most important commands, besides the Esc key and the `i` key, is the undo command. The undo command cancels the last command that you execute, whether you're changing, inserting, or deleting text. In `vi`, the undo command is executed by pressing *u*.

For an example of vi's delete and undo capabilities, use the following steps (if you're already running vi, skip to Step 2):

1. **At your command prompt, type** vi myfile **and press Enter.**

   vi runs and brings you to a blank screen with tildes (~) down the left column. You are now within the vi editor.

2. **Type** :set showmode **and press Enter.**

   The message Command appears in the bottom right corner. You are in command mode. The cursor is over the H in Hi there.

3. **Press *j* once.**

   The cursor moves to the beginning of the line Four score and seven years ago.

4. **Press *d* twice (this is the same as typing** dd**).**

   The line Four score and seven years ago disappears.

5. **Press *u* once.**

   The line Four score and seven years ago reappears. Pressing *u* after this either deletes or undeletes the line Four score and seven years ago, depending on whether a delete or an undelete was just performed.

6. **Type** :wq **and press Enter.**

   Your file is saved and is called myfile. vi exits.

elvis allows you to use undo multiple times if the command :set undolevels=# is typed while in command mode (when you type this, the command appears at the bottom of the screen), where # is some number greater than 0 and less than 100. (This command is not available in the original vi.) Remember to press Enter after typing any command that begins with a colon (:).

Replacing and substituting text

Replacing and substituting text is as important as typing text in. The difference between replacing text and substituting text is that you can substitute for as many characters as necessary, but you can only replace one character at a time.

Replacing and substituting commands requires that you're in command mode for them to work. To get to command mode, press Esc. If you're not sure if you're in command mode, press Esc anyway.

vi enables you to replace text easily by using the commands shown in Table 10-5.

Table 10-5	Replacing Text in vi
Key	***Description***
~	Change the case of the current character
R	Replace the current character

The tilde (~) command requires that you press Shift before typing that key. You can access the tilde on standard U.S. keyboards by pressing Shift+` (the backtick mark under the Esc key on the keyboard). The ~ command doesn't affect characters that cannot change case, like numbers, punctuation characters, or control characters.

For an example of `vi`'s replacement and case changing capabilities, use the following steps (if you're already running `vi`, skip to Step 2):

1. **At your command prompt, type** vi myfile **and press Enter.**

   `vi` runs and brings you to a blank screen with tildes (~) down the left column. You are now within the `vi` editor.

2. **Type** :set showmode **and press Enter.**

   The message `Command` appears in the bottom right corner. You are in command mode. The cursor is over the H in `Hi there`.

3. **Press *j* once.**

   The cursor moves to the beginning of the line `Four score and seven years ago`. The cursor is over the F in `Four`.

4. **Press ~.**

   The F changes to an f.

5. **Press *u* once.**

   The f changes back to an F.

6. **Press *r*.**

   The message at the bottom of the screen changes to read `Replc 1`.

7. **Press *z*.**

   The F changes to a z. The message at the bottom of the screen changes back to `Command`.

8. **Press *u* once.**

   The z changes back to an F.

9. **Type** :wq **and press Enter.**

   Your file is saved. `vi` exits.

While you can replace only one character at a time, you can substitute for any length or number of characters. The substitute commands place you in insert mode because you literally insert text where text already exists. Therefore you have to press Esc to go back to command mode when you are done with your substitution. A list of substitute commands is shown in Table 10-6.

Table 10-6 Substituting Text in vi

Key	Description
S	Substitute the current character
Shift+S	Substitute the entire current line
CH	Change the character to the left of the cursor
CL	Change the character to the right of the cursor
CW	Change the current word
CJ	Change the line below the cursor
CK	Change the line above the cursor
Shift+C	Change everything from the cursor to the end of the current line

You can preface any of the commands with a number to indicate how many characters or lines to change or substitute. The format for the command is `#{command}`, where # is any number greater than 1. For example, the command `5cl` changes the current character plus the next four characters to the right of the cursor (1 + 4 = 5). The command `5ch` will do the same for characters to the left of the cursor. However, the command `2ck` changes *three* lines — the line the cursor is on, and the two lines above it. The command `2cj` does the same for lines below the cursor.

For an example of `vi`'s substitution capabilities, use the following steps (if you're already running `vi`, skip to Step 2):

1. **At your command prompt, type** vi myfile **and press Enter.**

   `vi` runs and brings you to a blank screen with tildes (~) down the left column. You are now within the `vi` editor.

2. **Type** :set showmode **and press Enter.**

   The message `Command` appears in the bottom-right corner. You are in command mode. The cursor is over the H in `Hi there`.

3. **Press** ***j*** **twice.**

   The cursor moves to the beginning of the line `Would you like to play a game?`.

4. **Type** cw.

   The d in `Would` becomes a $, and the message at the bottom of the screen changes to `Input`. The $ designates the end of the word you are about to change.

5. **Type** Will **and press Esc.**

   The word `Would` changes to `Will`. The text shifts to the left to accommodate the missing character (only four letters in "Will," but five in "Would"). The message at the bottom of the screen changes to `Command`.

6. **Press** ***u*** **once.**

   The word `Will` changes back to `Would`.

7. **Type** :wq **and press Enter.**

   Your file is saved and is called `myfile`. `vi` exits.

Cutting, pasting, and copying text

Cutting and pasting text is one of the strengths of any good editor. Cutting and pasting enables you to remove text and place it in a different location in the file. Copying enables you to repeat phrases or paragraphs without having to type the entire phrase or paragraph again.

Cutting, pasting, and copying commands require that you're in command mode for them to work. To get to command mode, press Esc. If you're not sure if you're in command mode, press Esc anyway.

To cut text, you use the `dd` command (see Table 10-4). To copy text, use the `yy` command instead (see Table 10-7). Remember that you can add a number in front of either command to specify the number of lines to delete or copy.

If you want to paste the text elsewhere, after you cut text (the number of lines deleted isn't important), you move your cursor by using your arrow keys to the location in the file where you wish the text to be pasted. You can then use one of the commands listed in Table 10-7.

Table 10-7 Copying and Pasting Text

Key	*Description*
Shift+YY	Copies (yanks) a line of text
P	Pastes cut or copied text on the lines below the cursor
Shift+P	Pastes cut or copied text on the lines before the cursor

Notice the difference between the two commands — one is a lowercase `p`, the other is a capital `P`.

For an example of `vi`'s copying and pasting capabilities, use the following steps (if you're already running `vi`, skip to Step 2):

1. **At your command prompt, type** vi myfile **and press Enter.**

   `vi` runs and brings you to a blank screen with tildes (~) down the left column. You are now within the `vi` editor.

2. **Type** :set showmode **and press Enter.**

   The message `Command` appears in the bottom-right corner. You are in command mode. The cursor is over the H in `Hi there`.

3. **Press *d* twice (this is the same as typing** dd**).**

   The line beginning with `Hi there` is deleted.

4. **Press *j* once.**

   The cursor moves to the beginning of the line `Would you like to play a game?`.

5. **Press *p* once.**

   The line `Hi there. I am your computer!` appears on the line below the cursor. The cursor is now at the beginning of this line.

6. **Press *k* twice.**

   The cursor moves up two lines to the beginning of the line `Four score and seven years ago`.

7. **Press *y* twice (this is the same as typing** yy**).**

   Nothing happens.

8. **Press Shift+P.**

   The line `Four score and seven years ago` appears on the line above the cursor. The cursor is now at the end of this new line.

9. **Type** :q! **and press Enter.**

   Your file is not saved. `vi` exits.

Searching your file for text

One of the handiest parts of `vi` is the search feature. You can search a file for any string of characters that you want. Some characters, however, require a \ (backslash) in front of them because they are interpreted by the search program as the beginning of a command or metacharacter (metacharacters are explained in Chapter 9) — examples of this are the \ character itself, the asterisk (*), and the period (.). Placing a \ in front of a character is called *escaping* the character so the computer sees the character as a character, not as a command.

Search commands require that you're in command mode for them to work. To get to command mode, press Esc. If you're not sure if you're in command mode, press Esc anyway.

To search a file from beginning to end (called searching *forward*) for a string of characters, type a / (slash) followed by a string to search for. The / and the string you type appear at the bottom of the screen. This command causes `vi` to search for the string specified starting at the cursor and moving toward the end of the file. Remember to press Enter after your search string or `vi` waits patiently, doing nothing, until you do. When `vi` finds a string that matches what you're looking for, it places the cursor at the beginning of that string.

To search *backward* (from the end to the beginning), type a ? (question mark) followed by a string to search for. The ? and the search string you type appear at the bottom of the screen. Again, press Enter to start the search, otherwise `vi` waits until you do. When `vi` finds a string that matches your search, it places the cursor at the beginning of that string.

Suppose that you find the string of characters that you're looking for, but it's a common string and you're actually looking for it in another place in the document. If you press *n*, `vi` takes you to the next place that it finds your search string.

For an example of `vi`'s search capabilities, use the following steps (if you're already running `vi`, skip to Step 2):

1. **At your command prompt, type** vi myfile **and press Enter.**

   `vi` runs and brings you to a blank screen with tildes (~) down the left column. You are now within the `vi` editor.

2. **Type** :set showmode **and press Enter.**

   The message `Command` appears in the bottom-right corner. You are in command mode. The cursor is over the H in `Hi there`.

3. **Type** /computer **and press Enter.**

   The cursor moves to the beginning of the word `computer` in the first line.

4. **Press *n* once.**

   The message `(wrapped)` appears at the bottom of the screen. This indicates that the computer has searched from top to bottom for the search string and has come back to the top of the file.

5. **Type** ?Four **and press Enter.**

   The cursor moves to the beginning of the word `Four` in the line `Four score and seven years ago.`

6. **Type** :q! **and press Enter.**

   Your file is not saved. `vi` exits.

Make sure you place a \ in front of the following characters, if your search includes them: / (slash); ? (question mark); \ (backslash); | (pipe); ! (exclamation point); ((left or open parenthesis); [(left or open bracket);) (right or close parenthesis);] (right or close bracket); * (asterisk); & (ampersand); ; (semicolon); : (colon); and . (the period). For example, if you want to search for the string `(1:2)`, you type `/\(1\:2\)` and press Enter.

Joining lines and repeating commands

Joining lines of text is necessary if you're editing a file and need to bring together several separate lines onto one line. Joining brings the current line together with the line below the current line. Repeating commands is necessary if you find yourself retyping the same key commands over and over, like pasting the same line several times in a row.

Joining and repeating commands require that you're in command mode for them to work. To get to command mode, press Esc. If you're not sure if you're in command mode, press Esc anyway.

The join command is `J` (that's Shift+J). To join two lines, position the cursor anywhere on the line you need to join with the line below it and type `J`. The line below your current line is immediately added to the end of your current line.

The repeat command is the period (.). This command repeats the last command executed. The caveat is that the repeat command only repeats the *last* command you entered, not the command prior to that. In this respect, the repeat command is similar to the undo command.

For an example of `vi`'s join and repeat capabilities, use the following steps (if you're already running `vi`, skip to Step 2):

1. **At your command prompt, type** vi myfile **and press Enter.**

   `vi` runs and brings you to a blank screen with tildes (~) down the left column. You are now within the `vi` editor.

2. **Type** :set showmode **and press Enter.**

   The message `Command` appears in the bottom-right corner. You are in command mode. The cursor is over the H in `Hi there`.

3. **Press Shift+G and press Enter.**

   The cursor moves to the end of the file.

4. **Press *o*.**

   The message at the bottom of the screen changes to `Input`. A blank line is created under `Would you like to play a game?` and the cursor moves to the beginning of this new blank line. You are now in insert mode.

5. **Type** Some **and press Enter.**

   The word `Some` appears on a line by itself.

6. **Type** new **and press Enter.**

   The word `new` appears on a line by itself.

7. **Type** lines **and press Enter.**

   The word `lines` appears on a line by itself.

8. **Type** here **and press Enter.**

   The word `here` appears on a line by itself.

9. **Press Esc.**

   The message at the bottom of the screen changes to `Command`. You are now in command mode.

10. **Press *k* three times.**

    The cursor moves to the end of the word `Some`.

11. **Press Shift+J.**

    The word `new` moves to the end of the line after `Some`.

12. **Press . (the period).**

    The J command is repeated. The word `lines` moves to the end of the line after `Some new`.

13. **Press . (the period).**

    The J command is repeated again. The word here moves to the end of the line after `Some new lines`.

14. **Type** :q! **and press Enter.**

    Your file is not saved. `vi` exits.

Saving and exiting

Exiting and quitting are two different things. Exiting means that you've saved your file first before you stopped working in the editor. Quitting means you just stopped the editor cold without saving your work.

Commands that begin with a colon (:) need you to press Enter for them to work. You also must be in command mode for any colon (:) commands to work. If you're not in command mode, press Esc to change to command mode. If you're not sure what mode you're in, press Esc anyway.

If you want to save your file but still want to continue working on it, type the command `:w!` and press Enter. This command causes `vi` to write the changes you've made to the file to the hard drive. If you want, you can specify a filename to write to by typing `:w! filename` and pressing Enter. This command writes your work to the file called `filename`. Using the `:w!` command also means you can overwrite and destroy the contents of another file if you accidentally specify the wrong filename.

To save and exit, you can type either `:wq` and press Enter or type `ZZ` (that's holding down the Shift key and hitting *z* twice). If you want to quit without saving your file, type `:q!` and press Enter. When you save and exit or quit, you're taken immediately back to your trusty old command prompt (the prompt that ends in either a `>` or a `#`). Table 10-8 has a quick list of these commands.

Table 10-8 Saving and Exiting

Key	*Description*
:w! {filename}	Writes changes to file called filename
:wq	Saves changes to file and quits
Shift+ZZ	Saves changes to file and quits
:q!	Quits without saving changes to file

One drawback of using `vi` extensively is your fingers get used to pressing Esc every so often in order to move around the file. Pressing Esc and then pressing navigational keys like h, j, l, or k can make for interesting changes to your file in another editor like `emacs`, `pico`, or even a word processor like Microsoft Word.

For example, after working in `vi` for several hours, I found the following error:

```
One drawback of using bihhivi so extensivbely, hhhhiely, is
         that your
```

What this tells me is that I was hitting the Esc key and trying to move back to the incorrect text in order to correct it — I assumed I was in `vi`'s command mode. These kinds of keyboard errors also drop interesting tidbits in your file, like finding a `yy` or a `dd` in the middle of a paragraph (something I've been known to do) where something was copied or deleted.

The good thing about all this is the fact that the `vi` commands are so easy to use that they become second nature, even when using other word processors like Micforhhhrosoft Werhhord.

Playing with pico

`pico` is a new addition to the Slackware family. `pico` was born out of a need for a simple text editor because `vi` and `emacs` (`emacs` is described later in this chapter in the section "Taking Time with emacs") are both more complex than the average e-mail sender used or needed.

`pico` only uses insert mode and fakes a command mode by using Ctrl keys for its internal functions. Most of the Ctrl keys are listed at the bottom of your screen.

`pico` has several basic features:

- **Paragraph justification:** Forces text to fit predetermined margins.
- **Block cut-n-paste:** Cuts and pastes specific text from within paragraphs.
- **Spell-checking:** Checks your file for textual errors.
- **Text searching:** Finds words or phrases within your text.

To use `pico`, at your command prompt type **pico {filename}** and press Enter. After `pico` is running, you can start typing your text.

Getting around in pico

As with any editor, moving around in a file is crucial to editing text. To move around in `pico`, you use your arrow keys. The numeric keypad has no effect in `pico`.

To execute any of the functions listed at the bottom of your screen, press the Ctrl key and the key shown on the screen together. For example, if you wish to cut a line of text from the document, you press Ctrl+K.

The carat mark (^) at the bottom of the screen stands for the Ctrl key, so the key commands you see at the bottom all stand for Ctrl-something.

Table 10-9 lists some of the common commands in pico:

Table 10-9 Common Commands in pico

Key	*Description*
Ctrl+V	Scroll forward one page (screenful) of text
Ctrl+Y	Scroll backward one page (screenful) of text
Ctrl+W	Search text for string
Ctrl+J	Justify text to fit margins
Ctrl+T	Spellcheck your document
Ctrl+G	Get help
Ctrl+X	Exit

The justification command (^j) only justifies the paragraph that the cursor is currently on. Remember that justification is forcing text to fit into predetermined margins. Text that doesn't fit into these margins wraps onto the next line. Paragraphs are defined in pico as text in between blank lines. If the cursor is on a blank line and you issue the justification command, the paragraph immediately below the cursor is justified.

To exit and save your work, press Ctrl+X. pico asks you at the bottom of the screen if you want to save your work and prompts you for a yes or no answer with the message `Save modified buffer?`. If you answer yes (by pressing y), pico prompts you for a filename at the bottom of the screen. If you're editing an existing file, the filename fills in for you and you just press Enter. If this is a new file, you must enter a filename to call the file at the prompt at the bottom of the screen. If you answer no by pressing n, however, none of your changes are saved.

Cutting and pasting chunks of text

Cut-n-paste is one of pico's strengths. pico enables you to specify what text to cut and paste by visibly marking the beginning and ending of each block of text. On some monitors, this visible marking is highlighted text. On other monitors, the text may change colors instead. Either way, the text is very clearly marked. Table 10-10 lists the cut-n-paste commands for pico.

Table 10-10 Cut-n-Paste Commands

Key	*Description*
Ctrl+`	Set a mark for blocking of text
Ctrl+K	Cut line of text cursor is currently on
Ctrl+U	Paste (uncut) text at current cursor position

Cut-n-paste is done by first using your arrow keys to move the cursor to the beginning of the text to be marked or blocked. You must then press Ctrl+Shift+6 (the mark command). Then use your arrow keys to move the cursor to the end of the text to be cut. The text to be cut is now highlighted. The text directly underneath the cursor is not part of the mark. Press Ctrl+K (the cut command). The text between the point marked and your cursor is deleted. Using your arrow keys, move your cursor to the spot that you want the text pasted and press Ctrl+U. The text previously cut is now pasted.

For an example of `pico`'s cut-n-paste capabilities, use the following steps:

1. **At your command prompt, type** pico newfile **and press Enter.**

   `pico` runs and brings you to a blank screen with Ctrl key help commands at the bottom of the screen. You are now within the `pico` editor.

2. **Type** This is a test sentence. **and press Enter.**

   The line `This is a test sentence.` appears on screen.

3. **Use your arrow keys to move the cursor over the "T" in** This.

4. **Press Ctrl+^.**

   The message at the bottom of the screen changes to `Mark set.`

5. **Use your arrow keys to move the cursor to the space after the word "test."**

   The words `This is a test` become highlighted.

6. **Press Ctrl+K.**

   The highlighted text disappears.

7. **Use your arrow keys to move the cursor to the space after the word** sentence.

8. **Press Ctrl+U.**

   The previously cut text reappears at the end of `sentence`.

9. **Press Ctrl+X.**

   pico displays the message Save modified buffer? at the bottom of the screen.

10. **Type** n **and press Enter.**

    Your file is not saved. pico exits.

If you have another program that uses Ctrl keys also used in pico, you can get around this problem by pressing Esc twice, followed by the key in question. So, to execute a Ctrl+K command, you press Esc twice and then *k*.

Taking Time with emacs

emacs, which stands for Editor MACroS, is another powerful text editor. But emacs is much more than just an editor — emacs has built-in functions like an e-mail program, a Usenet news program, and a file browser. Like other software from the GNU Project (see the sidebar at the end of this chapter "Understanding the GNU Project"), emacs has its quirks. One of these quirks is that emacs is very slow to load on older computers (anything less than a Pentium 120 is considered older). For example, when I was a computer engineering student back in 1990 (when the Pentium hadn't been invented yet and Microsoft was barely getting Windows 3.1 released), if I typed emacs at a command prompt and pressed Enter, I could walk down the hall, grab a soda, talk on the phone, come back, and the program still wouldn't have finished starting. With the fast computers out now (Pentium III and AMD Athlon, for starters), emacs is much better.

emacs is *content sensitive* to file types, meaning emacs understands the difference between a plain-text file, an HTML (Web) document, and a file containing machine language code. emacs also supports many different languages, including all European languages, Russian, Japanese, Chinese, and Korean.

Running emacs

To run emacs, at your command prompt type **emacs {filename}**. emacs loads its program and takes you into the editor. From within the editor, you're always in insert mode, similar to pico. And, like pico, you can execute commands by pressing Ctrl and a letter, or Esc and a letter. Sometimes commands can be a combination of two or more Ctrl or Esc commands, which makes figuring out emacs a bit tricky.

Use your arrow keys to move around in the text. Some of the emacs commands are listed in Table 10-11. (To list all the emacs commands requires another book.) For more help on emacs, at your command prompt type

man emacs and press Enter to read the manual page. You can also read the complete `emacs` manual by going to `http://www.gnu.org/manual/emacs20.3/html_chapter/emacs_toc.html`.

Table 10-11 Some emacs Commands

Key	*Description*
Ctrl+K	Delete everything from cursor to end of line
Ctrl+G	Interrupt the command you are about to type
Ctrl+K	Cut text
Ctrl+Y	Paste text
Ctrl+HI	Built-in tutorial
Ctrl+X and then Ctrl+S	Save your work
Ctrl+X and then Ctrl+W	Save your work to a different file
Ctrl+X and then Ctrl+C	Exit without saving

The Ctrl+G command is intended to interrupt a multiple Ctrl command sequence. For example, if you start to enter the save and exit command (Ctrl+X and then Ctrl+S), after you press Ctrl+X you decide that you need to change something, so you press Ctrl+G to interrupt the Ctrl+X command.

You can get help on other Control keys for `emacs` by pressing Ctrl+H and then ?.

Managing meta-commands

`emacs` uses something called *meta-commands*. Meta-commands are commands that are intended for more complicated tasks that `emacs` can't do with simple Ctrl keys. Meta-commands are also reserved for more powerful `emacs` commands.

You can execute meta-commands for `emacs` by pressing Esc+X, and then the command and pressing Enter. When you press Esc+X, the bottom of the screen displays an `M-x` prompt (which stands for Meta-x). This is where you will type your meta-commands. To get a list of which meta-commands are available, press Esc+X and then type a character or two and press the space bar to force `emacs` to list all available commands on your screen beginning with the characters that you typed. This forced listing of available commands is similar to the command completion aspect of the `csh` shell (see Chapter 8).

After you type your meta-command, press Enter to make `emacs` run it. Your first meta-command should be the help list, so press Esc+X then type **help** and press Enter.

Inside the meta-commands are the `emacs` information files. To access these information files, press Esc+X and then type **info** and press Enter.

Other emacs functions

`emacs` has a host of other built-in functions, like the ability to read mail, Usenet news, and compile programs. Their use, however, is beyond the scope of this chapter, though you may run into them while reading through the `emacs` tutorial or browsing through the `emacs` information files.

For more help on `emacs`, at your command prompt type **man emacs** and press Enter to read the manual page. You can also read the complete `emacs` manual by going to `http://www.gnu.org/manual/emacs20.3/html_chapter/emacs_toc.html`.

Understanding the GNU Project

I would be remiss if I didn't include something about the GNU Project. The leader, Richard Stallman, has made it his personal crusade to get people to recognize the value of free software (free software being free as in freedom, not free as in beer). The downside to this crusade is that Stallman has managed to alienate people on both sides of the coin — those that value free software, and those that don't.

Founded in 1983, the GNU Project was envisioned as a way of bringing back the cooperative spirit of the computing community, before producing software become a commercial institution. The initial goal, a free operating system, has been acheived. Now the focus is on the rest of the spectrum of software, from applications to desktop publishing to games.

You can get much more information on the GNU Project by looking at the Web site `http://www.gnu.org/`. You may be able to help the GNU Project out. No contribution, regardless of how small or insignificant it may seem, is ever turned away, including offers to write or update documentation (which are always needed).

Chapter 11

Running X Ragged

In This Chapter

- Determining your hardware settings
- Using SuperProbe to find missing information
- Walking through your configuration
- Launching X Windows
- Taking control of your desktop

X Windows is the graphical display system for Slackware. The difference between X Windows and Microsoft Windows, however, is that X Windows is customizable to the point that it can resemble any graphical display or windowing system available, including Macintosh, Windows 95, or Sun Microsystem's OpenLook. You can also create new graphical displays for X Windows. (You can check out an entire Web site devoted to this idea at `http://www.themes.org/`.)

X Windows was once something of a mystery — running it was reserved for only those who had attained guru status and could puzzle out the arcane settings for configuration. With the hardware that has come out in recent years, however, configuring and using X Windows is actually pretty easy.

The X Windows system has two parts: the server, which controls the hardware, like the keyboard, mouse, and monitor; and the client (also called the X application), which controls the windows themselves. After these are in place, you can run add-ons, such as window managers, to customize your screen to your tastes. In this chapter, you will set up and run your own X Windows system.

For X Windows to run, you must install the X series of software programs during the installation process. (Information on the installation process is in Chapter 5. Installation of specific packages is covered in Chapter 7.) I also recommend that you install the `xvg16` package, which is the X server for 16-color VGA video cards. Almost every video card manufactured after 1995 works with the `xvg16` package, and the instructions in this chapter assume that you have this package installed.

If you're not sure of when your video card was made, install the `xvg16` package anyway. The `xvg16` package works with any video card other than monochrome (two color) video cards.

Uncovering Your Hardware

Before you start setting up X Windows, you need to have information about your video card, monitor, keyboard, and mouse. X Windows is very picky about its settings, and having this information ready can save you time and energy. You may already have some of this information if you went through the steps in Chapter 2.

If you don't have this information, you can still set up X Windows, but you need to first run SuperProbe to find your missing information. (See the next section, "Running SuperProbe," for the steps to run SuperProbe.)

You need the following information to set up X Windows:

- The make and model number of your video card, like *ATI All-in-Wonder Pro.*
- The chipset (type of microchips used) of your video card, if such information is available (for instance, if you still have the manual) — if you don't have this information, you can find it using SuperProbe. (There's more info on the SuperProbe program in the "Running SuperProbe" section later in this chapter.)
- The amount of video memory on your video card, like 2MB VRAM (video RAM).
- Whether or not your video card is VGA compatible — most are, but older monochrome (two color) cards may not be (any card made after 1995 should be VGA compatible).
- Your monitor's horizontal and vertical sync ranges — these determine exactly how X Windows displays images on the screen.
- Your monitor's maximum resolution, or the greatest amount of *pixels* (tiny little dots of light) your monitor can display on the screen.
- Whether or not your monitor is a *multiscanning* monitor, or able to handle multiple resolutions.
- If your mouse is a *PS/2* mouse (having a round connector at the end of the wire) or a *serial* mouse (having a rectangular connector).
- If your mouse is two-button or three-button — a two-button mouse can *emulate,* or fake, being a three-button mouse when you press both buttons together.

The resolution is a pair of numbers that tell X Windows how many pixels can be displayed horizontally and vertically. The higher the resolution (for example, 1280x1024), the fewer the number of colors that can be used, and the more video memory is used. A typical X Windows resolution is 800x600, though newer monitors can easily support 1280x1024. Older monitors (pre-1995) may only be able to handle 640x480 resolution.

Most monitors built in the last couple of years have built-in protections to keep them from melting key components when the monitor is used with settings outside of the monitor's standard settings. Don't assume, however, that your monitor has such protections. If you smell burning rubber, metal, or see smoke, turn off your monitor immediately, and then press Ctrl+Alt+ Backspace to turn off X Windows.

Running SuperProbe

If you don't have all the information about your video card and monitor handy, don't worry. You can find out the missing pieces by using a program included with X Windows called SuperProbe.

As the name implies, SuperProbe gets down to the smallest level it can to find out information about your hardware — this is called probing. SuperProbe can also detect more than just the hardware that X Windows needs to run.

Running SuperProbe can freeze your system, and the only way to unfreeze is to reboot. The freezing is due to SuperProbe's checking for information from your hardware and the hardware returning unexpected information or simply causing SuperProbe to endlessly ask for the same information over and over again (this is called an *endless loop*). SuperProbe causing your system to freeze, however, happens very seldom (and usually on extremely old hardware), so running SuperProbe is pretty safe.

To run SuperProbe, follow these steps:

1. **Log in as** root.
2. **At your command prompt (#), type** SuperProbe **and press Enter.**

   If you get an error message saying `SuperProbe: Command not found`, type **/usr/X11R6/bin/SuperProbe** and press Enter. (The error message is caused by the system not recognizing where the SuperProbe program is in the file system.)

SuperProbe starts to run. A screenful of information appears, mostly pertaining to its copyright and the e-mail address to which error reports are sent. After a couple of seconds, the screen goes blank, and then returns (if everything's okay) with information that looks similar to Figure 11-1 (the exact information depends on the type of video card that you have). If the screen doesn't return, SuperProbe has frozen your system and you must reboot.

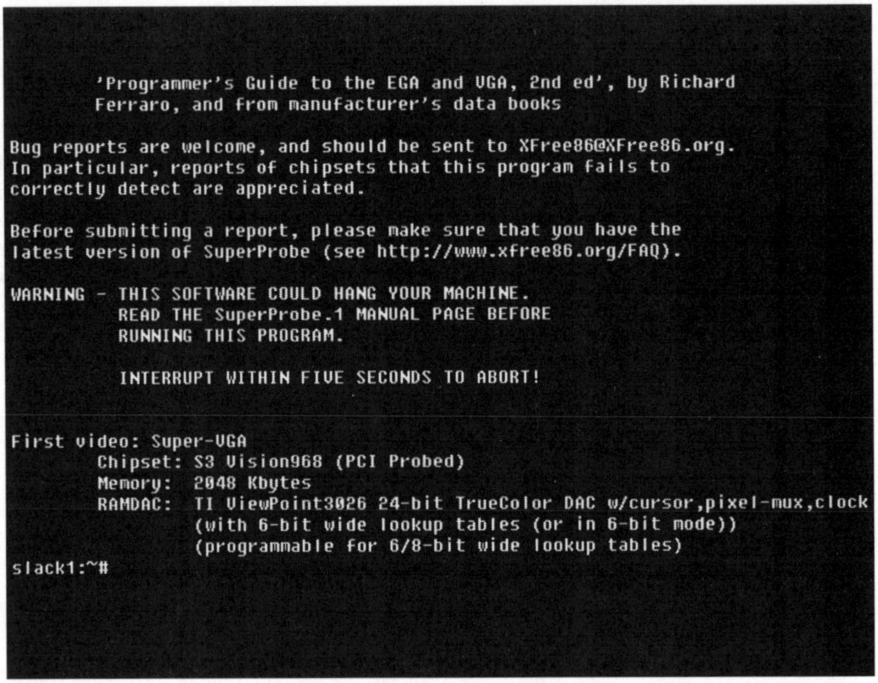

```
        'Programmer's Guide to the EGA and VGA, 2nd ed', by Richard
        Ferraro, and from manufacturer's data books

Bug reports are welcome, and should be sent to XFree86@XFree86.org.
In particular, reports of chipsets that this program fails to
correctly detect are appreciated.

Before submitting a report, please make sure that you have the
latest version of SuperProbe (see http://www.xfree86.org/FAQ).

WARNING - THIS SOFTWARE COULD HANG YOUR MACHINE.
          READ THE SuperProbe.1 MANUAL PAGE BEFORE
          RUNNING THIS PROGRAM.

          INTERRUPT WITHIN FIVE SECONDS TO ABORT!

First video: Super-VGA
        Chipset: S3 Vision968 (PCI Probed)
        Memory:  2048 Kbytes
        RAMDAC:  TI ViewPoint3026 24-bit TrueColor DAC w/cursor,pixel-mux,clock
                 (with 6-bit wide lookup tables (or in 6-bit mode))
                 (programmable for 6/8-bit wide lookup tables)
slack1:~#
```

Figure 11-1: Resulting information from running SuperProbe.

Write down the information that you see, starting from "First video." This is most likely the information that you're missing. If you're missing any other information, chances are that the information is the horizontal and vertical refresh rates, something that SuperProbe can't detect.

Walking Through Your Configuration

After you have the necessary information about your hardware, you're ready to set up X Windows. (If you don't have this information or have skipped ahead, you need to back up and read the section at the beginning of this chapter, titled "Uncovering Your Hardware.") Setting up X Windows is a long process and you may make mistakes (like mistyping a letter here or there). Take your time.

You can configure X Windows two ways: the `XF86Setup` program and the `xf86config` program. `XF86Setup` is a graphical program and is the easier program to use. If, however, you have a video card that isn't VGA compatible or have a fixed-frequency monitor, which cannot display high frequencies or resolutions, you must use `xf86config` instead. `xf86config` is a text-based program.

Running away with XF86Setup

`XF86Setup` is a graphical utility that aids in setting up X Windows. `XF86Setup` requires that you first install the `xvg16` package and the `xset` package on the system. (See Chapter 7 for information on installing packages.) If you don't want to install either package due to disk space concerns, skip to the next section in this chapter titled "Walking around with xf86config." `XF86Setup` also uses the mouse to move through the configuration, though you can use the keyboard if you prefer.

To configure `XF86Setup`, follow these steps:

1. **Log in as** root.
2. **At your command prompt (#), type** XF86Setup **and press Enter.**

   `XF86Setup` runs. A message appears asking if you want to use the existing `XF86Config` file to set default values for various settings. If you have already set up some values in `/etc/XF86Config` (like if you're rerunning this to redo your configuration), use your arrow keys to highlight yes, and then press Enter.
3. **Use your arrow keys to highlight** No **and press Enter.**

   A message appears saying that `XF86Setup` is about to switch to graphics mode. A single OK button is at the bottom of the screen, but your mouse will not work yet so you can't click on it.
4. **Press Enter.**

   The screen blinks for a moment, and then a notice appears saying "Loading, please wait . . ." The introduction for `XF86Setup` then appears, as shown in Figure 11-2.

   Six buttons run across the top of your screen. Each button corresponds to a category of configuration. The buttons are: Mouse, Keyboard, Card, Monitor, Modeselection, and Other.

   At the bottom of your screen are three buttons: Abort, Done, and Help. Abort exits `XF86Setup` without saving any changes that have been made. You select Done when you finish all the various categories' configurations. Help gives you online help regarding the current screen.

   If you don't get a graphics screen similar to Figure 11-2 within one minute (older computers may need a couple of minutes), press Ctrl+Alt+Backspace to exit XF86Setup. You now have to use `xf86config` because XF86Setup is not responding. Skip to the next section in this chapter, titled "Walking around with xf86config."
5. **Press Enter.**

   A dialog box pops up that describes the steps necessary to configure your mouse. Read this carefully.

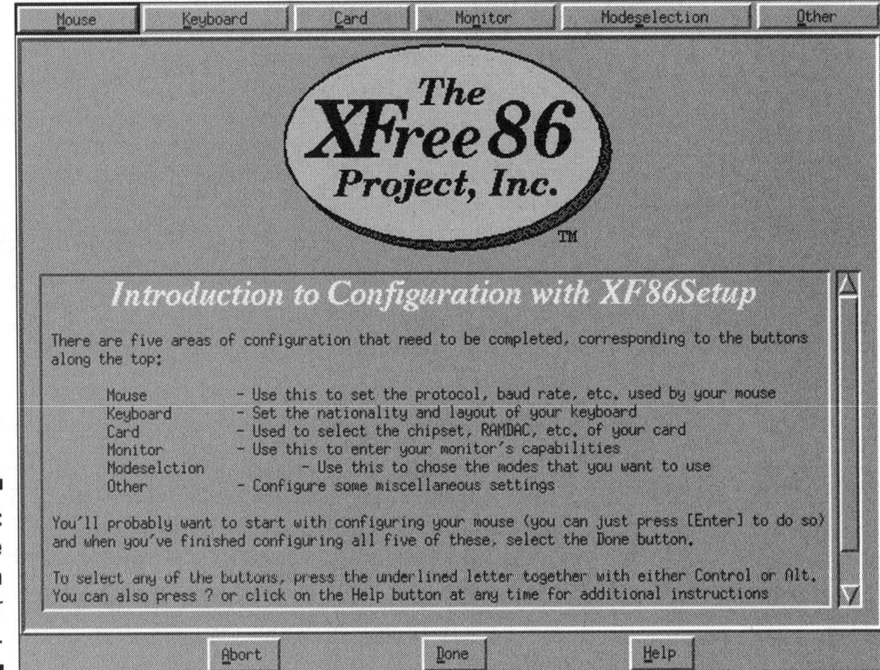

Figure 11-2: The Introduction screen for XF86Setup.

6. **Press Enter.**

   The Mouse configuration screen appears. `XF86Setup` highlights the type of mouse that it thinks you're using with a blue background, as shown in Figure 11-3.

   Move your mouse around the screen. If your mouse pointer responds, test the buttons by moving the mouse pointer over the picture of the mouse on the right side of the screen (the three small boxes on top of the larger box) and clicking your buttons. If the buttons respond (the buttons on the picture of the mouse will change color), you can safely exit this configuration without having to do anything. You can skip to Step 14. If your mouse doesn't respond, continue with Step 7.

7. **Press *p* until your mouse protocol (the manufacturer of your mouse or generic mouse type) is highlighted.**

   Your mouse protocol is now highlighted.

8. **Press *a* to apply the setting.**

   Nothing happens on the screen.

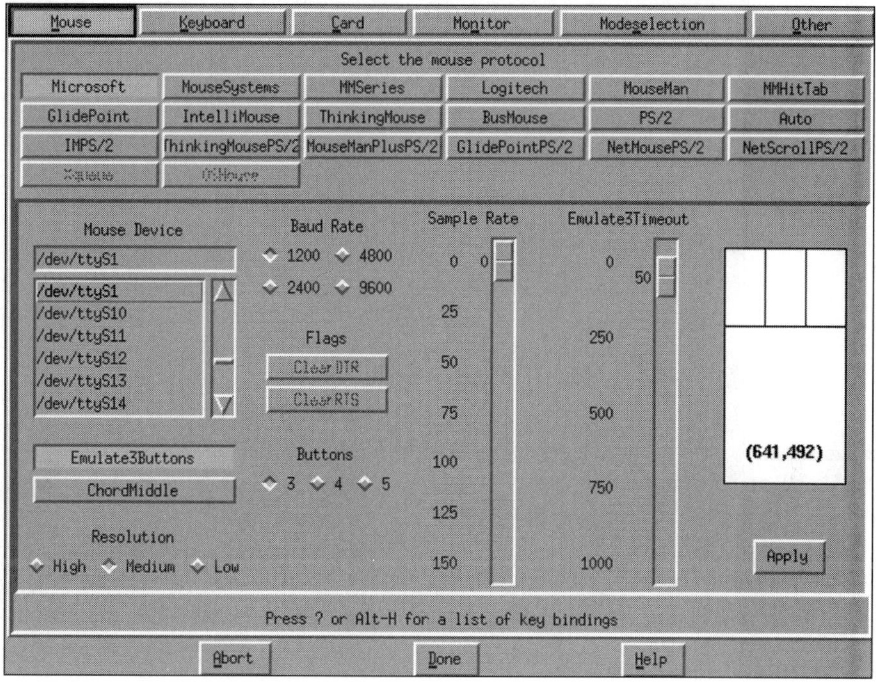

Figure 11-3: The Mouse configuration screen for XF86Setup.

9. **Press *n*.**

   Nothing happens on the screen.

10. **Press Tab.**

    The Mouse Device list is highlighted.

11. **Use your arrow keys to highlight your mouse device and press Enter.**

    For example, if your mouse is a PS/2 mouse, use your arrow keys to highlight `/dev/psaux` and press Enter.

12. **Press *a* to apply the setting.**

    Now move your mouse. If it responds correctly (meaning, it doesn't zoom off to one side of the screen), continue with Step 13. Otherwise, repeat Steps 7 through 12 until your mouse pointer responds correctly.

13. **If your mouse only has two buttons, click Emulate3Buttons.**

    If you're using a Logitech mouse, click ChordMiddle instead.

14. **Click the Keyboard button at the top of the screen.**

    The Keyboard configuration screen appears, as shown in Figure 11-4.

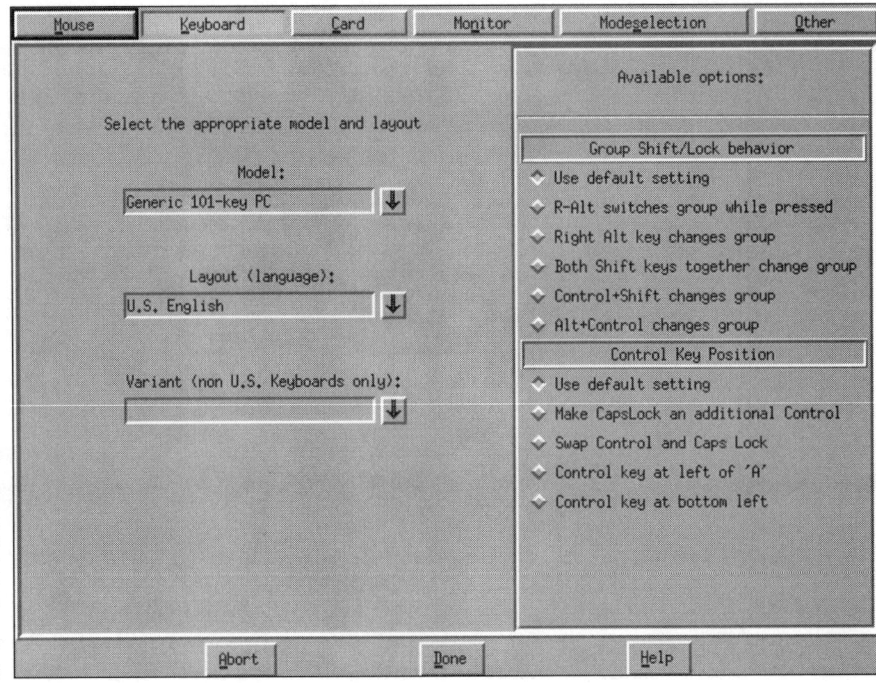

Figure 11-4: The Keyboard configuration screen for XF86Setup.

If the Model and Layout of your keyboard are already correct (they are unless you're using a non-English keyboard), skip to Step 19.

15. **Click the Model text box down-arrow.**

    A pull-down menu appears.

16. **Select the model of your keyboard from the pull-down menu.**

    The pull-down menu disappears and the model that you selected appears in the Model text box.

17. **Click the Layout (language) text box down-arrow.**

    A pull-down menu appears.

18. **Select the layout of your keyboard from the pull-down menu.**

    The pull-down menu disappears and the model that you selected appears in the Layout (language) text box.

19. **Click the Card button at the top of the screen.**

    The Video Card configuration screen appears, as shown in Figure 11-5.

    This list is long, so use the scrollbar on the right to navigate up and down the list.

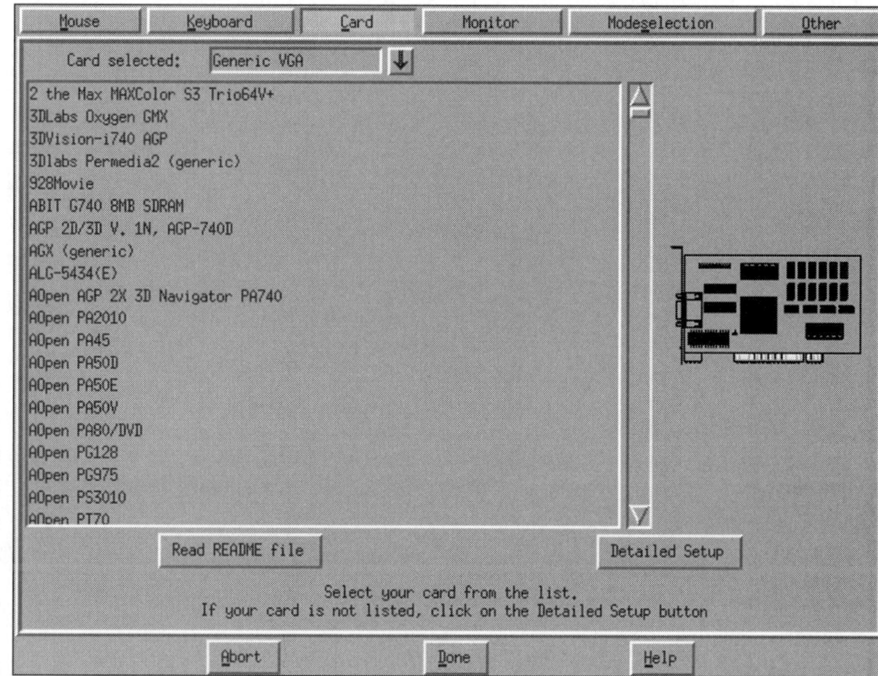

Figure 11-5: The Video Card configuration screen for XF86Setup.

20. **Select your card from the scroll-box list.**

    If you don't know what your card is, or have forgotten, press Ctrl+Alt+Backspace and run SuperProbe to find out. (See the section in this chapter, titled "Running SuperProbe," for more help.)

21. **Click the Monitor button at the top of the screen.**

    The Monitor configuration screen appears, as shown in Figure 11-6.

    You must enter settings for your monitor, specifically the *vertical refresh rate*, which is the rate at which the whole screen is redrawn, and the *horizontal sync rate*, which is the rate at which lines of dots are displayed.

    The two ranges (horizontal and vertical) are documented in your monitor's manual. If you don't have this manual available, you can check the monitor database file (press Ctrl+Alt+Backspace, and then at your command prompt, type **more /usr/X11R6/lib/X11/doc/Monitors** and press Enter) to see if your monitor is listed there. You can also go to `http://www.griffintechnology.com/monitor.html` and check this database.

22. **Click once in the Horizontal text box.**

    A black line outlines the text box, and the cursor begins blinking inside the text box.

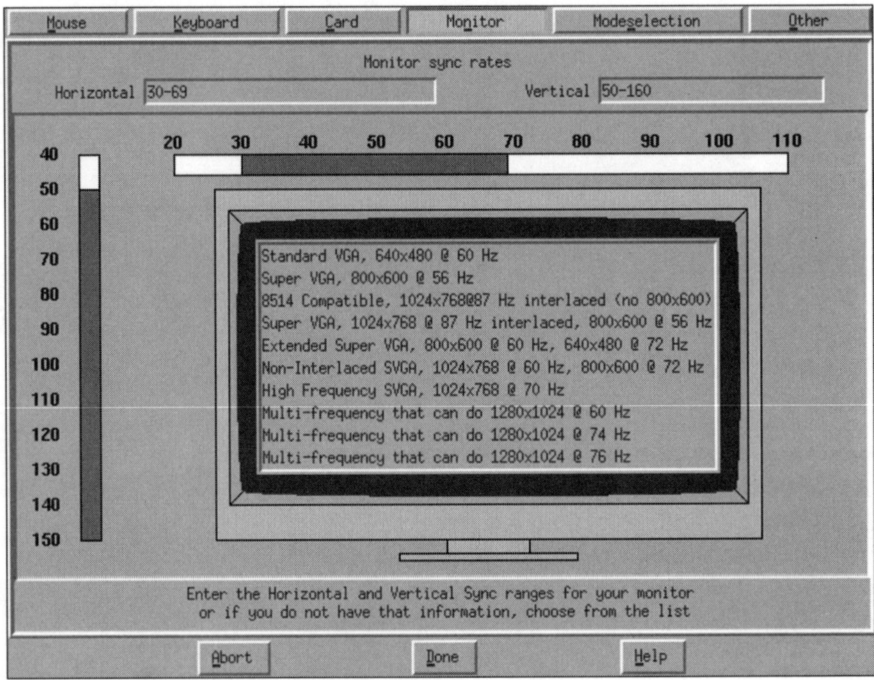

Figure 11-6: The Monitor configuration screen for XF86Setup.

23. **Delete the old number listed.**

    Use your backspace key to delete the number.

24. **Type the range of your horizontal sync rate (for example, 30-64) and press Enter.**

    The horizontal bar changes from white to red for the range you just entered.

25. **Click once in the Vertical text box.**

    A black line outlines the text box, and the cursor begins blinking inside the text box.

26. **Delete the old number listed.**

    Use your backspace key to delete the number.

27. **Type the range of your vertical sync rate (for example, 50-160) and press Enter.**

    The vertical bar changes from white to red for the range you just entered.

28. **Click the Modeselection button at the top of the screen.**

    The Modeselect configuration screen appears, as shown in Figure 11-7.

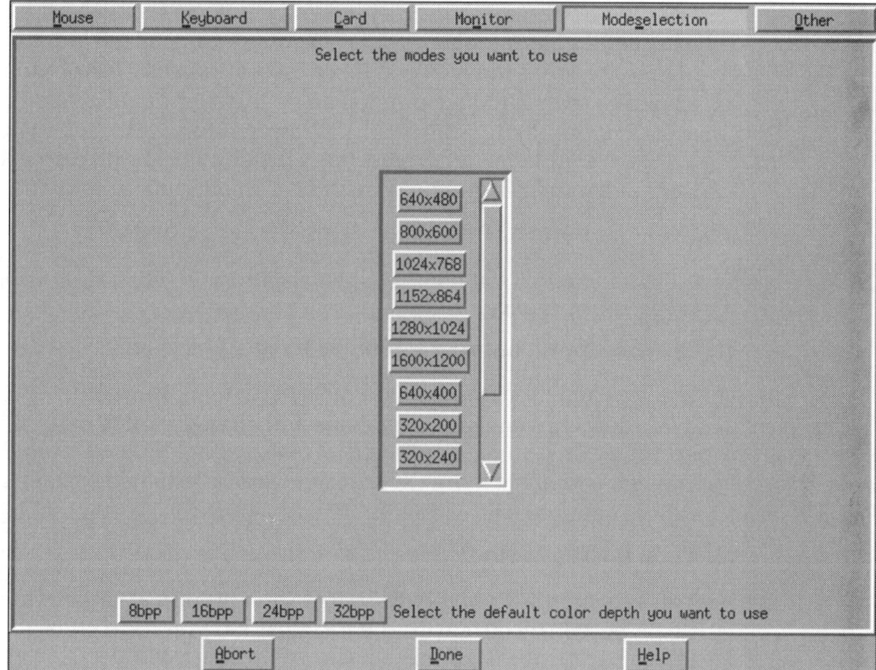

Figure 11-7: The Modeselect configuration screen for XF86Setup.

You can choose multiple resolutions (size of your screen) to be used.

29. **Click the buttons of the resolution(s) you want to use.**

    When you click a resolution button, it becomes highlighted. Some good choices to start out with are 640x480 and 800x600 (but probably not together unless your video card has a lot of memory). 640 x 480 is the easiest resolution with which to read text and see icons, but takes up a lot of room on your desktop. 800 x 600 is a little smaller, but you can get more icons on the screen, and thus more windows. The higher the resolution, the smaller everything becomes on the screen. Choose a resolution that won't strain your eyes.

Your video card and monitor may not be able to support all the depth and mode combinations that can be selected. The X server automatically rejects any unsupported combinations when it starts. Note that if you select multiple modes, you get a *virtual screen* as large as the largest of the usable modes. A virtual screen is a screen that's larger than the monitor, so you have areas on the virtual screen that are outside the border of the monitor.

Near the bottom of the screen are four buttons that determine the number of colors (color depth) available. You can select only one. A higher color depth gives you more colors available for programs (which also uses more RAM). However, many programs can't handle too many colors (more than 16-bit depth). A lower color depth gives you less colors available for programs, but a lower color depth also uses less RAM and more programs can handle a smaller number of colors.

30. **Click the button of the color depth you want to use.**

    Your selection is highlighted. If you're just starting out, the 8bpp button is the safest choice.

31. **Click the Done button at the bottom of the screen.**

    A notice appears asking if you believe that you have finished configuring X Windows. If you want to go back and change something, click the button at the top of the screen corresponding to the section you wish to change; do *not* click the OK button. If you're satisfied with your configuration, continue with Step 32.

32. **Click the OK button.**

    The screen is switched back to text (non-graphical) mode for a moment. The X server restarts with the settings that you have chosen. Three buttons and a text box appear, as shown in Figure 11-8.

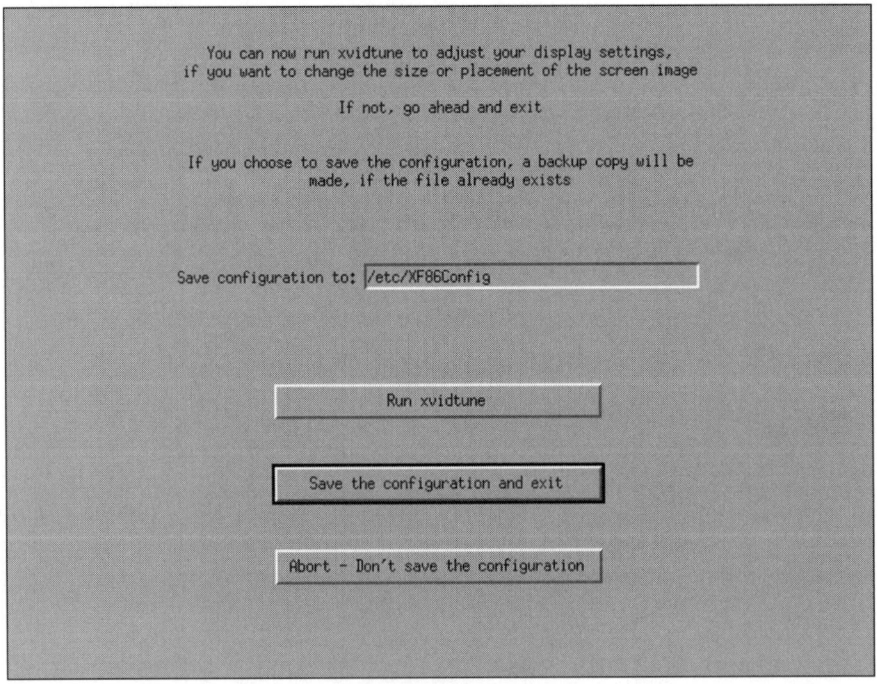

You can now run xvidtune to adjust your display settings,
if you want to change the size or placement of the screen image

If not, go ahead and exit

If you choose to save the configuration, a backup copy will be
made, if the file already exists

Save configuration to: /etc/XF86Config

Run xvidtune

Save the configuration and exit

Abort - Don't save the configuration

Figure 11-8: Time to save your settings.

The text box is the location to save the `XF86Config` configuration file. The first button runs `xvidtune`, which fine-tunes your monitor settings. See the manual page on `xvidtune` for more information (at your command prompt, type **man xvidtune**). The second button saves your settings, and the third button aborts without saving anything.

33. **Click the Save the Configuration and Exit button.**

    A small text message appears saying "Configuration complete."

34. **Click OK.**

    `XF86Setup` exits.

Your setup of X Windows by using `XF86Setup` is complete.

Walking around with xf86config

Another method of configuring X Windows is to use the `xf86config` program, which is the text-only process of creating your X Windows configuration file. X Windows can't run without this file, and if this file has incorrect information, X Windows may display strangely — like only displaying its screen on one half of the monitor or having all the characters so tiny that you need a magnifying glass to read them. In a worst-case scenario, incorrect information in this configuration file can cause your monitor to burn up. The reason for the `xf86config` program is so you can set up your configuration file correctly the first time around.

You can press Ctrl+C at any time to stop the program, if you need to stop and gather more information about your hardware. Each time you press Ctrl+C, however, you must start again at Step 2.

To run `xf86config`, follow these steps:

1. **Log in as** root **(see Chapter 6 for more info on the super user account).**

   You're now at the command prompt (the # prompt).

2. **Type** xf86config **and press Enter.**

   `xf86config` runs. The program tells you that it can help you set up an `XF86Config` file, which is the X Windows configuration file, or that you can do the job yourself with an editor.

3. **Press Enter.**

   `xf86config` asks you to specify the type of mouse that you have. A list of common mouse types appears on your screen, as shown in Figure 11-9.

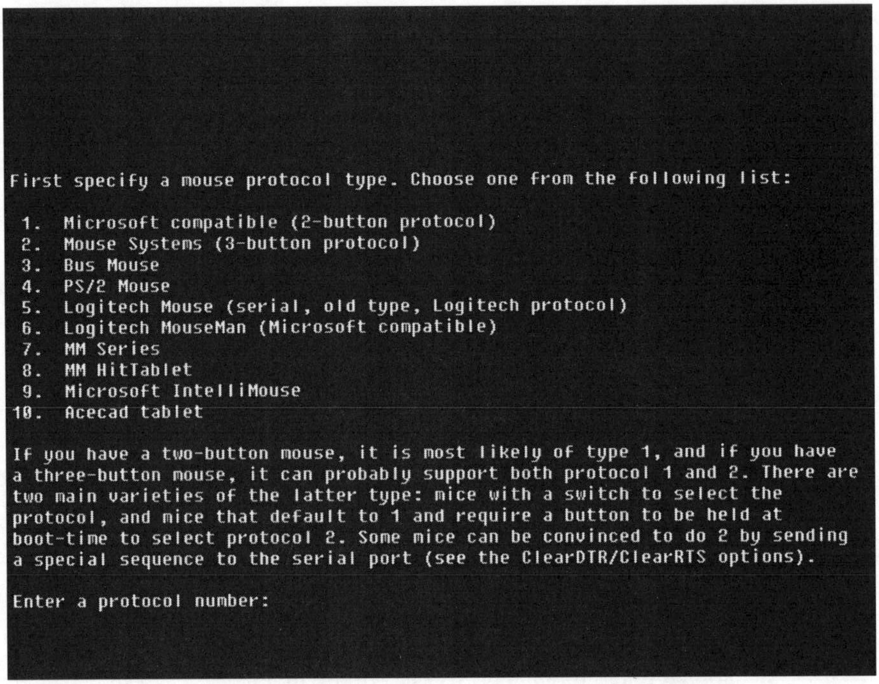

```
First specify a mouse protocol type. Choose one from the following list:

 1.  Microsoft compatible (2-button protocol)
 2.  Mouse Systems (3-button protocol)
 3.  Bus Mouse
 4.  PS/2 Mouse
 5.  Logitech Mouse (serial, old type, Logitech protocol)
 6.  Logitech MouseMan (Microsoft compatible)
 7.  MM Series
 8.  MM HitTablet
 9.  Microsoft IntelliMouse
10.  Acecad tablet

If you have a two-button mouse, it is most likely of type 1, and if you have
a three-button mouse, it can probably support both protocol 1 and 2. There are
two main varieties of the latter type: mice with a switch to select the
protocol, and mice that default to 1 and require a button to be held at
boot-time to select protocol 2. Some mice can be convinced to do 2 by sending
a special sequence to the serial port (see the ClearDTR/ClearRTS options).

Enter a protocol number:
```

Figure 11-9: Determining your mouse type.

4. **At the Enter Protocol Number prompt, type in the number corresponding to your mouse protocol and press Enter.**

   `xf86config` asks you if you wish to enable a protocol called ChordMiddle or Emulate3Buttons. Both of these protocols enable a two-button mouse to *emulate* (fake) being a 3-button mouse.

5. **At the Enable Emulate3Buttons prompt, press *y* and then press Enter.**

   If you already have a 3-button mouse, press *n* instead.

   `xf86config` asks you what the device name is for your mouse (for example, `/dev/tty00`). `/dev/mouse` is the device you want to use, and `xf86config` uses it as the default if you don't enter anything.

6. **Press Enter.**

   `xf86config` asks if you want to change your keyboard layout.

7. **At the Change Keyboard Layout prompt at the bottom of your screen, press *n* and then press Enter.**

   `xf86config` tells you that if you set your Alt keys to be Meta keys, you can enter in language-specific characters, such as ö, è, and ç using a combination of your Alt key and another key. `xf86config` then asks if you want it to set the Alt keys in such a way.

8. **At the Set Alt Keys prompt at the bottom of your screen, press *n* and then press Enter.**

   If you want to have the ability to use characters from other languages, type *y* instead.

   `xf86config` now tells you that you're about to enter settings for your monitor, specifically the *vertical refresh rate*, which is the rate at which the whole screen is redrawn, and the *horizontal sync rate*, which is the rate at which lines of dots are displayed.

   The two ranges (horizontal and vertical) are documented in your monitor's manual. If you don't have this manual available, you can check the monitor database file (press Ctrl+Alt+Backspace, and then at your command prompt, type **more /usr/X11R6/lib/X11/doc/Monitors** and press Enter) to see if your monitor is listed there. You can also go to `http://www.griffintechnology.com/monitor.html` and check their database.

9. **Press Enter.**

   A list of common horizontal sync rates for monitors appears on your screen, as shown in Figure 11-10.

```
You must indicate the horizontal sync range of your monitor. You can either
select one of the predefined ranges below that correspond to industry-
standard monitor types, or give a specific range.

It is VERY IMPORTANT that you do not specify a monitor type with a horizontal
sync range that is beyond the capabilities of your monitor. If in doubt,
choose a conservative setting.

    hsync in kHz; monitor type with characteristic modes
 1  31.5; Standard VGA, 640x480 @ 60 Hz
 2  31.5 - 35.1; Super VGA, 800x600 @ 56 Hz
 3  31.5, 35.5; 8514 Compatible, 1024x768 @ 87 Hz interlaced (no 800x600)
 4  31.5, 35.15, 35.5; Super VGA, 1024x768 @ 87 Hz interlaced, 800x600 @ 56 Hz
 5  31.5 - 37.9; Extended Super VGA, 800x600 @ 60 Hz, 640x480 @ 72 Hz
 6  31.5 - 48.5; Non-Interlaced SVGA, 1024x768 @ 60 Hz, 800x600 @ 72 Hz
 7  31.5 - 57.0; High Frequency SVGA, 1024x768 @ 70 Hz
 8  31.5 - 64.3; Monitor that can do 1280x1024 @ 60 Hz
 9  31.5 - 82.0; Monitor that can do 1280x1024 @ 76 Hz
10  31.5 - 95.0; Monitor that can do 1280x1024 @ 85 Hz
11  Enter your own horizontal sync range

Enter your choice (1-11):
```

Figure 11-10: Listing common horizontal sync rates for monitors.

If your horizontal sync rate doesn't match any of the listed choices, type **11** in Step 10 and press Enter. The screen prompts you to type in the range of your horizontal sync rate, as shown in Figure 11-11. Otherwise, continue with Step 10.

10. **At the Enter Your Choice (1-11) prompt, type the number corresponding to your horizontal sync rate and press Enter.**

    A list of common vertical refresh rates for monitors appears on your screen, as shown in Figure 11-12.

    If your vertical refresh rate doesn't match any of the listed choices, enter *5* in Step 11 and press Enter. The screen again prompts you to type in the range, as shown in Figure 11-13. Otherwise, continue with Step 11.

11. **At the Enter Your Choice prompt, type the number corresponding to your vertical refresh rate and press Enter.**

    `xf86config` asks you to give this definition of horizontal and vertical ranges a name for easier reference, should you choose to go back and edit the configuration file later.

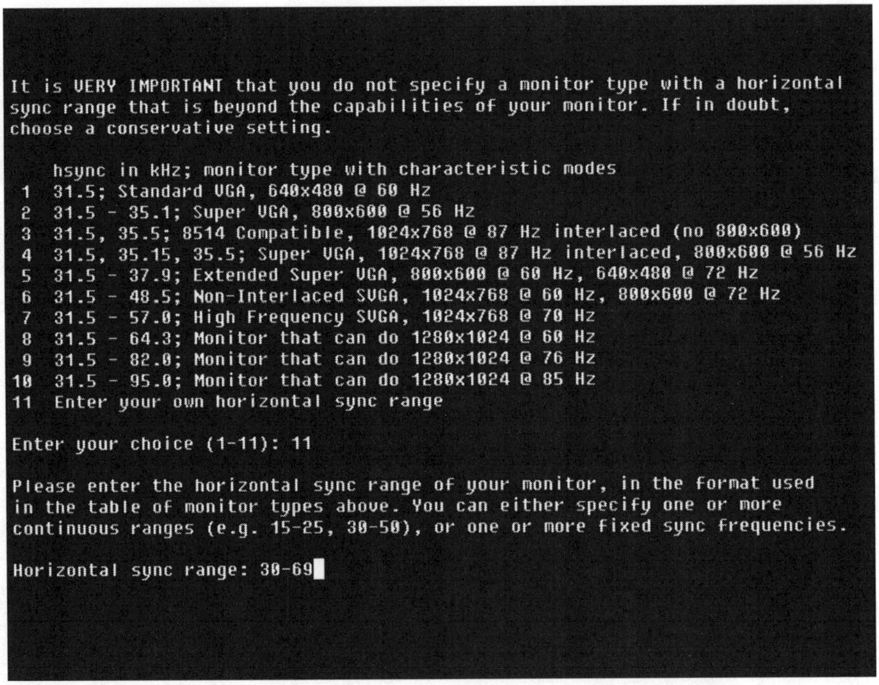

```
It is VERY IMPORTANT that you do not specify a monitor type with a horizontal
sync range that is beyond the capabilities of your monitor. If in doubt,
choose a conservative setting.

    hsync in kHz; monitor type with characteristic modes
 1  31.5; Standard VGA, 640x480 @ 60 Hz
 2  31.5 - 35.1; Super VGA, 800x600 @ 56 Hz
 3  31.5, 35.5; 8514 Compatible, 1024x768 @ 87 Hz interlaced (no 800x600)
 4  31.5, 35.15, 35.5; Super VGA, 1024x768 @ 87 Hz interlaced, 800x600 @ 56 Hz
 5  31.5 - 37.9; Extended Super VGA, 800x600 @ 60 Hz, 640x480 @ 72 Hz
 6  31.5 - 48.5; Non-Interlaced SVGA, 1024x768 @ 60 Hz, 800x600 @ 72 Hz
 7  31.5 - 57.0; High Frequency SVGA, 1024x768 @ 70 Hz
 8  31.5 - 64.3; Monitor that can do 1280x1024 @ 60 Hz
 9  31.5 - 82.0; Monitor that can do 1280x1024 @ 76 Hz
10  31.5 - 95.0; Monitor that can do 1280x1024 @ 85 Hz
11  Enter your own horizontal sync range

Enter your choice (1-11): 11

Please enter the horizontal sync range of your monitor, in the format used
in the table of monitor types above. You can either specify one or more
continuous ranges (e.g. 15-25, 30-50), or one or more fixed sync frequencies.

Horizontal sync range: 30-69
```

Figure 11-11: Entering a custom horizontal sync rate.

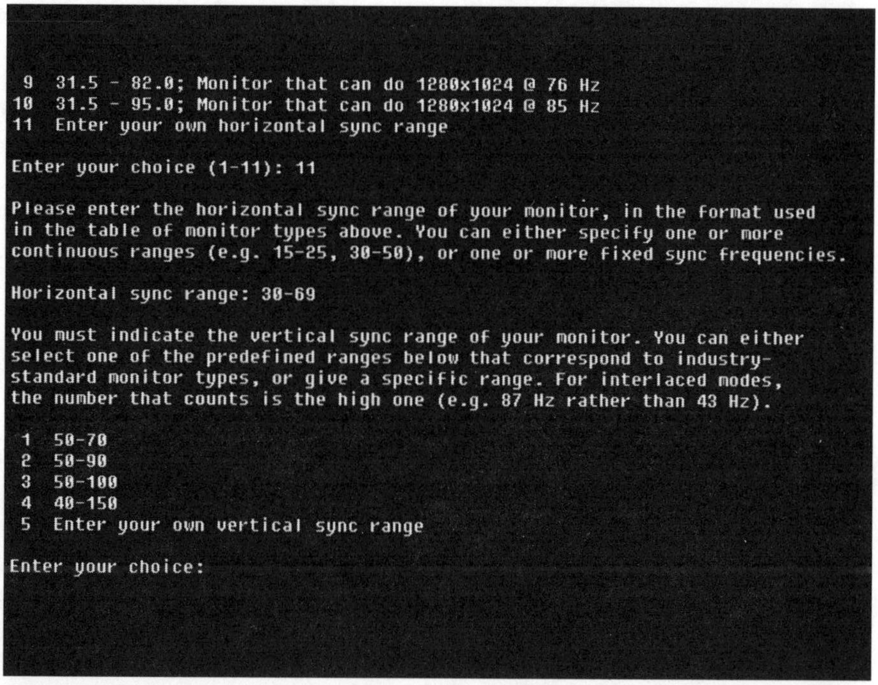

```
 9  31.5 - 82.0; Monitor that can do 1280x1024 @ 76 Hz
10  31.5 - 95.0; Monitor that can do 1280x1024 @ 85 Hz
11  Enter your own horizontal sync range

Enter your choice (1-11): 11

Please enter the horizontal sync range of your monitor, in the format used
in the table of monitor types above. You can either specify one or more
continuous ranges (e.g. 15-25, 30-50), or one or more fixed sync frequencies.

Horizontal sync range: 30-69

You must indicate the vertical sync range of your monitor. You can either
select one of the predefined ranges below that correspond to industry-
standard monitor types, or give a specific range. For interlaced modes,
the number that counts is the high one (e.g. 87 Hz rather than 43 Hz).

 1  50-70
 2  50-90
 3  50-100
 4  40-150
 5  Enter your own vertical sync range

Enter your choice:
```

Figure 11-12: Listing common vertical refresh rates for monitors.

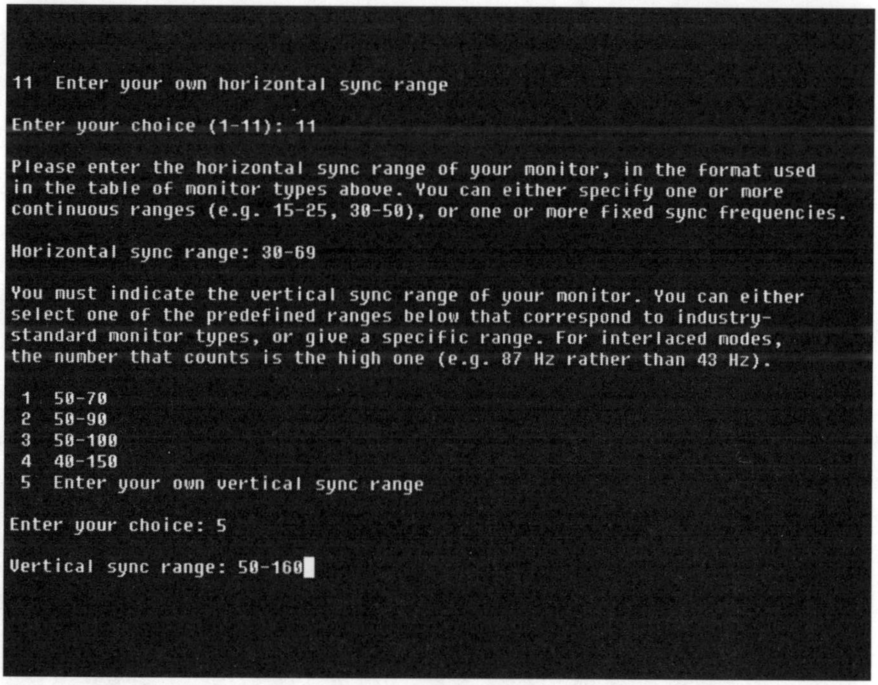

```
11  Enter your own horizontal sync range

Enter your choice (1-11): 11

Please enter the horizontal sync range of your monitor, in the format used
in the table of monitor types above. You can either specify one or more
continuous ranges (e.g. 15-25, 30-50), or one or more fixed sync frequencies.

Horizontal sync range: 30-69

You must indicate the vertical sync range of your monitor. You can either
select one of the predefined ranges below that correspond to industry-
standard monitor types, or give a specific range. For interlaced modes,
the number that counts is the high one (e.g. 87 Hz rather than 43 Hz).

 1  50-70
 2  50-90
 3  50-100
 4  40-150
 5  Enter your own vertical sync range

Enter your choice: 5

Vertical sync range: 50-160
```

Figure 11-13: Entering a custom vertical sync rate.

12. **At the Monitor Definition prompt at the bottom of the screen, type** def1 **and press Enter.**

    `xf86config` asks you to enter the manufacturer name of your monitor. This is something like Philips, ViewSonic, or maybe HP, depending on which company made your monitor.

13. **At the Monitor Manufacturer prompt at the bottom of your screen, type the manufacturer name of your monitor and press Enter.**

    `xf86config` asks you to enter the model number of your monitor. This is something like 17A, G773, or A4331A, depending on the exact model number.

14. **At the Model Number prompt at the bottom of the screen, type the model number of your monitor and press Enter.**

    `xf86config` asks if you want to view the database of cards. Picking your card from the list can save a little time.

    Don't pick a card that looks similar to your card. In other words, if you have a RadVid 128 card, don't pick RadVid 128-A — the two cards are different (unless there is a listing for RadVid 128 series).

15. **At the Yes or No prompt at the bottom of your screen, press *y* and then press Enter.**

    A list of video cards arranged in alphabetical order appears, as shown in Figure 11-14.

```
 0  2 the Max MAXColor S3 Trio64V+                 S3 Trio64V+
 1  3DLabs Oxygen GMX                              PERMEDIA 2
 2  3DVision-i740 AGP                              Intel 740
 3  3Dlabs Permedia2 (generic)                     PERMEDIA 2
 4  928Movie                                       S3 928
 5  ABIT G740 8MB SDRAM                            Intel 740
 6  AGP 2D/3D V. 1N, AGP-740D                      Intel 740
 7  AGX (generic)                                  AGX-014/15/16
 8  ALG-5434(E)                                    CL-GD5434
 9  AOpen AGP 2X 3D Navigator PA740                Intel 740
10  AOpen PA2010                                   Voodoo Banshee
11  AOpen PA45                                     SiS6326
12  AOpen PA50D                                    SiS6326
13  AOpen PA50E                                    SiS6326
14  AOpen PA50V                                    SiS6326
15  AOpen PA80/DVD                                 SiS6326
16  AOpen PG128                                    S3 Trio3D
17  AOpen PG975                                    3dimage975

Enter a number to choose the corresponding card definition.
Press enter for the next page, q to continue configuration.
```

Figure 11-14: The beginning of the video card database.

In the left column of the listing are numbers that correspond to each entry. The far-right column is the video chipset that corresponds to each entry.

If you don't see your card listed, press Enter to get the next page (screenful) of card listings. If you don't see your card listed after viewing the entire list, press *q* and then press Enter to continue. Skip to Step 17.

16. **Type the number corresponding to your video card and press Enter.**

    Some information about your selected card appears, as shown in Figure 11-15.

    Notice that the type of X server is listed (in Figure 11-15, the server is XF86_S3). Make a note of this by writing it down somewhere, or keeping it fresh in your mind. Also, if the Clockchip line is listed (some cards don't have this entry in the database), write it down as well.

You can go back and install the correct server package that corresponds to this listing if the listing is different than what you have already installed (which is probably either `xvg16`, the XF86_VG16 server, or `xsvga`, which is the XF86_SVGA server). See Chapter 7 for help on installing packages.

```
243  Diamond Stealth 64 Video VRAM (TI RAMDAC)          S3 968
244  Diamond Stealth II S220                            Verite 2100
245  Diamond Stealth II/G460 AGP                        Intel 740
246  Diamond Stealth Pro                                S3 928
247  Diamond Stealth VRAM                               S3 911/924
248  Diamond Stealth Video 2500                         Alliance AT24
249  Diamond Stealth Video DRAM                         S3 868
250  Diamond Stealth64 Graphics 2001 series             ARK2000PV
251  Diamond Stealth64 Graphics 2xx0 series (864 + SDAC)S3 864

Enter a number to choose the corresponding card definition.
Press enter for the next page, q to continue configuration.

247

Your selected card definition:

Identifier: Diamond Stealth VRAM
Chipset:    S3 911/924
Server:     XF86_S3
Clockchip:  icd2061a
Do NOT probe clocks or use any Clocks line.

Press enter to continue, or ctrl-c to abort.
```

Figure 11-15: Information about your selected card.

In some cases, like in Figure 11-15, the following warning message appears on your screen:

```
Do NOT probe clocks or use any Clocks line.
```

If you get this warning message, make yourself a reminder because in Step 25, you're asked what Clockchip to use.

17. **Press Enter.**

    `xf86config` asks you which server you wish to run. From your information in Step 16, the correct server appears as the fifth choice listed, as shown in Figure 11-16.

    If you skipped Step 16, you only have the first four options listed in Figure 11-16.

18. **At the prompt at the bottom of the screen, which asks you which screen type you intend to run by default, enter *5* and then press Enter.**

    If you skipped Step 16, change the 5 to 2.

    `xf86config` asks if you want the computer to create a link between the server program and the directory where all the programs reside.

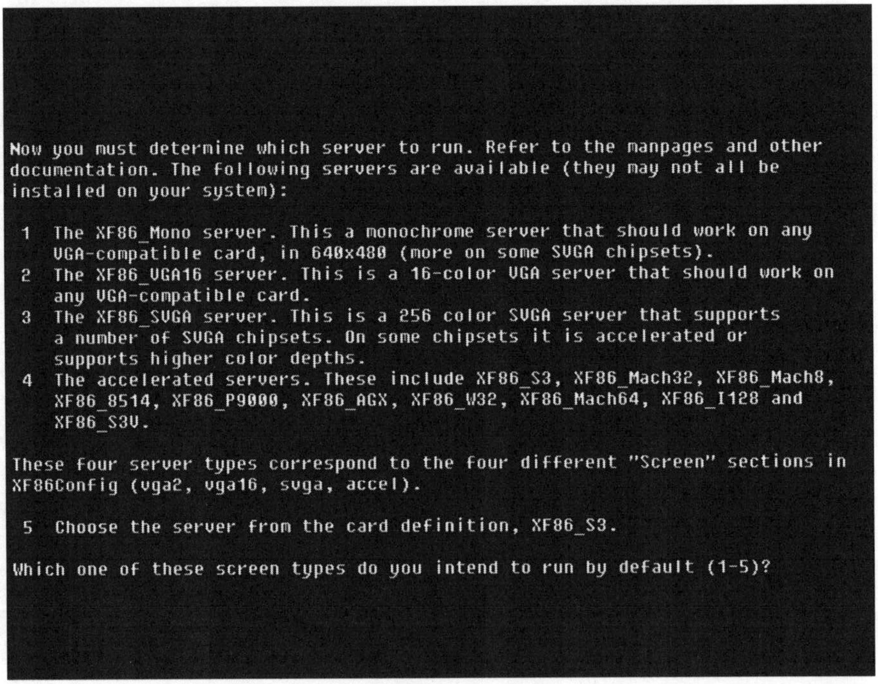

```
Now you must determine which server to run. Refer to the manpages and other
documentation. The following servers are available (they may not all be
installed on your system):

 1  The XF86_Mono server. This a monochrome server that should work on any
    VGA-compatible card, in 640x480 (more on some SVGA chipsets).
 2  The XF86_VGA16 server. This is a 16-color VGA server that should work on
    any VGA-compatible card.
 3  The XF86_SVGA server. This is a 256 color SVGA server that supports
    a number of SVGA chipsets. On some chipsets it is accelerated or
    supports higher color depths.
 4  The accelerated servers. These include XF86_S3, XF86_Mach32, XF86_Mach8,
    XF86_8514, XF86_P9000, XF86_AGX, XF86_W32, XF86_Mach64, XF86_I128 and
    XF86_S3V.

These four server types correspond to the four different "Screen" sections in
XF86Config (vga2, vga16, svga, accel).

 5  Choose the server from the card definition, XF86_S3.

Which one of these screen types do you intend to run by default (1-5)?
```

Figure 11-16: Entering a server selection.

19. **At the Create a Link in /usr prompt at the bottom of the screen, press *y* and then press Enter.**

    `xf86config` asks if you want the computer to create another link to an alternate directory, just in case the first one doesn't work.

20. **At the Create Alternate Link prompt at the bottom of the screen, press *y* and then press Enter.**

    `xf86config` asks how much video memory your video card has, as shown in Figure 11-17. Common amounts are listed with a selection number in the left column.

    WARNING!

    If you don't know this information, you should press Ctrl+C now and run SuperProbe (see the section entitled "Running SuperProbe" earlier in this chapter for instructions); then start these steps over from Step 2.

    If you have more video memory than 4096K (which is 4MB), then press *6*. The screen prompts you to enter the number in kilobytes. To calculate this number, multiply the amount of video memory you have by 1024. For example, if you have 8MB of video memory, multiply 8 x 1024 = 8192. This is the number you enter.

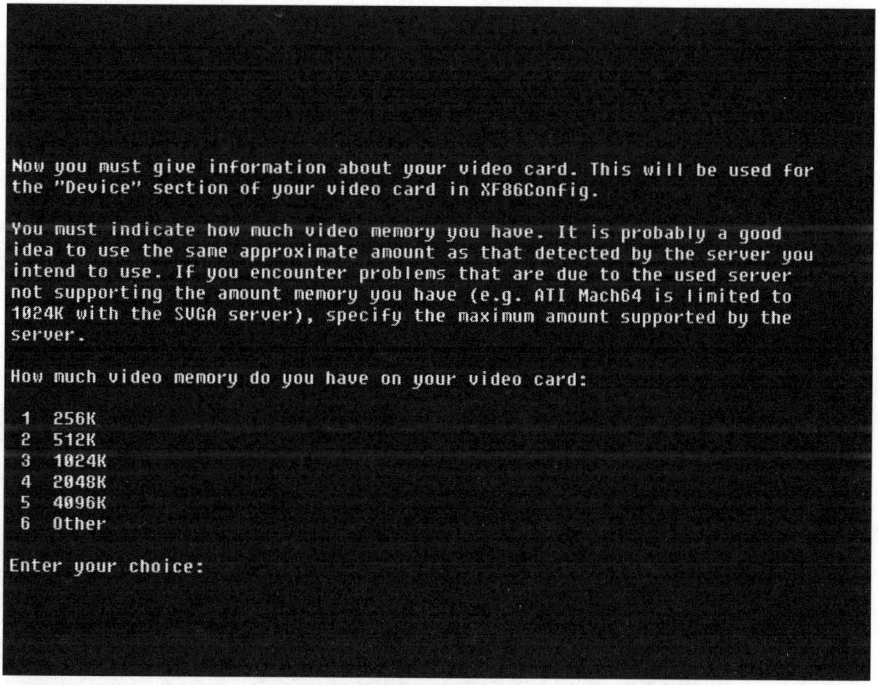

```
Now you must give information about your video card. This will be used for
the "Device" section of your video card in XF86Config.

You must indicate how much video memory you have. It is probably a good
idea to use the same approximate amount as that detected by the server you
intend to use. If you encounter problems that are due to the used server
not supporting the amount memory you have (e.g. ATI Mach64 is limited to
1024K with the SVGA server), specify the maximum amount supported by the
server.

How much video memory do you have on your video card:

 1  256K
 2  512K
 3  1024K
 4  2048K
 5  4096K
 6  Other

Enter your choice:
```

Figure 11-17: Common video memory amounts on your video card.

21. **At the Enter Your Choice prompt, type the number corresponding to the amount of video memory that you have and press Enter.**

    `xf86config` asks you to give this definition of your video card's settings a name for easier reference, should you choose to go back and edit the configuration file later.

22. **At the Video Card Definition prompt at the bottom of your screen, type** viddef1 **and press Enter.**

    `xf86config` asks you to enter the manufacturer name of your video card. This is something like Diamond, ATI, or maybe 3dfx, depending on which company made your monitor.

23. **At the Video Card Manufacturer prompt at the bottom of your screen, type the manufacturer name of your video card and press Enter.**

    `xf86config` asks you to enter the model number of your video card. Again, this is something like Stealth, All-in-Wonder, or Voodoo, depending on the exact model number.

24. **At the Video Card Model prompt at the bottom of your screen, type the model number of your video card and press Enter.**

    `xf86config` asks for the type of RAMDAC that your video card uses, as shown in Figure 11-18. RAMDAC stands for Random Access Memory Digital-to-Analog Converter and is used to convert digital image data into the analog data that your monitor needs in order to display the image correctly.

```
The RAMDAC setting only applies to the S3, AGX, W32 servers, and some
drivers in the SVGA servers. Some RAMDAC's are auto-detected by the server.
The detection of a RAMDAC is forced by using a Ramdac "identifier" line in
the Device section. The identifiers are shown at the right of the following
table of RAMDAC types:

  1  AT&T 20C490 (S3 and AGX servers, ARK driver)          att20c490
  2  AT&T 20C498/21C498/22C498 (S3, autodetected)          att20c498
  3  AT&T 20C409/20C499 (S3, autodetected)                 att20c409
  4  AT&T 20C505 (S3)                                      att20c505
  5  BrookTree BT481 (AGX)                                 bt481
  6  BrookTree BT482 (AGX)                                 bt482
  7  BrookTree BT485/9485 (S3)                             bt485
  8  Sierra SC15025 (S3, AGX)                              sc15025
  9  S3 GenDAC (86C708) (autodetected)                     s3gendac
 10  S3 SDAC (86C716) (autodetected)                       s3_sdac
 11  STG-1700 (S3, autodetected)                           stg1700
 12  STG-1703 (S3, autodetected)                           stg1703

Enter a number to choose the corresponding RAMDAC.
Press enter for the next page, q to quit without selection of a RAMDAC.
```

Figure 11-18: Common RAMDAC listings.

Press Enter to get the next page (screenful) of available choices for RAMDAC types. If you don't know this information, just press *q* and then press Enter.

If you used SuperProbe to find your video card's information, the RAMDAC type appears with that information.

25. **At the RAMDAC Type prompt at the bottom of the screen, type the number corresponding to your video card's RAMDAC type.**

    `xf86config` asks for the type of Clockchip your video card uses, as shown in Figure 11-19. A Clockchip is the microchip that calculates the frequency (or number of pulses of light per second) necessary to display images on your monitor.

    If you don't want a Clockchip setting, or your card doesn't require one, press Enter. X tries to determine a Clockchip setting, if one exists, automatically when X is started.

In Step 16, one of the items returned was the Clockchip type for your video card, if one existed in the database. If you received a warning that said:

```
Do NOT probe clocks or use any Clocks line.
```

```
A Clockchip line in the Device section forces the detection of a
programmable clock device. With a clockchip enabled, any required
clock can be programmed without requiring probing of clocks or a
Clocks line. Most cards don't have a programmable clock chip.
Choose from the following list:

 1  Chrontel 8391                                                  ch8391
 2  ICD2061A and compatibles (ICS9161A, DCS2824)                   icd2061a
 3  ICS2595                                                        ics2595
 4  ICS5342 (similar to SDAC, but not completely compatible)       ics5342
 5  ICS5341                                                        ics5341
 6  S3 GenDAC (86C708) and ICS5300 (autodetected)                  s3gendac
 7  S3 SDAC (86C716)                                               s3_sdac
 8  STG 1703 (autodetected)                                        stg1703
 9  Sierra SC11412                                                 sc11412
10  TI 3025 (autodetected)                                         ti3025
11  TI 3026 (autodetected)                                         ti3026
12  IBM RGB 51x/52x (autodetected)                                 ibm_rgb5xx

The card definition has Clockchip "icd2061a"

Just press enter if you don't want a Clockchip setting.
What Clockchip setting do you want (1-12)?
```

Figure 11-19: Listing of Clockchips for video cards.

you *must* select a Clockchip type, otherwise `xf86config` will probe your video card! Probing your video card after being warned could cause irreparable damage to your video card.

26. **At the What Clockchip Setting Do You Want prompt at the bottom of the screen, type the number corresponding to your video card's Clockchip type.**

    A screen of information about clocks and probing appears.

    If you didn't select a Clockchip type, `xf86config` asks if you want the system to probe your video card. (This may damage your video card, especially if you have a warning that says `The card definition says to NOT probe clocks`.) You can safely get away with not having a Clockchip line, so press *n* and then press Enter.

    If you selected a Clockchip type, you can safely ignore this.

27. **Press Enter.**

    Some common resolutions that should work with your video card appear, as shown in Figure 11-20.

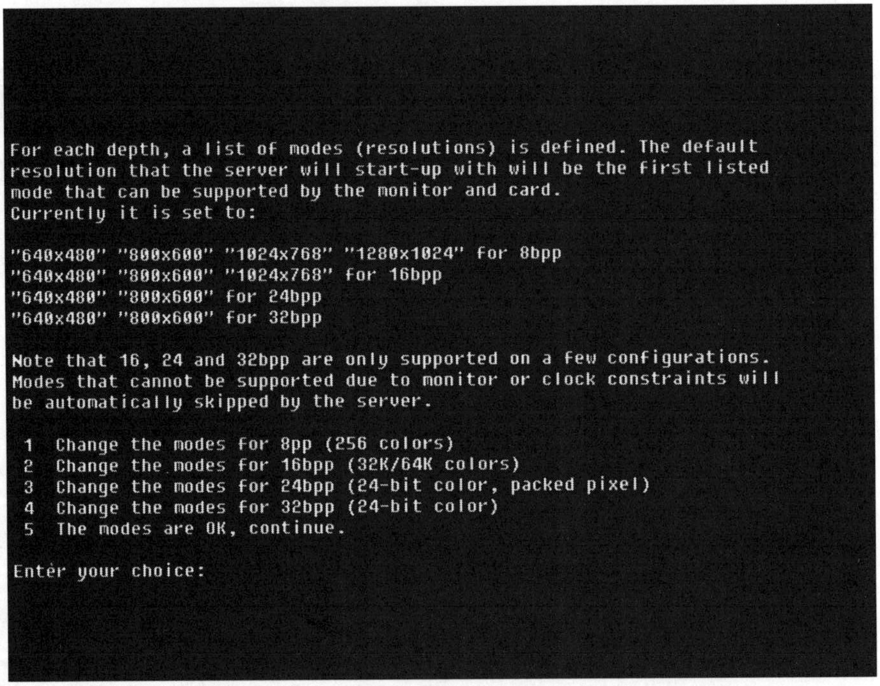

```
For each depth, a list of modes (resolutions) is defined. The default
resolution that the server will start-up with will be the first listed
mode that can be supported by the monitor and card.
Currently it is set to:

"640x480" "800x600" "1024x768" "1280x1024" for 8bpp
"640x480" "800x600" "1024x768" for 16bpp
"640x480" "800x600" for 24bpp
"640x480" "800x600" for 32bpp

Note that 16, 24 and 32bpp are only supported on a few configurations.
Modes that cannot be supported due to monitor or clock constraints will
be automatically skipped by the server.

 1  Change the modes for 8pp (256 colors)
 2  Change the modes for 16bpp (32K/64K colors)
 3  Change the modes for 24bpp (24-bit color, packed pixel)
 4  Change the modes for 32bpp (24-bit color)
 5  The modes are OK, continue.

Enter your choice:
```

Figure 11-20: Common resolutions available for most video cards.

28. **At the Enter Your Choice prompt at the bottom of the screen, press *5* and then press Enter.**

    `xf86config` asks if the computer can write the configuration file now.

29. **At the Save Configuration prompt at the bottom of the screen, press *y* and then press Enter.**

    The computer writes the configuration file to `/etc/XF86Config`. You can look at this file later if you want by typing at your command prompt `more /etc/XF86Config` and pressing Enter.

The `xf86config` program is complete. Congratulations! Go find yourself something tall and cool to drink because you've earned it.

Running X Windows

After you're satisfied that the configuration is correct, you want to run X Windows to see what happens. To do so, at your command prompt type **startx** and press Enter. You now have a running X server. If it's running but the display doesn't look too good, turn to Chapter 21 for troubleshooting X Windows.

X Windows has some common terms that you should familiarize yourself with:

- **Desktop:** the whole screen is your desktop
- **Root window:** the background of your desktop
- **Window manager:** interface between you and the X Windows system, providing window borders, menus, icons, buttons, and tool bars
- **Pointer:** the arrow that moves with your mouse
- **Window:** a frame in which an application resides, and is managed by the window manager.
- **Active window:** the window that you're currently using

These terms are used whenever something references the X Windows system.

One other application that is widely used is the `xterm`, which is a command prompt within a window in X Windows. All X Windows systems give you the option of running an xterm from a menu on the desktop. To run an `xterm` in KDE, choose K⇨Non-KDE Apps⇨Utilities⇨X Terminal. In GNOME, choose G⇨Utilities⇨Color Xterm or Regular Xterm. In either case, a new window titled `xterm` appears. To exit an `xterm`, type **exit** at the command prompt within the xterm window. For more information on KDE and GNOME, turn to Chapter 12.

Changing colors

X Windows gives you the ability to change colors around in windows. You can experiment with some simple tasks like changing the background and foreground colors of an `xterm`. To open an `xterm` in KDE, choose K➪Non-KDE Apps➪Utilities➪X Terminal. In GNOME, choose G➪Utilities➪Color Xterm or Regular Xterm. At the command prompt that appears within the `xterm` window, type **xterm -bg yellow -fg black &**.

This command opens a hopelessly ugly yellow `xterm` with black text. You can try other settings by typing **more /usr/X11R6/lib/X11/rgb.txt** at the command prompt. Note that the settings are actually hexadecimal numbers that have names assigned to them! This is because the computer only knows things in numbers, not names like we do, so it has to translate the string *yellow* into something it understands, like 255 255 0.

Other useful programs

Slackware comes with several useful programs to run within X Windows. Some are just silly, but some have real use.

For example, Slackware comes with a screen saver, but only if you install the `xlock` package from the X series of Slackware software. `xlock` is a basic screen saver that does all the normal functions, like blanking the screen after so many minutes and locking the screen until a password is entered.

Another program is `xclock`, which displays the time and date on your desktop. You can set the time and date on your system by using this program.

Some other interesting programs are listed in the file `/cdrom/slakware/xap1/diskxap1` on the Slackware CD-ROM included with this book. These programs include:

- **xman:** A man page browser for X
- **xpaint:** A paint program for X
- **xsetroot:** Enables you to change the color of your desktop
- **xwininfo:** Enables you to get information about any window

Install some of these (by using the instructions from Chapter 7) and play with them at your leisure. None of these programs can cause your system to crash, so you don't have to worry about messing something up.

Controlling the Desktop

Customizing the desktop is something every user should do. (Remember that the entire screen is your desktop.) Customization is a key item for Slackware; however, the system has a default in case users don't want to mess with the customization.

A single file in `/var/X1R6/lib/xinit/` called `xinitrc` controls the system-wide default desktop. Usually, this file is a link to another `xinitrc` file in the same directory, like `xinitrc.kde` (for the KDE desktop) or `xinitrc.fvwm95` (for the fvwm95 desktop, which looks eerily similar to Windows 95).

If you want to change which desktop you use, make sure that you install the correct software series for the desktop in question — for KDE you need to install the KDE series, for GNOME the GTK series. fvwm95 has its own package in the XAP series (`fvwm95.tgz`), and twm comes with the `xbin`, `xcfg`, and `xlib` packages.

After you install the correct series and packages, you must change the link in `/var/X11R6/lib/xinit` to the `xinitrc` file for the particular desktop in question (for example, `xinitrc.twm`).

Suppose that you want to change the twm desktop (the default X Windows desktop) to the fvwm95 desktop, which makes your desktop look like Windows 95. To do so, you must follow these steps:

1. **Log in as** root.
2. **At your command prompt (#), type** `cd /var/X11R6/lib/xinit` **and press Enter.**

   You have changed directories to the `/var/X11R6/lib/xinit` directory.
3. **At your command prompt (#), type** `rm xinitrc` **and press Enter.**

   This removes the `xinitrc` file.
4. **At your command prompt (#), type** `ln -s xinitrc.fvwm95 xinitrc` **and press Enter.**

   The `xinitrc` file for fvwm95 now links to the system-wide `xinitrc` file.

You can now type the command **startx** at your command prompt and press Enter. Your desktop is now fvwm95.

Chapter 12

Launching KDE and GNOME

In This Chapter

- Starting KDE
- Applying Kapplications
- Managing KDE
- Using GNOME
- Running GNOME utilities
- Managing GNOME

X Windows System (X) is an extremely useful graphics display system. You can tailor X to meet your requirements by using a desktop environment. Several desktop environments exist, but the two most popular are KDE and GNOME. Both come with their own sets of utilities, such as paint programs, terminal emulators, and calculators.

KDE and GNOME each have strong points that directly contrast the other. GNOME, for example, uses less computer memory (RAM) than KDE. GNOME also supports more emerging industry standards than KDE. KDE, on the other hand, has had more time to develop and is more stable (crashes less often) than GNOME. Additionally, KDE looks more like Windows than GNOME, meaning that KDE users have a shorter learning curve than GNOME users. In this chapter, you receive a short introduction to both environments and become familiar with some of the common options available to both.

KDE and GNOME use standard UNIX conventions in terms of the mouse: the left button selects items (and drags them if it's held down on a selected item); the right button shows a menu for an item if one exists; and using both buttons together (or the middle button if you have a three-button mouse) pastes items that are copied.

The CD-ROM at the back of the book includes both KDE and GNOME. To use KDE, you must install the KDE series of software packages. To use GNOME, you must install the GTK series of software packages.

Be careful about installing both packages — you can do so, but your hard drive must have at least 1.5GB of space for both to exist in addition to your other software.

Starting With KDE

The Internet hosts many heated discussions regarding whether KDE or GNOME is the better desktop environment. No clear-cut winner ever emerges because both have heavy support from users. KDE, however, has won several awards for its stability and robustness.

The name KDE stands for K Desktop Environment (the K doesn't stand for anything). KDE isn't a window manager, although one is included with it (called KWM). KDE is a desktop suite of applications that provides a file manager, an integrated help system for help on almost every KDE application, and an integrated configuration system. The KDE software series on the Slackware CD enclosed with this book contains all the files necessary to run the KDE desktop.

To start KDE, you must first install KDE and correctly set up the `xinitrc` file (see Chapter 11 for more help on setting up your `xinitrc` file). Then at the command prompt, type **startx** and press Enter. KDE runs automatically. If you've never run KDE before, KDE displays a message on the screen saying it's creating a subdirectory to store your user-specific settings.

After KDE runs, its desktop appears along with the K File Manager, as shown in Figure 12-1.

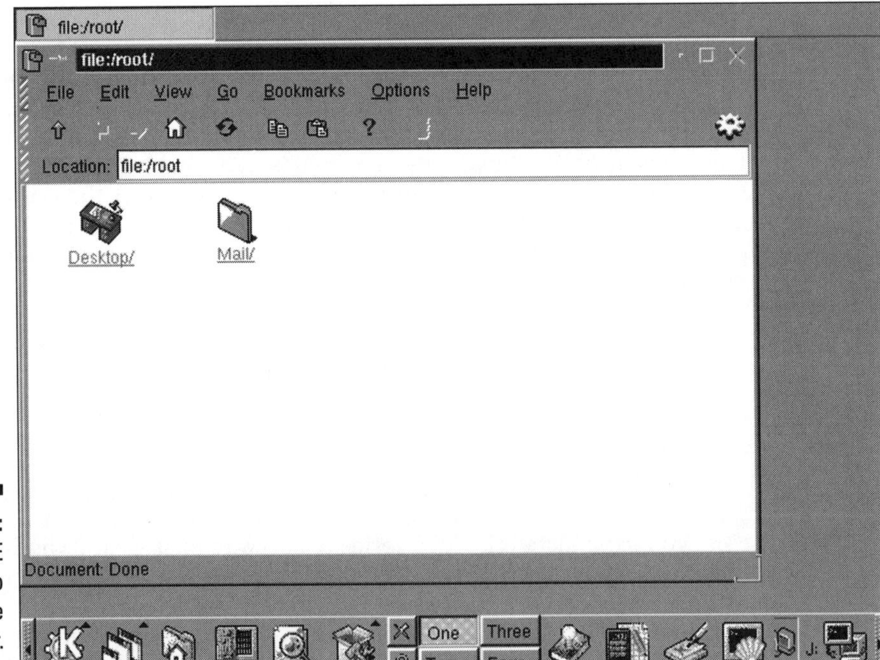

Figure 12-1: The KDE desktop and file manager.

The K File Manager, shown in Figure 12-1, shows two icons that represent directories on your hard drive: Desktop (which is the KDE desktop currently running), and Mail (where e-mail is stored). Note that the Location bar shows the current directory — `/root`.

A desktop environment is useless without some way of accessing the programs that you wish to use. KDE makes the switch from Windows seamless by placing a large K button in the far-left corner of the panel that runs across the bottom of your desktop. Applications are available by clicking the K button. Clicking the K brings up the main menu for KDE.

One of the things necessary for use in KDE is a command prompt, which is gotten from an `xterm` window. To create an `xterm` for use in KDE, choose K⇨non-KDE Apps⇨Utilities⇨X Terminal. A new window appears with a command prompt (it will be a # prompt if you logged in as the root user, or a > or % prompt if you used a personal account).

To log out of KDE, choose K⇨Logout, as shown in Figure 12-2.

Many Slackware applications have entries accessible from the K button. You can browse through these menus and applications at your leisure.

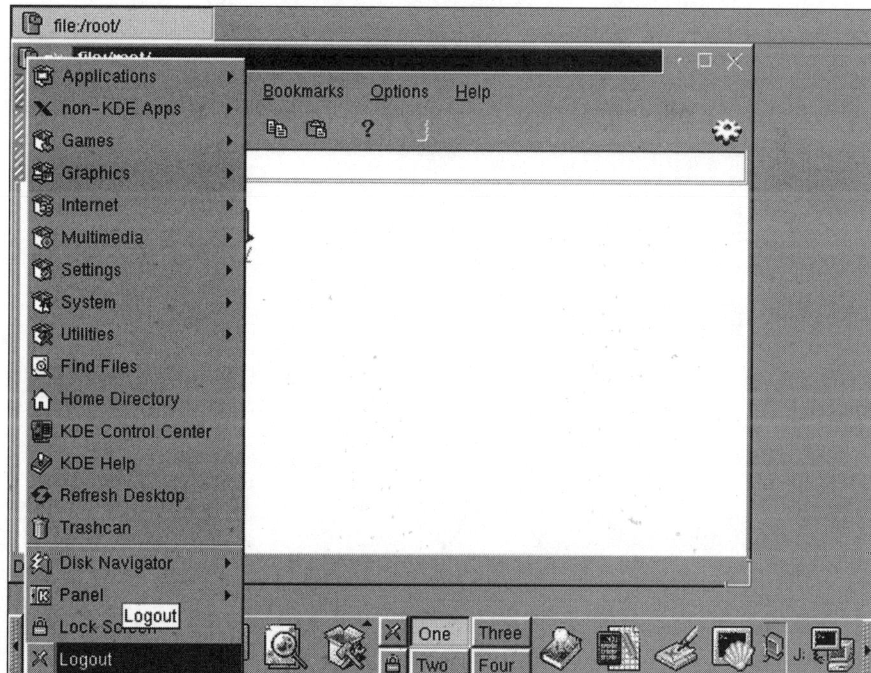

Figure 12-2: Logging out of the KDE desktop.

The top right corner of each window has three icons — a dot, a square, and an X. Clicking the dot minimizes the window and places it in the taskbar at the top of the screen. Clicking the square maximizes the window to fill the entire screen. Clicking the X closes the window and exits whatever program was running inside it. You can move a window around by placing your mouse pointer on the title bar at the top of each window, clicking and holding down the left mouse button, and then moving your mouse around the screen.

Playing with Kapplications

A desktop environment is useless without some way of accessing the programs that you wish to use. KDE makes the switch from Windows seamless by placing a large K button in the far-left corner of the panel that runs across the bottom of your desktop. This K button is similar to the Windows 9*x* Start button, so a menu pops up when the button is pressed. Applications are available by clicking the K button. Additional icons along the bottom panel represent some of the more common applications. Figure 12-3 shows a standard set of icons in the panel.

Figure 12-3: The standard KDE desktop with no applications running.

Some of the more common applications visable on the panel are the K Control Center (fourth icon from the left), the K Help utility (icon with the light bulb and book), and the Konsole — which gives you a command prompt (icon of monitor and seashell). The K Control Center is discussed in the next section, “Controlling KDE.”

Placing your mouse over one of these icons causes a brief description of the icon’s utility to appear, as shown in Figure 12-4.

One quirk of KDE is the ability to run multiple desktops. You can choose how many desktops you want to run by clicking a number button in the center of the panel. The number of desktops that you can create is limitless, though the KDE default is four. Applications can run in all four desktops at the same time. To switch to a different desktop, click on the button representing the desktop number (One, Two, Three, or Four) in the middle of the panel at the bottom of the screen. If you run an application and don’t want to clutter your desktop with its window, you can send the application to a specific desktop, as shown in Figure 12-5.

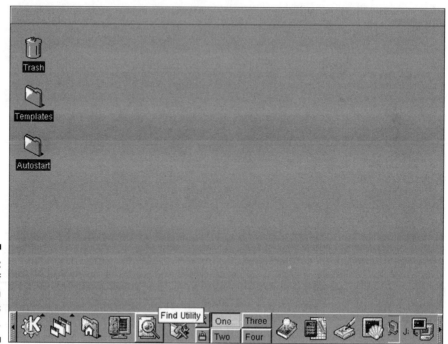

Figure 12-4: A brief description of the icon’s utility.

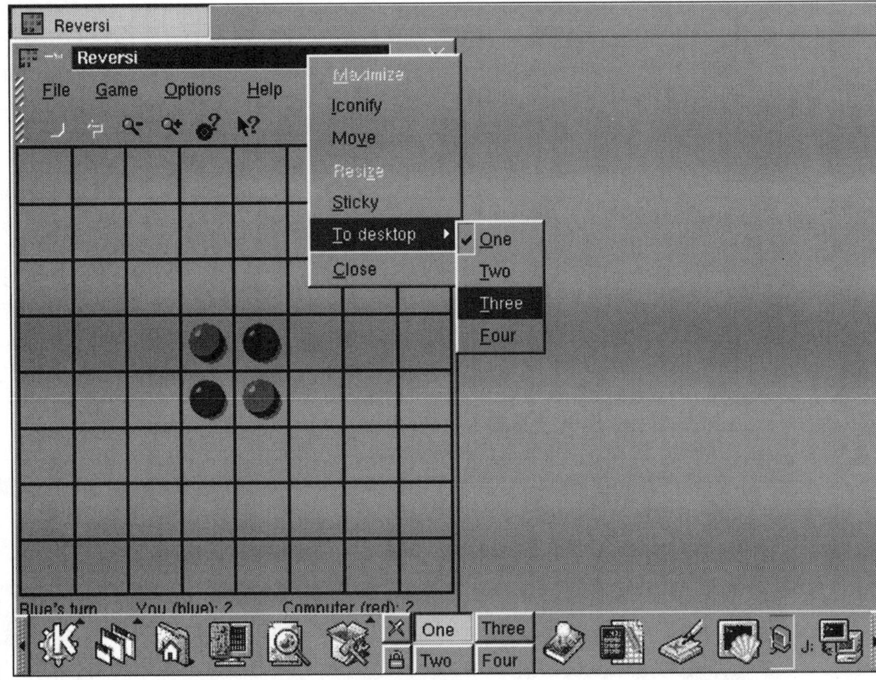

Figure 12-5: Sending an application to another desktop.

Other applications that come with KDE include:

- **K Organizer:** A calendar and scheduling program.
- **kscd:** A CD audio player.
- **kpaint:** A simple paint program.
- **kedit:** A text editor similar to Windows Notepad.
- **kworldwatch:** A toy that shows where daylight is on the planet. (See Figure 12-6.)
- **kreversi:** K's version of the Othello game.

You can access all these applications by clicking the K button and navigating through the menus. A partial list of applications available for the KDE desktop is available on the CD-ROM in the `packages.txt` file. You can also visit KDE's home page at `http://www.kde.org/`.

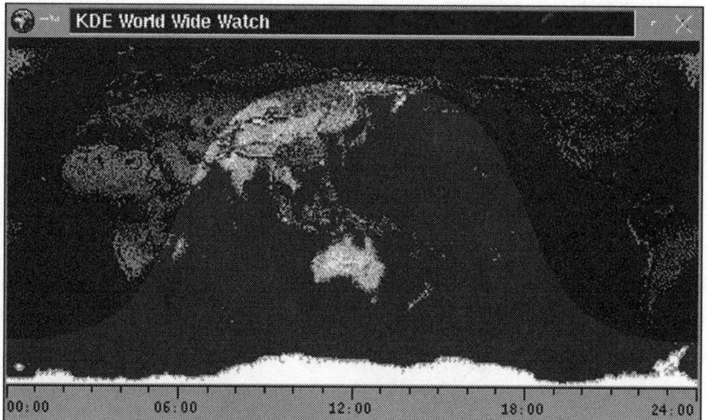

Figure 12-6: kworldwatch — the KDE World Wide Watch application.

Controlling KDE

You can change how your desktop looks and feels with the KDE Control Center. The Control Center configures everything from how applications interact with KDE to what sounds play when you make an error.

To access the KDE Control Center, click the fourth icon from the left on the bottom panel. Figure 12-7 shows the KDE Control Center when it is first opened.

Suppose that you want to change how your desktop looks. First, you double-click the Desktop entry in the white categories box. A new set of entries appears under Desktop, including Background, Fonts, and Screensaver. Each entry is a category that you can set. Double-click the Fonts entry, and you see the types of fonts that you can change (general, window title, and so on). You can even try out the fonts by changing the font type and clicking the Apply button at the bottom of the K Control Center window. Your changes are seen immediately.

The best way to configure your desktop is to explore all the options available and choose as you go. You can set up your desktop any way you like — it's a reflection of your personal tastes.

Close the Control Center by clicking the OK button at the bottom of the K Control Center window or the X at the top-right corner. See *KDE For Linux For Dummies,* by Michael Meadhra, Kate Wrightson, and Joe Merlino (IDG Books Worldwide, Inc.), for more information on the KDE desktop environment.

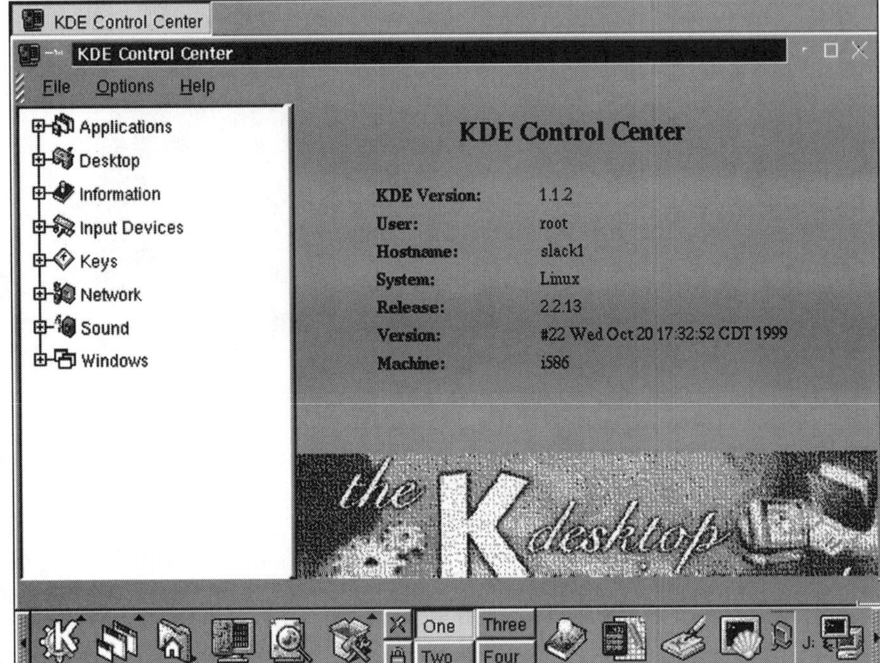

Figure 12-7: The KDE Control Center.

Going with GNOME

GNOME stands for GNU Network Object Model Environment and is part of the GNU Project. (See Chapter 1 for more info on the GNU Project.) GNOME, unfortunately, is slow in developing, even though it has monetary backing from Red Hat, Inc. (another distributor of Linux).

GNOME's lengthy development doesn't mean that you shouldn't use GNOME — GNOME has many advantages, some of which may be better suited to you than KDE. One of these advantages is its ease of integration with new utilities, such as the gimp, which is a powerful image manipulation program on par with Adobe Photoshop or Corel Draw. GNOME also works with almost any window manager (which is the interface between you and the X Windows system — see Chapter 11 for help with the X Windows system). A third factor is GNOME's ease of customization.

To use GNOME, you must first install the GTK series of Slackware software and make sure that your `xinitrc` file is pointing to the correct `xinitrc` file (see Chapter 11 for more info on setting up the `xinitrc` file). Then type **startx** at the command prompt and press Enter.

The panel at the bottom lists common programs and applications — this gives you quick access to frequently used programs. The arrows on either side of the panel hide (or show) the taskbar. You can drag-and-drop programs onto the panel from the file manager to place them there for later use.

The button in the bottom-left corner that looks like a foot is the GNOME main menu button (it's abbreviated as the letter G), similar to the Windows Start button. By clicking on the GNOME main menu button (the G button), a pop-up menu appears that lists many categories of applications, ranging from Administration to Utilities. GNOME and common Slackware utilities are listed in the sub-menus from this pop-up menu.

You also have a folder on your desktop labeled Home Directory. Clicking it runs the GNOME File Manager. Using the file manager, you can drag-and-drop files, edit or delete files, and place programs or applications on the desktop.

To log out of GNOME, click the G button and choose Log out, or click the large X on the bottom panel. Refer to Figure 12-2.

The top right corner of each window has three icons — a square with three horizontal lines, an X, and a triangle. Clicking on the three horizontal lines forces the window to "stick" or not move. Clicking the X closes the window and exits whatever program was running inside it. Clicking the triangle brings up another pop-out set of buttons with which to control the window. Move the window around by clicking and holding down the left button on the title bar at the top of each window, then moving your mouse around the screen. Some programs, like gEdit, have pull-down menus inside their windows.

Discovering Other GNOME-ish Utilities

GNOME has many utilities that come prepackaged with Slackware's version of GNOME. GNOME has a pop-up menu accessible from the G button on the panel at the bottom of the screen. Having a main menu accessible from a single button on the screen makes GNOME similar to its counterpart KDE, or at the very least Windows 9*x*. Clicking this button presents a directory of categories and applications.

You can run any GNOME program by opening up an `xterm` and typing in the name of the program. And like KDE, moving the mouse over any of the icons in the panel at the bottom of the screen causes a snippet of info to be displayed about that icon. However, if you move the mouse over a button at the top of a window, GNOME displays another small help feature about that window button.

GNOME for Slackware comes with some very useful utilities, such as:

- **Gnumeric:** A spreadsheet that looks eerily similar to Microsoft Excel.
- **gnotepad+:** A simple text editor that resembles Wordpad.
- **gnomepim:** The GNOME Personal Information Manager to keep your personal calendars, to-do lists, and business cards.
- **GnomeICU:** A clone of the Mirabilis ICQ program.
- **gmc:** An enhanced version of the Midnight Commander file manager, which in itself is a clone of Norton Commander.
- **The gimp:** The GNU Image Manipulation Program, a powerful presentation and imaging program rivaling Adobe Photoshop and Corel Draw.

You can access all these applications by clicking the GNOME button and navigating through the menus.

Controlling GNOME

Changing the appearance of GNOME is a must-have for users that want more from their desktop than a vanilla setup. In GNOME, you're given the ability to change your settings through the GNOME Control Center.

To access the GNOME Control Center, choose G⇨System⇨GNOME Control Center.

Suppose that you want to change how your desktop looks. First, you double-click the Desktop entry in the white categories box. A new set of entries appears under Desktop, including Background, Screensaver, Theme Selector, and Window Manager. Each entry is a category that you can set. Click the Background entry, and you see the types of backgrounds that you can set (plain colors to shapes and even pictures). You can preview your choices before they're applied to your current desktop by clicking the Apply button at the bottom of the GNOME Control Center window.

The best way to set up your desktop is to explore the options within the Control Center and change things at your leisure.

Close the Control Center by clicking the OK button at the bottom of the GNOME Control Center window or the X at the top-right corner.

Part IV
Networking and the Web

"I don't mind dealing with Slackware's little quirks, Martin, but I'd appreciate it if you kept yours to yourself."

In this part . . .

You're now ready to connect to the Word Wide Web. Chapter 13 shows you what ISPs are for and how to use them. You then walk through the process of setting up your modem and connecting to your ISP. Chapter 14 guides you through configuring Netscape to browse the Web and to send and receive e-mail. This chapter also provides information on junk e-mail (spam).

Chapter 13

Setting Up Your Internet Connection

In This Chapter

- Understanding ISPs and why you need them
- Setting up your modem
- Communicating with your communications software
- Dialing the number

One of the more important aspects of Slackware is its ability to connect to the Internet through a modem. Slackware was first designed for direct plug-in connections to the Internet, but with so many people using Slackware at home, communications programs for connecting computers to the Internet via modem naturally sprang up. Soon after, Internet Service Providers began cropping up in an effort to capitalize on Internet growth. These providers began offering a level of support between the home user and the Internet that previously didn't exist.

You must have an Internet Service Provider (ISP) available in order for your Slackware machine to connect to the Internet. An ISP is like a rental company — unless you're one of the few that has your own direct Internet connection, you must rent a connection from the ISP. In this chapter, you get to know your ISP, set up your modem and communications software, make your connection to the ISP, and hook up to the Internet.

Investigating Internet Service Providers

Internet Service Providers (ISPs) ensure that people can connect to the Internet. ISPs make their money by charging you an hourly or monthly rate for connecting to them, and they, in turn, connect you to the Internet. You can't connect to the Internet without an ISP, unless you shell out around $900 per month for a T1 (very, very fast) connection to your house from the phone company.

The easiest way to find a good ISP is to ask friends that have computers. Find out how much each ISP charges and whether it's per month or per hour (I'd avoid the ones that have hourly charges). Also find out whether the ISP's lines are often busy (which means that they have more customers than they can handle) or whether their technical support is any good. A small ISP that has excellent technical support is better than a large ISP that has subpar technical support.

When you call an ISP, ask them whether they can handle a Slackware (or just plain Linux) connection. If they can, tell them you're interested in PPP (point-to-point protocol) services and e-mail. You also need to tell them the speed of your modem. Finally, make sure that the ISP has a local number for you to call in your area, because long distance charges, in addition to a monthly ISP fee, really add up.

After you choose your ISP, you must have the following information:

- **A login name:** You usually get to choose this yourself.
- **A password:** You have to change this later, so make sure that you ask the ISP's technical support or help line how to do so.
- **The DNS server of the ISP:** This is the Domain Name Server that the ISP uses to translate names of computers (like `www.idgbooks.com`) into numbers that the computer understands.
- **The name of the e-mail server for the ISP:** This is the server that receives and processes all e-mail and is usually called something like *mailhost*, *smtp*, or even just *mail*.
- **The type of PPP authentication that the ISP requires:** The ISP can require PAP (Password Authentication Protocol) or CHAP (Challenge/Handshake Authentication Protocol) authentication.
- **The name of a POP3 (Post Office Protocol version 3) server:** The POP3 server downloads e-mail from the ISP to your Slackware machine.

Make sure you write this information down and keep it in a safe place — you don't want visitors to see this information.

Your e-mail address is usually of the form `login@ISP.com`, where `login` is your login name and `ISP.com` is the domain of the ISP. For example, `support@aol.com` is the e-mail address for technical support (`support`) at AOL (`aol.com`). Remember your e-mail address, because that's what you end up giving your friends to send and receive e-mail.

Configuring Your Modem

After you choose an Internet Service Provider (ISP), the next task is to connect your Slackware computer to the ISP. Your computer needs a device that enables it to talk to another computer over a phone line. Enter your *modem*, which stands for MOdulator/DEModulator. A modem translates analog waves (sound waves) into digital transmissions and vice versa, thus enabling your computer to talk to another computer over a phone line.

Typecasting your modem

Many styles of modems exist, but they all boil down to two categories — *external* and *internal*. The external modem is a piece of hardware that sits outside the computer and plugs into the PC, while the internal modem is a card (like your video card) that you install inside the computer.

If you use an external modem, Slackware requires that it be a *serial* modem, which is a modem that connects to a serial port on your computer — this is the 9-pin rectangular connector on the back of your computer. If you use an internal modem, Slackware requires that the modem be either an ISA (Industry Standard Architecture) modem — Plug-and-Play (PnP) ISA modems are completely compatible — or a PCI (Peripheral Component Interconnect) modem that works with Linux. You can find more help on ISA PnP modems in the file `/usr/doc/Linux-HOWTOs/Plug-and-Play-HOWTO`. You can find PCI help in the file `/usr/doc/Linux-HOWTOs/PCI-HOWTO`.

Other modems, called *Winmodems*, exist, but do not work in Slackware. Winmodems require Windows in order to work because almost all the work normally done by the modem is actually done by Windows (hence the name Winmodem). Check out `http://www.o2.net/~gromitkc/winmodem.html` for a list of modem makes and models that work and don't work with Slackware.

Modems that say "For Windows only" don't work with Slackware.

Recognizing your modem

If you have an external modem, plug it into the serial port on the back of your computer. The serial port is a 9-pin rectangular connector. If you have an internal modem, it's probably already plugged in to your computer. You most likely have an internal modem.

Your modem should have been set up during Slackware installation. (You can check the Slackware installation procedures in Chapter 5.) If, however, you did not set up your modem during installation, you can do so now if you know the following information:

- The communications (COM) port that your modem uses
- The interrupt signal number (IRQ) that your modem uses

Table 13-1 provides information to help you set up your modem.

Table 13-1 Slackware Devices, COM Ports, and IRQs

Device	*COM port*	*IRQ*
/dev/ttyS0	COM1	4
/dev/ttyS1	COM2	3
/dev/ttyS2	COM3	4
/dev/ttyS3	COM4	3

The IRQ is the number that a device (like /dev/ttyS0) uses to tell the computer that it has data to be processed. When the computer receives the number 4, for instance, the computer knows that the information is coming from /dev/ttyS0. No two devices can have the same IRQ number at the same time. /dev/ttyS0 and /dev/ttyS2 cannot be used at the same time, but they can be used separately.

After you know which COM port your modem uses (if you're unsure, follow the steps in Chapter 2), you must make a link from /dev/modem to the correct Slackware device. At your command prompt (the # prompt), type **ln -s /dev/ttyS$ /dev/modem** and press Enter. ($ is the device number in Table 13-1.)

Nothing happens on the screen after you press Enter, but if you type **ls -la /dev/modem** and press Enter, you see the following:

```
lrwxrwxrwx   1 root     root              4 Feb 20  2000
          /dev/modem -> ttyS$
```

(Again, $ is the device number in Table 13-1. The date will differ from your screen.) The arrow pointing from /dev/modem to the ttyS port you specified in the ln command verifies that a link has been made.

Some of the documentation that comes with Slackware may reference /dev/cua0. Using /dev/cua is outdated, so make sure that you're using /dev/ttyS devices instead.

Configuring Communications Software

You must install the ppp package from the N series of Slackware software packages. (You can find instructions for installing specific packages in Chapter 7.) In the ppp package is a program called pppsetup. You use pppsetup to configure your point-to-point (PPP) connection to your ISP. Before you start, make sure that you have contacted an ISP in your area. The "Investigating Internet Service Providers" section earlier in this chapter lists the questions you must ask and the information you need in order to complete this setup.

To run pppsetup, follow these steps:

1. **Log in as** root.

   You're now at the command (#) prompt.

2. **At the command prompt, type** pppsetup **and press Enter.**

   pppsetup runs. An introduction screen appears.

3. **Press Enter.**

   The Phone Number dialog box appears, as shown in Figure 13-1. The dialog box asks you the phone number of your ISP.

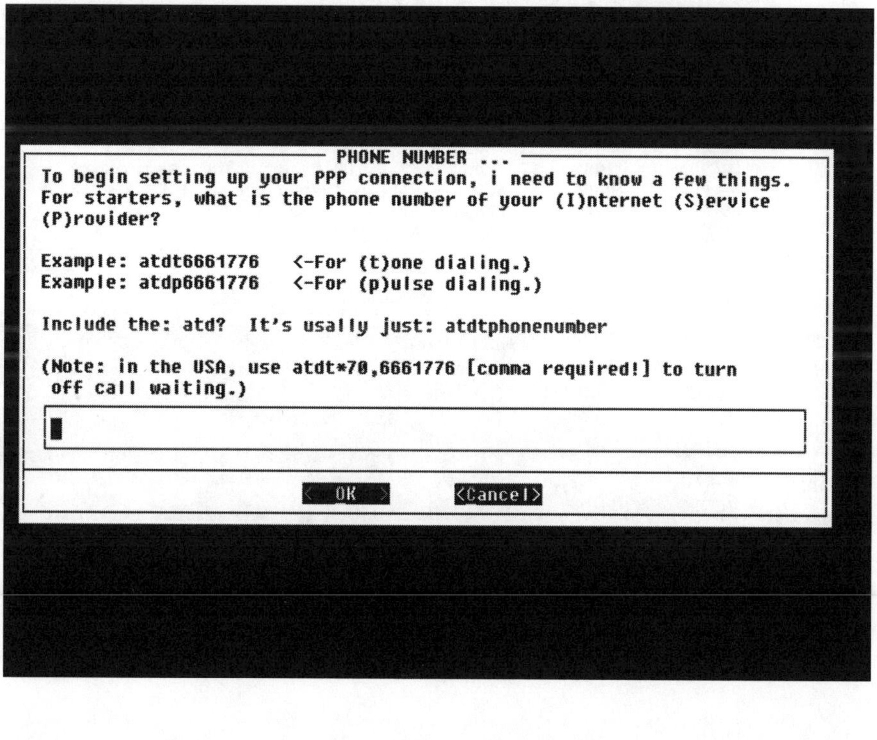

```
PHONE NUMBER ...
To begin setting up your PPP connection, i need to know a few things.
For starters, what is the phone number of your (I)nternet (S)ervice
(P)rovider?

Example: atdt6661776   <-For (t)one dialing.)
Example: atdp6661776   <-For (p)ulse dialing.)

Include the: atd?  It's usally just: atdtphonenumber

(Note: in the USA, use atdt*70,6661776 [comma required!] to turn
 off call waiting.)

< OK >   <Cancel>
```

Figure 13-1: Enter your ISP's phone number.

If you're in the United States and wish to disable call waiting, type ***70,** (including the comma) before the ISP's telephone number.

4. **In the text field, type** atdt **and the phone number of your ISP, and then press Enter.**

   For example, the ISP `Foo.com` phone number is 555-1485. In the text field, type **atdt5551485** and press Enter.

   The Modem Device dialog box appears, asking you what device your modem uses. Use the arrow keys to move up and down the list.

5. **Using your arrow keys, highlight the device corresponding to your modem and press Enter.**

   The Modem Baud Rate dialog box appears, as shown in Figure 13-2. The dialog box asks you for your modem speed.

   Use your arrow keys to move up and down the list. If your modem's speed isn't listed, select a speed slightly higher than your modem's baud rate.

```
MODEM BAUD RATE ...

                 What baud rate is your modem?

   460800   460KBps  - ISDN modem...
   230400   230KBps  - 56Kbps modem... or ISDN modem...
   115200   115KBps  - 28.8, 33.6, or 56Kbps modem...
   57600    57.6KBps - 28.8, 33.6, or 56Kbps modem...
   38400    38.4KBps - Hangin ten on the net! 28.8 or 33.6...
   19200    19.2KBps - Better known as 14.4...
   9600     9600bps  - No comment...

                 <  OK  >        <Cancel>
```

Figure 13-2: Select the speed of your modem.

6. **Using your arrow keys, highlight the baud rate (speed) of your modem and press Enter.**

   The Callback dialog box appears, asking you if your ISP uses the callback method for verifying your identity. (It's 99.9 percent likely that your ISP does not.)

7. **Use your arrow keys to highlight** No **and press Enter.**

   The Modem Init String dialog box appears, asking you for your default modem initialization string. The initialization string is a list of commands for the modem to get itself ready for a connection. Don't make any changes here if this is your first time using `pppsetup`.

8. **Press Enter.**

   The Domain Name dialog box appears, as shown in Figure 13-3. The dialog box asks you for the domain name of your ISP.

   Several examples are given in Figure 13-3. Generally, the domain name is the name or acronym of the ISP followed by either `.com` or `.net`. Examples include `att.net` (for AT&T) or `netcom.com` (for Netcom, Inc.).

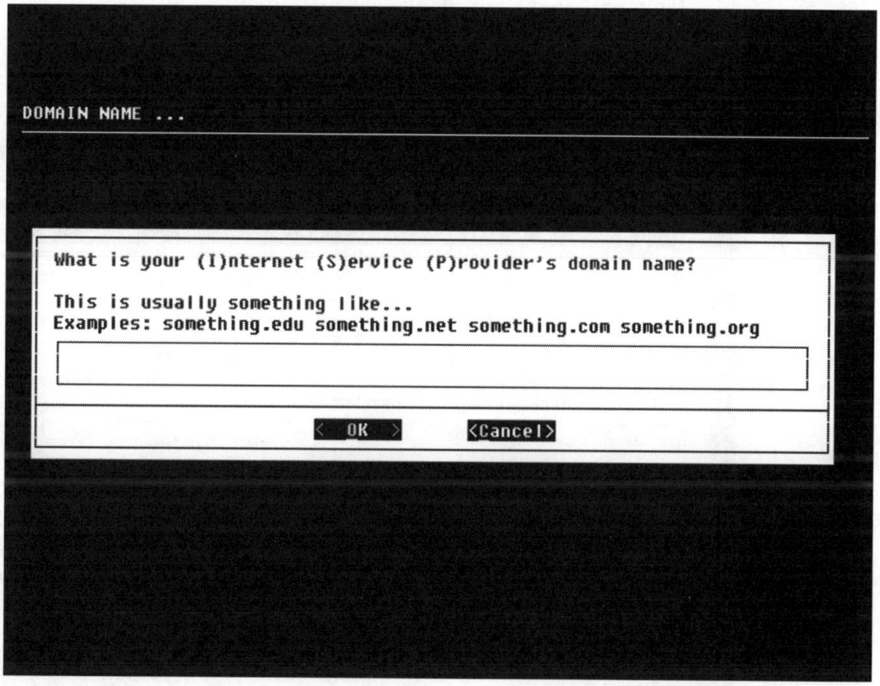

DOMAIN NAME ...

What is your (I)nternet (S)ervice (P)rovider's domain name?

This is usually something like...
Examples: something.edu something.net something.com something.org

< OK > <Cancel>

Figure 13-3: Enter the domain name of your ISP.

9. **In the text field, type the domain name of your ISP and press Enter.**

   The DNS IP Address dialog box appears, as shown in Figure 13-4. The dialog box asks you for the Domain Name Server (DNS) address for your ISP.

   Make sure that the address given to you by your ISP is a series of numbers and dots (like 123.456.789.012) and not a name (like `dns.myISP.com`).

10. **In the text field, type the address of your ISP's DNS server and press Enter.**

    The PAP, CHAP, or SCRIPT dialog box appears, as shown in Figure 13-5. The dialog box asks whether your ISP uses an authentication system.

    PAP (Password Authentication Protocol) and CHAP (Challenge/Handshake Authentication Protocol) are the common authentication schemes. SCRIPT is outdated and being phased out.

11. **Use your arrow keys to highlight your ISP's authentication scheme and press Enter.**

    The PAP Or CHAP Login dialog box appears. The dialog box asks you for your login name on the ISP. Note that this may be different than your login name for your Slackware machine!

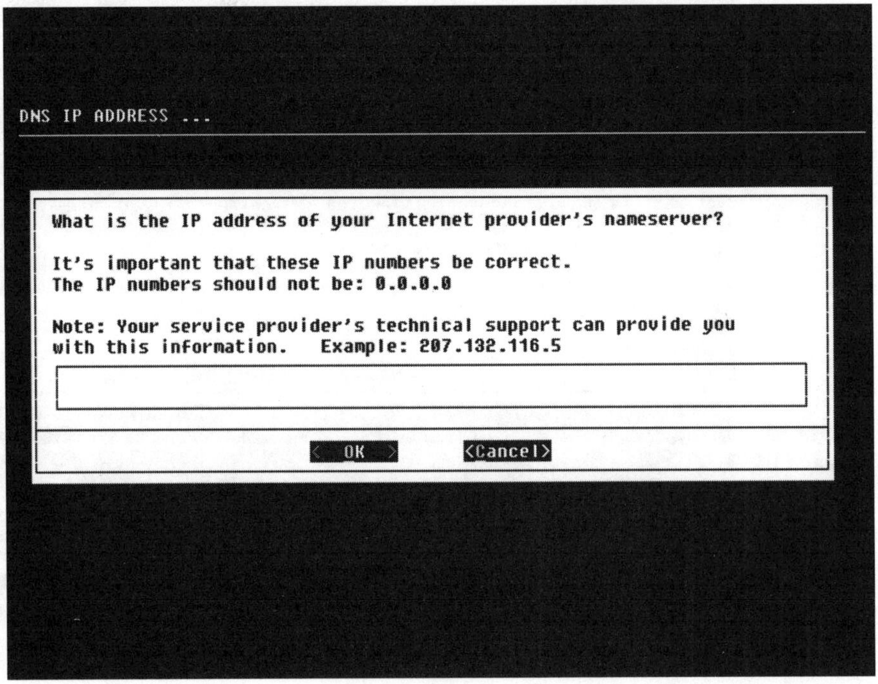

DNS IP ADDRESS ...
What is the IP address of your Internet provider's nameserver?
It's important that these IP numbers be correct.
The IP numbers should not be: 0.0.0.0
Note: Your service provider's technical support can provide you
with this information. Example: 207.132.116.5
< OK >
<Cancel>

Figure 13-4: Enter your ISP's DNS server address.

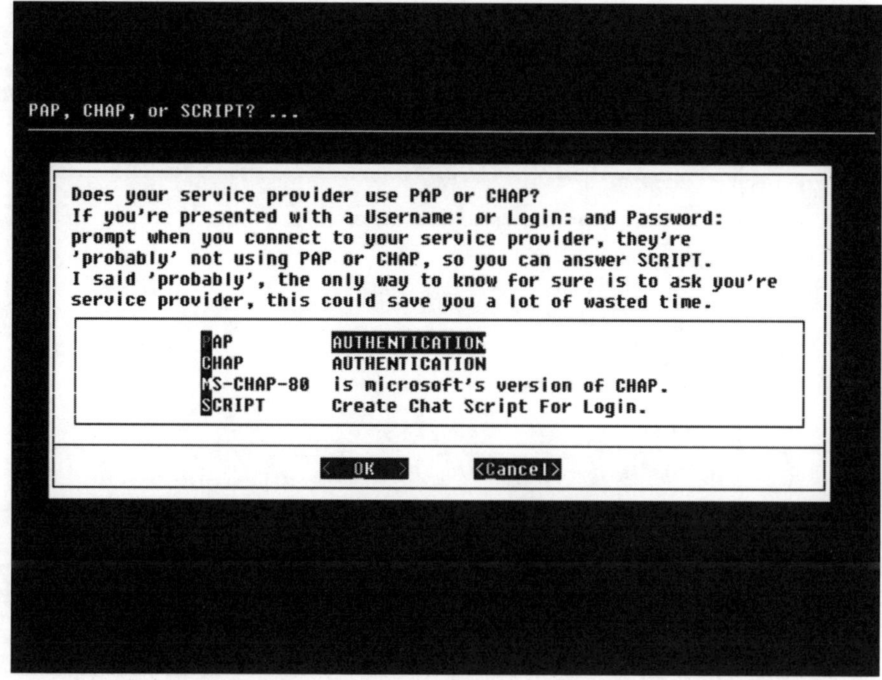

PAP, CHAP, or SCRIPT? ...
Does your service provider use PAP or CHAP?
If you're presented with a Username: or Login: and Password:
prompt when you connect to your service provider, they're
'probably' not using PAP or CHAP, so you can answer SCRIPT.
I said 'probably', the only way to know for sure is to ask you're
service provider, this could save you a lot of wasted time.
PAP AUTHENTICATION
CHAP AUTHENTICATION
MS-CHAP-80 is microsoft's version of CHAP.
SCRIPT Create Chat Script For Login.
< OK >
<Cancel>

Figure 13-5: Select your ISP's authentication system.

12. **In the text field, type your login name for your ISP and press Enter.**

    The PAP or CHAP Password dialog box appears. The dialog box asks you for the password to your ISP. Again, this may be different than the password that you use for your Slackware machine!

13. **In the text field, type your password for your ISP and press Enter.**

    `pppsetup` presents your configuration files, as shown in Figure 13-6. Use your arrow keys to navigate up and down the files.

    The numbers and settings in Figure 13-6, like the phone number, DNS server, and login name and password, will differ depending on your ISP's information.

Your PPP setup is complete.

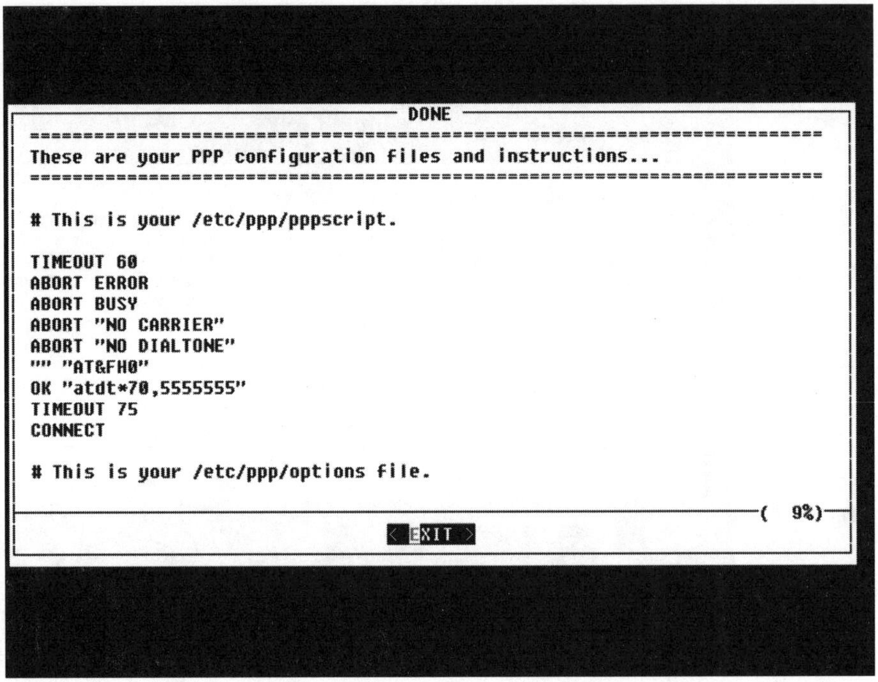

```
DONE
==========================================================================
These are your PPP configuration files and instructions...
==========================================================================

# This is your /etc/ppp/pppscript.

TIMEOUT 60
ABORT ERROR
ABORT BUSY
ABORT "NO CARRIER"
ABORT "NO DIALTONE"
"" "AT&FH0"
OK "atdt*70,5555555"
TIMEOUT 75
CONNECT

# This is your /etc/ppp/options file.
( 9%)
< EXIT >
```

Figure 13-6: Your configuration files for PPP.

Making the Connection to Your ISP

After you complete your PPP configuration, you're ready to connect to your ISP. To make the connection to your ISP, follow these steps:

1. **Log in to your own personal account.**
2. **At the command prompt (the > or % prompt), type** startx **to start X Windows.**

   See Chapter 11 for more help on running X Windows.

   After X Windows is running, you must open an xterm window.
3. **In KDE, click K, then choose Non-KDE Apps⇨Utilities⇨X Terminal. In GNOME, click the Main Menu Button, then choose Utilities⇨Color Xterm or Regular Xterm. In either case, a new window titled xterm appears.**

4. **Within the xterm window, type** ppp-go & **and press Enter.**

   Do not leave off the `&` in the command unless you don't want to use your xterm window again! The `&` puts the command in the background, where it runs without any more input from you (you can find more info on background processes in Chapter 16).The `ppp-go` program sends messages to your xterm window the entire time that you're connected to your ISP.

Your modem picks up your phone line, dials, and makes loud screeching noises as the ISP's modem on the other end of the line picks up and connects. After a few moments, you're connected to the Internet.

Now you need to check if the ISP's DNS server is running. To do so, type **ping -c 5** followed by the DNS server address. For example, if your ISP's DNS server is 1.2.3.4, you type

```
ping -c 5 1.2.3.4
```

The ping program sends five test queries (pings) to the DNS server 1.2.3.4 and exits.

A positive response looks like the following (numbers will vary depending on several factors, ranging from how busy your ISP is to how far away you physically are from the ISP's office):

```
slack1:~> ping -c 5 1.2.3.4
PING 1.2.3.4 (1.2.3.4): 56 data bytes
64 bytes from 1.2.3.4: icmp_seq=0 ttl=255 time=0.5 ms
64 bytes from 1.2.3.4: icmp_seq=1 ttl=255 time=0.4 ms
64 bytes from 1.2.3.4: icmp_seq=2 ttl=255 time=0.4 ms
64 bytes from 1.2.3.4: icmp_seq=3 ttl=255 time=0.4 ms
64 bytes from 1.2.3.4: icmp_seq=4 ttl=255 time=0.4 ms

-- 1.2.3.4 ping statistics --
5 packets transmitted, 5 packets received, 0% packet loss
round-trip min/avg/max = 0.4/0.4/0.5 ms
```

A positive response means that the server is responding to the ping and is available for use. You're on the Internet!

A negative response features the message `100%" packet loss` under the statistics line. If you get a negative response, either the connection between your computer and the ISP, or the server 1.2.3.4 isn't working properly. At this point, call your ISP's support or help desk for more information.

Disconnecting from Your ISP

When you're done playing on the Internet, open up another xterm window, or use the same window in which you ran `ppp-go`, and type **ppp-off** and press Enter to disconnect from your ISP.

You can find more help on PPP and the `ppp-go` and `ppp-off` programs by looking at the file `/etc/ppp/pppsetup.txt`. At a command prompt, type **more /etc/ppp/pppsetup.txt** and press Enter.

Chapter 14

Web Browsing and E-Mail

In This Chapter

- Configuring Netscape Communicator as your Web browser
- Using Netscape Navigator to surf the Web
- Using Lynx to read just the text
- Setting up Netscape Messenger for e-mail

Netscape — the very name is synonymous with the World Wide Web. At one time, Netscape's Navigator browser was available only for those who used Windows computers. Linux users were forced to use either Lynx or old versions of Mosaic (the predecessor to Navigator).

Netscape Communicator is now part of the Slackware distribution. You must install the `netscape` package from the XAP series and the X Windows programs from the X series in order for Netscape to work. (See Chapter 7 for help on installing specific packages. You may also need to see Chapter 11 for help in getting X Windows started.) In this chapter, you set up Netscape Communicator to browse the Web and send and receive e-mail. You're also introduced to Lynx, the text-only Web browser.

Setting Up Netscape Communicator

The Slackware system treats Netscape Communicator just like any other program, even though Communicator is an X Windows application. This means that you can run Communicator from the command prompt or from within an X Windows window manager. But before you can run Communicator, you must first configure it.

These instructions assume that you have an ISP and all information necessary to connect to the Internet. For more information on ISPs and the information needed, see Chapter 13.

To run Netscape from the command prompt, follow these steps:

1. **Log in as any user,** root **or otherwise.**
2. **At the command prompt, start X Windows by typing** startx.

   See Chapter 11 for more help on running X Windows.

   You must now open an xterm window.
3. **In KDE, choose K⇨Non-KDE Apps⇨Utilities⇨X Terminal. In GNOME, choose G⇨Utilities⇨Color Xterm or Regular Xterm. In either case, a window titled xterm opens with a command prompt.**
4. **At the command prompt in the xterm, start your PPP connection by typing** ppp-go & **and pressing Enter.**

   Your modem calls your ISP and connects. (You can find more detailed information on the `ppp-go` command in Chapter 13.)
5. **At the command prompt in the xterm, type** netscape & **and press Enter.**

   If you're running KDE, you can run Netscape by choosing K⇨ non-KDE apps⇨Internet⇨Netscape. In GNOME, choose G⇨Internet⇨ Netscape Communicator. In either case, Communicator appears in a separate window.

After Communicator is running, you must set it up for use. To do so, follow these steps:

1. **In the Netscape Navigator window (Navigator is the browser part of Communicator), choose Edit⇨Preferences.**

   The Netscape Preferences window appears, as shown in Figure 14-1.
2. **In the left pane, under Category, click Navigator.**

   The Navigator screen appears to the right of the Category listing, as shown in Figure 14-2.
3. **In the Location text box, type the URL of the Web page that you want to set as your home page.**

   You can type any Web page URL that you want. (The example in Figure 14-2 is a personal Web page.)

   URL stands for Uniform Resource Locator, which is the Web address for a Web page. URLs typically look like this: `http://somewhere.someplace.com`. The `http://` means that the page uses the HyperText Transfer Protocol (HTTP).You may see URLs that begin with `ftp://` as well — FTP stands for File Transfer Protocol, which is used for file servers that supply files to the Internet. A home page is the Web page that automatically appears when Navigator opens. The default Web page when Netscape starts for the first time is Netscape's Netcenter Web page at `http://www.netscape.com`.

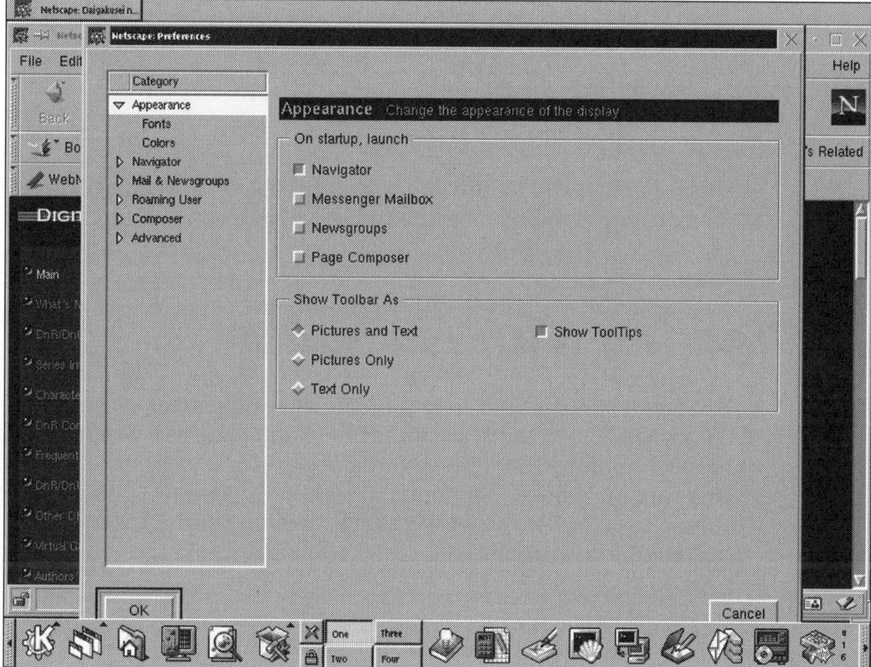

Figure 14-1: The Netscape Preferences window.

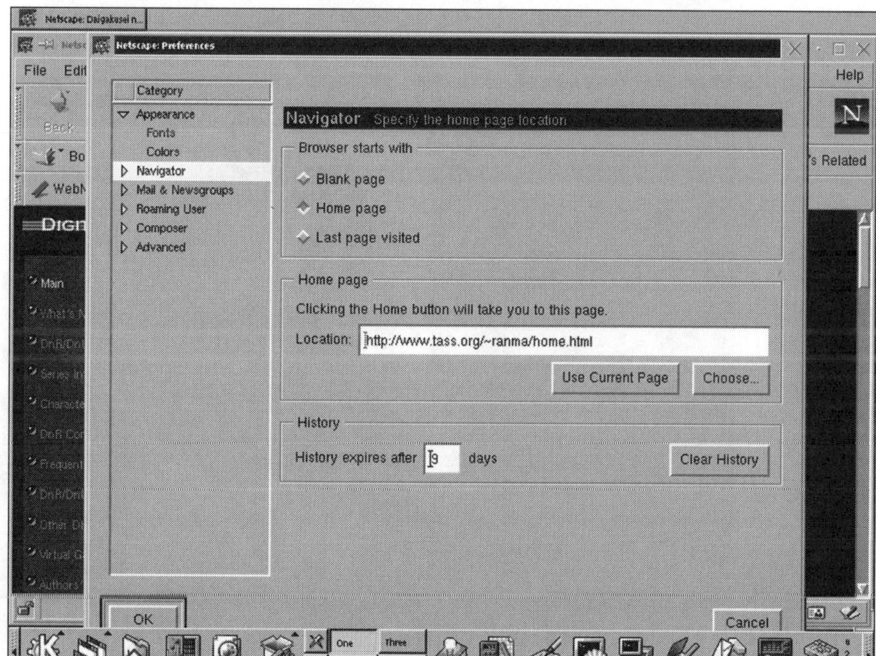

Figure 14-2: Setting up preferences for the Navigator browser.

For example, type **http://www.slackware.com** in the Location text box to change the home page to the Slackware home page.

4. **Click OK.**

   The Netscape Preferences window closes.

You are now ready to surf the Internet. To view a Web page, type the URL in the Location text box near the top of the Netscape window and press Enter.

Navigating with Navigator

When you surf the Web, pages of information appear on your screen. Some of the words or sentences are underlined and shown in a different color than the surrounding text. These words or sentences are *links* to other Web pages. Links are invisible connections to Web addresses or URLs of other Web pages. To go to the linked Web page, click the underlined portion of the link (or the differently colored portion). Navigator takes you to the new Web page.

Web pages can also contain graphics, as shown in Figure 14-3.

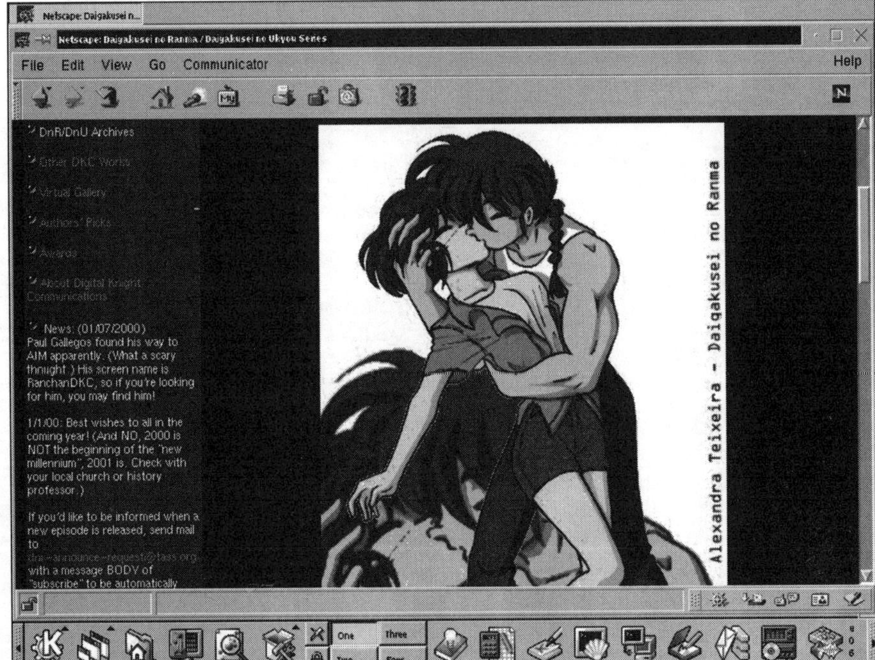

Figure 14-3: A Web page with graphics.

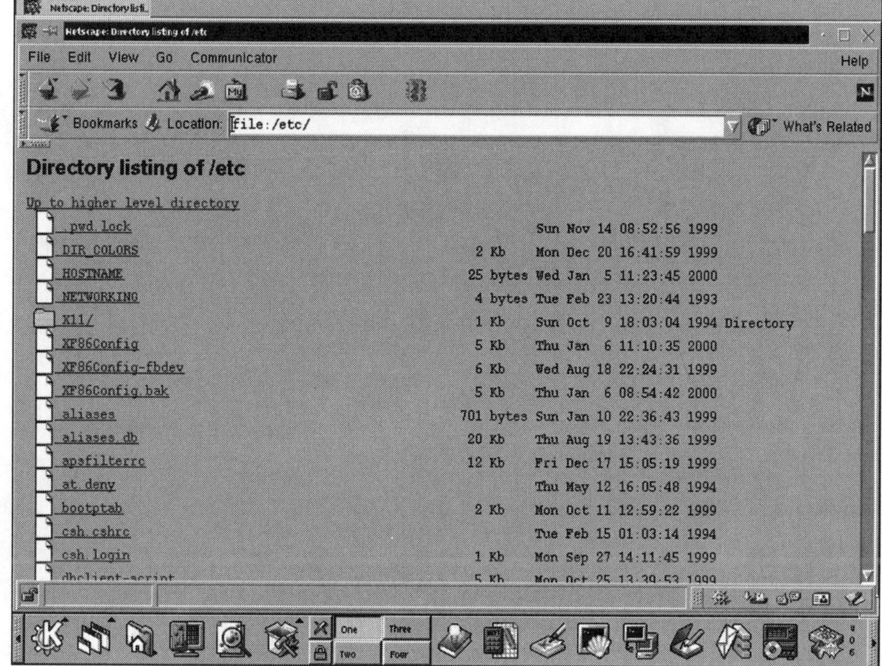

Figure 14-4: Browsing through directories on your Slackware machine.

Navigator doesn't care whether the graphics on a Web page are big or small — all Navigator does is display them. Web sites can contain animated graphics, graphics that are links to other Web pages, and interactive graphics. You're likely to run into these new graphics as you explore the Web.

You can also use Navigator as a File Browser. To use Navigator in this fashion, type **file:/etc** in the Location text box. A listing of the contents in the `/etc` directory on your Slackware machine appear, as shown in Figure 14-4.

Web Surfing for the X Windows-Impaired

If you have an ISP but haven't yet gotten the hang of X Windows, you can still surf the Web. Slackware has a text-based Web browser called Lynx that's been around for quite a while. While you don't get to see neat-o graphics with Lynx, you *do* get to read Web pages. Lynx requires that you install the `lynx` package in the N series of Slackware software. (See Chapter 7 for information on installing specific packages.)

To run Lynx, at your command prompt type **lynx http://www.slackware.com** and press Enter. The resulting screen is shown in Figure 14-5.

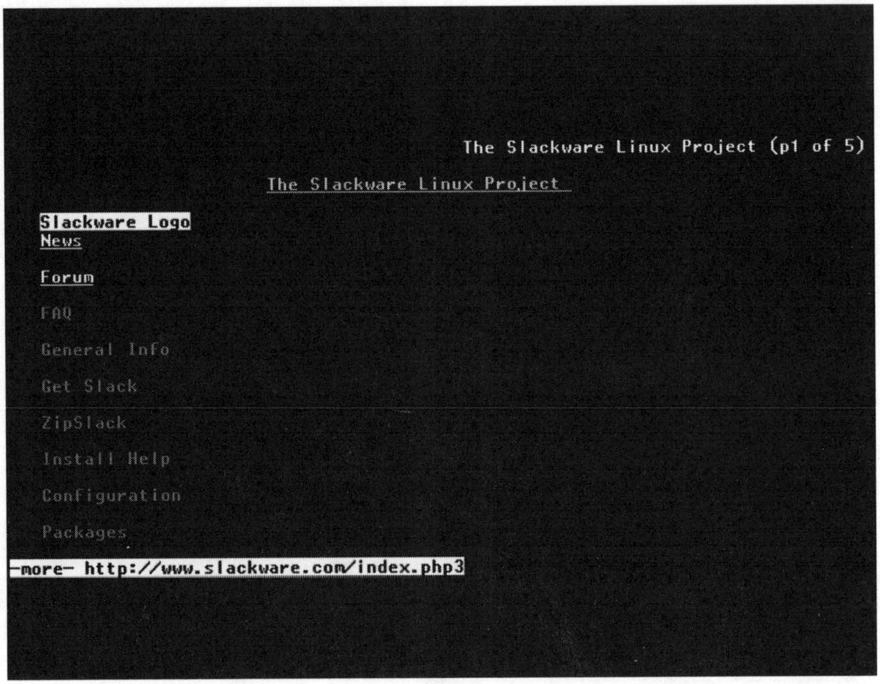

Figure 14-5: Using Lynx to surf the Web.

What a difference no graphics makes! Use the space bar to move forward through pages of information, or use the up and down arrow keys to navigate line by line. The highlighted areas are links to other Web pages. When you use the up and down arrows, the highlighted area jumps to the next available link. Use your right arrow key to follow a link, and use your left arrow key to go back a Web page.

Lynx enables you to view URLs of different protocols (HTTP, FTP, and so on) just like Netscape Navigator. Lynx is often good if you want to surf certain Web pages but don't want to read the advertising windows that pop up. Because Lynx can't open any windows, none of the pop-up advertisements appear. Plus, any advertisements built in to the Web page that you're viewing only appear as the phrase `[ Advertisement ]`, or something similar (what appears in the space depends on what the creators of the Web page make it say — some say `Ad`, `Image`, or even `Image Goes Here`).

Sending and Receiving E-Mail

Another nice feature of Netscape Communicator is its Messenger e-mail client, which you can set up to send and receive e-mail so that you don't have to use multiple programs in order to surf the Web and read e-mail.

The following instructions assume that you have the following information from your ISP:

- E-mail address
- POP server name
- Mail server name

If you don't have this information, turn to Chapter 13 to find out how to get it.

You must configure Messenger before you can use it for e-mail. To do so, follow these steps:

1. **Run Netscape Communicator, either from the desktop manager (KDE, GNOME, or another manager), or from an xterm window.**

   In KDE, you can run Netscape by choosing K⇨non-KDE apps⇨Internet⇨Netscape. In GNOME, choose G⇨Internet⇨Netscape Communicator. Or from an xterm window, type **netscape &** and press Enter.

2. **Choose Edit⇨Preferences.**

   The Netscape Preferences window appears.

3. **In the left pane, under Category, click Mail & Newsgroups.**

   A new listing appears underneath Mail & Newsgroups, as shown in Figure 14-6.

4. **Click Identity.**

   The Identity screen appears to the right of the Category listing.

5. **Type your name and your e-mail address in the Name and E-mail Address text boxes.**

   You can skip the Reply-To Address, Organization, and Signature File text boxes.

6. **Click Mail Servers in the Category listing.**

   The Mail Servers screen appears to the right of the Category listing, as shown in Figure 14-7. Several buttons appear on the right of this screen.

7. **Click the Edit button.**

   The window titled Netscape appears, as shown in Figure 14-8.

8. **In the Server Name text box, type the POP server name supplied by your ISP.**

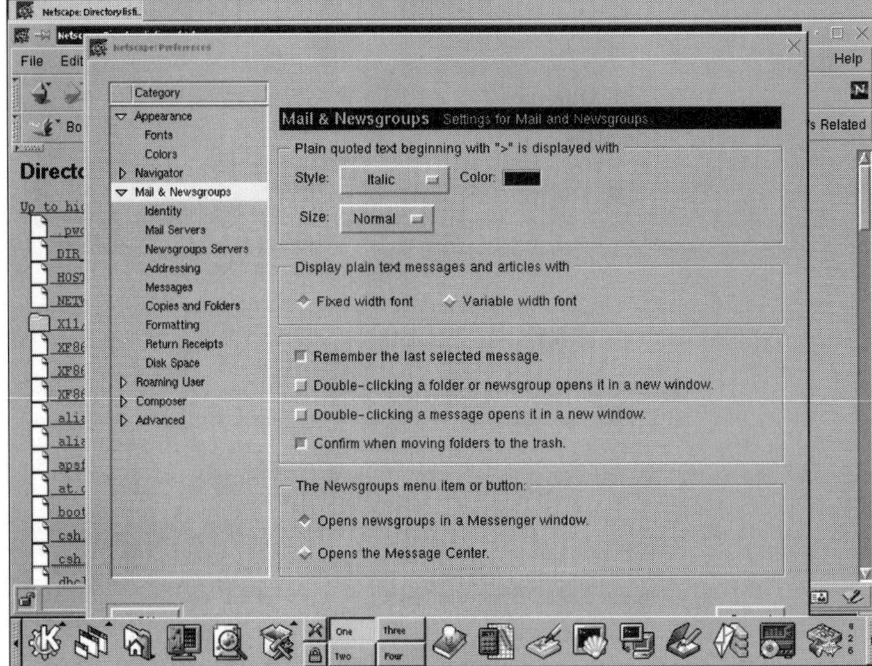

Figure 14-6: The Mail & News-groups listing.

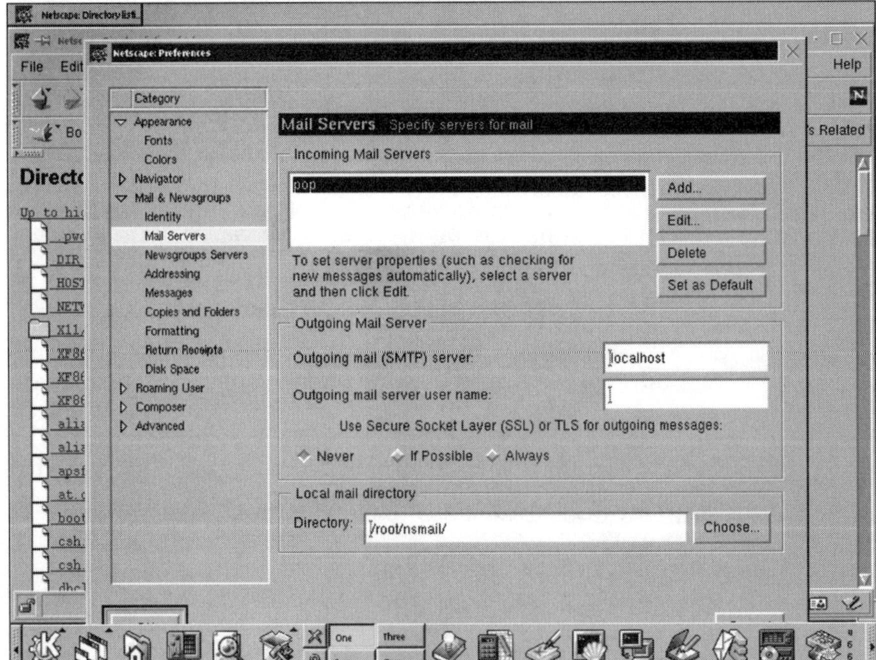

Figure 14-7: The Mail Servers screen.

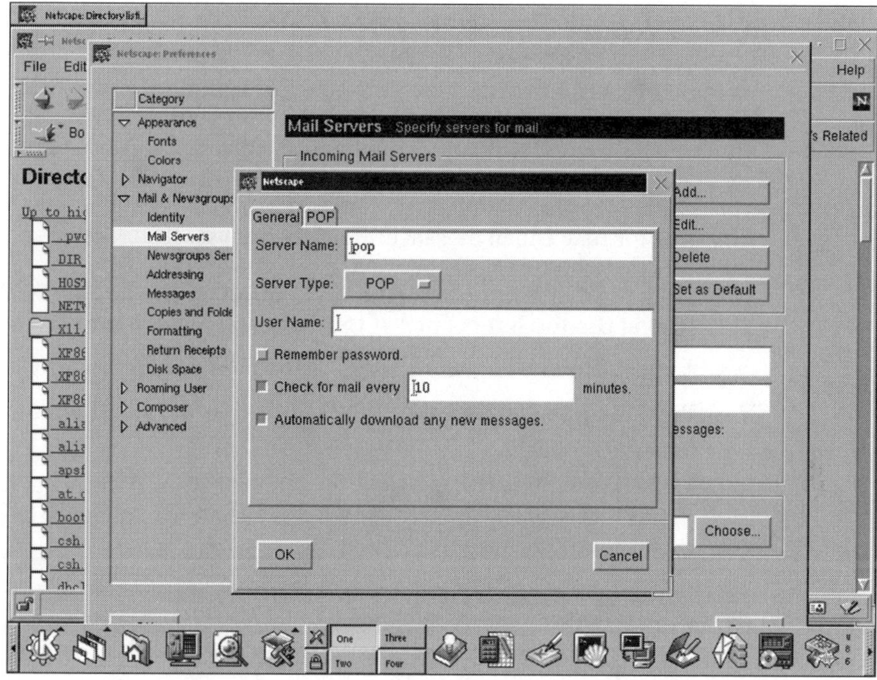

Figure 14-8: Editing your mail server settings.

9. **Type your POP user name in the User Name text box.**

   Your ISP supplies the POP user name information.

10. **Click the Remember Password option.**

11. **Click OK.**

    The Edit window disappears. The name of your POP mail server appears in the Incoming Mail Servers box.

12. **In the Outgoing Mail (SMTP) Server text box, type the name of the mail server supplied by your ISP.**

    Your ISP supplies the STMP mail server information.

13. **Type your mail server user name in the Outgoing Mail Server User Name text box.**

    This is usually the same as your login name on the ISP.

14. **Click the OK button in the bottom-left corner of the Preferences window.**

    The Preferences window closes.

Messenger is now set up to send and receive e-mail.

Checking for e-mail

In the bottom-right corner of your Netscape window are five icons. The second icon from the left is the Inbox icon. (If you look closely, it resembles a tiny envelope and a tray for incoming mail.) Clicking this icon brings up the Netscape mail utility, as shown in Figure 14-9.

To check for new e-mail messages, follow these steps:

1. **Click the Get Msg button (the first button on the left under the word File) at the top-left corner of the Netscape Messenger window.**

   A small window appears asking for the password to your POP account.

2. **Type the password to your POP account in the small window and click OK.**

   If you have any new messages, they appear in an orderly list in the top-right section of the Messenger window, as shown in Figure 14-10.

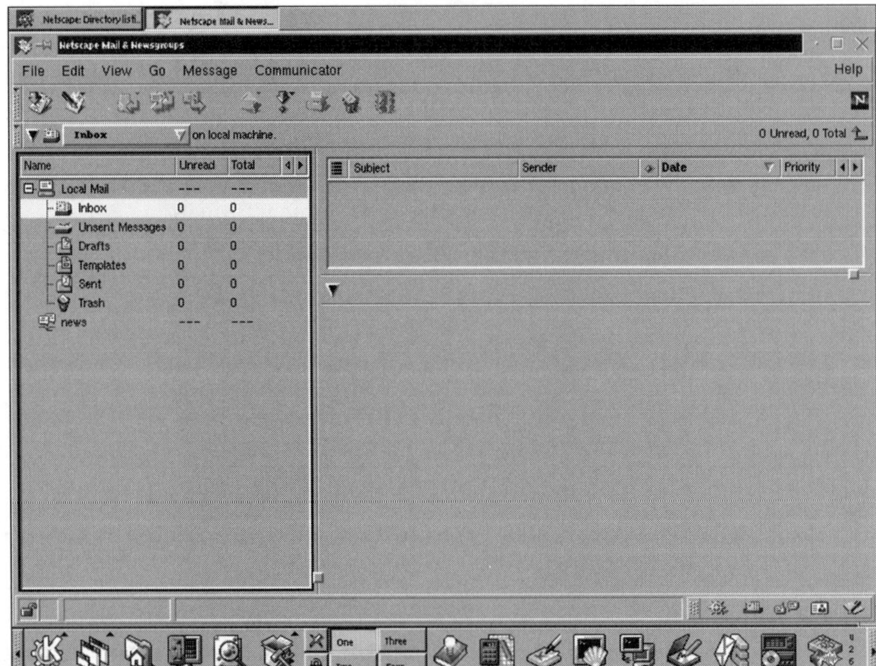

Figure 14-9: Behold Netscape Messenger.

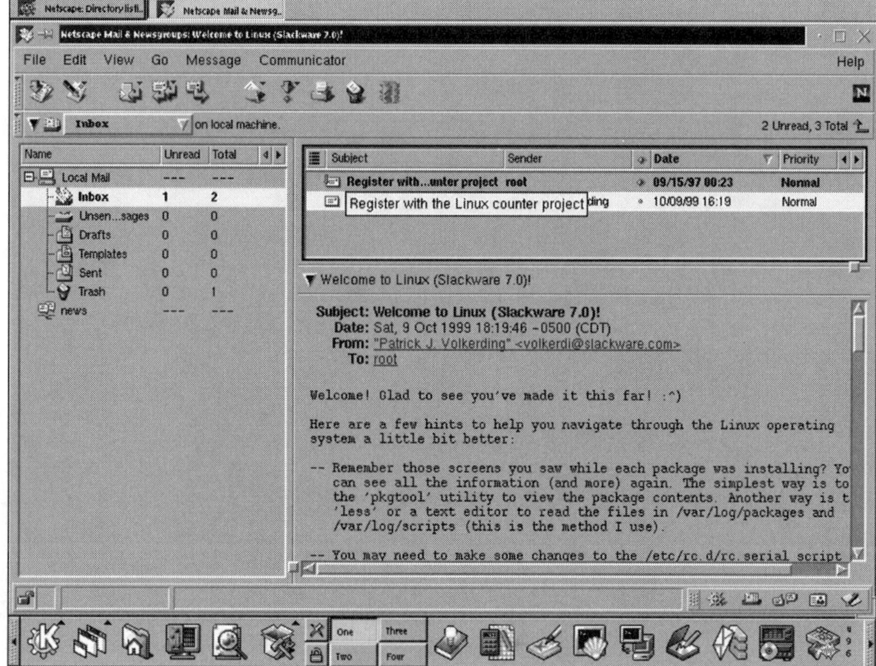

Figure 14-10: You've got mail! The Netscape Messenger window.

3. **Click once any of the messages in bold font. The message appears in the section below.**

   You can also double-click any message to open a new window and read the message in the new window.

You've mastered reading e-mail! Now it's time to send some.

Sending e-mail

Sending an e-mail message is the same as sending a letter — you need to know the recipient's e-mail address.

To send an e-mail message, follow these steps:

1. **Click the New Msg button (the second button from the left under the word Edit).**

   The Compose window appears, as shown in Figure 14-11.

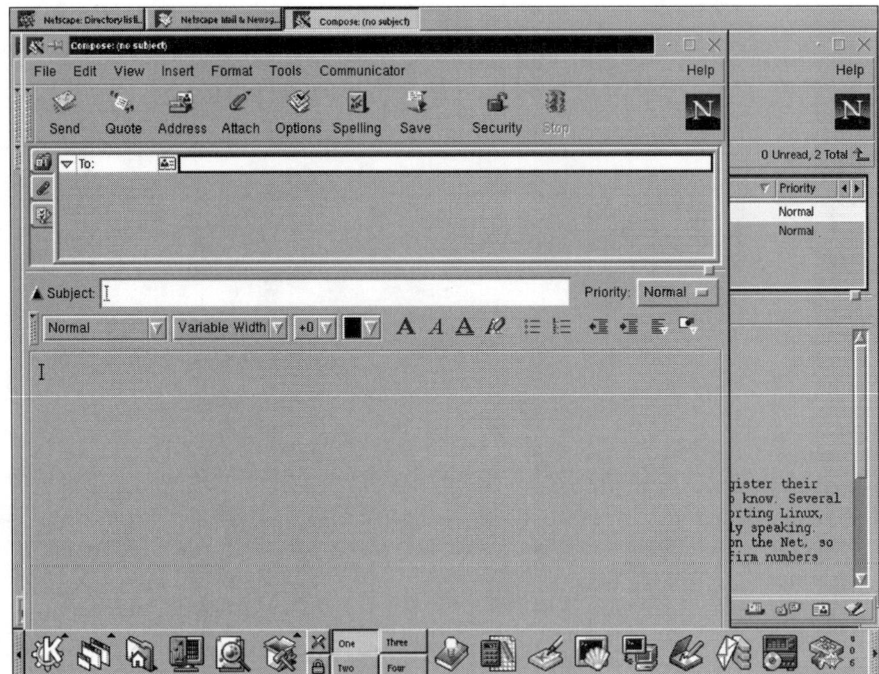

Figure 14-11: Sending an e-mail message.

2. **Click inside the To: text box.**
3. **Type the e-mail address of the person you wish to send the message to.**

   For example, to send to your friend John Doe at `company.com`, you would type `johndoe@company.com`.
4. **Click inside Subject: text box.**
5. **Type a subject for your e-mail.**
6. **Click inside the large text field below the `Subject:` line.**
7. **Begin typing your e-mail message.**

   Your e-mail can be as long or as short as you want.
8. **When you finish, click the Send button at the top of the window.**

   Your e-mail is sent.

A good test to see if your e-mail works is to send yourself a test message. Type your e-mail address in the `To:` text box, as shown in Figure 14-12. Then click the Send button. If everything is working correctly, your test message appears in your inbox.

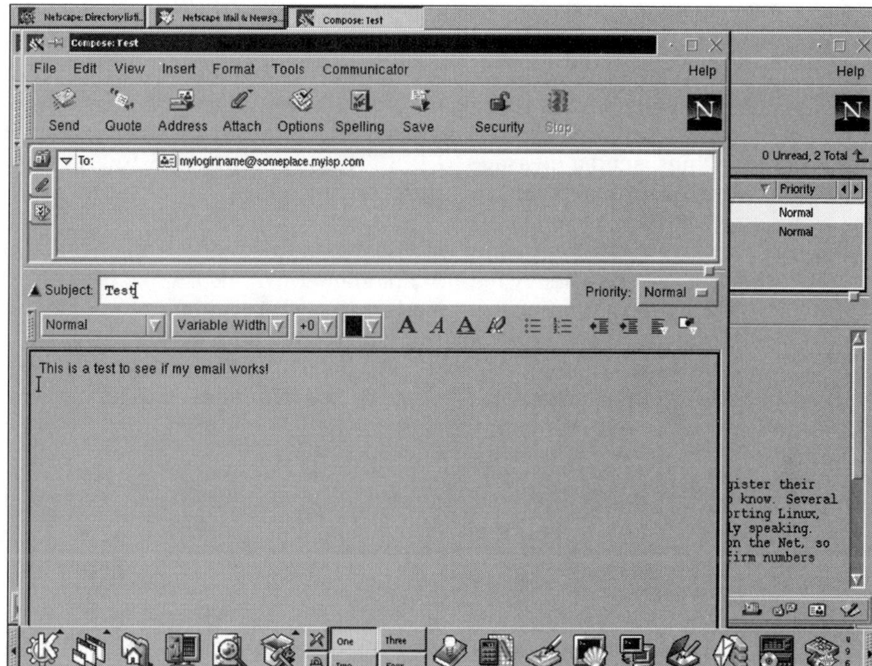

Figure 14-12: A test message.

Avoiding spam

Invariably, you will receive unwanted e-mail, called *spam*. Spam is electronic junk mail and is very, very annoying. Most spam comes from mailing lists that you're added to when you fill out an electronic form on a Web page or when you write down your e-mail address in a promotion at the mall.

Getting off these mailing lists is next to impossible because your e-mail address is sold to new people almost instantaneously. You can, however, do the following to curb the influx of spam:

- Never give your e-mail address to people that you don't know. If an online company requests your e-mail address, ask to see their Privacy Policy to see what they may or may not do with your e-mail address. All good companies have a Privacy Policy.
- Call your ISP when you receive spam to ask them to block the sender from sending you any more spam.
- Delete the messages without reading them.

Whatever you do, *don't* reply back to the sender saying "Take me off this list." Most senders monitor their lists to see if the e-mail addresses actually exist. If they get a response back, then the sender marks you as someone who read their spam (which, technically, you did by replying). Also, don't send e-mail to any addresses listed in a spam e-mail that say "To be removed from our mailings, send a message to . . . ." This is another ploy to grab a real e-mail address for placement on future mailing lists.

Legislators are proposing laws designed to eliminate spam and force the senders to pay heavy fees for spamming. Who knows — in the next couple of years, the amount of spam may drop as more and more people become informed. You can do your share by informing your ISP about any and all spam e-mail that you receive. You can also check with your local government to see if any legislation is being enacted in your area to deal with spam e-mail.

Part V

Managing Your System

In this part . . .

You're now ready to handle some of the intricacies of Slackware. You get to play with the advanced system administration techniques, possibly eking out that extra bit of performance, or potentially crashing your system.

Chapter 15 discusses the file system, where you find out about hard drives, special drives such as CDs and floppies, and backing up your system. Chapter 16 goes into file and directory permissions and job process control.

Chapter 17 demonstrates some tuning you can do with your system, including recompiling the kernel. You also uncover more about the necessity of RAM and see the importance of using `tune2fs`.

Chapter 18 is the *what to do in case of an emergency* chapter. This chapter includes tips that may help you stave off a complete failure of your system.

Chapter 15

Working with the File System

In This Chapter

- Understanding drive space
- Working with hard drives
- Handling special drives
- Backing up your data in Slackware

The amount of space on your hard drive limits what software you can install on your Slackware machine. But even if you run out of space, you can always add more drives to your machine. These drives can be normal hard drives, or special drives like floppy disk drives, Zip drives, or CD-ROM drives. In this chapter, I show you what drive space truly means, guide you through handling hard drives, and introduce you to other special drives.

Another key to running a successful Slackware system is doing automatic backups. In this chapter, I show you how to perform these backups without breaking a sweat.

Journeying into Free Space

Free space determines exactly how much data you can place on your computer. All systems, including Windows and DOS, have a problem with free space. But these operating systems don't have the tools to manage it as well as Slackware. As the super user in Slackware, you can choke your system by installing too much software for the amount of space that you have. Doing so causes errors and makes programs unable to run. Slackware provides you with several ways to check your free space to make sure that you aren't going over the limit.

In Slackware, you can use the `df` command to determine how much space is in use. To run `df`, at your command prompt type **df** and press Enter. You don't have to be the super user to look at the system's disk space.

You receive information similar to the following (the actual numbers will differ depending on your system):

```
slack1:~> df
Filesystem    1k-blocks      Used Available Use% Mounted on
/dev/hda1        432591     98395    311115  24% /
/dev/hda3        432623    414076         0 100% /usr
/dev/hda4        943656    784610    108646  88% /home
```

In this case, the /usr partition is almost full — the system considers the partition close enough that it's listed at 100% in the Use% column. But if you compare the 1k-blocks column (which lists the total amount of disk space available on the partition in blocks of 1024 bytes) against the Used (the amount of disk space used, also measured in blocks of 1024 bytes) column, some space is still available (432623 - 414076 ≠ 0). This means that the machine needs cleaning up, and quickly!

You can also use the du command, which estimates disk space usage for particular directories. At the command prompt, type **du** and press Enter. du calculates the total space used in each directory, starting from the current directory and moving through all the subdirectories contained in the current directory.

For example, to determine the amount of disk space used in the /var/log/packages directory (which is the listing of all the packages installed on the system), you would type the following commands:

1. **At your # command prompt, type** cd /var/log/packages **and press Enter.**

   /var/log/packages appears at the prompt.

2. **Type** du **and press Enter.**

   A numerical response similar to the following appears (the numbers may differ depending on the number of Slackware software packages you have installed on your system):

   ```
   1869    .
   ```

The directory is using 1.8MB (1869KB) of space in the /var/log/packages directory, or just under 2MB of space. That's not bad. As a comparison, if 75 percent of the packages are installed from the CD-ROM, the typical amount of disk space usage is around 5MB.

Working with Hard Drives

Each hard drive on your system can have multiple partitions. The advantage of having multiple hard drives and partitions is that you can always add new drives at any time to your Slackware system by creating a place for them to connect to in your file system (these are called mount points, a concept covered in more detail in Chapter 9). After you mount the drives, you can configure the drives at your leisure.

You must also be able to clean up the drives as needed. The `fsck` program does this for you when you boot your machine, but you can run it manually when necessary.

Mounting and unmounting

Mounting is the act of connecting a drive partition to an existing system. But you must have a *mount point,* or location, for the new drive to connect.

You must be the super user to mount a new drive. At your command prompt (the # prompt), you type **mount {device} {mount point}** and press Enter.

Suppose that you have a hard drive, called `/dev/hdb`, with three partitions, and you want to mount another partition to the directory `/mnt`. Type the following at your # prompt:

```
mount -t auto /dev/hdb3 /mnt
```

The `-t auto` flag tells the `mount` command to check the partition `/dev/hdb3` and see if the partition is a recognized type (the partition should be recognized — Slackware recognizes almost every partition in existence). After `mount` recognizes the partition, `mount` adds `/dev/hdb3` to the system as the directory `/mnt`.

After you mount a partition, the partition is considered a normal directory that you can access by using the `cd` command. The partition also appears in the system table of disk usage listed when the `df` command is issued. After you mount a partition, you cannot remount it elsewhere on the system — only one mount per partition is allowed. So if `/dev/hdb3` is already mounted as `/mnt`, it cannot be simultaneously mounted as `/mnt2`.

If you need to create a new mount point for a partition, simply generate a new directory via the `mkdir` command. For example, typing **mkdir /newpoint** at your command prompt creates a directory called `newpoint` in the `/` directory. Now you can mount new partitions to this directory.

When you're done with a partition and don't want it mounted any longer, type **umount {mount point}** at your command prompt and press Enter. You must be the super user to use the `umount` command. Note also that the command is `umount`, not unmount! To unmount the `/mnt` partition that is being used by `/dev/hdb3`, type

```
umount /mnt
```

Typing this command unmounts the /mnt partition and frees /dev/hdb3 for use on another part of the system.

Sometimes you cannot unmount a partition because another program or user is using the partition. You can determine which program (and user) is using the partition by typing **fuser -u {mount point}**. This command lists all the programs that are using the partition in question. For example, to check who or what is using /mnt before attempting to unmount it, type

```
slack1:~# fuser -u /mnt
```

The result will look something like the following (results vary depending on what programs are running on your machine):

```
/mnt:                14800c(root)
```

This means that a program owned by root is using /mnt, and that its process ID (PID) is 14800.

After you know the process ID using the partition, you can kill the program (if you're the super user or owner of the program) by typing kill -9 14800 and pressing Enter. See Chapter 16 for help on killing processes.

Configuring

Mounting partitions manually is tedious. You can automate this process by adding your new partitions to the system-wide file /etc/fstab, which is the file system table. To add a new partition to the /etc/fstab file, use an editor (like vi or pico) on the /etc/fstab file and make your new entry look like one of the entries already in the file. For example, if you prefer the pico editor, at your # command prompt, you would type **pico /etc/fstab** and press Enter. The /etc/fstab file would then be ready for editing. (You can find more help on editors in Chapter 10.)

A typical /etc/fstab table looks like this:

```
/dev/hda2       swap      swap      defaults   0   0
/dev/hda1       /         ext2      defaults   1   1
/dev/hda3       /usr      ext2      defaults   1   1
/dev/hda4       /home     ext2      defaults   1   1
none            /proc     proc      defaults   0   0
```

The first column is the partition name. A none entry instead of a /dev entry means that the partition in question is a virtual partition on the system — no physical partition exists for the virtual partition.

The second column is the mount point. A `swap` entry means that Slackware is using the partition as swap space (see Chapter 4 for more information on swap).

The third column is the type of file system that the device is being used for. Again, a `swap` entry means that the file system is a swap file system. A `proc` entry means that the `proc` file system is in use (see Chapter 9 for more info on the `proc` file system).

The fourth column is the specifications for the partition. This column may list several options, all of which are comma-separated. Table 15-1 lists some of the options available:

Table 15-1 Options for /etc/fstab

Code	*Description*
rw	Partition is read/writable
ro	Partition is read-only
dev	Treat special files on this partition as special files
nodev	Treat special files on this partition as filenames
exec	Binary files can be executed from this partition
noexec	Binary files cannot be executed from this partition
auto	Allow the system to automatically mount this partition
nouser	Only the super user can mount this partition
suid	Allow programs to become the owner of the program (called *setuid programs*) on this partition
nosuid	Disallow setuid programs on this partition
async	Write data to the partition in asynchronous fashion
defaults	A combination of rw, suid, dev, exec, auto, nouser, and async

The fifth column is the dump frequency, which is the frequency with which the partition's data can be backed up using the `dump` command. The use of this command is outdated.

The sixth column is the `fsck` pass number, which tells the system in what order `fsck` is supposed to look at this partition. `fsck` is the file system checking utility that clears up errors on the partition, if any exist. More information on how to use the `fsck` program is found in the next section.

fscking

fsck stands for FileSystem ChecK, and is the equivalent of Windows Scandisk and Defrag rolled into one program. (Remember that Scandisk and Defrag are file system and disk error-checking utilities.) fsck, however, can't help you if you have corrupt data — it can only fix problems with the hard drive. fsck does attempt to move data on corrupt sections of a partition into a safer location on the hard drive. Usually, fsck is successful, but occasionally a disk is too damaged for fsck to recover any information. (You can usually tell when fsck is not going to be successful when you hear a horrid scraping sound as the disk is spinning. This sound signifies a *head crash*, where the hard drive's magnetic head has dropped and is touching — actually more like scratching, tearing, or ripping — the disk itself.)

You must unmount a partition before you can check it by using fsck. Running fsck on a mounted file system isn't recommended because a mounted file system can have its data changed by any program or user during recovery. An unmounted file system cannot have its data changed during recovery because no user or program other than fsck can see the file system.

fsck uses several flags to help with its tasks, as shown in Table 15-2:

Table 15-2 Options (Flags) for fsck

Flag	*Description*
-p	Perform automatic repairs that don't change the contents of files
-n	Do not repair any problems, just list them
-y	Repair all problems
-A	Check all the file systems listed in /etc/fstab
-f	Force a file system to be checked

To run fsck, at your command prompt type **fsck [options] {partition to be checked}**. For example, if you want to check the /dev/hdb2 partition, and you want to run the check automatically, you type

```
fsck -y /dev/hdb2
```

The results of this command appear as follows:

```
Parallelizing fsck version 1.12 (9-Jul-98)
e2fsck 1.12, 9-Jul-98 for EXT2 FS 0.5b, 95/08/09
/dev/hdb2: clean, 816/27440 files, 48566/109466 blocks
```

Remember that the `-y` flag tells `fsck` to repair all problems. The third line of output states that no problems were found (`/dev/hdb2` is clean). If problems are found, `fsck` lists what the problems are and then what it did to fix them.

The `/proc` file system never needs to be checked with `fsck` because `/proc` is not a physical partition. `fsck` can only check physical disk partitions.

If you need to check the / directory, you must first boot using an emergency floppy disk before running `fsck`. See Chapter 18 for more information on emergency disks.

Handling Removable Disks

Slackware treats floppy disks and CDs as normal drives, even though they're removable. In fact, Slackware treats all drives, whether they're hard, floppy, CD-ROM, or Zip, as normal drives. The only difference between hard drives and other drives is the removable aspect — that is, you can walk away with a floppy disk, but you can't walk away (easily) with a hard drive.

Floppy and Zip disks

You must mount (make a file system available for use by the system) a floppy or Zip disk, regardless of what operating system is on the disk (DOS, Windows, OS/2, or Slackware) before you can use it. But you need to give the `mount` command a flag to tell `mount` what type of file system it's about to use, because by default `mount` assumes that the file system in question is a Slackware file system.

To mount a floppy disk in your `A:` drive, type

```
mount -t auto /dev/fd0 /floppy
```

(For disks in your second floppy drive, change the 0 to 1 so the `mount` command uses `/dev/fd1` — Zip drives can be mounted the same way using `/dev/iomega` instead of `/dev/fd0`.) The `-t auto` flag tells the `mount` command that `mount` is supposed to check the disk and make a determination as to what type of operating system created the disk.

Floppy disks can serve as tiny directories if you want to save small bits of information, or floppy disks can become another mounted file system if you're in need of an extra 1.44MB of space. You make Slackware file systems on floppy disks by typing the command

```
fdformat /dev/fd0; mke2fs /dev/fd0
```

This command formats your floppy disk and then makes the floppy disk a Slackware disk. (Again, change the 0 to 1 in `/dev/fd0` if you're using your secondary floppy disk drive instead of your primary floppy disk drive — Zip disks use `/dev/iomega` instead of `/dev/fd0`.)

CD-ROMs

CD-ROMs are a bit more complicated. CD-ROMs are mounted read-only. This means that you can't copy or write data to a CD-ROM, even if your CD-ROM is a CD-ROM writer. Writable CD-ROMs require a special program to use the writing capabilities — the use of such programs is beyond the scope of this book, but you can find more information on them at `http://www.linuxdoc.org/HOWTO/CD-Writing-HOWTO.html`. Mounting CD-ROMs, however, is just as easy as any other partition — at your command prompt, type

```
mount /dev/cdrom /cdrom
```

After you issue this command, Slackware replies with a message that it has mounted the CD-ROM as a read-only device. You can navigate the CD as if it was a normal directory on the system, but the difference is that you can't create or change any files on the CD. Automatically mounting your CD-ROM at boot is a good idea if you have a CD that you need continual access to.

To automatically mount your CD-ROM, add the following line to your `/etc/fstab` file (use an editor like `pico` or `vi` to edit this file by typing **vi /etc/fstab** and pressing Enter):

```
/dev/cdrom      /cdrom    auto        ro         0   0
```

This line tells Slackware to mount `/dev/cdrom` as the directory `/cdrom` and make it a read-only (ro) partition. The information on this line also tells Slackware that the type of CD is to be automatically detected and the CD-ROM is not to be checked by `fsck`, nor backed up by the `dump` command.

Backing Up Your Data in Slackware

System crashes happen, though with Slackware, crashes happen considerably less frequently (like almost never) than with Windows. But to be on the safe side, consider backing up your important files, such as your e-mail or personal files, to another location, like a floppy disk.

The best way to back up files is to use your floppy drive in conjunction with the `tar` command. `tar` stands for tape archive, but hardly anyone uses it to back up files to magnetic tapes anymore — the more common use is to create archive files with tar. (See Chapter 9 for more information on tar.) Some of the flags for tar are listed in Table 15-3:

Table 15-3 Options (Flags) for the tar Command

Flag	*Description*
-c	Create archive
-x	Extract archive
-v	Verbose mode — display more information than normal
-f	Use file instead of tape (does anyone use magnetic tape anymore?)
-z	Compress the tar archive
-M	Multiple disk spanning

Suppose that you want to back up your personal directory on the /home partition (because that's where personal directories are located). At your command prompt, type

```
tar -cvfzM /dev/fd0 /home/yourloginname
```

Using -M in conjunction with the floppy disk forces tar to prompt you to insert the next floppy disk when the current floppy disk being used is full.

To restore your backup from floppy disk(s), type

```
tar -xvfzM /dev/fd0
```

You must be careful when restoring backups because tar restores your backup to the directory specified inside the backup. For example, say you created a tar file with the command

```
tar -cvf paul.tar /home/paul
```

Later, you decide to unarchive the paul.tar file in the /tmp directory. The result is a directory called /tmp/home/paul! This is because the directory /home/paul was archived, not the directory paul. (Remember, the two are different because the *full path*, or explicit directory listing, for each is different.)

Chapter 16

Controlling and Directing Data

In This Chapter

- Establishing permissions
- Redirecting output with links
- Controlling jobs and processes

One of the finer details of using Slackware is setting up permissions. Permissions can enable or prohibit users from executing system-wide programs, reading certain files, and accessing specific directories. In this chapter, I show you how permissions play a huge role in user administration.

A process is the path a program takes from the moment it is executed until its completion. Slackware users must understand how to redirect the output of a process to other locations, including saving output that normally appears on screen into a separate file. Programs can also send the results of their processes to another user's terminal, window, or even to another computer. This chapter familiarizes you with process output redirection.

Finally, you can control the programs you're running in Slackware via *job control*, or telling a program how it is supposed to run. This includes telling processes to run in the *background* (behind the scenes so you don't have to deal with it) and suspending and killing processes. In this chapter, I show you the joys of controlling your own processes.

Issuing Permissions

Permissions establish what takes place on your system, such as what programs are run, and which files are read. Besides the super user (who, of course, can do anything), only the owner of a file can set permissions. Several different file types exist, and permissions are preset on many of them. You can, however, change or override the default when necessary. (For more information on the different file types in Slackware, turn to Chapter 9.)

The basics of permissions

All files have three types of permissions: owner, group, and world. The owner permissions belong to the user account that creates the file. In addition, each user account is part of a larger group of users on the system, so that group of users are also assigned permissions. World permissions classify everyone that doesn't fall into the first two categories.

Each permissions group contains three more explicit permissions: read (`r`), write (`w`), and execute (`x`). An active read permission means that a file can be read by the user or group granted access by the permission. An active write permission means that a file can be modified by the user or group granted access by the permission. Finally, an active execute permission means that a file can be executed like a program by the user or group granted access by the permission.

If you type **ls -ld /bin** at your command prompt and press Enter, you see something like the following (the exact response depends on your computer):

```
drwxrwxr-x   2 root     bin          2048 Dec 15 14:28 /bin
```

(The `ls` command supplies a directory listing, and the `-l` flag tells `ls` to use the long format of the listing. The `-d` flag tells `ls` to list the directory name instead of the contents of the directory.)

This result from the `ls -ld` command means that the directory `/bin` is owned by `root` (shown by the root entry in the third column), and that the group listed for this directory is `bin` (the bin entry in the fourth column). The far-left column tells you what permissions are in place.

Starting from the left, the `d` means that the file in question is a directory. A `l` appears instead of the `d` if the file is a link; otherwise a `-` is shown to indicate a regular text file or a program.

The next three letters determine the permissions granted to the owner of the file. In this case, root has read (`r`), write (`w`), and execute (`x`) permissions for the `/bin` directory, which means that root has *full permissions* on the `/bin` directory and can read the directory's contents, write to the directory, and execute programs within the directory.

The second set of three letters indicate the group permissions. Again, the `bin` group has all three types of permissions (read, write, and execute).

The last three letters are the permissions for everyone else. If a user is not `root` and not a member of the `bin` group, then that user is everyone else. In this case, everyone else has read and execute permissions for the `/bin` directory, but not write permissions — this means that everyone else cannot create, copy, or move files into the /bin directory. Whenever a specific permission is made inactive, a - appears in place of the inactive permission.

The execute permission is the most complicated permission. Shell scripts (see Chapter 8) need both read and execute permissions enabled before they can function; binary (compiled programs in machine language code) files only need the execute permission. If the execute permission is enabled on a directory, the contents of that directory are viewable via the ls command.

Changing permissions

Eventually you may need to change the permissions of some file or directory on the system. Slackware enables you to do this by using the chmod command (which stands for *change mode*). Before you use the chmod command, however, you must determine what permissions you want to enable or change. To do so, follow these steps:

1. **Assign the read, write, and execute permissions the values 1, 2, and 4, respectively. Write this down on a piece of paper.**
2. **Add the numbers that correspond to specific permissions to get a unique number.**

   For example, if you want to give a file read, write, and execute permissions, add 1 + 2 + 4 = 7. If you want to give a file read and execute permissions only, add 1 + 4 = 5.
3. **Repeat Step 2 for each set of permissions — owner, group, and world.**
4. **At your command prompt, type** chmod +++ {filename} **to change the permissions on the file called filename. Each + stands for the number you determined in Step 2 for each set of permissions (owner, group, and world).**

Suppose that you have the file myfile. Typing **ls -la myfile** and pressing Enter returns the following output:

```
-rw-r—-   1 paul      users       364 Dec 15 17:18 myfile
```

You want to change the permissions of myfile so that it looks like the following:

```
-rwxrw-r–   1 paul      users       364 Dec 15 17:18 myfile
```

This means that you have all permissions, the group users can read and write to myfile, and world (everyone else) can only read myfile. To change permissions on myfile, follow these steps:

1. **Calculate owner permissions.**

   You want all permissions as the owner of the file, so add 1 + 2 + 4 = 7.

2. **Calculate group permissions.**

   You want group permissions to be read and write only, so add 4 + 2 = 6.

3. **Calculate world permissions.**

   You want world (everyone else) permissions to be read only, so add 4 = 4.

4. **At your command prompt, type** chmod 764 myfile **and press Enter.**

   You have changed the permissions for `myfile`.

5. **At your command prompt, type** ls -la myfile **and press Enter.**

   The following information appears:

   ```
   -rwxrw-r—   1 paul     users         364 Dec 15 17:18 myfile
   ```

   The first column states that: `myfile` is a file (`-` as the first character in the column); owner (`yourlogin`) has all permissions (the first `rwx` letters); group (`users`) has read and write permissions (`rw`); and world has read-only permissions (`r—`).

Changing owners

Changing the ownership of a file so it's accessible by the new owner is a common task. Changing ownerships is usually completed from the super user account, though you can change ownerships of any file that you have owner permissions on from your personal account. The command to change ownership is `chown {new owner} {filename}`. Note that the new owner *must* be an existing user account on the system. (You can find a list of user accounts that exist on the system by typing **more /etc/passwd** at your command prompt and pressing Enter.) The following is an example of changing the ownership of `myfile` to your friend Keith (who has the user account `keith`):

```
slack1:~# chown keith myfile
```

If, however, you try to change ownership of `myfile` to Keith and misspell his user account name, you get the following error:

```
slack1:~# chown keih myfile
chown: keih: invalid user
```

If you change the ownership of a file to someone else and you aren't the super user, you cannot later change the ownership back.

Changing groups

Changing groups is similar to changing ownership. Type **chgrp {new group} {filename}** at your command prompt and press Enter in order to change the group of a file or directory. Note that the new group must be an existing group on the system. (You can find a list of groups on the system by typing **more /etc/group** at the command prompt and pressing Enter.)

For example, to change the group of the file `myfile` from its current group to the `games` group, type the following at your command prompt:

```
slack1:~# chgrp games myfile
```

If you aren't the owner of the file (or the super user) or a member of the group that the file belongs to, you cannot change the group of the file.

Putting owners and groups together

You can change both the owner and the group of a file at the same time. To do so, use the `chown` command, but give it a new twist:

```
slack1:~# chown keith.games myfile
```

This command changes the ownership of myfile to the user account `keith`, and then changes the group of the file to `games`. Both `keith` and `games` are existing user accounts and groups on the system, so you must place a `.` between the user account and group. The `chown` command knows that when it encounters a `.`, it's supposed to separate the two words and use them as user and group. If you make a typo, `chown` prints an error message and exits without changing anything.

Redirecting with Links

Redirection is changing what a program does with its output. Redirection also means forcing a program to take input from another source. Redirection is useful if you want to make a program do something with its output other than place it in a predetermined location, or if you want a program to use data from another source. By using links, you can accomplish redirection.

You probably have seen links in Slackware and didn't even know it. If you look at the directory listing for `/dev/mouse` (by typing **ls -la /dev/mouse** at your command prompt and pressing Enter), you see the following:

```
/dev/mouse -> /dev/ttyS1
```

This says that /dev/mouse is *linked* to the device /dev/ttyS1. In other words, the device /dev/mouse doesn't actually exist, it's just a pointer to /dev/ttyS1 — hence the pointer arrow (->) in the directory listing.

Using links is an excellent way of moving files and data throughout the system. You can create links in any directory on the system for which you have write permissions (the super user can create links anywhere on the system). To create a link, type **ln -s {real file} {link name}** at your command prompt and press Enter.

For example, if you want to create a link called whee to point to myfile, you type the following:

```
ln -s myfile whee
```

Now if you edit whee, your changes actually appear in myfile. This same concept holds true if you have a program send its output to whee — the output ends up in myfile. If you change the permissions on the link whee, the real file myfile is changed as well. This concept of output redirection is useful when you have two programs that cannot change where their output is being sent, but you want their output to end up in one file.

Suppose that you want to send the output of a directory listing to the file /home/mylogin/directory/directory2/dirlist on a daily basis, but typing that long string of characters every day is a pain. To redirect with links, follow these steps:

1. **At your command prompt, type** ln -s /home/mylogin/directory/directory2/dirlist link **and press Enter.**

   This command creates the link link.

2. **At your command prompt, type** ls > link **and press Enter.**

   The directory listing is sent to the link link, which actually points to the file /home/mylogin/directory/directory2/dirlist.

This looks like the following on your screen:

```
slack1:~> ln -s /home/mylogin/directory/directory2/dirlist
            link
slack1:~> ls > link
```

Now you can type **more link** at your command prompt and press Enter to see the contents of the file /home/mylogin/directory/directory2/dirlist.

If the real file myfile is removed from the system, the link whee no longer works because it points to a file that no longer exists. But if whee is removed or renamed, myfile remains intact.

Controlling Jobs and Processes

Any program that runs on your Slackware system is a *process*. Each program you run, every system task, and even your shell is a process. Processes are run until they complete or are *killed*, meaning that either you or the system has interrupted the process and forced it to abort.

Slackware enables you to manage processes to the point where you can run them in the background (which means they run without intervention on your part, leaving you free to run another program) or when you're not logged in to your computer. Running processes in the background is a good idea when you have to run multiple programs at the same time — if you had to wait for each program to finish before running the next, your work may take twice as long!

Backgrounding and foregrounding

To make a process run in the background, add a `&` after the command. The `&` is a special character that tells the shell that the command is to run without intervention.

For example, say you want to run a process called `analyzepi` that calculates the exact value of π (and some people do). To run this process in the background, at your command prompt type **analyzepi &** and press Enter. Slackware presents the following message:

```
slack1:~# analyzepi &
[1] 2072
slack1:~#
```

The `[1] 2072` means that you're running a job in the background, it's the first job you have in the background (the number 1 in brackets), and its *process identification number* (PID) is 2072.

If you place processes in the background, you need to have a way to list them. The command `jobs` lists all processes currently running in the background.

After running the `analyzepi` program in the background, type **jobs** at your command prompt and press Enter. The following appears:

```
[1]  + Running                          analyzepi
```

This tells you that `analyzepi` is running.

If you want to bring a process or job from the background into the foreground, type **fg** and press Enter. If you have more than one job in the background, you need to indicate which process to bring to the forefront by typing **fg $**, where $ is the number of the job to bring back to the foreground.

For example, if you want to bring the `analyzepi` process to the foreground, type **fg 1** and press Enter.

You may run a program and find you need that command prompt or xterm window to do something else. At the same time, you don't want to stop your program. Slackware provides a way to get around this: press Ctrl+Z to suspend the program. This command doesn't stop the program, it just momentarily halts it. After you press Ctrl+Z, type **bg** to place the program in the background. Slackware responds with the following message:

```
[1]+ analyzepi &
```

This means that the program `analyzepi` is now running in the background as job number 1.

Now you can continue working.

Listing processes

As you continue to use backgrounding and foregrounding, eventually you want to determine what you are running, both in the foreground and in the background. Slackware contains the `ps` command to list processes. If you use the `ps` command without any flags, `ps` lists all the processes you currently own. An example of the results from a `ps` command is shown in Figure 16-1.

The first column is the process ID (PID) of each process. The second column lists which terminal controls the process (in Figure 16-1, it's a *pseudoterminal*, which is a terminal that's used when someone connects to your machine from a remote location). The third column is the time taken to run the process, and the fourth column is the actual name of the program.

Using flags with the `ps` command causes Slackware to list all the processes currently running on the system. These processes include information, such as who owns the process, how long the process has been running, and how much memory and CPU the process is using. These flags are `-aux` (the -a flag stands for show processes of other users also, the -u flag stands for display user name, and the -x flag stands for show noninteractive processes), and an example run of the command `ps -aux` is shown in Figure 16-2.

You see in Figure 16-2 that a lot of processes run on your computer that you didn't know about — some are processes owned by other system users, like `bin` or `daemon`, but most are owned by root. You should always know what is running on your system.

```
-rwxr-xr-x   1 root     bin         15532 Jul 28 15:14 zipcloak*
-rwxr-xr-x   1 root     bin          1180 Jul 28 15:14 zipgrep*
lrwxrwxrwx   1 root     root            5 Nov 14 06:54 zipinfo -> unzip*
-rwxr-xr-x   1 root     bin         18648 Jul 28 15:14 zipnote*
-rwxr-xr-x   1 root     bin         20504 Jul 28 15:14 zipsplit*
-rwxr-xr-x   1 root     bin            49 May 19  1994 zless*
-rwxr-xr-x   1 root     bin          3500 May 19  1994 znew*
-rwxr-xr-x   1 root     bin         63428 Sep 20 13:38 zoo*
ucchan:~# talk &
[2] 513
ucchan:~# Usage: talk user [ttyname]

[2]    Exit 1                        talk
ucchan:~# talk ranma &
[2] 514
ucchan:~#
[2]  + Suspended (tty output)        talk ranma
ucchan:~# ps
  PID TTY          TIME CMD
  364 pts/0    00:00:00 tcsh
  505 pts/0    00:00:00 lynx
  514 pts/0    00:00:00 talk
  515 pts/0    00:00:00 ps
ucchan:~#
```

Figure 16-1: Process listing from ps.

```
ucchan:~# ps -aux
USER       PID %CPU %MEM   VSZ  RSS TTY      STAT START   TIME COMMAND
root         1  0.0  0.0   344   52 ?        S    10:33   0:03 init
root         2  0.0  0.0     0    0 ?        SW   10:33   0:00 [kflushd]
root         3  0.0  0.0     0    0 ?        SW   10:33   0:00 [kupdate]
root         4  0.0  0.0     0    0 ?        SW   10:33   0:00 [kpiod]
root         5  0.0  0.0     0    0 ?        SW   10:33   0:00 [kswapd]
root        76  0.0  0.0   196    0 ?        SW   10:34   0:00 [dhcpcd]
bin         78  0.0  0.0  1076    0 ?        SW   10:34   0:00 [rpc.portmap]
root        82  0.0  0.3  1360  220 ?        S    10:34   0:00 /usr/sbin/syslogd
root        85  0.0  0.0  1468    0 ?        SW   10:34   0:00 [klogd]
root        87  0.0  0.3  1332  216 ?        S    10:34   0:00 /usr/sbin/inetd
root        89  0.0  0.1  1380   84 ?        S    10:34   0:00 /usr/sbin/lpd
root        91  0.0  0.2  1540  148 ?        S    10:34   0:00 /usr/sbin/rpc.mou
root        95  0.0  0.2  1556  148 ?        S    10:34   0:00 /usr/sbin/rpc.nfs
root        98  0.0  0.4  1172  312 ?        S    10:34   0:00 /usr/sbin/crond -
daemon     100  0.0  0.1  1180  116 ?        S    10:34   0:00 /usr/sbin/atd -b
root       107  0.0  0.5  2016  328 ?        S    10:34   0:00 sendmail: accepti
root       114  0.0  0.0  2156   52 ?        S    10:34   0:00 /var/lib/apache/s
root       123  0.0  0.1  1088   88 ttyS1    S    10:34   0:00 gpm -m /dev/mouse
root       125  0.0  0.6  2068  412 tty1     S    10:34   0:00 -tcsh
root       126  0.0  0.1  1048   68 tty2     S    10:34   0:00 /sbin/agetty 384
root       127  0.0  0.0  1048    0 tty3     SW   10:34   0:00 [agetty]
root       128  0.0  0.0  1048    0 tt 4     SW   10:34   0:00 [a ett ]
```

Figure 16-2: Process listing from ps -aux.

Killing processes without a gun

Killing a process stops it cold — well, mostly. You can actually tell the process to do certain things besides just dying, such as reloading its configuration files (if it has any) or changing modes (like to debug mode).

The command for killing processes is `kill -{signal} {PID}`. You can only kill processes that you own. (The super user can kill any process on the system — see the sidebar at the end of this chapter titled "Killing number 1.")

The `kill` command needs some kind of signal to indicate how a process is to be killed. A partial list of signals used for the `kill` command is shown in Table 16-1:

Table 16-1 Signals for the kill Command

#	*Signal*
1	HUP — Reread configuration and restart
2	INT — Interrupted via keyboard control
3	QUIT — Quit via keyboard control
4	ILL — Illegal instruction detected
5	TRAP — Trap signal
6	ABRT — Abort signal
7	BUS — Bus error
8	FPE — Floating point exception
9	KILL — Die

For signals 1 through 4, `kill` sends the process a message describing the reason for its imminent termination, and then terminates the process. The intent is so processes are able to document, if documenting is built into the process, how the process was killed, the reason for the kill, who killed the process, and the time of termination. Slackware includes signals 5 and 7 to be compatible with older programs. Signals 6 and 8 also create a core file containing the output of the program at the time of termination. The core file is then dismantled with other programs and examined for debugging purposes. Signal 9 kills the process instantly.

You can use either the signal number or the signal name in the `kill` command. Suppose that you're running the process `analyzepi` in the background. Type the command **ps** (remember that the `ps` command lists processes on the system, and without flags it lists only the processes you own), and you get the following information:

```
slack1:~> ps
  PID TTY          TIME CMD
  105 tty1     00:00:00 csh
  136 tty1     00:00:00 ps
 2072 tty1     00:01:15 analyzepi
```

The first column lists the process ID (PID) of each process. The second column lists the `tty` or virtual console the process is running on. (For more on virtual consoles, see Chapter 6.) The third column shows how long the process has been running (hours:minutes:seconds) and the fourth column is the name of the process.

Suppose that you want to reset the `analyzepi` program to make it reload its configuration files. Type **kill -HUP 2072** at the command prompt and press Enter. You can also type **kill -1 2072** to accomplish the same thing.

Now suppose that you've been running `analyzepi` for a while now, and you want to quit. You type **kill -KILL 2072** at your command prompt and press Enter to stop the process completely. You can also type **kill -9 2072** to do the same thing.

Killing number 1

I know, you're probably thinking that the title of this sidebar is a lame reference to Star Trek: The Next Generation. Actually, I'm referring to the program that runs with process ID number 1 on the system — `init`.

`init` purges zombie processes. System daemons (programs) are run after consulting with `init`. `init` assigns programs process ID's. In short, `init` runs the show that is your Slackware system.

The only way for `init` to run is for it to use the user ID of the super user (root). In fact, many processes on the system run under root's user ID. If you type **ps -aux | grep root** at your command prompt and press Enter, you see what processes are running under the root user ID.

Because many important processes run under the root user ID, a typo in your `kill` command can accidentally stop an important system daemon or, worse, bring the system to its knees. In fact, if you `kill -9 1`, you immediately halt your system causing `init` to die. Running this command is almost like intentionally crashing your computer. Another typo that's just as bad is `kill -1 1`, which resets the system, causing all sorts of errors (it's happened to a lot of administrators I know — the phrase "typing too fast for your own good" comes to mind). Be very careful using the `kill` command while logged in as the root user.

After a program has been *kill -9'd,* it can do two things: die — in which case it won't show up on a `ps` listing any longer; or become an undead process. Undead processes are known as *zombie* processes (because zombies are undead, naturally) and show up on a `ps` listing with a Z in the STAT (status) column. Not even the super user can `kill -9` a zombie process. Zombie processes only go away when the system purges them over time, or when the machine is rebooted.

Chapter 17

Tuning Your System

In This Chapter

- Managing RAM
- Tuning with tune2fs
- Getting the best out of your hardware
- Checking system performance
- Boosting your processes

The Slackware operating system runs well, but you can make it run better. Slackware provides a set of tools that enable you to squeeze the most performance out of your system. In this chapter, I cover some of these tools and show you how to use them to manage your memory, tune your hard drive, and maximize your CPU usage. I also discuss how to check your system's current statistics and what it takes to compile your own Linux kernel.

Regulating RAM

RAM stands for Random-Access Memory, which is the working memory of a computer. Until the release of Windows 95, machines running the Windows operating system had an upper limit of 64MB of RAM — any more memory than that and the performance increase was negligible. Microsoft finally bypassed the memory problem with the advent of Windows 98.

Slackware doesn't have a problem with memory — unlike Windows 95, having more than 64MB of RAM doesn't present a problem. Slackware can take advantage of the extra RAM. In fact, with the use of swap space (space on your hard drive set aside for virtual memory — see Chapter 4 for information on swap space), even an 8MB Slackware machine can outperform an old Windows 3.1 system with double the amount of RAM. Imagine what a Slackware machine with 128MB of RAM can do.

The optimum amount of RAM for your system depends on what you're doing with your system. If you're planning to create computer-assisted drawings (CAD), you want 512MB of RAM or more. If you're a serious gamer, 128MB to 256MB suits you perfectly. And if you're a home office user, 64MB to 128MB is a suitable amount. Some people set up Slackware machines as servers (Web, file, e-mail, and so on) — machines set up in such a capacity should always have more than 128MB of RAM to handle the amount of work created by serving clients.

The optimum swap space is 2½ times the amount of physical RAM of your system. So if you have 32MB of RAM, the best swap space amount to use is 32 x 2.5 = 80MB. Remember, though, that the maximum amount of swap space you want is 128MB. Also remember that having more swap space isn't necessarily bad, but it detracts from the amount of free space you have available on your system for data. You want the best performance from your computer while having the maximum amount of space available for your use, so you must find a happy medium — if you want better performance, be prepared to sacrifice a bit more disk space.

The more memory that your system has, the better its performance is going to be running multiple applications simultaneously. More memory also helps when running memory-intensive processes like a CAD program. And remember, computer memory is cheap — if you need more, you can always go to the store and get more.

Using tune2fs

The `tune2fs` command adjusts file system parameters on Slackware file systems (ext2fs file systems). Many administrators are unaware that you can adjust file system parameters, while others feel that the ext2fs file system is optimized by default, and thus the parameters do not need adjusting. In either case, `tune2fs` is an extremely useful tool for system administration.

Never adjust parameters of a currently mounted file system. Make sure that you unmount the system before using `tune2fs`!

You must be the super user to use `tune2fs`. After you log in as the super user, type **tune2fs [options] {device to tune}** at the command prompt and press Enter.

For example, to view the current settings for /dev/hda1, use the -l flag (the -l flag stands for list settings) and type **tune2fs -l /dev/hda1**.

The most important options for tune2fs are listed in Table 17-1.

Table 17-1 Options for tune2fs

Option	*Description*
-e $	Changes how the system reacts to errors on the file system — whether to continue (*continue*), to remount the file system as read-only (*remount-ro*), or to cause a kernel panic (*panic*) and shut the machine down to single-user mode (substitute continue, remount-ro, or panic for the $)
-c #	Sets the number of times the file system can be mounted before a file system check (fsck) is forced (enter a number in place of the #)
-m #	Sets the percentage of reserved space on the file system for the super user — the default is 5 percent (enter a number in place of the #)

A *kernel panic* is when the kernel (the core of the operating system) stops everything it's doing because it feels that the error encountered is severe enough to warrant bringing down the system. This is *not* a crash — Slackware brings the system down to *single-user mode*, which is the mode where Slackware has very minimal resources (similar to Windows Safe Mode). When you encounter a kernel panic, run the fsck program on your hard drives (see Chapter 15 for help on this program) and reboot.

Make certain that you have backups of the data on the file system partition in question before attempting to use tune2fs on it.

For example, suppose that you want to set your /dev/hda2 partition so it remounts itself as read-only when errors are encountered, and you want the system to run fsck every tenth time the partition is mounted. Remounting a partition as read-only upon an error doesn't let any more data be added, changed, or deleted until the partition is checked and errors are fixed. Specifying how often fsck runs is an option given to system administrators in the case that the hard drives are still working, but more and more errors are cropping up — this ensures that errors are caught and fixed while still minimal. Type **tune2fs -e remount-ro -c 10 /dev/hda2** at your command prompt and press Enter.

Optimizing Hardware Configuration

Increasing the performance of your system is a priority if you're planning to use your computer for strenuous tasks, such as computer-assisted drawing (CAD). One way to increase your system's performance is to strip your kernel of any unnecessary hardware support, such as ISDN and Ham radio, leaving only the support necessary for your specific hardware. (Yes, Slackware actually has Ham radio support.) This is called *recompiling* your kernel, which means that you're making a new kernel by using the blueprint of the old one.

An advantage of recompiling your kernel is that the kernel becomes smaller and faster. Recompiling also enables you to add more hardware support for your computer, like support for Windows NT file systems or infrared modems (assuming you have a hard drive with an NT file system on it or an infrared modem, like on a laptop).

Recompiling your kernel is beyond the scope of this book. You can, however, get much more information about the recompilation procedure by looking at the file `/usr/doc/Linux-HOWTOs/Kernel-HOWTO`. (At your command prompt, type **more /usr/doc/Linux-HOWTOs/Kernel-HOWTO** and press Enter.)

To walk through a quick summary of the recompilation process, follow these steps:

1. **Log in as root.**
2. **At your command prompt, type** cd /usr/src/linux **and press Enter.**

   `/usr/src/linux` appears at your prompt.
3. **At your command prompt, type** make menuconfig **and press Enter.**

   The kernel configuration menu runs. You can walk through each category for the kernel, from hardware support to network support. Use your arrow keys to select Help at any time to see what each section entails. You also see what is currently supported in your system's kernel. If you know you have hardware in your computer that the current configuration does not show any support for, you can now add support. When you're done looking and configuring, use your arrow keys to select Done. You're then returned to your command prompt.
4. **At your command prompt, type** make dep **and press Enter.**

   Slackware creates all the hardware dependencies for the options you selected during the `make menuconfig` process in Step 3.

5. **At your command prompt, type** make zImage **and press Enter.**

   Slackware begins the long process of recompiling your kernel. Just how long depends on your CPU and amount of RAM. If you have a Pentium 120 with 32MB of RAM, go get yourself a bite to eat and a cup of coffee. If you have an AMD Athlon 800 with 512MB of RAM, you may have time to look out the window for about five minutes before it's done.

Follow the instructions found in `Kernel-HOWTO` to see how to set up your kernel for the next time that you reboot your machine. If you want more information on recompiling the kernel, or other expert kernel parameters, you should check out a copy of the *Linux Bible* (IDG Books Worldwide, Inc.).

Evaluating System Performance

You determine how the system is currently working by its *load,* or number of processes that are running. The system load is a single number (called the *load average*) that shows the approximate amount of time for a process to run.

Slackware comes with several utilities to display the current system load, which are listed in Table 17-2.

Table 17-2 Utilities to Show the System Load

Command	*Description*
uptime	Shows the number of days since last reboot, how many users are currently logged in, and several load averages based on time intervals of 1, 5, and 15 minutes.
top	Shows a continuous view of the most CPU-intensive processes, and gives the super user the ability to kill processes.
w	Shows the current users on the system, what those users are currently doing, and the load average.

To use these utilities, you must enable the `proc` file system. You use the `proc` file system to immediately change the state of various settings throughout the system. The information in the `proc` file system information is a snapshot of the processes running through the kernel at any one point in time. In the `/proc` directory, each process has its own directory entry corresponding to its process ID (PID). These directory entries, in turn, list information about the state of the process, the process's current memory, and the process's CPU usage.

Other /proc directories have information about the state of various kernel subsystems. /proc/net lists the status of your network according to Slackware, and /proc/ide lists the status of your hard drives, if they're IDE drives — SCSI drives have their own directory in /proc/scsi. proc is a dynamic system, which means that all values in proc are constantly updated to provide an accurate view of the current system state.

Using this information, you can determine what processes are eating up abnormal amounts of memory or CPU. You can then adjust these processes accordingly, whether that means you kill the process, adjust the priority level of the process (see next section) or run a different process altogether.

The w command lists the users logged in to the machine and what these users are doing. The following is the result of a w command (this is not a typical result, because the machine being used hasn't been turned off in over a week):

```
8:31pm  up 11 days,  1:44,  2 users,  load average: 4.18,
           4.06, 4.00
```

From left to right, the result shows the current time, how long the machine has been running (days, hours:minutes), the number of users logged in, and the load averages. The load averages shown are measures of the load in 1-minute, 5-minute, and 15-minute increments. Typical load averages should average 1.00 or less. A load average above 2.00 is cause for wonder — what's running on your system that's making it so slow? In this example, the load averages are above 4.00, which means that processes are running that are eating up more CPU and memory than necessary.

Issuing a ps -aux command to see all the processes running on the machine results in the following:

```
USER    PID %CPU %MEM   VSZ   RSS TTY      STAT START   TIME
           COMMAND paul  4485 72.3 65.5 46212 39968 tty1     R
           Dec28 226:28 netscape
```

ps -aux returns results in this format: the user (owner) of the process; the process ID (PID) of the process; the percentage of CPU being used by the process; the percentage of memory used; the total virtual memory used in bytes; the number of kilobytes of the program currently in memory; the terminal number the process is running on; the current status of the process (R = running, Z = zombie, S = sleeping); the date and time the process was started; and the name of the command itself.

The results of this particular ps -aux command indicate that a runaway netscape process is eating just over 72 percent of my CPU and over 65 percent of my available memory. This netscape process is probably waiting for some information from a Web page, but has not yet received it. In this instance, killing the process (via a kill -9 4485 command) is a good idea because the CPU and memory are freed up immediately for use by other processes on the system.

Tuning Processes

As the super user, you can assign resource limits (limits on the amount of system resources available for use by processes) or give certain processes preferential treatment. This is called *process tuning* and enables you to maintain supreme control over how Slackware is executing programs.

Slackware provides two utilities to accomplish process tuning: `nice` and `renice`. These utilities enable you to change the *priority* of a process. The priority of a process is how the computer deals with processes — processes with a higher priority get more time to work on the CPU (obviously, this is the advantage of running with a higher priority). By default, all processes have a priority of 0 (zero). The highest priority is -20, and the lowest is +19.

As a normal user, you can only *lower* the priority of your processes — you can *never* raise the priority of any process, including processes that you just lowered. The super user is the only one on the system that can raise *and* lower priorities of processes. To lower the priority of a program that you're about to run, you use the `nice` command. At the command prompt, you would type **nice -n {level} {program}**, where level is any number greater than 0 and less than (but not equal to) +20. In mathematical terms, your new level is: 0 < level < 20. The `-n` flag means that you are specifying a set number adjustment for the level — omitting the `-n` {level} lowers the priority of the program by 10.

For example, if you want to set the priority level of the program `analyzepi` to 15 (remember that the default is 0) so that `analyzepi` doesn't use as much CPU, you would type the following at your command prompt:

```
nice -n 15 analyzepi
```

If, however, you already have a process running, and you want to change its priority, you use the `renice` command. At the command prompt, you would type **renice {level} {PID}**, where level is the new priority and PID is the process ID number of the process in question.

Suppose that you have the following `netscape` process running (you can tell what the name of the process is by looking at the far right column):

```
USER    PID %CPU %MEM   VSZ   RSS TTY      STAT START   TIME
            COMMAND
paul   4485 72.3 65.5 46212 39968 tty1     R    Dec28 226:28
            netscape
```

Instead of killing this process, you want to make it run at the lowest priority possible, so other processes can get their work done. To do so, at your command prompt type:

```
renice 19 4485
```

This changes the priority of process ID (PID) 4485, which is the runaway `netscape` process, to the lowest priority possible (19).

If you want to raise the priority back to normal (you must be the super user to do this!), type the following at your command prompt:

```
renice 0 4485
```

This changes the priority of PID 4485 back to normal (0). If you want the process to go even faster, change the 0 to -20.

Chapter 18

Calling 911! In Case of Emergency

In This Chapter

- Booting from an emergency disk
- Recovering the root password
- Recovering a crashed file system
- Recovering lost files

The information in this chapter is extremely valuable, but I hope you never have to use it. This chapter covers the steps you need to take in case you encounter some serious problems with Slackware.

In this chapter, I show you how to use an emergency boot disk, recover from forgetting the super user password, and attempt to salvage lost files.

Using Emergency Disks

The boot and root disks are essential tools for the system administrator. The boot and root disks are floppy disks that contain a copy of the Slackware system. In case of emergency (your Slackware system doesn't boot, or the file system becomes corrupt), you can boot your system from the boot and root disks. (Refer to Chapter 3 for instructions on making boot and root disks.)

You should also place backup copies of your important system configuration files onto a floppy disk in case you need to copy them back to the main system in the event of a disk failure. This is so you don't have to recreate your configuration files for your programs or your hardware. Flip to Chapter 15 for information on making a floppy disk a Slackware-friendly file system.

Table 18-1 is a list of some recommended files a back up on a floppy disk. After you make the floppy disk a Slackware-compatible file system, you can use the `cp` command to copy the recommended files to the disk. Label this disk *backup*.

Table 18-1 Files to Place on a Floppy Disk

Name	*Description*
/etc/groups	The list of groups on the machine
/etc/XF86Config	X Windows configuration file
/etc/passwd	The password file for the system
/etc/shadow	The shadow password file
/etc/fstab	The file system table
/etc/*.conf	Miscellaneous configuration files for the system (the *.conf means any file that ends with .conf)
/etc/hosts*	Computer name definitions and access permissions (the hosts* means any file that begins with hosts)
/etc/ppp/*	The PPP configuration files (the * means all files in this directory)

After you copy all your essential configuration files to this disk, you use the disk to replace missing files on the system in case of a crash or failure. In case of a failure or system crash, follow these steps:

1. **Power on (boot) your machine with your boot disk in the floppy drive.**
2. **Switch disks to the root disk when prompted.**
3. **At the login: prompt, type** root.
4. **At the command prompt (#), type** mount /dev/hda1 /mnt **and press Enter. (Substitute your root partition for /dev/hda1.)**

   The root file system is mounted as the `/mnt directory`.
5. **Insert your backup disk into the floppy drive.**
6. **At the command prompt (#), type** mount /dev/fd0 /floppy **and press Enter.**

   The floppy disk's contents are mounted as the `/floppy` directory.
7. **At the command prompt (#), type** cp /floppy/{missing/damaged file} /mnt/etc **and press Enter.**

   The backup copy of the file or files is copied to your Slackware system. For example, if you wanted to copy the `groups` file from the backup disk, you type **cp /floppy/groups /mnt/etc** and press Enter to copy the file.

You can now reboot your system normally (without using floppy disks). Your configuration files are restored.

Any changes you made to any configuration files since the time you copied them onto a floppy disk will be lost. This means that if you copied your config files to floppy on Thursday and made changes to them on Friday, the changes will be lost because the copies are Thursday's copies.

Fixing a Crashed File System

When Slackware crashes (and it does happen occasionally), Slackware is usually nice enough to bring itself down to its maintenance mode, or *single-user mode*, in order for you to fix things with the `fsck` program (see Chapter 15 for more info on `fsck`). But sometimes single-user mode isn't enough. This is because the location containing all the critical information about the file system (size, status, and free space) may be corrupt. This location is called the *superblock*, and the master copy of the superblock resides in block 0 of your hard drive partition. Fixing the superblock is the highest priority in recovering your crashed system.

If the superblock is corrupt, the file system is unrecognizable to Slackware. `fsck` can't fix problems on a system it doesn't recognize — it's like trying to speak Chinese without knowing any of the language.

Slackware's file system, however, prepares for such an emergency by making backup copies of its superblock and placing them all over the file system. To use one of these backup copies, you must use a variant of the `fsck` program called `e2fsck`.

In case your master superblock cannot be used, you can make `e2fsck` look at a backup superblock by using the `-b` flag with the `e2fsck` command. Slackware normally places a copy of the superblock every 8192 blocks, meaning 8192 blocks separate the superblocks. Therefore, a superblock copy appears at 1 (of course), 8193, 16385, and so on. But you count the 8192nd block as part of each set of blocks, and the superblock is the first block in the set. Thus, the first set is 1-8192, the second set is 8193-16384, the third set is 16385-24576, the fourth set is 24577-32768, and so on. Mathematically, the starting and ending blocks of each set can be shown by the formula `{((8192 * n) - 8191), (8192 * n)}`, where *n* is any integer greater than or equal to 1.

Suppose that you need to recover a superblock and recreate the file system. At your command prompt, type **e2fsck -b 8193 /dev/hda2** and press Enter. (Change `/dev/hda2` to whatever disk partition is affected.) `e2fsck` then gives you the following information:

```
Pass 1: Checking inodes, blocks, and sizes
Pass 2: Checking directory structure
Pass 3: Checking directory connectivity
Pass 4: Checking reference counts
Pass 5: Checking group summary information

/dev/hda2: ***** FILE SYSTEM WAS MODIFIED *****
/dev/hda2: 736/27440 files (1.0% non-contiguous),
           49500/109466 blocks
```

This means that e2fsck found no major errors and that the superblock was recoverable. A summary of the number of files on the disk and the number of blocks used appears at the bottom.

Don't use e2fsck if you don't need to! You should only use e2fsck if fsck displays the error Invalid superblock or Could not find superblock, after which, fsck will abort and bring you back to your command prompt.

You can find more help on e2fsck by typing **man e2fsck** at any command prompt and pressing Enter. The manual page for e2fsck appears, listing all the flags available for the command and describing what the program does using each flag.

Fixing the root Password

What happens if you forget the password for the super user, or it's changed or removed without your knowledge? You need that password, but the problem is that normally you must have the root password to be able to change the root password! Instead of reinstalling Slackware from scratch (which is an option if you *really* want to do so), you can reset the root password by using your boot and root disks.

Resetting the password with this method requires the use of the vi editor. Turn to Chapter 10 for help with the vi commands.

To fix the root password, follow these steps:

1. **Power on (boot) your machine with your boot disk in the floppy drive.**
2. **Switch disks to the root disk when prompted.**
3. **At the login: prompt, type** root.
4. **At the command prompt (#), type** mount /dev/hda1 /mnt **and press Enter. (Substitute your root partition for /dev/hda1.)**

   The root file system is now mounted as the /mnt directory.

5. **At the command prompt (#), type** vi /mnt/etc/passwd **and press Enter.**

   The `vi` editor runs with `/etc/passwd` as the file to be edited. `/etc/passwd` contains several entries, one entry per line. Each entry has several fields — these fields are separated by colons (:). Completely remove the `x` in the second field (see Chapter 10 for more help on editors) for the `root` entry.

6. **At the command prompt (#), type** vi /mnt/etc/shadow **and press Enter.**

   The `vi` editor runs with `/etc/shadow` as the file to be edited. `/etc/shadow` contains the actual password, but the password is encrypted. The encryption makes the password look like a string of garbage text, like `S7!gb61bM8x`. Again, the entry fields are separated by colons (:), so remove the garbage text in the second field of the `root` entry.

   Under no circumstances will Slackware ever be able to tell you what the password actually was. Encryption of passwords is one-way only — Slackware takes the password, encrypts it, and stores it. It can never decrypt a password.

7. **Reboot normally (without floppy disks).**

   The computer reboots.

The `root` account now has no password. When you reach the `login:` prompt, type **root** and press Enter. You aren't prompted for a password, though you should change that immediately by typing **passwd root** and giving the `root` account a password once again. (Turn to Chapter 6 for more information on changing passwords.)

Salvaging Lost Files

Every so often, you may accidentally delete a file from the system. Unfortunately, there's no way to undelete them. If the files deleted were system files, the best thing you can do is copy those files from another source, like the CD-ROM or from a backup floppy disk.

A good way to help prevent accidental file deletion is to use a desktop file manager, such as KDE or GNOME, that throws things in the trash can (similar to Windows). If you throw files in the trash can, you can still recover them. If, however, you're at a command prompt (either in KDE or GNOME, or not running X Windows at all) and use the `rm` command, you're out of luck. Files don't get moved to the trash can with the `rm` command; they get removed, period.

You can make the `rm` command ask you if you want a file to be deleted by using the `-i` flag (the `-i` stands for inquire). Using the `-i` flag forces the `rm` command to ask if you really want the file removed, giving you a second chance to say no if you accidentally mistyped. Using `rm -i` is a good way to help minimize the damage you can do.

For example, if you type **rm -i myfile** and press Enter, the following message appears:

```
rm: remove `myfile'?
```

At this point, if you type anything other than just **y**, the file `myfile` will not be removed.

Part VI
The Part of Tens

"Slackware does a lot of great things, I'm just not sure running a word processing program sideways without line breaks on butcher's paper is one of them."

In this part . . .

The Part of Tens features easy-to-read tips designed to help optimize your Slackware experience. Chapter 19 focuses on the ten most common problems found during or after installation, Chapter 20 answers some questions about X Windows, Chapter 21 explores packages in a bit more detail, and Chapter 22 lists the top ten places in which to seek out additional help with Slackware.

Chapter 19

Ten Common Installation Problems

In This Chapter

- A faulty CD-ROM
- Missing password
- Disappearing CD-ROM
- A full device
- Hanging LILO at *LI*
- No directory errors
- Typing at the boot: prompt
- fsck-ing drives
- Finding programs
- Typing rm *

Every installation has its share of quirks — minor problems that may put a hitch in an otherwise smooth setup. This chapter lists ten common problems that may crop up with Slackware installations, and how you can easily solve them.

If your trouble spot isn't listed below, you can always look through the HOWTOs on the CD-ROM. You can sometimes solve even the most unlikely problem in a HOWTO because someone else previously experienced it and wrote up the solution.

My CD-ROM Doesn't Work

Problem: During the Slackware installation, `setup` doesn't find your CD-ROM.

Solution: Make sure that you're using the right boot disk, which has support for your particular CD-ROM. The `bare.i` or `scsi.s` boot disk images don't contain extra support for certain manufacturer's CD-ROM drives.

If you're sure that you have an ATAPI CD-ROM drive (ATAPI stands for *AT Attachment Packet Interface* — an interface between your computer and the CD-ROM drive that provides additional commands needed for controlling the CD-ROM drive) and used the correct boot disk, try typing the following at the LILO `boot:` prompt:

```
linux hdb=cdrom
```

(Change `hdb` to `hdc` if you have more than one hard drive.)

I Don't Know the Password

Problem: After booting with boot and root disks, you're presented with a `login:` prompt.

Solution: Type **root** and press Enter. Slackware doesn't prompt you for a password because this is a brand-new installation.

If you're asked for a password, it usually means that you don't have enough memory to complete the installation.

After Installation, My CD-ROM Disappeared

Problem: Slackware is installed, but upon reboot, the CD-ROM isn't found.

Solution: You didn't install a kernel with the correct drivers for your CD-ROM. You probably used the `bare.i` or `scsi.s` kernel instead of the kernel necessary for your CD-ROM. You can try and compile a new kernel with support (see Chapter 17 for a quick walk through on kernel compiling), or you can try and use modules for your CD-ROM driver. See the file `/etc/rc.d/rc.modules` for examples on how to use modules.

The Device Is Full

Problem: During installation, the message `device is full` flashes across the bottom of the screen.

Solution: You've run out of drive space. Make a note of what disk series you were installing at the time, and then cancel setup. You have to run through the steps in Chapter 4 again by using `fdisk` or `cfdisk` to repartition your drives and give yourself more space. This means that you have to delete and recreate your partitions.

You can also cut back on the number of software packages you install. Remember, everything that you install uses disk space.

LILO Prints Just LI and Hangs

Problem: Upon boot, the letters *LI* appear, and the computer does nothing else.

Solution: The partition LILO was told to use as a boot partition isn't set as bootable. Use a rescue or emergency floppy or your backup boot disks to get the `boot:` prompt. At the prompt, type the following:

```
mount root=/dev/hda1
```

(Replace `hda1` with whatever your bootable partition is supposed to be, such as `hda2`, `hdb1`, and so on.)

Your Slackware machine boots. You have to edit the `/etc/lilo.conf` file to change the bootable partition to the correct one.

If, however, your partition is listed correctly, you must run `cfdisk` and toggle the bootable flag next to your boot partition.

I Get No Directory Errors When I Log In

Problem: Upon login, Slackware shows the message `No directory! Logging in with home = /`.

Solution: This message appears because of an invalid or missing entry in the system password file for your account. Switch users to the super user account and edit the `/etc/passwd` file to give yourself a home directory. You can use the root entry as an example of an account with a home directory. (root's home directory is `/root`. Your home directory should be something like `/home/username`.)

I Never Get to Type Anything at the boot: Prompt

Problem: At power up, the computer presents the LILO greeting, and then promptly boots to Windows or DOS.

Solution: Your delay setting in LILO is either not set or set to 0. This means that LILO is going to boot the first operating system listed, which is usually DOS or Windows.

To fix this, boot from your boot disk (rescue, emergency, or otherwise) and at the `boot:` prompt, type:

```
mount root=/dev/hda1
```

(Replace `hda1` with whatever your bootable partition is supposed to be, such as `hda2`, `hdb1`, and so on.)

Your Slackware machine boots. You have to edit the `/etc/lilo.conf` file and change or add the following line:

```
timeout = 1200
```

Your system waits patiently for you to tell it which operating system to boot.

My Drives Keep fsck-ing When I Boot

Problem: Upon boot up, Slackware forces a file system check (`fsck`) on every partition.

Solution: Your file systems are not unmounting properly before shutdown. This is usually caused by turning off the power before doing a proper shutdown or by doing the "three-finger-salute" too often (Ctrl+Alt+Delete).

Always type **shutdown -h now** to shut down your Slackware system, and **shutdown -r now** to reboot your system.

I Can't Find a Program

Problem: Typing in the name of a program returns the error message `Command not found`.

Solution: Make sure that the program is actually installed. To do this, you can search the installed packages lists in /var/log/packages by typing **grep {program name} /var/log/packages/* | more** (to save sanity, pipe the output to more) and pressing Enter.

If your program name is installed, Slackware returns a list of places where it placed a file with the name of your program. You can then attempt to run the program by typing the *full path* to the program (like /usr/bin/myprog or /usr/local/bin/myprog).

Another reason for the error message is that the program is not in your system's *path*, or in places that it looks for programs. To determine what your path is, type **printenv PATH** and press Enter. A colon-separated list like the following appears (your list may have more or less entries than this):

```
/usr/local/sbin:/usr/local/bin:/sbin:/usr/sbin:/bin
```

If Slackware doesn't find your program in one of those directories, just typing the name doesn't run the program. You must either type the *full path* (see previous paragraphs) or add the program to one of the directories with the **mv** command:

```
mv myprg /usr/local/bin
```

You must then log out and log back in for the change to take effect.

I Accidentally Typed rm *

Problem: You accidentally typed rm * and all your files disappear.

Solution: If the files were of a personal nature, then they've gone to the giant bit bucket in the sky. If the files were system files, you can reinstall the specific software package(s) from the CD.

Chapter 20

Ten Common Problems with X Windows

In This Chapter

- The gray screen
- Immobile mouse
- In a blink, it was gone
- Running X Windows when I boot
- The scrolling screen
- A shy mouse
- Fuzzy edges
- Improving color
- Slow xterms
- What about emacs?

You may have difficulty setting up X Windows after installation. This chapter addresses ten typical problems with the X Windows setup that you may (hopefully never) experience.

If you continue to have problems, check out the X Windows HOWTO in `/usr/doc/Linux-HOWTOs` or on the CD-ROM.

I Get a Gray Screen

Problem: X Windows starts and presents a gray screen, but then nothing happens.

Solution: If you have less than 8MB of RAM, you're lucky that X Windows is running at all. Your best bet is to shell out the cash for more RAM.

If RAM isn't the problem, then X Windows may be having difficulty reading the configuration files from your home directory. To fix this problem, follow these steps (substitute your personal account name where it says username):

1. **Log in as root.**
2. **Type** chown -R username ~username **and press Enter.**
3. **Type** chgrp -R users ~username **and press Enter.**
4. **Log out and log back in to your personal account.**

My Mouse Won't Move

Problem: X Windows starts, but the mouse doesn't move.

Solution: The mouse may not be plugged in correctly in the back of the computer. Barring that, make sure that the correct device is being linked to from `/dev/mouse`. If you have a PS/2 mouse, `/dev/mouse` should point to `/dev/psaux`. If your serial mouse uses COM1, `/dev/mouse` should point to `/dev/ttyS0`.

My Screen Blinks, Then Nothing

Problem: Typing **startx** starts X Windows; then the program aborts.

Solution: Your `/etc/XF86Config` file isn't set up correctly. You have to rerun the `XF86Setup` program or the `xf86config` program to redo your configuration.

I Want X Windows to Run When I Boot

Problem: Getting X Windows to automatically run upon boot-up.

Solution: Use an editor like `pico` or `vi` (see Chapter 10 for more help on editors) to edit the `/etc/initial` file by typing **pico /etc/inittab** and pressing Enter. (You must be logged in as the super user to edit this file.) Look for the following line:

```
id:3:initdefault:
```

Change the 3 to 4 and save. The number 3 is the default level for normal text-only mode. Number 4 is the default run level for X Windows.

When I Move the Mouse, the Screen Scrolls

Problem: Moving the mouse around the screen makes the screen scroll.

Solution: You have the virtual desktop setting higher than the screen size. You can attempt to correct this by pressing Ctrl+Alt+plus sign or Ctrl+Alt+minus sign (the + or - keys on your numeric keypad) until the screen stops moving around when you move the mouse.

You also need to fix this setting in the `/etc/XF86Config` file. Run `XF86Setup` and correct your screen size (resolution) that way.

The Mouse Stays in a Corner

Problem: The mouse pointer moves, but only stays in one corner of the screen. The pointer will not move anywhere else on the screen except in the one corner.

Solution: You've selected the wrong protocol for your mouse. Exit X Windows by pressing Ctrl+Alt+Backspace and rerun `XF86Setup` to redo your mouse settings.

I Have Fuzzy Edges

Problem: The edges of the screen are somewhat out of focus.

Solution: You're using the wrong values for your monitor or video card. You may need to redo your configuration by rerunning `XF86Setup`.

You can also try running X by itself by typing **X >& /tmp/x.err** and pressing Enter. X starts again, so you have to press Ctrl+Alt+Backspace to kill the X server. You can then look at the file `/tmp/x.err` and see what was written there by the X server. Lots of information is listed, some of which may be useful for debugging why your monitor is fuzzy. Look for screen resolutions that may be out of range for your monitor (a common culprit is setting your resolution to 1024x768x64000 when the video card can only handle 800x600x256).

As a last resort, you can install a different X server like `xsvga`, which is more generic and supports more video cards.

I Need More Color

Problem: Some applications won't run or have problems displaying graphics in the correct colors in your current configuration.

Solution: X, by default, uses 256 colors for its server. You can specify how many colors to use by using the `-bpp` flag with the `startx` command, which tells startx how many bits per pixel (bpp) it is to use for the colors. Start your X server by typing **startx -- -bpp 16** and pressing Enter (16 bpp = 65,356 colors). Be warned — not all applications work with 65,356 colors.

xterms are Soooo Slooooow

Problem: Running `xterm` takes forever to bring up a window. Sometimes using `xterm` makes it take a while for anything you type to appear on the screen, or the cursor is about three characters behind what you're typing.

Solution: You may have a slow video card or a video card with not a lot of video memory. The obvious choice is to upgrade your video card.

Outside of spending money, you can use the `rxvt` program in lieu of `xterm`. `rxvt` doesn't emulate as many graphics modes as `xterm`, but then again, you may not need all the functionality in `xterm` anyway. To use `rxvt`, type **rxvt &** and press Enter. A new `rxvt` window appears.

emacs Doesn't Work in X

Problem: You want to run `emacs` in X mode, but it won't run.

Solution: Make sure that you installed the correct packages for `emacs`. By default, X support is installed with `emacs` in the E series. But if you installed the package `emacs_nox.tgz`, then you uninstalled your X support. Use `pkg-tool` to install the `emacsbin.tgz` package in the E series, which reinstalls the X support.

Chapter 21

Ten Questions About Packages

In This Chapter

- Installing and removing packages
- Creating new packages
- Acquiring and sharing packages
- Fixing packages

Packages can be confusing, because multiple packaging methods exist and not all packages are the same. This chapter covers some basic questions about Slackware packages, package format, and packaging tools, such as how to check packages, where to get packages, and how to upgrade older packages.

Why .tgz?

The `.tgz` extension is actually a contraction of `.tar.gz`. You can uncompress and unarchive `.tgz` packages with `gunzip` and `tar`, though this is not the usual practice. I recommend using `pkgtool` to do this kind of work for you.

Can I Check My Package Before Installing It?

Yes. Using the `-warn` flag for `installpkg`, you can make installpkg display what you will install if the installation were to take place now. For example, if I want to check where the files for `mypackage.tgz` will install, I type **installpkg -warn mypackage.tgz** and press Enter. The screen then displays exactly where all the files would be installed, if this were an actual install. At the end of the list, a message appears saying "You've been warned."

Can I Check My Package Before Removing It?

Yes. Using the same flag as `installpkg` (`-warn`), `removepkg` shows what will be eliminated if you remove the package from the system. You would type **removepkg -warn mypackage**. You must be in the `/var/log/packages` directory to remove a package.

Do I Have to Remove My Package Before Installing a New Version?

No. If the packages have the same name, type **upgradepkg {packagename}** and press Enter. Slackware does all the work for you of checking the older version against the newer version and adding the appropriate files to the system.

If the packages have different names, type the following instead:

```
upgradepkg oldpackagename%newpackagename
```

Only one space exists in the command, after `upgradepkg`.

Can I Make My Own Package?

Yes. If you have everything you want ready to go in your current directory, type **makepkg**. You should probably read the manual page on the `makepkg` command first, as there are tips and tricks listed to help speed up the package creation process (type **man makepkg** and press Enter).

What if I Need to See What's Inside a Package?

Run `pkgtool` (type **pkgtool** at your command prompt and press Enter) and select the View option with your arrow keys. (Turn to Chapter 7 for more help on pkgtool and its related programs.) This lists all the files in a package. `pkgtool` works best when the package in question is in the current directory that you are in.

Can I Use .rpm Packages?

Yes, but you must first convert them to `.tgz` format. Use the `rpm2tgz` command by typing **rpm2tgz [package].rpm** and pressing Enter. This command creates a `[package].tgz file`, which you can then use `pkgtool` or `installpkg` to install.

Can I Use .deb Packages?

No, `.deb` packages are for the Debian version of Linux and are not compatible with Slackware. Most `.deb` packages, however, are usually available as `.rpm` packages — and you can certainly use the `.rpm` packages. You can get a list of comparable packages for any program by surfing the Web to `http://freshmeat.net/`.

Where Do I Get Packages From?

This is a tough question. Packages are compiled versions of a program specific for a certain type of Linux system. For example, you don't want packages that are listed for Linux 1.2.13 if you're using the version of Slackware on the enclosed CD-ROMs.

You can grab packages from sites that let you download programs from them, like Walnut Creek (`ftp://ftp.cdrom.com/pub/linux/slackware`). Another place to look for new programs is Freshmeat (`http://freshmeat.net`), which keeps an active index of programs for Linux.

Can I Send Packages Via E-Mail?

Sending packages by e-mail isn't a good idea. The person on the receiving end of your e-mail may not like his mailbox filled with one message — packages can be large. Another reason is that some older mail servers filter out long e-mails as *spam,* or junk e-mail, and your package can go to the wastebasket immediately.

A better method is to send the *location* of the package (a Web address or an FTP site) to your friend instead.

I Found a Bug — Is There a Patch?

It depends on how fast you send an e-mail to support@slackware.com. If you really think it's a bug in a package or program, you should send e-mail to Slackware support. If you're not sure, check the Slackware Forum (http://www.slackware.com/forum/list.php3?num=2) and see if your bug is mentioned there. You can also check the Change Logs (http://www.slackware.com/changelog/stable.php3) to see if a patch is released.

Chapter 22

Ten Sources of Help

In This Chapter

- Online solutions
- Offline solutions

In the course of working with Slackware, you may experience a problem that you just can't seem to solve. Don't worry — I still encounter questions that I need assistance in figuring out. This chapter lists ten minus one places that you can go for help in deciphering these dilemmas.

The Slackware Forum

```
http://www.slackware.com/forum/list.php3?num=2
```

Slackware users gather at this site to help each other answer questions about the system. Most questions that you may have were likely asked before. Use the forum's Search function to check on your questions or concerns.

Be specific about your problem! Posting a message saying that your computer doesn't work isn't going to get many responses. A message saying that your SoundBlaster 16 card won't work with IRQ 7, on the other hand, will probably result in a better response.

The Linux Documentation Project

```
http://www.linuxdoc.org/
```

You can find every Linux manual page or HOWTO under the sun at this site. (You also have copies of all the HOWTOs on your CD-ROM, and you can install the man pages as well.) If you can't get relief from the Slackware Forum, then this is a good second choice.

Manual Pages (man pages)

man pages exist for 99 percent of the commands or programs for Slackware. man pages are very detailed in explaining how commands work and what flags or arguments are used with the command. Not only that, but at the end of the man page is a list of related commands and files. Sometimes you may even find e-mail addresses or Web page addresses to help you with your questions. With all this information, you can get a lot of help from a man page.

XFree86

```
http://www.xfree86.org/
```

This site, which is the location of the XFree86 project, is the place to go to solve problems with X Windows. You can find extensive — and I do mean extensive — lists of compatible hardware, problems users have encountered with X Windows, and many other solutions.

Freshmeat

```
http://freshmeat.net/
```

If you're having difficulty running an application, check out Freshmeat. Freshmeat is an all-purpose troubleshooting site that includes links to other helpful Web sites and information on application updates.

Other Books

Visit the IDG Web site at `http://www.idgbooks.com` and check out the following books that may be helpful:

- *Linux For Dummies*, 3rd Edition
- *Linux Bible*
- *Discover Linux*
- *Linux Administration For Dummies*
- *GIMP For Linux Bible*
- *GNOME For Linux For Dummies*
- *KDE For Linux For Dummies*

Consultants

If you decide to pay someone to help you with Slackware, first check out the Consultants-HOWTO on your CD-ROM or in the `/usr/doc/Linux-HOWTOs` directory. Consultants typically have extensive knowledge on what might seem to be arcane subject matter. In reality, they know the minute trivia that may escape even the most detailed instruction sheet or manual page. Consultants usually have many years of experience in their chosen fields, so make sure when you call one to ask how long the person has been working with Slackware or Linux in general.

```
Slashdothttp://www.slashdot.org/
```

If you haven't heard of Slashdot, that's about to change. Slashdot is the information source for anyone who wants up-to-the-nanosecond Linux news. If the information is available, you are assured that Slashdot has the news and there's already a discussion about it as well.

Linux User Groups

If you live in a major city, like Phoenix, you probably have a Linux User Group (LUG) in your area. Check your grocery store for a free computer magazine (you usually find these in the same place as the free real estate and car sales publications) and browse through it for information on the local LUG. If a LUG exists, make a note of the contact information, meeting locations and times, and membership info. Most LUGs have Web sites that you can go to as well.

Trade Magazines

Industry and trade magazines are a valuable resource because they review new equipment and programs as they come out. If you have a top-of-the-line, bleeding-edge video card and want to know about what can run on it, a trade magazine may have the information you need.

Part VII
Appendixes

"Philip- come quick! David just used Slackware to connect the amp and speakers to his air-guitar!"

In this part . . .

I just couldn't finish without some last-minute details. Here you find some information that didn't quite fit anywhere else, such as an abridged hardware compatibility list in Appendix A and some info about the CD-ROMs that come with this book in Appendix B.

Appendix A

Common Hardware Compatibility List

Slackware contains support for an extraordinary amount of hardware, old and new. The entire list is too long to be included here, but some of the more common older pieces of hardware are listed.

The list in its entirety is available on the Installation CD-ROM in the file `[CD-ROM drive letter]:\docs\Linux-HOWTOs\Hardware-HOWTO`. Word processors in all operation systems (Linux, Unix, DOS, or Windows) can read this file.

Because Slackware is continuously adding new hardware support, do not look at this listing as the final list of compatible hardware. As a precaution, double-check any hardware not cataloged here against the Hardware Compatibility-HOWTO.

The Linux Hardware Database at `http://lhd.datapower.com/` has a more extensive list, plus a rating system to show how well certain hardware works with Linux. You can search their database by product name, model, manufacturer, rating, or category (like video card, sound card, motherboard, and so on). I strongly suggest visiting this site if you have questions about hardware that aren't answered here.

If you have a laptop or are thinking of using Slackware on a laptop, I urge you to visit the Linux on Laptops site at `http://www.cs.utexas.edu/users/kharker/linux-laptop/`. This site contains information on the nuances of using Slackware on a laptop.

Central Processing Units (CPUs)

Slackware supports the following CPUs:

- Intel 386, 486, Pentium, Pentium Pro, Pentium II, and Pentium III
- AMD 386, 486, 5x86, K5, K6, K6-2, K6-3, and Athlon
- Cyrix 486 and 5x86
- IDT Winchip C6

Memory

You can use all memory, such as DRAM, EDO, and SDRAM, with Linux. If you have large amounts of RAM, however, you may have to add the following line to your LILO configuration file (`/etc/lilo.conf`):

```
append="mem=<number of Mb>M"
```

Therefore, if you have 512MB of memory, the line becomes

```
append="mem=512M"
```

Video Cards

Slackware works with any video card in text (non-graphical, no X Windows) mode. In addition, most video cards work with monochrome (two color) VGA displays.

Slackware supports the following video cards:

- Any card by Diamond Multimedia manufactured after 1995 (earlier cards may work as well, but these cards are not officially supported by XFree86 — the creators of X Windows)
- ATI VGA Wonder series, Mach8, Mach32, Mach64
- Trident 8800CS, 8200LX, 8900x, 9000, 9420, TVGA8900/9000, 9440, 96xx
- S3 732 (Trio32), 764 (Trio64), 801, 805, 866, 868, ViRGE series
- Matrox Millenium, Mystique
- Cirrus Logic 542x, 543x, 544x, 546x, 754x
- Western Digital WD90C24/24A/24A2/31/33, Paradise, WD90C00/10/11/30

Hard Drive Controllers

Slackware works with any IDE hard drive controller. In fact, any hard drive works in Slackware if the controller is supported.

When it comes to SCSI controllers, however, Slackware is a little pickier. Slackware supports the following SCSI controllers:

- Almost any controller by Adaptec (unsupported controllers are the Adaptec AHA 2940UW Pro, AAA-13x RAID, AAA-113x Raid Port, and AIC-7810)

- All BusLogic controllers
- Quantum ISA-200S, ISA-250MG
- Seagate ST-01/ST-02
- Western Digital WD7000

Joysticks and Other I/O Controllers

Slackware works with any standard serial, parallel, joystick, or combo card. You can also use cards that support nonstandard IRQs (IRQs > 9).

Network Interface Cards (NICs)

NICs, also called ethernet adapters, vary depending on make and model. In general, the newer the card, the better it functions. Be careful with clones, as bad clones cause lockups in Slackware.

Avoid the 3Com 3C501 card, as it very, very old and may not work with your hardware even if it is supported in Slackware.

Slackware supports the following NICs:

- Almost any 3Com card (unsupported cards are the 3Com 3C359 Velocity XL PCI and the 3C339 Velocity PCI)
- Cabletron E21xx
- DEC DE425/DE434/DE435/DE450/DE500, EtherWORKS, and EtherWORKS3
- Intel EtherExpress and EtherExpress Pro series
- SMC Ultra/EtherEZ, 9000 series, EtherPower II
- Western Digital WD80x3

Sound Cards

Slackware supports the following sound cards:

- Ensoniq Soundscape
- Gravis Ultrasound series
- Crystal Audio cards

- Logitech SoundMan 16, Wave, and Games
- OPTi 82C924/82C925, 82C928/82C929
- SoundBlaster, SoundBlaster 16, Pro, 32/64/AWE, AWE63/Gold
- MPU-401 MIDI

CD-ROMs

Most CD-ROM drives are moving to the worldwide ATAPI (AT Attachment Packet Interface) standard, so this list may become obsolete in another couple of years. But some drives using proprietary hardware still exist.

Slackware supports the following CD-ROM drives:

- Creative Labs CD-200(F)
- GoldStar R420
- Panasonic CR-521/522/523/562/563
- Mitsumi CR DC LU05S and FX001D/F
- Sanyo CDR-H94A
- Sony CDU31A/CDU33A, CDU-510/CDU-515, CDU-535/CDU-531
- Teac CD-55A SuperQuad

Slackware has also begun supporting CD-ROM writers. For an up-to-date list of supported CD-ROM writers, check the CD-Writing mini-HOWTO at `http://www.linuxdoc.org/HOWTO/CD-Writing-HOWTO.html`.

Slackware supports the following CD-ROM writers:

- HP CD-Writer+ 7100, SureStore 4020i, SureStore 6020es/i
- Mitsubishi CDRW-225
- Mitsumi CR-2600TE
- Philips CDD-522/2000/2600/3610
- Plextor CDR PX-24CS
- Sony CDU 920S/924/926S
- Yamaha CDR-100, CDR-200/200t/200tx, CDR-400t/400tx

Mice

You may think that mice are so simple — but the mouse must use one of the following protocols:

- Microsoft serial mouse, busmouse, or Intellimouse
- Mouse Systems serial mouse
- Logitech serial mouse, busmouse, or Mouseman serial mouse
- PS/2 mouse

Printers/Plotters

All printers and plotters connected to the parallel or serial port should work. A plotter is a printer used specifically for drawing graphs or charts. Some manufacturers, however, have created Windows 9x-only printers, like Lexmark, Sharp, and Brother.

Slackware supports the following printers:

- Any HP DeskJet or LaserJet series
- Most Canon BubbleJet series (unsupported is the Canon LBP-465)
- Epson Stylus Color/Color II/500/800
- Okidata MicroLine 182
- Apple Imagewriter

Scanners

Slackware supports SANE (Scanner Access Now Easy) for scanner support. You can find information on this package at `http://www.mostang.com/sane/`. This is a universal scanner interface (meaning that it is accepted as the standard for every scanner) and comes complete with documentation and several frontends and backends.

Slackware does *not* (repeat, *not*) support the following scanners:

- Acer
- Escom 256 (Primax Lector Premier 256) handheld scanner
- Genius ScanMate/256, EasyScan handheld scanners

- Mustek CG8000 handheld scanner
- Trust Ami Scan handheld scanner

Notice that four of the five unsupported scanners are handheld. Slackware doesn't handle handheld scanners too well.

Other Hardware

By no means is this a complete list of supported hardware. Slackware also supports things like Amateur Radio, VESA Power Savings Protocol (DPMS) monitors, touch screens, terminals on serial ports, digital cameras, video capture boards/frame grabbers/TV tuners, and uninterruptible power supplies (UPS).

For listings of any of these hardware specifications, go to the Hardware Compatibility HOWTO or check out `http://www.linuxdoc.org/HOWTO/Hardware-HOWTO.html`.

Appendix B

About the CD-ROMs

The CD-ROMs that come with this book contain the full distribution of Slackware Linux 7.0, as well as Netscape Communicator 4.7, FIPS 2.0, KDE 1.1.2, and GNOME.

System Requirements

Make sure that your computer has the minimum system requirements listed here. If your computer doesn't meet most of these requirements, you may have problems using the contents of the CDs:

- A PC with a 486 or faster processor.
- At least 16MB of total RAM installed on your computer. For the best performance, we recommend that people who want to use X Window System have at least 32MB of RAM.

  At least 800MB of hard drive space available to install all the software from the CD. You'll need less space if you don't install every program on the CDs. For example, if you want to install only the the base system and X Window System, you can do that in about 250MB.
- A CD-ROM drive.
- A 3½-inch floppy disk drive and at least three blank 3½-inch disks.
- A monitor capable of displaying at least 256 colors or grayscale.
- An IDE or a SCSI disk.
- A keyboard and a mouse.
- A modem with a speed of at least 14,400 bps if you want to go online.

Appendix A lists all the hardware compatible with Slackware Linux.

If you need more information on the basics of computer operation, check out *PCs For Dummies,* 7th Edition, by Dan Gookin; *Windows 98 For Dummies, Windows 95 For Dummies,* 2nd Edition, or *Windows 3.11 For Dummies,* 4th Edition, all by Andy Rathbone; all published by IDG Books Worldwide, Inc.

For more basic Linux information, you can also check out *Linux For Dummies*, 2nd Edition, by Jon "maddog" Hall.

Using the CDs

The instructions for installing the CDs are detailed in Part II. After you install the software, return each CD to its plastic jacket for safekeeping.

What You'll Find

The CDs contain the full distribution of Slackware Linux 7.0. The documentation is found on the first CD (the installation CD) in the directory `[CD-ROM drive letter]:\docs\`. You may view the documentation on the CD through your favorite word processor or through Netscape. The CDs are readable from other operating systems, such as DOS, Windows, or Unix.

Because the CD-ROMs have a full implementation of Slackware Linux, listing all the programs and tools included would take too much room. Briefly, the CDs include the basic software you need to access the Internet, write programs in several computer languages, create and manipulate images, create, manipulate, and play back sounds (if you have a sound card), and play games. And of course, the source code for everything is included.

If You Have Problems (Of the CD Kind)

We tried our best to test various computers with the minimum system requirements. Alas, your computer may differ, and Slackware Linux may not install or work as stated.

The two likeliest problems are that you don't have enough RAM for the programs you want to use, or you have some hardware that Slackware Linux doesn't support. Luckily, the latter problem occurs less frequently each day as more hardware is supported under Slackware Linux. (Check out Appendix B for a list of compatible hardware.) You may also have hardware that is simply too new for the Slackware Linux development team to have given it the proper support at the time the CDs were pressed.

If you have trouble with corrupt files on the CDs, please call the IDG Books Worldwide Customer Service phone number: 800-762-2974 (outside the United States: 317-572-3342). Customer service won't be able to help with complications relating to the program or how it works.

Index

• D •

• E •

• J •

• K •

• L •

• Q •

• R •

• S •

• T •

• U •

• V •

• W •

• Z •

IDG BOOKS WORLDWIDE BOOK REGISTRATION

We want to hear from you!

Visit **http://my2cents.dummies.com** to register this book and tell us how you liked it!

- Get entered in our monthly prize giveaway.
- Give us feedback about this book — tell us what you like best, what you like least, or maybe what you'd like to ask the author and us to change!
- Let us know any other *For Dummies*® topics that interest you.

Your feedback helps us determine what books to publish, tells us what coverage to add as we revise our books, and lets us know whether we're meeting your needs as a *For Dummies* reader. You're our most valuable resource, and what you have to say is important to us!

Not on the Web yet? It's easy to get started with *Dummies 101®: The Internet For Windows® 98* or *The Internet For Dummies®* at local retailers everywhere.

Or let us know what you think by sending us a letter at the following address:

For Dummies Book Registration
Dummies Press
10475 Crosspoint Blvd.
Indianapolis, IN 46256

BESTSELLING
BOOK SERIES

GNU GENERAL PUBLIC LICENSE

Version 2, June 1991

Preamble

The licenses for most software are designed to take away your freedom to share and change it. By contrast, the GNU General Public License is intended to guarantee your freedom to share and change free software—to make sure the software is free for all its users. This General Public License applies to most of the Free Software Foundation's software and to any other program whose authors commit to using it. (Some other Free Software Foundation software is covered by the GNU Library General Public License instead.) You can apply it to your programs, too.

When we speak of free software, we are referring to freedom, not price. Our General Public Licenses are designed to make sure that you have the freedom to distribute copies of free software (and charge for this service if you wish), that you receive source code or can get it if you want it, that you can change the software or use pieces of it in new free programs; and that you know you can do these things.

To protect your rights, we need to make restrictions that forbid anyone to deny you these rights or to ask you to surrender the rights. These restrictions translate to certain responsibilities for you if you distribute copies of the software, or if you modify it.

For example, if you distribute copies of such a program, whether gratis or for a fee, you must give the recipients all the rights that you have. You must make sure that they, too, receive or can get the source code. And you must show them these terms so they know their rights.

We protect your rights with two steps: (1) copyright the software, and (2) offer you this license which gives you legal permission to copy, distribute and/or modify the software.

Also, for each author's protection and ours, we want to make certain that everyone understands that there is no warranty for this free software. If the software is modified by someone else and passed on, we want its recipients to know that what they have is not the original, so that any problems introduced by others will not reflect on the original authors' reputations.

Finally, any free program is threatened constantly by software patents. We wish to avoid the danger that redistributors of a free program will individually obtain patent licenses, in effect making the program proprietary. To prevent this, we have made it clear that any patent must be licensed for everyone's free use or not licensed at all.

The precise terms and conditions for copying, distribution and modification follow.

TERMS AND CONDITIONS FOR COPYING, DISTRIBUTION AND MODIFICATION

This License applies to any program or other work which contains a notice placed by the copyright holder saying it may be distributed under the terms of this General Public License. The "Program", below, refers to any such program or work, and a "work based on the Program" means either the Program or any derivative work under copyright law: that is to say, a work containing the Program or a portion of it, either verbatim or with modifications and/or translated into another language. (Hereinafter, translation is included without limitation in the term "modification".) Each licensee is addressed as "you".

Activities other than copying, distribution and modification are not covered by this License; they are outside its scope. The act of running the Program is not restricted, and the output from the Program is covered only if its contents constitute a work based on the Program (independent of having been made by running the Program). Whether that is true depends on what the Program does.

1. You may copy and distribute verbatim copies of the Program's source code as you receive it, in any medium, provided that you conspicuously and appropriately publish on each copy an appropriate copyright notice and disclaimer of warranty; keep intact all the notices that refer to this License and to the absence of any warranty; and give any other recipients of the Program a copy of this License along with the Program.

   You may charge a fee for the physical act of transferring a copy, and you may at your option offer warranty protection in exchange for a fee.

2. You may modify your copy or copies of the Program or any portion of it, thus forming a work based on the Program, and copy and distribute such modifications or work under the terms of Section 1 above, provided that you also meet all of these conditions:

   (a) You must cause the modified files to carry prominent notices stating that you changed the files and the date of any change.

   (b) You must cause any work that you distribute or publish, that in whole or in part contains or is derived from the Program or any part thereof, to be licensed as a whole at no charge to all third parties under the terms of this License.

   (c) If the modified program normally reads commands interactively when run, you must cause it, when started running for such interactive use in the most ordinary way, to print or display an announcement including an appropriate copyright notice and a notice that there is no warranty (or else, saying that you provide a warranty) and that users may redistribute the program under these conditions, and telling the user how to view a copy of this License. (Exception: if the Program itself is interactive but does not normally print such an announcement, your work based on the Program is not required to print an announcement.)

   These requirements apply to the modified work as a whole. If identifiable sections of that work are not derived from the Program, and can be reasonably considered independent and separate works in themselves, then this License, and its terms, do not apply to those sections when you distribute them as separate works. But when you distribute the same sections as part of a whole which is a work based on the Program, the distribution of the whole must be on the terms of this License, whose permissions for other licensees extend to the entire whole, and thus to each and every part regardless of who wrote it.

Thus, it is not the intent of this section to claim rights or contest your rights to work written entirely by you; rather, the intent is to exercise the right to control the distribution of derivative or collective works based on the Program. In addition, mere aggregation of another work not based on the Program with the Program (or with a work based on the Program) on a volume of a storage or distribution medium does not bring the other work under the scope of this License.

3. You may copy and distribute the Program (or a work based on it, under Section 2) in object code or executable form under the terms of Sections 1 and 2 above provided that you also do one of the following:

(a) Accompany it with the complete corresponding machine-readable source code, which must be distributed under the terms of Sections 1 and 2 above on a medium customarily used for software interchange; or,

(b) Accompany it with a written offer, valid for at least three years, to give any third party, for a charge no more than your cost of physically performing source distribution, a complete machine-readable copy of the corresponding source code, to be distributed under the terms of Sections 1 and 2 above on a medium customarily used for software interchange; or,

(c) Accompany it with the information you received as to the offer to distribute corresponding source code. (This alternative is allowed only for noncommercial distribution and only if you received the program in object code or executable form with such an offer, in accord with Subsection b above.)

The source code for a work means the preferred form of the work for making modifications to it. For an executable work, complete source code means all the source code for all modules it contains, plus any associated interface definition files, plus the scripts used to control compilation and installation of the executable. However, as a special exception, the source code distributed need not include anything that is normally distributed (in either source or binary form) with the major components (compiler, kernel, and so on) of the operating system on which the executable runs, unless that component itself accompanies the executable.

If distribution of executable or object code is made by offering access to copy from a designated place, then offering equivalent access to copy the source code from the same place counts as distribution of the source code, even though third parties are not compelled to copy the source along with the object code.

4. You may not copy, modify, sublicense, or distribute the Program except as expressly provided under this License. Any attempt otherwise to copy, modify, sublicense or distribute the Program is void, and will automatically terminate your rights under this License. However, parties who have received copies, or rights, from you under this License will not have their licenses terminated so long as such parties remain in full compliance.

5. You are not required to accept this License, since you have not signed it. However, nothing else grants you permission to modify or distribute the Program or its derivative works. These actions are prohibited by law if you do not accept this License. Therefore, by modifying or distributing the Program (or any work based on the Program), you indicate your acceptance of this License to do so, and all its terms and conditions for copying, distributing or modifying the Program or works based on it.

6. Each time you redistribute the Program (or any work based on the Program), the recipient automatically receives a license from the original licensor to copy, distribute or modify the Program subject to these terms and conditions. You may not impose any further restrictions on the recipients' exercise of the rights granted herein. You are not responsible for enforcing compliance by third parties to this License.

7. If, as a consequence of a court judgment or allegation of patent infringement or for any other reason (not limited to patent issues), conditions are imposed on you (whether by court order, agreement or otherwise) that contradict the conditions of this License, they do not excuse you from the conditions of this License. If you cannot distribute so as to satisfy simultaneously your obligations under this License and any other pertinent obligations, then as a consequence you may not distribute the Program at all. For example, if a patent license would not permit royalty-free redistribution of the Program by all those who receive copies directly or indirectly through you, then the only way you could satisfy both it and this License would be to refrain entirely from distribution of the Program.

   If any portion of this section is held invalid or unenforceable under any particular circumstance, the balance of the section is intended to apply and the section as a whole is intended to apply in other circumstances.

   It is not the purpose of this section to induce you to infringe any patents or other property right claims or to contest validity of any such claims; this section has the sole purpose of protecting the integrity of the free software distribution system, which is implemented by public license practices. Many people have made generous contributions to the wide range of software distributed through that system in reliance on consistent application of that system; it is up to the author/donor to decide if he or she is willing to distribute software through any other system and a licensee cannot impose that choice.

   This section is intended to make thoroughly clear what is believed to be a consequence of the rest of this License.

8. If the distribution and/or use of the Program is restricted in certain countries either by patents or by copyrighted interfaces, the original copyright holder who places the Program under this License may add an explicit geographical distribution limitation excluding those countries, so that distribution is permitted only in or among countries not thus excluded. In such case, this License incorporates the limitation as if written in the body of this License.

9. The Free Software Foundation may publish revised and/or new versions of the General Public License from time to time. Such new versions will be similar in spirit to the present version, but may differ in detail to address new problems or concerns.

   Each version is given a distinguishing version number. If the Program specifies a version number of this License which applies to it and "any later version", you have the option of following the terms and conditions either of that version or of any later version published by the Free Software Foundation. If the Program does not specify a version number of this License, you may choose any version ever published by the Free Software Foundation.

10. If you wish to incorporate parts of the Program into other free programs whose distribution conditions are different, write to the author to ask for permission. For software which is copyrighted by the Free Software Foundation, write to the Free Software Foundation; we sometimes make exceptions for this. Our decision will be guided by the two goals of preserving the free status of all derivatives of our free software and of promoting the sharing and reuse of software generally.

NO WARRANTY

11. BECAUSE THE PROGRAM IS LICENSED FREE OF CHARGE, THERE IS NO WARRANTY FOR THE PROGRAM, TO THE EXTENT PERMITTED BY APPLICABLE LAW. EXCEPT WHEN OTHERWISE STATED IN WRITING THE COPYRIGHT HOLDERS AND/OR OTHER PARTIES PROVIDE THE PROGRAM "AS IS" WITHOUT WARRANTY OF ANY KIND, EITHER EXPRESSED OR IMPLIED, INCLUDING, BUT NOT LIMITED TO, THE IMPLIED WARRANTIES OF MERCHANTABILITY AND FITNESS FOR A PARTICULAR PURPOSE. THE ENTIRE RISK AS TO THE QUALITY AND PERFORMANCE OF THE PROGRAM IS WITH YOU. SHOULD THE PROGRAM PROVE DEFECTIVE, YOU ASSUME THE COST OF ALL NECESSARY SERVICING, REPAIR OR CORRECTION.

12. IN NO EVENT UNLESS REQUIRED BY APPLICABLE LAW OR AGREED TO IN WRITING WILL ANY COPYRIGHT HOLDER, OR ANY OTHER PARTY WHO MAY MODIFY AND/OR REDISTRIBUTE THE PROGRAM AS PERMITTED ABOVE, BE LIABLE TO YOU FOR DAMAGES, INCLUDING ANY GENERAL, SPECIAL, INCIDENTAL OR CONSEQUENTIAL DAMAGES ARISING OUT OF THE USE OR INABILITY TO USE THE PROGRAM (INCLUDING BUT NOT LIMITED TO LOSS OF DATA OR DATA BEING RENDERED INACCURATE OR LOSSES SUSTAINED BY YOU OR THIRD PARTIES OR A FAILURE OF THE PROGRAM TO OPERATE WITH ANY OTHER PROGRAMS), EVEN IF SUCH HOLDER OR OTHER PARTY HAS BEEN ADVISED OF THE POSSIBILITY OF SUCH DAMAGES.

END OF TERMS AND CONDITIONS

Installation Instructions

The *Slackware Linux For Dummies* CD-ROM 1 contains the full freeware distribution of Slackware Linux. CD-ROM 2 contains source code for the distribution.

Important Information About Using Linux: Linux supports many IBM-compatible PCs, but some PCs and components aren't supported. Appendix A lists the hardware compatible with Linux. Please review the appendix before attempting to install Linux from *Slackware Linux For Dummies* CD-ROM 1.

The Linux operating system and its applications are collaborative products of a worldwide community of independent users. IDG Books Worldwide, Inc. doesn't guarantee the fitness of the Linux operating system, Linux applications, or the *Slackware Linux For Dummies* CD-ROMs for any computer system or purpose. IDG Books Worldwide, Inc. doesn't provide additional installation support or technical support for the Linux operating system, Linux applications, or the *Slackware Linux For Dummies* CD-ROMs.

Part II of this book describes the installation process for Slackware Linux.

Limited Warranty

IDGB warrants that the Software and Software Media are free from defects in materials and workmanship under normal use for a period of sixty (60) days from the date of purchase of this Book. If IDGB receives notification within the warranty period of defects in materials or workmanship, IDGB will replace the defective Software Media.

IDGB AND THE AUTHOR OF THE BOOK DISCLAIM ALL OTHER WARRANTIES, EXPRESS OR IMPLIED, INCLUDING WITHOUT LIMITATION IMPLIED WARRANTIES OF MERCHANTABILITY AND FITNESS FOR A PARTICULAR PURPOSE, WITH RESPECT TO THE SOFTWARE, THE PROGRAMS, THE SOURCE CODE CONTAINED THEREIN, AND/OR THE TECHNIQUES DESCRIBED IN THIS BOOK. IDGB DOES NOT WARRANT THAT THE FUNCTIONS CONTAINED IN THE SOFTWARE WILL MEET YOUR REQUIREMENTS OR THAT THE OPERATION OF THE SOFTWARE WILL BE ERROR FREE.

This limited warranty gives you specific legal rights, and you may have other rights that vary from jurisdiction to jurisdiction.